Trial
and Error

SUNY Series in Israeli Studies
Russell Stone, Editor

Trial
and Error

Israel's Route from War to
De-Escalation

Yagil Levy

State University of New York Press

Cover art by Asnat Haddas.

Published by
State University of New York Press, Albany

© 1997 State University of New York

For information, address State University of New York
Press, State University Plaza, Albany, N.Y., 12246

Production by E. Moore
Marketing by Bernadette LaManna

Library of Congress Cataloging-in-Publication Data

Levy, Yagil, 1958–
    Trial and error : Israel's route from war to de-escalation / Yagil
Levy.
        p.   cm. — (SUNY series in Israeli studies)
    Includes bibliographical references and index.
    ISBN 0-7914-3429-X (hc : alk. paper). — ISBN 0-7914-3430-3 (pbk.
: alk. paper)
    1. Israel—Military policy. 2. Social classes—Israel. 3. War
and society—Israel. 4. Israel—Ethnic relations. 5. Israel-Arab
conflicts—Social aspects. 6. Social conflict—Israel. I. Title.
II. Series.
UA853.I8L446 1997
355'.03355694—dc20
                                                                96-42064
                                                                CIP

For my parents, Esther and Yair Levy

Contents

Figures and Tables

Acknowledgments

I have incurred many debts over the period while writing this book.

I would like to express my appreciation to Eti Leneman of the Department of Political Science at Tel Aviv University for generous administrative support and to Ralph Mandel for translating part of the manuscript. I am especially grateful to Kim Geiger who devotedly edited this book, to Lizabeth Zack, Nina Reshef, and Maria den Boer who completed the job, to Ido Keren who prepared the artwork, and to Asnat Haddas who designed the cover art.

I thank SUNY Press, particularly the series editor Russell Stone, four reviewers, and the editors Clay Morgan and Elizabeth Moore for guiding this manuscript into print.

My formal and informal advisers at Tel Aviv University, Jose Bruner, Yoav Peled, and Yonathan Shapiro, helped design the conceptual framework of this book. Aluf Benn, Dan Friel, Andy Grossman, Hanna Herzog, Gur Huberman, Jeffrey Isaac, Ian Lustick, David Nachmias, James Nolt, Zeev Rosenhek, and James Rule commented on various parts of the manuscript and helped me clarify my arguments. As critical listeners, my students at Tel Aviv University and colleagues at the Center for Studies of Social Change at the New School for Social Research, New York, gave me multifarious opportunities to test my arguments.

I am especially thankful to Michael Barnett, Yinon Cohen, Lev Grinberg, Baruch Kimmerling, Uri Ram, and Michael Shalev for their enduring support and, above all, to Asher Arian who attended the writing of this book from the beginning.

The intellectual inspiration, guidance and support of Charles Tilly have made this book much more than it would have been otherwise.

Finally I offer gratitude to my sister, Michal Keren, and my friend and partner, Sigal Bonano for immeasurable support. I dedicate this book to my parents.

CHAPTER 1

Introduction

Over the past forty-five years, the State of Israel has undergone a striking shift. After embracing the premise that its Arab neighbors could only grasp the language of violent force, it moved toward policies that gradually de-escalated the enduring Arab-Israeli conflict. At the same time, Israel became one of the most inegalitarian societies in the Western world. Is the occurrence of these two processes coincidental, or are they related? To what extent has the conflict played a role in molding the social structure? And has that structure had any impact on foreign-military policies regarding peace and war? This book tackles this neglected linkage.

The linkage between social structure and foreign policy in Israel reflects the broad theoretical project that explores the conditions under which a state selects its preferred mode of action in the external arena. Considering the trends toward demilitarization and de-escalation of violent interstate conflicts that seem to have prevailed during the past decade, understanding this linkage becomes more important than ever. Echoing some of the current criticism of the most prominent international relations (IR) theory, neorealism, this book emphasizes the role of internal forces in shaping external policy choices.

The next section discusses the analytical gaps in IR and statist theories. It is followed by two sections outlining the theoretical framework in which I ground the empirical analysis. The final section presents the implications of the lacunas in the above general theories for the case of Israel and sketches my general argument.

THE ANALYTICAL GAP

The manner in which state security interests are defined and the way such interests are executed have inspired broad writing. This writing has been largely embraced in IR studies and, to some extent, in statist theories. Interestingly, the point of departure for strands of thought in both fields is the fact that international politics is deeply anarchic.

Explicitly, the central claims in the neorealist paradigm (the dominant one among international relations) is that the international system is anarchic in the absence of a central authority above the individual states that comprise the international system. Anarchy is the ordering principle of international politics, a principle from which the notion of self-help results, the belief that "force is the ultimate arbiter of disputes" (Levy, 1989, 224). This means that since anarchy leads to uncertainty among states regarding each other's intentions, the hierarchy of a state's interests is dominated by ensuring survival, by its security interests. Security interests motivate every single state to maximize its power position over other states (to achieve relative gains/relative power), which predisposes each state to competition in zero-sum international politics. Naturally, an arms race or even a slide toward war might be one of the outcomes of this structure, patterned by the logic of security dilemmas[1]; international institutions cannot prevent war by changing states' innate patterns of behavior.

In a self-help environment, the distribution of material capabilities in the international system is the focal factor determining the behavior of individual states. Distribution of power imposes constraints on and, hence, changes the operations of states according to their relative power. State policies are rationally assessed by decision-makers informed by material and nonmaterial capabilities and future expectations (see Gilpin, 1984; Keohane, 1986; Levy, 1989, 224–228; Mearsheimer, 1994/95; Waltz, 1979; Wohlforth, 1994/95, 96–98). As we will see below, constructivists also share some of these assumptions.

Implicitly, theories of state formation have attributed the power of the modern state to the state's position in the anarchic global system; its monopoly on the use of the societal resources of violence is the ordering principle of the state's internal control (Weber, 1972, 78). Monopoly control over violence is also the basis of a state's sovereignty relative to other members of the international system. Sovereignty, in turn, gives the state powers of coercion over internal activities (see Mann, 1984, 1988; Rosenberg, 1990; Schmitt, 1976; Shaw, 1984; Thomson, 1990, 1994; Tilly, 1985a). In practice, states exploited the state of anarchy that unintentionally resulted in the creation of bureaucratic coping mechanisms (Tilly, 1985b; see also Lake, 1992).

Historically, needs originating externally and state rulers' manipulation of domestic power centers worked together to centralize the modern state. The introduction of massive artillery and gunpowder in warfare in the sixteenth and seventeenth centuries propelled state agencies to extract resources for military buildup whenever (competition-oriented) geopolitical conditions necessitated or permitted it (Tilly, 1985a, 1992). Conscription was imposed on the domestic population when growing needs for disciplined manpower could no longer be met by mercenaries (Thomson, 1994). The state then became the exclusive entity able to underwrite and maintain a military (Andreski, 1971, 98–99; Finer, 1975; Tilly, 1985b; Weber, 1972, 221–223). At the same time, state activities aimed at preparing for and legitimizing war also became a lever for internal state expansion. Civilian bureaucracies dealing with mass conscription, tax collection, military production, and territorial centralization were products of this process (Barnett, 1992; Giddens, 1985; Hooks, 1990; Porter, 1994; Tilly, 1992).[2]

Overall, for neorealists, global anarchy determines the state's relations with other states in the international arena, while for statist theorists, global anarchy determines the state's relations with internal forces. Nevertheless, in each school, one arena is seen as a major causal factor while the other one remains a "black box."

For neorealists, the black box is the state's internal features facilitating and shaping external moves. That goes beyond the level at which state capacities cumulatively change the distribution of power in the international system, which in turn determines the state's relative power. As it has become more and more established among IR scholars and acknowledged by most neorealists, neorealism is a theory that pertains to the "properties" of the international system rather than individual states (Schweller, 1993, 75). Since global anarchy permits the state to opt for more than one mode of action within a self-help system (Waltz, 1988), anarchy as such is not a structural cause (Wendt, 1995, 77–78). Theorizing about individual state priorities thus requires an attempt to identify mediating mechanisms between global systems and state behavior in situations where global constraints by themselves do not force a specific mode of state action.

In an attempt to build such a bridge between structural variables and a theory of foreign policy, neorealists have largely focused on states' rational mechanisms of decision-making. Assuming that states possess internal autonomy to administer foreign policy (see mainly Krasner, 1978), neorealists imply that strategists exclusively conduct their countries' politics. Strategists consider the concentration of power in the international system, other states' intentions, and their own state power. They then calculate several alternative policies in terms of the costs/risks and benefits relative to previously defined security interests.

Nonetheless, distinctions between objective facts and the way agents reach an understanding of them are absent in the neorealist analysis, which confines itself to presumably objective realities alone. Expressing qualitative judgments rather than quantitative measurements, terms like "risks" and "gains" acquire meaning only through the dynamic political interaction between the state and domestic groups that goes beyond the narrow circle of decision-makers. Risks, costs, and gains differentially impact on, and, hence, are appreciated by, different domestic groups on which the implementation of state policies is grounded. Those groups' members function as soldiers, taxpayers, or at least voters. That is exactly the analytical gap between global structures and the manner in which they determine an individual state's activity (see Gaddis, 1992/93, 34; Wendt, 1987). No wonder that some neorealists admit that under countervailing external pressures, that is, when the international system permits more than one option, "other levels of analysis will necessarily play a more important role in explaining state behavior," such as the effects of external policies on domestic politics (Glaser, 1994/95, 86; see also Mearsheimer, 1990, 25, on the role of nationalism). In short, neorealists imperfectly lay out the causal chain linking the features of the international system to a state's assessment of that system.

How a state assesses the reality of the international system has been partly illuminated by the neoliberal and constructivist wing of IR studies. Rejecting the neorealist perspective that privileges exogenous structure (anarchy) over processes, constructivism in particular—as a self-perceived critical theory—broaches an alternative way of thinking. For constructivists, "world politics is 'socially constructed' which involves two basic claims: that the fundamental structures of international politics are social rather than strictly material . . . and that these structures shape actors' identities and interests, rather than just behavior" (Wendt, 1995, 72–73). While for neorealists self-help causally follows from anarchy as the very nature of the international system, for constructivists, self-help is one possible institution created by what "states make of anarchy." Socialization mediates the international system to influence the action of individual states. States respond to the actions of other states and "learn" the international system. Through this form of international socialization, intersubjective concepts (like sovereignty), identities, interests, and expectations are created through which states distinguish between "friend" and "foe." Reciprocal effects of states' behavior on each other thus affect the social structure within which individual states are embedded. In turn, this structure socializes individual states (see mainly Wendt, 1992, 403–410). The distribution of material capabilities matters but it acquires meaning through the structure of interstate shared knowledge (according to which states interpret their counterparts' intentions) rather than exogenously dictating state behavior. War, then, is a possible, not a probable, outcome (Wendt, 1992, 1995).

Drawing on the reorientation of the Soviet Union under the leadership of Gorbachev, constructivists highlight the key role played by the flow of values and ideas in reshaping national interests and inducing leaders to autonomously reassess the nature of the international system beyond the predicament of built-in anarchy. After all, Gorbachev could have embarked on the opposite road and become more aggressive in the face of the Soviet Union's decline.

Accordingly, neoliberal and constructivist scholars have partially addressed the domestic debates, informed by external events, among Soviet decision-makers that shaped political reality (see, for example, Deudney and Ikenberry, 1991; Lebow, 1994; Risse-Kappen, 1994).[3]

Though I accept the constructivist stand that international socialization plays a key role in shaping states' behavior, the analytical trajectory along which constructivism marshals a state's selection of its priorities is credible only in part. For example, the domestic structural change that brought the USSR to a crossroads where reassessment became critical, is overlooked. So are the conditions under which the Gorbachev faction successfully mobilized domestic support beyond the decision-making circle in order to prevail over other groups. This is the very process through which a certain set of ideas wins out over other alternatives.

Similar to neorealists, constructivists implicitly perceive the state as a unitary, internally autonomous actor while its domestic dimension plays a secondary role in shaping behavior relative to the international system (as reflected in Wendt, 1994, 385–387). The role of domestic groups, whether autonomous relative to the state or not, in filtering external information through the lenses of their social interests, identities, expectations, and concepts, and converting it into action has not been theorized in either school—even though this information contributes to the construction of shared knowledge about threats and risks.

Significant in particular is that constructivists overlook the relations among social forces, forms of state, and the world order whereby hegemonic social forces champion their worldviews through global institutions and thus create intersubjective meanings of world order (such as protectionism, free trade, sovereignty, etc.; see Cox, 1981, 135–141; Mann, 1993, 35–42; and also the classical analysis by Polanyi, 1944). Such processes, moreover, cumulatively change the features of the international system, particularly the distribution of power (Gaddis, 1992/93, 34). At this stage, moreover, neorealism adduces a problem-solving perspective based on a previously created global structure (Cox, 1981, 128–129).

Also, both wings of IR studies have given little attention to the historical processes that originally led to interstate competition (see Levy, 1989, 227, on realism). After all, real assets are generally at stake, not just images of systems, values, and ideas. Moreover, in addition to state agencies, other internal actors evaluate those assets and correspondingly inform state institutions of them. Nonetheless, having tended to reduce particularist interests to state interests, IR statist theories are inclined to overlook the role of particularist interests in inducing state action (see the critique by Ashley, 1984, 239–240).[4] So, in the absence of a full conceptualization of the relative weight of internal versus external factors—with their impacts on decision-making (in neorealist terms) or on state identity (in constructivist terms)—during moments in which two or more strategic (not only situational) options for external action exist, we are left in the dark regarding the conditions under which states cling to competition or cooperation, or how a competition-driven state elevates war. State mechanisms of assessment should be further theorized.[5]

This brings us to military capabilities. Although they play a pivotal role in shaping and executing state security interests—they are the crucial pillar in a state's assessment of its relative power—scholars from both IR wings have not addressed the internal features that determine the military capabilities of a state. Although domestic resources account for a state's capacity to act externally (see Organski and Kugler, 1980), their explicit conceptualization is missing (see mainly the critique by Barnett, 1990, 529–535). IR scholars have a lot to say about how states mold and change the international system but less about the internal structure that facilitates a state's action within that system.

Statist theorists have partially filled the gap left by IR scholars by focusing on state features. Scholars illuminate how states extract domestic resources through their position vis-à-vis the organization of major social classes (see mainly Tilly, 1992) and the strategies employed to convert those resources into military power. These are strategies of war preparation, which include taxation, production, and conscription (Barnett, 1992). Employment of these strategies impacts on the internal status of the state relative to societal and political forces, which, in turn, further affects state features.

While a state's strategies of war preparation matter, more significant is the legitimation that allows these processes to take place and permits the use of—or threat to use—violent force (see Mann, 1993, 258–261).[6] The satisfaction of domestic groups with the effects of war and war preparation on society plays a key role in this regard. Wars not only make states (to use Tilly's dictum); they also make societies by reshaping social groups' interests and identities and, hence, social relations of power. By addressing these issues, we may move further than statist theoreticians (such as Giddens, 1985; Tilly, 1992) toward linking the consequences of war, both actual and potential, to the causes of war, the black box of statist theories. Who gains from certain outcomes of war and thus might be motivated to sustain them? Facilitating or impeding war preparation, group interests are also a component of state features.

Consequently, although the anarchic nature of the international system leads to internal state expansion mediated by previously created state capacities, statist scholarship as such has not explained *how* states fuel wars. Noting that the international system allows states considerable freedom to administer foreign-military policies, the creation of a militarized state and its propensities toward resource extension do not necessarily dictate a selection of certain policies.

To sum up, the "black boxes" of one school serve, at least partially, as the causal factors in the other school and vice versa, as figure 1.1 shows. We may infer from the figure that the transition from a state's internal features to its actual performance (conduct of policies) in the external arena, via the selection of foreign-military policies is inadequately linked in the causal chain—that is, as long as IR theories do not delve beyond the level of the state as a unitary actor. As for proponents of the statist theories, they directly pass from either the material features (theories of state formation) or legitimation (militarism) to actual performance (war preparation), skipping over processes of selection of policies. Both schools, however, address how actual performance affects the state's status internally and externally, and its impact on the properties of the international system (IR) and the features of a single state (statist studies). To tie the loop, it is necessary to blend both schools and move further in examining the manner in which domestic variables decrease the scope of freedom states enjoy in the international system, with implications for decision-making systems. Evaluating external assets, filtering external information, enabling extraction of domestic resources to facilitate external activities, legitimizing the use of violent force, and the like are among the roles domestic agents play. By doing so, they drive, facilitate, harden, and impede state policies. Socially constructed interests engineer agents' actions, as I now show.

INTERESTS

This and the following section introduce the basic theoretical concepts that guide the empirical analysis informed by five schools—neorealism, constructivism, state formation, neo-Marxist statist approaches, and scientific realism. Additional concepts will be suggested later along with problems springing from empirical observation.

Scientific realists have generally established the idea that agency and structure are mutually constitutive elements. The constitution of agents and structure represents a duality in which social structures are both the medium and the outcome of human action. Structures do not exist apart from the practices they recursively organize or the social agents' conceptions of these practices (which also include a discursive dimension). It is the agents' recognition of certain rules that enables structures to exist. But structures also condition social activity by socializing agents, creating preconditions for their behavior, setting restrictions on their activities, and giving meaning to their participation (for instance, as family/community members, citizens, individual states composing the international system, etc.) (for scientific realism see Isaac, 1987a, 1987b, 1987c; Outhwaite, 1987; Shapiro and Wendt, 1992; Wendt, 1987, mostly following the concept of "structuration" in Giddens, 1984). Though social structures depend on the self-understanding of the agents involved, they are not "reducible to what agents think they are doing, since agents may not understand

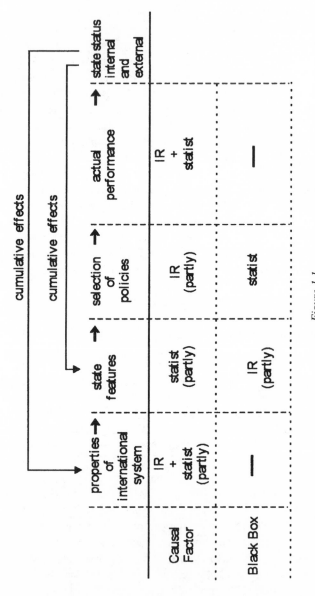

Figure 1.1
The Causal Chain of State External Action

the structural antecedents or implications of their actions" (Wendt, 1987, 359). Structures are therefore real, not empirical.

Scientific realism suggests four implications for the understanding of agentic interests.[7] First, assuming that agents are motivated by their interests, agents produce/reproduce/transform structures through their very interest-driven, partly purposive behavior. In turn, agents' interests are constituted through the agents' participation in the production/reproduction of social structures. Interests are a product of social experience through which an individual learns to internalize interests as though they were his or her own, even if doing so is unconscious. Interests emanate from norms, values, and logic subsumed in social practices and bound up with social roles and identities (Isaac, 1987a, 97–99; see also Connolly, 1993, 45–74; Wendt, 1992, 396–399). Interests, then, are "those purposes implied in the performance of social practices and therefore implicitly and practically held by participants in these practices" (Isaac, 1987a, 99, defining "real interest"). It is this form of interest that sustains social relations (see ibid., 97–100).

Second, and interrelatedly, assuming that agents are simultaneously involved in different structural relations, agents construct different sets of interests with possibilities for noncohesiveness, even contradictions, between them. Tension between consciously defined, short-term interests and undefined long-term interests is a typical symptom. An agent's involvement in the production/reproduction/transformation of structures might thus entail prioritizing certain sets of structural relations relative to others. No wonder that "many groups appear to be unaware of their own real interests . . . or articulate them falsely . . . [or] say conflicting things" (Tilly, 1978, 61).

Third, the very dialectical nature of structural relations also means that reproduction of structures unavoidably embraces *relations of exchange* between agents in which agents implicitly exchange readiness to harmonize their personal/group interests to structural orders in return for structure-produced gains. Subjectively perceived, unbalanced exchange might thus generate agents' exit from structural relations, particularly in a situation in which agents are motivated by conflicting interests. As much as interests refer to a structurally embedded orientation, relations of exchange embody a structural pattern; groups do not necessarily bargain over the terms of exchange (see more below).

As for the fourth and concluding implication, if socially constructed and unconsciously held conflicting interests govern agentic action, a space is then opened not only for the *construction* but also for the *reconstruction* of agents' interests. A perceived unbalanced relation of exchange might shift agents' behavior, particularly through interaction with other agents, creating new commitments, identities, possibilities of, or expectations for action owing to the creation of newly available resources or the drying up of old ones, and so on.

It is the strategic effect of other agents' moves that fuels the agents' satisfaction with the newly created reality relative to the previous one, a satisfaction that does not necessarily entail explicit reformulation of interests. Enduring satisfaction generates the reconstruction of interests, while agents neglect their former interests and structural affiliations. A transformation of structures might be the result. Alternatively, reconstruction of interests might encourage agents to neglect their intention to exit, a reconfirmation of relations of exchange.

So, the more interests were harmonized, the less likely that agents would have been motivated to replace old structural relations with new ones, that is, to mitigate innate tensions between interests; hence, the less likely that reconstruction would have taken place. A similar result would have occurred had agents been aware, from the outset, of the structural relations within which they were embedded. In such cases, structures would have become visible and thus solidly tied. This will have the implications of making agents' interests more self-conscious. Agents then might have been more aware of the cost of the exit option created by the pressures and incentives of their counterparts. Likewise, agents would have been less subject to the manipulation by others through which they indirectly transferred their loyalties from one set of commitments to others.

Finally, had structures and interests been visible, agents would not have made errors in their relations with others. Errors relate to: (1) a failure to calculate invisible structural limitations imposed on other agents, limitations such as commitments, expectations, loyalties, identities, and so on; agents' moves then might provoke others' antagonism; and (2) a failure to calculate other agents' capacities to accumulate power owing to the pattern of exchange, which might generate a realignment of power relations.[8] Reconstruction thus is also an error-correction mechanism, that is, agents' reaction to situations in which their actions overtly produce unanticipated consequences. Reconstruction of interests, I contend, is what a state unintentionally does in its pursuit of mitigation of intergroup conflicts and creation/aversion of structural exits with it.

Methodologically, defining and identifying interests is always a problem because interests are observable only in part, that is, at the level where agents express conscious, rational preferences and intentions. Identification of agents' interests might be drawn from a general analysis of the connection between interests and social position. Further, focus on mechanisms of error correction helps identify structural constraints on agentic action, hence, interests as well (see Tilly, 1978, 60; 1995a). By doing so, we can avoid a self-confirming explanation—interests are what agents do. But the ultimate analytical test is *interpretive* rather then *empirical*, done by measuring certain explanations against alternative theories that have been ruled out. If war preparation is a process of structural production then, arguably, factoring in of agentic interests matters.

THE THREE DOMAINS OF STATE ACTION

The role social agents play in shaping the state's foreign-military policies is relevant to the three domains of state action, as figure 1.2 proposes. The first domain exhibits the IR elements in the underlying causal chain (see figure 1.1): the state's actual, externally oriented performance, directly and intentionally motivated by the rational calculation of self-help-guided security interests and by previously understood threats and previously created material power. In short, this approach focuses on the problem-solving perspective of statecraft (see Cox's critique of neorealism, 1981, 128–129). State policies produce war or peace, which result in victories, defeats, casualties, loss of resources, and so on. IR scholars, notably neorealists, credibly address activity in this domain.

Domains II and III embrace state features. In the second domain, the actual outcomes of external activities or the expectations of such outcomes affect domestic agents, be they social groups, political parties, particular state agencies, business organizations, and the like. Those agents reconcile their interests, consciously or unconsciously, to those outcomes. Hence, their attitudes toward issues of peace and war, competition and cooperation, are shaped by and determine—via their willingness to legitimize and be mobilized for carrying out state policies—state strategies of war preparation.

This process starts with the evaluation of external assets domestic agents expect to gain regardless of who initiates state action: state agencies or domestic agents themselves. Assets might be raw material resources (Krasner, 1978), markets, religious sites, territories (Kocs, 1995), and so on. They might be new holdings to be possessed by the state or existing holdings that are imperiled by other states. When pushing the state to compete with other states to attain those assets (if a fine tuning of existing policies is inadequate), agents are inclined to present their particularistic interests as universalistic, national security interests serving a vast social group. The level of universalization determines the level of legitimization domestic forces confer on state actions, especially costly ones.

Collective action, lobbying, manipulation, provocation, and the like are all means through which groups attempt to universalize security interests in their concurrent effort to gain the support of state agencies; as does the state when working to mobilize agents (the movement from evaluation to universalization and mobilization in figure 1.2). Universalization of military establishments' activities by means of tight political supervision dovetails with this process if the military takes part in marking external targets as interests. With the support of state agencies, universalization is more workable, as is the capacity to mobilize the society to support, and in many times even to carry out, the burden state policies prescribe (a two-way movement from universalization

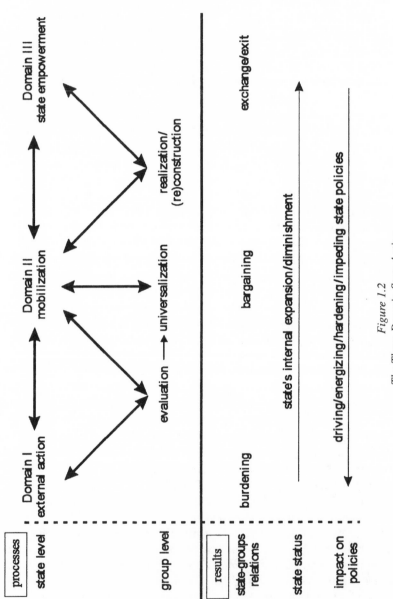

Figure 1.2
The Three-Domain State Action

to mobilization).[9] Though the extent of interstate competition might go beyond the agents' initial intentions, real interests, not anarchy as such, spark interstate competition from the outset.[10]

Nevertheless, universalization of particularistic interests is a necessary but not a sufficient condition for enduring costly competition. It is particularly so if competition elevates war without a tangible, immediate, existential danger. And as long as modern warfare relies on the mass mobilization of citizens functioning as soldiers, taxpayers, or at least voters, and the extraction of huge domestic resources, the groups involved in the initial phase (i.e., evaluation), and those who are expected to carry out the burden that results from this phase, do not necessarily overlap. On the other hand, intimidation by means of threat is also an insufficient instrument for mobilizing long-term support unless it involves a state's pledge to protect values, rights, identities, and interests against an external threat (Lake, 1992), all required to shape popular consent (Tilly, 1995b, 167). So, a state's capacity to act externally is determined by its capacity to improve the well-being of the mobilized groups. Improvement means realization of both the existing domestic interests and the construction of new interests. The latter are adapted to the newly expected/created situation shaped by external action. Bettering groups' well-being is, in many cases, an *unintended consequence* of external, intended action.

To provide benefits to groups, the state may utilize three sources (a two-way movement from mobilization to realization/construction): (1) direct production of new material resources by means of external extraction (for example, by seizing new raw material resources or by being given foreign aid; it is a movement from external action to mobilization); (2) indirect production through the process of state extraction for war preparation, enabling the state to reallocate resources, for instance, by creating new jobs or increasing budgets (see Mastanduno et al., 1989; Starr, 1994); (3) production of symbolic resources from wars/interstate competition. Allocation of citizenship, access to political power via the expansion of political participation, social prestige, construction of identities, militarism (including access to arms), and national pride are among the resources states allocate to social groups as a result of the latter's military participation (i.e., participation in war and war preparation). Since these three sources are dynamically created or expanded through military participation, agents create resources for themselves when mobilized by the state. Realization and construction of interests are endogenous, not exogenous, to mobilization.

Concurrently, as the above state theorists have established, the resulting status of war/war preparation affects the third domain: empowerment or disempowerment of the state via expansion or diminishment, respectively, of its domain. Both effects go beyond the direct functional needs of conducting foreign-military policies.

But the movement from realization/construction to state empowerment goes in the opposite direction as well, inasmuch as state expansion affects social relations by benefiting social agents differentially. In many instances, this process oversteps the context of mobilization for war. Two issues are relevant: (1) as I have suggested above, the enhancement of the state's internal extraction to maintain the war effort results in the reshuffling of domestic resources, from which there are new gainers and losers; and (2) the state's preoccupation with collective existence works to cement its image as an essentially rational and universalistic entity. A universalistic military, with professional rather than affiliational recruitment, is instrumental in bolstering this image. Also instrumental is the augmentation of state's relative autonomy over internal agents through the possession of resources aimed at war preparation. This makes the state (as long as it retains a high degree of cohesiveness) less constrained by those agents' preferences, as state-centered theories have established (see, for example, Ellis, 1992; Krasner, 1978, 10; Nordlinger, 1981; Poggi, 1978; Skocpol, 1985; Trimberger, 1977).

As neo-Marxist scholars argue (albeit without dealing directly with the military domain of the state), the state's construction of social inequality (within previously established relations of social power between the state and dominant groups) becomes more legitimate when based on that universalization and rationalization. State universalism blurs the exploitation of peripheral groups by installing the interests of dominant groups as incarnations of the general interests of the seemingly unified political community (see, for example, Althusser, 1976; Ditomaso, 1978; Domhoff, 1986; Gold et al., 1975; Habermas, 1971, 81–122; Poulantzas, 1978; Therborn, 1976; Zeitlin, 1980, 22–28).[11] Hence, the existence of cultural-ideological barriers to political action demanding all-encompassing reallocation of the societal resources. Reproduction of inequalities is the result.

War preparation, it follows, creates social structures rather than being just an administrative process. Discourse, by which agents, in a mutual manner, passively acquire meaning from, and actively bring and constitute meaning to their action and modes of allocation and extraction of resources, are among the structures created by a state of war that affect social relations of power. Agents' collective identities, concepts, and interests are constructed or solidified at this stage.

Within this structure, state action constructs particularistic interests when agents consider *exchanging* their support for the state's bellicose policies, with the internal burden and the state's internal expansion that it entails, in return for a share in the possible profits of this process and the supply of protection. Groups and the state bureaucracy do not necessarily bargain over the terms of exchange. Overtly, albeit subtly, groups take advantage of their elevated role owing to war/war preparation while state agencies have less leverage to halt group demands. After all, "the voice of the people is heard loudest when governments require either their gold or their bodies in defense of the state" (Porter, 1994, 10).[12] Indirectly, however, agents' well-being is altered for better or for worse owing to state-designed structures. Internalizing those changes, agents adjust their interests accordingly, as we have already noted.

Moving one step further, to the extent that agents (including the military establishment and its constitutive social groups) acquire benefits, they gradually shift from being merely mobilized for shouldering state policies to possessing interests in retaining, even furthering, those policy outcomes. A reversal of policy in the external arena that is not backed by internal change or compelled by external change is then hardly able to be implemented. Those reversals actually entail structural change, rather than just a change at the level of strategic doctrine. The reversal comes to be at odds with the parties' mutual commitments.[13] That is the meaning of interests as durably hardening state action, reducing the scope of possibilities the international system permits, beyond just energizing episodic, short-term action. All in all, the main movement—a two-way one from external action to realization of interests via mobilization with implications for state's internal expansion—is set in motion.

But agents have an "exit" option, too. Notwithstanding the expected gains from external moves, agents, driven by short-term calculations, might hinder the state's attempts to mobilize their support or resources for such moves, especially costly bellicose moves. Short-term sacrifice is not necessarily mitigated by long-term considerations—hence, the creation of unbalanced exchange. Unsatisfied agents would then be more prone to recalculate gains and risks of alternative routes of external action, deem their previous commitments as an error, and reconstruct their interests accordingly. Drawing from Hirschman (1970, 106–119), the absolute "exit" option might be emigration. Still, by legally voicing their dissatisfaction with the gains from war, agents might cause, even without resorting to forms of massive disobedience, the breakdown of structures maintaining the state of war, that is, delegitimization of war preparation. This is a moderate version of exit by means of breaking the "rules of the game."

Subordination of short-term interests to long-term goals is precisely what social institutions, first and foremost the state, customarily do. In line with our general understanding of interests, we maintain that the state, through its dynamic, long-term accumulation of resources, not only realizes or constructs group interests, but also *reconstructs* interests. States do this by creating alternative sources of satisfaction for agents when the original ones dry up, thus inducing agents to change their exit-prone conduct for another set of interests. If the state ultimately fails, an agent's exit from the state-constructed structural relations of exchange is set in motion, bringing about a reverse course in the external arena. By making war preparation less legitimate, the decline of relative power in IR terms is the likely result. This is a *negative* movement in figure 1.2, from the failure to realize interests to the state's diminishment in its external domain, via the failure of mobilization, with implications for internal state power. Unavoidably, this process entails the deuniversalization of previously deemed national interests or the devaluation of assets for which the state competes.[14]

We see that agents may read and interpret external events differently based on their position relative to the expected outcomes of those events. Domestic interests actually filter information from the international system into societies. Information ranges from assets appearing as external, actual gains to losses inflicted on the society by another state, whether by warfare or economic means. Converting information to political action, domestic agents transmit, indirectly in general, the extent of their willingness to carry out foreign-military policies. Traditional distinctions between hawks and doves, expansionists and nonexpansionists, or isolationists and internationalists should be seen within this context; they are socially constructed.[15]

Clearly put, the external arena matters only by virtue of the manner in which internal agents filter this arena's "objective impacts" via their interests and take advantage of the setting (material or discursive) that it creates. It is the state that selects between conflicting signals, functioning as a mediator between global trends externally and social group preferences internally.[16] Seeing interests as both engines and filters, through which domestic forces drive, energize, or harden foreign-military policies or reverse them by impeding their implementation, partly fills gaps created by IR students.

In turn, internal agents reciprocally affect the realities of the international system via the state. In this regard, constructivists give a plausible explanation of the nature of the dynamic construction of global structures. They claim that states are socialized through interstate interactions by responding to the actions of other states (see Wendt, 1992, 1994). And cumulatively, as other scholars maintain, internal changes within individual states impact on the distribution of power in the international system, even changing the structure of power (Cox, 1981; Gaddis, 1992/93, 34). So, states possess the capacity to utilize external action to reconstruct interests internally as much as states take part in molding their surrounding international structure by utilizing their domestically accumulated material power.

In sum, processes taking place in Domains II and III cyclically affect Domain I. Given the preexisting limits set by the international system, a competition-oriented posture becomes a possible, even preferred mode of action to the extent that groups gain from this type of state action. At the minimum, groups that benefitted from the outcomes of bellicosity accept moves initiated by competition-geared, hawkish state agencies; at a higher rate of involvement they directly drive/impede moves or passively/actively hinder reversal and thus harden polices. Escalation and a slide toward war become potential outcomes within the pattern of security dilemmas. Domain I embraces the direct causal force behind foreign-military polices; Domains II and III make those policies possible and indirectly fuel them. Domestic interests in conjunction with international constraints generate the contingencies of particular outcomes; they are determinants but not deterministic (see Isaac, 1987a, 49–50, on causal mechanisms).[17] The two main motions in figure 1.2, the positive and negative, are at the heart of this book.

It is with this conceptualization as the foundation that I use the term "state." Although it refers to the state's institutional system (including the military)—acting both internally and externally—it does so in linkage with the structural arrangements that are affected by and affect the direction of its activity. I address a problematic arising from this conceptualization pertinent to the borders between the state and other agencies in chapter 2.

Overall, dialogue between the different schools, mediated by the concept of interests, may convert black boxes into factors. So, the present study proposes to draw on several schools of thought, particularly those embraced by IR and critical statist theories, rather than positing a distinct alternative. By integrating several schools of thought, I hope to gain in scope more than I might lose in accuracy.

A focus on Israel's conduct in the conflict with bordering Arab countries presents a typical case in which the regional and international arenas have permitted a state to select from among several alternatives. Domestic considerations played their part in inducing the state to act within the boundaries of the external arena. We now proceed with analytical gaps in the study of the case of Israel.

THE EXOGENOUS CONFLICT

At first glance, Israel is a classic case of a state guided by principles of self-help. A prolonged Jewish-Palestinian intercommunal conflict in Palestine under the British Mandate and the 1948 War against the neighboring Arab countries subsequent to the state's formal establishment set the direction: Israel's interest was defined in military terms. It was geared toward expanding security margins beyond ensuring the sheer survival of the state against the perceived existential threat posed by fundamentally hostile and unreliable Arab countries. With this vision of threat, self-help left no space for flexibility toward bordering states. Retaining military superiority over the Arab states, sustaining high capabilities for deterrence, and conducting retaliatory behavior underlay Israel's doctrine. This was the Israeli version of "relative power" within the evolving security competition.

From these principles, Israel derived its strategies. A defensive posture prevailed during the state's first years, guided by Israel's lack of resources in the face of similarly deficient Arab armies. Israel insisted on basing its security on territorial holdings, especially those acquired during the 1948 War, rather than making concessions for attaining peace with the Arab states. An aggravated threat, compounded by the emergence of militant regimes in some Arab states, led Israel to a massive military buildup conducted under French auspices, including the acquisition of nuclear armaments to establish opaque deterrence. In doing so, Israel extended the security margins through an offensive doctrine. Israel initiated the Suez War (1956) and the Six-Day War (1967), signaling the crescendo of its offensive policies. After 1967, with control over huge conquered territories and a regional monopoly on nuclear capabilities, Israel could retake a defensive posture. Ensuring "defensible borders" was entwined with Israel's insistence that any future peace agreement include Israeli control over part of the territory conquered during the Six-Day War.

Nevertheless, a number of events induced a reorientation of Israel's strategic doctrine, central to which was a change in the distribution of material capabilities at the regional level. Diminishment of the threat posed to Israel by the bordering Arab states, which ensued after the fall of the Soviet Union (the Arabs' chief ally) and Iraq's defeat in the Gulf War of 1991, signified an opportunity to settle conflicts from an advantageous position. At the same time, new limitations were imposed on Israel's capacity to exploit its military capabilities. Among these limitations were the proliferation of nuclear weapons among radical states in the region; the costs and losses that Israel absorbed due to wars, beginning with the October War (1973); and the switch in the posture of the United States—on which the Israeli military depended—from permitting Israel's bellicosity to checking Israel's activities as a means of terminating regional conflicts. This mélange of opportunities and limitations prompted Israel to gradually prioritize strategies of de-escalation of the conflict with the relatively moderate bordering countries as a means of reducing the conflict's costs and containing both the radical Islamic movement and the spread of nuclear weapons in the region (see Inbar and Sandler, 1995; see also Peres, 1993, 1–32). The first signs of the overall change accounted for Israel's concessions producing the Israel–Egypt peace accord (1979). Later, a more intensive appearance of the phenomena accounted for the Israel–PLO interim agreements (1993–95) and (at the time of writing) a tacit approval to withdraw from the Golan Heights in exchange for peace with Syria (on Israel's doctrine from the IR perspective see Aronson, 1992; Evron, 1987; Handel, 1973, 1994; Horowitz, 1985, 1987; Levite, 1988; Safran, 1978; Shimshoni, 1988; Yaniv, 1994).

Elegant arguments of this kind are hardly disputable. Nevertheless, one could argue that Israeli IR scholars reflect the neorealist strand of thinking and replicate some of the same flaws—thinking that regional anarchy causally generates an objectively defined security interest constituted on self-help principles on which Israel's military doctrine was built. The external system does not appear to the state as anything more than "conditions of possibility for state action" (Wendt, 1987, 342); Israel, IR scholars stipulate, reacts to an external reality that constrains its behavior. Thus, the very sources of security competition and Israel's part in crafting it remain unexamined.

Most conspicuous is how scholars have overlooked the crossroads at which Arab leaders displayed pragmatism, when they did not force the reality of conflict on Israel, opening, even if only a little, the vista of alternative paths. In the early 1950s, Israel did not want to grant territorial and demographic concessions in return for peace before Arab hostility hardened (see Morris, 1993; Pappe, 1992; Rabinovich, 1991).[18] In the post-1967 period, Israel again impeded the possibility for withdrawal from the territories it had occupied in the Six-Day War in return for peace treaties, or for interim agreements, at least with Egypt, that might had been attainable and could have prevented the October War (see, Gazit, 1984; Rabin, 1979, 338–360; Shlaim, 1994, 41–47; Touval, 1980, 71–77; Yaacobi, 1989). The situation was aggravated by the Israel-initiated Lebanon War in 1982 against both the PLO and Syria, perceived as an unnecessary "war by choice" by the Israeli Center-Left (see Horowitz, 1983; Yariv, 1985). Likewise, massive colonization of the occupied territories and the use of an "iron fist" against local Palestinians were instrumental in keeping the conflict alive up to the time of the Intifada—the Palestinians' violent resistance against Israel's rule in the West Bank and the Gaza Strip (1987–93).

Alternatively, drawing from *contingent realism*—a version of neorealism more optimistic about the likelihood of establishing interstate cooperation (Glaser, 1994/95)—Israel could employ either strategies of de-escalation/cooperation or escalation/competition.[19] Moderate strategies could have tested the Arabs' willingness for peace, communicating nonoffensive signals as a means of lessening the other side's fears, and establishing cooperative institutions to reduce the uncertainty innate in regional politics. The adoption of moderate strategies might have helped Israel accommodate its security interest by political means and avoid enduring losses, an economic burden, and a risky arms race.

Nevertheless, scholars have not weighed the costs and risks of an arms race relative to those entailed in de-escalation against the fact that Israel actually failed in coping with the security dilemma by aggravating the threat to its security. This failure went from a conventional, regional threat in the early 1950s to a global, conventional threat and a restricted nuclear one from the mid-1950s with the incorporation of the Israeli-Arab conflict into the Cold War. The latter grew into a regional, poorly restricted proliferation of nuclear weapons in the Middle East that became apparent subsequent to the Gulf War. Risks of competition rather than only risks of cooperation might have concerned Israel. Its "selection of concerns" merits an explanation. Still, all of this is not to historically judge whether Israel really could have advanced the peace process in these periods—we cannot evaluate the Arab side's possible reaction; it is only to address Israel's failure to fully exhaust the potential for furthering the process. Hereinafter, setting Israel's rigidity against Arab pragmatism serves this line of analysis rather than implying historical judgment.

This being the case, we are left in the dark regarding the main question: why did Israel strategically prioritize force-oriented policy over more pacifist strategies, not only how did Israel manage its everyday policies in the face of external threats (on which IR accounts are considerably plausible)?

Adhering to the IR analytical avenue, Israel's shift toward peace is not fully understandable, either. At last, presented with opportunities for peace and the limitations and threats of the status quo, Israel again faced a crossroads from the late 1970s on. Opportunities for peace, however, could also have been read as opportunities to maintain the status quo. As a security-seeking state, Israel could have remained jealous of its militarily defined security interest when the regional system seemed to have changed significantly and then could have displayed a tough position toward the Arabs insofar as they were viewed as accepting Israel's unquestionable military superiority. This particularly holds true when taken against Israelis' increasing awareness of the spread of nuclear weapons in the Middle East. The United States, after competition with the Soviet Union ended, imposed pressures to halt offensive moves. But Israel's recognition of the PLO (1993) and the apparent Israeli endorsement of a complete withdrawal from the Golan Heights went beyond America's direct pressures. In short, the international system did not compel Israel to change its policies. Indeed, the force-oriented logic was proposed by the Israeli right wing (see Netanyahu, 1995) but was practically rejected by Israel's government.

To sum up, both strategies at each historical milestone—cooperation-prone in the 1950s–80s and competition-prone in the 1980s–90s—were equally rational. The regional arena offered an array of options, each of which had costs and benefits. So, the regional system does not provide a sole determinant for Israel's choice other than by addressing the alternative calculations and the values on which each possible route was grounded. In this regard, neorealism in general and neorealist explanations for Israel's shift in particular do not furnish us with plausible explanations. (I will introduce more IR explanations along with the empirical discussion. My purpose here is just to whet the reader's appetite for further examination.)

Not only have IR scholars neglected the question of "why," but also the intersecting question of "how." This refers to the state's *execution* of its defined security interests, the manner in which the state mobilizes the internal legitimacy and resources on which its military power is built. In this process are grounded Israel's assessment and reassessment of its own relative power, which might have inclined it to overlook past options for de-escalation and reverse its stand later (on the latter, see Inbar and Sandler, 1995). To a large extent, IR scholars have actually echoed the way in which mainstream Israeli sociologists and historians focus on the social domain of the conflict. Whereas for IR students the conflict was exogenously imposed, for their counterparts the conflict is taken as a given, a starting point for explaining certain domestic developments and not as a reality that itself merits explanation.

Israeli sociologists and historians believe that the roots of the conflict lie in the regional reality the Zionists encountered from the outset of their project. They then proceed to analyze Israeli society's responses to a situation of conflict as if the conflict was *exogenous* to the society and only *interfered* with the normal development of the Zionist project. Analysis then focuses on how the society copes with the conflict or how it is shaped by the conflict (prominent examples of this approach are Arian, 1995a; Barzilai, 1992; Eisenstadt, 1967, 1985; Galnoor, 1982; Horowitz and Lissak, 1978, 1989; Keren, 1989a; Migdal, 1989; Peri, 1983; Shapira, 1992; Shapiro, 1984a, 1991, 1996). Even relatively critical scholars tend to slip into an implicit understanding of the conflict as "spoiling" the normal evolution of Israeli society, particularly by "corrupting" the civilian/socialist/statist posture of the labor movement (Ben-Eliezer, 1995; Carmi and Rosenfeld, 1993; Lustick, 1993, respectively). Hence, the absence of discussion attempting to relate the etiology of the conflict to that of the social order in Israel and to examine to what extent Israeli society itself shaped the conflict and who benefited (see the critiques by Deutsch, 1985, 3–4; Ehrlich, 1987; Levy and Peled, 1994).

For sociologists and political scientists, moreover, the self-help system presents itself through the conception of Israel as a "society under siege." Scholars who have uncritically internalized this conception have not considered the roots of that situation or its impact on the social relations of power. This is consistent with the tendency of many scholars to uncritically grasp the images of the dominant elites that have been injected into the political discourse (see critique by Kimmerling, 1992; Shapiro, 1985).

No wonder that Israeli students from both wings have not problematized the question of "how." For Israeli students, internal forces unquestionably carried out an externally imposed conflict under conditions of broad political consensus (see Horowitz and Lissak, 1989, for a clear example). Political consensus is then taken as a point of departure instead of being analyzed as a process dynamically shaped through multidimensional state strategies of war preparation, as our theoretical framework suggests. Problems of legitimation have been highlighted only when disputes were amplified, mainly from the Lebanon War on, but the manner in which they had been previously regulated and how the winning formulas for dealing with external challenges came into being are overlooked.[20] Hence, missed opportunities for political agreements with the neighboring countries have not been questioned by Israeli sociologists and political scientists. They have not scrutinized the political mechanisms that leave immense autonomy in leaders' hands and prevent public groups from reading and interpreting external, moderate signals.

My purpose is also to fill gaps in the critical scholarship of Israeli society on which this study broadly draws. Critical scholars have made only half the journey. They thoroughly analyze internal mechanisms to account for the prolongation of the conflict; in part, critical scholars explicitly treat the conflict as an endogenous component of the social order in Israel. Those mechanisms range from the conflict's impacts on regulation of the labor market and the social order that it constructed (Grinberg, 1993a; Peled, 1990; Shalev, 1992) to groups' capacities to promote their status by identifying their raison d'être with force-oriented symbols such as militarism or traditionalism (see Ben-Eliezer, 1995; Kimmerling, 1989, 1993a, 1993b; Lustick, 1993, 417–436). Nevertheless, similar to the broad deficiency found in statist theories, a causal linkage between internal utilization of war and external moves has not been established. Scholars focus on how the conflict nourishes power relations in the state's internal arena; they do not redirect their analyses in order to examine whether, and how, those power relations determined the management of the conflict (the exception is Shafir, 1989, but his work is confined to the first years of the pre-state Zionist project). Moreover, their tendency to discern a hardening in the functioning of the intrastate mechanisms that nourish the conflict, especially after the 1967 War, is not easily reconciled with the functional change that has occurred in these mechanisms during the 1980s and 1990s. They now nourish an opposite process of downscaling the conflict. Because of these problems, the existing scholarly accounts cannot provide an adequate explanation for either the shape of Israel's military policies or the current shift in those policies.

A social interests–centered approach as outlined in this chapter can fill gaps and build bridges between the theories in the Israeli context. Evidently, the Israeli state, regardless of domestic disputes, demonstrated an effective capacity to mobilize the required domestic support and material resources for carrying out the conflict up until the Lebanon War. The same success repeated itself during 1993–96 with the peace moves, notwithstanding the previous hawkish thrust and the deeply inculcated perception of the Arab threat. Accordingly, I propose to analyze Israel's shift by examining how the prolongation of the conflict benefited the main social interests and then investigating how those interests were reconstructed to induce agents to work toward, or to accept, the downscaling of the conflict. This shift suggests that the domestic arena dramatically fluctuated no less than did the regional system; hence, the diminishing degree of freedom enjoyed by decision-makers to act externally. Clearly, studying the peace process also means studying the conflict.

THE ARGUMENT

Simply put, this book denounces the commonly accepted view that Israel's military policies were crafted only as a direct and inevitable response to neighboring Arab states' hostility. Instead, Israel's security interests were also largely determined by the social interests of a rising middle class composed of Western Israelis (mostly Ashkenazis), Jews of European descent who founded the pre-state society. Due to the protracted state of war, this class achieved its dominant status over other groups: Oriental Jews, who immigrated from Arab countries during Israel's first years, and the minority of Palestinian citizens both of whom comprised the peripheral classes. The state of war dynamically enabled these three groups to gain, materially and symbolically, from the outcomes of bellicose policies, unintentionally resulting in the construction of durable inequality.[21] Inequality rested on three pillars: (1) state-led differential gains by the different ethno-class groups; (2) Western groups' exploitation of the other groups within the labor market; and (3) legitimation of inequality owing to the war-driven internal empowerment of the state. The state could then play a key role not only in constructing the social structure through socioeconomic policies but also in reproducing it by three means: universalization of its action by means of a state ideology, Mamlachtiyut (statism), in which the highly prestigious Israel Defence Forces (IDF) played a large part; sustaining a high degree of social mobility in the aftermath of wars; and splitting, hence politically dismantling, the peripheral groups between mobile and nonmobile ones (the foundations of the social structure outlined in chapter 2).

As a result of this social structure, a sturdy link was created between increasing inegalitarianism in Israeli society and bellicosity up to the 1980s. Satisfied with their preferential position, the Western groups, which benefited the most from the conflict and were the only ones possessing the capacity to contain state moves, supported the internal empowerment of the Israeli state and the preference it lent to the military mind-set. This process produced policies that in turn bolstered the Westerners' dominance. These structural relations of exchange between the state and Western groups worked to energize the conflict; they hardened even further Israel's force-oriented posture as long as social groups gained and external geopolitical conditions permitted. Israel's domestic considerations then played a focal role in tipping the scale for bellicose policies at critical crossroads when the international system permitted Israel to employ more moderate policies. These could have led to the realization of security interests by political instead of military means but, at the same time, jeopardized social gains and to a large extent the entire social order. Thus, not just the strategic setting and Israel's military power went into the making of Israeli foreign policy. Missed opportunities for peace/de-escalation along with reprisal raids against bordering Arab countries, culminating in the Suez War and the entrenchment of the occupation that resulted from the Six-Day War, put obstacles on the road toward de-escalation of the conflict (this history will be discussed in chapters 2 and 3).

State empowerment, externally and internally, dialectically bore within it the seeds of its own decline. Military rigidity stimulated Arab reactions, inflicting heavy losses on Israel and increasing the conflict's burden beginning with the War of Attrition (1969–70). Paradoxically, as the benefits produced by the 1967 War served to elevate the consumerist life style of the Westerner-dominated middle class, the burden of war became less appealing to it.

Through multiple forms of political action, middle-class groups bolstered restraints imposed by the United States (on which Israel had become heavily dependent) on using force and amplified the costs and losses Arab countries inflicted on Israel. Together with echoing the more attractive political and economic opportunities innate in the post–Cold War international system, especially as the war-produced internal gains declined (mainly following the 1987–93 Intifada), this class again narrowed the state's relative freedom to act externally, channeling it toward de-escalation of the conflict. Internal constraints again reduced the state's relative freedom to act externally (discussed in chapters 5–6).

As I will repeatedly emphasize, as long as structurally embedded domestic interests played their role in driving, energizing, hardening, and hindering the state's external moves, rational calculations did not solely dominate statecraft. Rather, an aggregation of unintended consequences accounted for piloting Israel's policies through a pattern of "trial and error" (see concluding remarks in chapter 7).

This book thus proposes an alternative option for examining the Arab-Israeli conflict—its conduct and possible termination—and other interstate conflicts as well. By placing the conflict within the Israeli sociopolitical order rather than in an exogenous position, the state's "dual face" is brought into focus: The state manages a violent conflict in the external arena but, at the same time, shares in regulating a potential nonviolent interethnic conflict in the internal arena. I will try to show that understanding each conflict enhances our knowledge of the other. If the reader wishes, he or she may therefore turn the problem with which this piece struggles on its head, may read the book as an explanation of the role played by bellicose policies in the reproduction of social structure. To these two optional problems, however, this book furnishes a tentative explanation by exposing the web of possibilities, not determinants, for certain actions.

The analysis of Israel's first years will give us an opportunity for testing this theoretical framework.

CHAPTER 2

The State's Construction of an Inequitable Social Structure

This chapter analyzes the structural arrangements that evolved in the State of Israel's first years of existence. Construction of a state-regulated inequitable social structure was the main outcome. The Arab-Israeli conflict with the Israeli military in the center simultaneously fueled and was fueled by the new social order. Thus, this chapter focuses on the third domain of state action.

HISTORICAL BACKGROUND: EXTERNAL CONFLICT AND PRE-STATE FORMATION AS ONE STORY

The Arab-Israeli conflict was instrumental to the evolution of the State of Israel. According to Shafir (1989), the roots of the conflict go back to the Second *Aliyah* ("Ascent")—the influx of Jews into Palestine from 1905 to 1914—which heralded the onset of the Zionist colonial project. The conflict developed as a result of the attempt made by these immigrants to fulfill their material needs. This group was at a disadvantage in the labor market vis-à-vis the Palestinians, the people that inhabited Palestine before the start of the Zionist enterprise. Because Palestinians worked for lower wages than Jews, they were preferred by Jewish employers (those who had arrived in earlier small-scale influxes). Failing to compete with Palestinians, the Jewish workers organized on a political-national basis, propelling the formation of a separate Jewish economic sector, neutralizing their disadvantage in the labor market. To a large extent, the means by which this group sought to gain access to land and make a living in a country previously occupied by Palestinians left them little freedom to choose the option of Jewish-Palestinian cooperation (see Shalev,

1996, 7–9). The segregation between the two economic sectors gave rise to two concurrent processes: frictions between the two ethnic communities, gradually evolving into a violent intercommunal conflict, and crystallization of a pre-state pattern of rule, later known as the *Yishuv*.

Contradictory interests fueled the Arab-Israeli conflict. Each side sought to establish an autonomous political framework in Palestine, controlling both territory and a homogeneous population. Hence, the Arab community opposed Jewish immigration and Jewish land purchases, while the Jews insisted on their right to advance both processes unimpeded (see Kimmerling, 1983). At the same time, exigencies of conflict management contributed to the parallel development of various centralistic control mechanisms in the hands of the Yishuv's institutions to facilitate the mobilization of the community for the carrying out of the conflict. Both the need to establish a separate labor market and to deal with scarcity of territorial resources were instrumental factors in the formation of the pre-state order.

The labor parties played a pivotal role in this process. Most significant was the status of Mapai (short for The Party of Land of Israel Workers, the dominant party in the Yishuv/Israel from the 1930s until the 1970s) and the labor parties' umbrella organization, the *Histadrut Haklalit*, or the General Federation of Labor. The Histadrut, created to meet the material needs of the Jewish workers, worked to gain control over the labor market by running labor exchange and developing an independent infrastructure on which to build an economic sector and a welfare system. This infrastructure gave rise to the durable political dominance of the labor parties controlling the Histadrut. To aid its efforts to achieve and maintain effective control, the Histadrut invoked national symbols. Such symbols, by injecting meaning into the segregation between the Jewish and Arab communities, validated the centralistic control exercised by the Histadrut and the labor parties, nowhere more blatantly than in the labor market. At the same time, owing to the nationalization of control over the labor market, the Histadrut also lay the foundations for an alliance between the labor parties and wealthy diaspora Jews. With the help of this funding from overseas, the labor parties were able to underwrite the economic-social system that had been set up by the Histadrut, the very system that promoted the labor parties' dominance (see more below). Since it was based on nationalist elements, this alliance further heightened the Jewish segregation from the Arab community (this outline drawn from Carmi and Rosenfeld, 1993; Grinberg, 1993a, 19–35; 1993b; Shalev, 1992, 32–44; Shapiro, 1976, 1977).

The Jewish community gradually established a pre-state pattern of rule under the government of the British Mandate, embodied by the Jewish Agency. Although not vested with formal sovereignty, the Yishuv's institutions proved highly effective in administering Jewish autonomy due in large degree to patterns of cooperation and political exchange between the political camps, gradually shaping a democratic configuration (see Horowitz and Lissak, 1978; Shapiro, 1977, 1984b). In consequence, the Yishuv's institutions controlled the main underground armed force of the Jewish community, the Haganah ("Defense") and the Palmach; raised money to underwrite the army's activities; were responsible for Jewish immigration, the regulation of the labor market, and land acquisitions; and established an autonomous system supplying social services. Naturally, a huge bureaucracy gradually evolved driven by the empowerment of the Yishuv's institutions. Notwithstanding the formal power granted by the British rulers to the Jewish institutions with the Jewish Agency in the center (due to a large extent to world Jewry's growing influence subsequent to World War I; see Love, 1969, 27–43), both its translation into practical performance and its expansion into areas beyond Britain's formal empowerment (particularly the gradual formation of a military) were made possible due to the utilization of the conflict.

Both processes—the development of the conflict and the evolution of the Jewish control structure—culminated in two major events in 1948: the establishment of the State of Israel, in which the Yishuv's power structure was reproduced in the constitution of the state on democratic-parliamentary foundations (see Migdal, 1989); and the outbreak of war between the Jewish community and the neighboring Arab states. Taking advantage of high capacity for mobilization and extraction of resources, the Jewish state achieved victory over the Arab armies by which Israel expanded its original boundaries. This also marked the conflict's transformation from the intercommunal to the interstate level.

Kimmerling (1976) concludes that the congruent management of the two processes helped reduce the costs that would have accrued from the separate management of each. Equally significant, the underlying interconnectedness served the political and material interests of the main groups in Israeli society. Social groups enjoyed a constantly improving standard of living due to the pre-statist capacity to both exploit the conflict to avert unequal Jewish-Palestinian interethnic competition in the labor market and to raise funds to be channeled to the erection of bureaucracies in which laborers enjoyed mobility (Shapiro, 1984a). At the same time, political groups benefited from the capacity to utilize external conflict for internal control and a permanent flow of resources to be converted to political support. The case of Israel was thus characterized by a parallel unfolding of processes: before there was a conflict there had not been a society and vice versa.

THE CREATION OF SOCIAL STRUCTURE

The Yishuv community was mainly composed of Jews from Central and Eastern Europe who had arrived in Palestine in a series of waves beginning in

1882. By 1948 there were 650,000 Jews in Israel. At bottom, the Yishuv did not have a rigid inegalitarian class structure. It was composed of a working class (urban and agrarian), an enormous middle class, and a petty bourgeoisie. Social disparities were not fixed because of several factors. First, the social structure of the Yishuv allowed agricultural and urban manual laborers to move into the bureaucratic class. In practice, new immigrants, initially placed on the periphery of the labor market, were "pushed" up the social ladder by the latest influx of new arrivals. The conflict-driven erection of an economic infrastructure and a huge bureaucracy absorbed manual workers and supported the bourgeoisie. This situation virtually precluded the emergence of a fully formed, fixed peripheral social class.

Second, the accumulation of power by the Yishuv's institutions involved the establishment of a quasi-state welfare system as a part of a centralist pre-state frame of rule. This system provided employment, education, and health services to most of the Jewish community. The effectiveness and inclusiveness of these services was the basis for the effective control of the Yishuv's institutions, primarily the Histadrut, by which it exchanged social services for political support. Insofar as a basic standard of living was guaranteed, social groups could focus their expectations on improving their lot. Third, the dominant social status in the Yishuv was epitomized by the *Chalutz* (pioneer) image—that of a settler engaged in manual labor whose contribution was crucial to the Zionist project. Consequently, a low social position not only reflected a temporary situation; it was also offset by the social prestige appropriated for the pioneering act (on the Yishuv's structure, see Shalev, 1992, 81–130; Shapiro, 1984a, 35–53).

The transition from pre-state to a state structure affected, inter alia, the reproduction of these arrangements assuring perpetual social mobility, rather than entrenchment of the dominance of specific groups. This was the uniform interest primarily of the post-Yishuv elites identified with the bureaucratic middle class. That interest took precedence over specific groups' interests, including those of political parties whose leaders and rank and file also belonged to this social class. Nevertheless, this transition entailed a crucial challenge to the original social structure.

The state, inspired by both the Zionist vision and the need to increase the Jewish population over against the Arab world, absorbed during the 1948–58 period about one million Jews, almost twice the existing number of Jewish citizens. Half of the immigrants streamed from Arab countries (mainly Iraq, Yemen, and North Africa) and were known as the Orientals. Most of them were encouraged to emigrate from their countries by Israel, which emphasized the possible implications for local Jews of growing nationalism in those countries. In the 1970s, the Orientals became the majority of the Jewish community in Israel owing to their higher birth rates relative to their counterpart Western

Israelis. Moreover, the state absorbed and granted formal Israeli citizenship to about 155,000 Palestinians living in areas mostly annexed by the State of Israel as a result of the 1948 War.[1]

Practically, the Western elites now staffing the new state institutions devised—partly by trial and error—three alternative strategies of absorption of the Oriental immigrants. The first was to absorb the Orientals on an egalitarian basis, involving equal allocation of state resources. But then the Westerners' dominant social position would be jeopardized, as absorption would have entailed drastic erosion of their standard of living. In practice, from 1949 to 1951, faced with a massive influx of immigrants and lacking a well-developed economic infrastructure, the state introduced an austerity and rationing regime. In effect, vital commodities were rationed equally for new immigrants and the veteran population by means of issuing government stamps to the population, irrespective of their differential economic ability. This partially egalitarian approach was inspired by the social-democratic tradition of Mapai but provoked the wrath of the veteran Western population, who increasingly complained about the lowering of their standard of living. They looked for alternative ways to purchase commodities freely and circumvent the state-imposed restrictions. A flourishing black market developed that the government was unable to eradicate, in no small measure because of both poor cooperation by officials in the civil service and the covert cooperation of the Histadrut's economic institutions with the black market. The Mapai machine demanded the abolition of the austerity policy, fearing the loss of its traditional supporters, the middle-class Westerners, a trend that was pronounced in the 1950 municipal elections and the elections to the Second Knesset (the Israeli parliament) held in 1951. This policy then was gradually abolished beginning in 1951 (Segev, 1986, 296–323; Shapiro, 1984a, 128–132). Had the state enforced another equality-oriented policy, it would have created a sharp tension with the Western middle-class groups. Their very empowerment under pre-state auspices was sufficient to contain any attempt to jeopardize their material achievements.

A second alternative was to openly discriminate against the Orientals, who would be treated as ordinary immigrants as in other capitalist countries. The state could, moreover, even employ selective immigration, suitable to the country's economic needs and capacity, an option that some Yishuv leaders raised, questioning the Jewish Agency's inclination to encourage mass immigration of Orientals and even Westerners (Hacohen, 1994, 113–116, 214–215). However, this market-oriented path meant decentralization of state control and thus was at odds with the pre-state pattern of rule. No wonder that the market-oriented alternative was in part echoed by the General Zionists Party. Although overt discrimination and selective immigration were not part of this party's rhetoric, it challenged the social-democratic posture of Mapai and voiced support for letting market rules govern the absorption of immigrants and economic development (see Abramov, 1995, 97–112). The costs entailed by embarking on a more liberal avenue, moreover, would have not only inflamed an interethnic/interclass conflict but, equally significant, have precluded the Orientals' (low-cost) roles—presented as national missions—in the economy, agrarian settlement, and the military. Consequently, mobilization for these missions would have to be left to limited but costly market-oriented, rather than nationally invoked, low-cost mechanisms.

Overt discrimination or selective immigration also contradicted the Zionist vision of equal absorption for all Jews, a vision that legitimized the state's successful fundraising and mobilization of political support among world Jewry. At the same time, ethnic categorization was unnecessary as long as Westerners' control over the state institutions paved the road to effective economic and political control over the unorganized Orientals. So, a competitive position between Westerners and Orientals in the labor market that might have stimulated ethnic policies, similar to those of the United States and South Africa (see Marx, 1996), was averted.

Practically rejecting options 1 and 2, the Western elites opted for a third, middling option: to employ methods that would treat the Orientals on a seemingly equal basis while leaving intact the pre-state sociopolitical structure, entrenching the arrangements that assured the Westerners' perpetual social mobility *despite* the mission of mass absorption. Such methods would reduce the structure's inherent potential to incubate an active ethnic class conflict by blurring to the utmost the inegalitarian image of the ethno-class division of labor. Conditions were then created to mold an interventionist state carrying out a dual mission—running the absorption in a manner making inequalities a durable phenomenon and legitimizing the inequitable ethno-class structure that resulted. This worked to create political-ideological barriers to Orientals' political action in demand of all-encompassing reallocation of the societal resources. *Reproduction* of inequality was the result.

It should be emphasized that the ethno-class structure that resulted from the opted trajectory was not necessarily a product of a deliberate, defined plan but, rather, an outcome of power relations finding their expression in conditions of convergence between the two ethnic groups in the labor market under the direction of a state in the process of being built. This model of state–society relations underlined the state's internal position and mode of action. The remainder of this chapter deals with this trajectory of state-building.

Absorption was based on the government's policy of settling—in many cases, even forcibly—the incoming Orientals in remote border towns and in the peripheral neighborhoods of the large cities, some of them abandoned Palestinian villages lacking infrastructure and services. A policy of this kind could not be carried out effectively by market mechanisms alone. Furthermore, state agencies worked to fulfill a mission beyond absorption, namely, to populate and, thus, to fix, the state's new borders with the Arab countries. By 1974 Orientals accounted for about 70 percent of the total population in peripheral settlements—small, developing towns and agricultural villages (*Moshav Olim*) (Swirski, 1981, 62–63).

Oriental immigrants received inferior services from the state, particularly in housing and education. A survey in 1968 (about fifteen years after the immigration wave) indicated that only about 5.5 percent of the Oriental immigrants lived in housing with a density of less than one person per room, relative to 24 percent among the veteran Westerners and 14 percent among the Westerners who immigrated during the same period (Swirski, 1981, 31). At the same time, the isolation of many Orientals in peripheral, developing towns and villages meant that schools in their neighborhoods were mostly staffed by underqualified teachers, many of them women soldiers. Moreover, while the young generation faced difficulties dealing with the dominant, Western content of education, their achievements within this system were what would determine their mobility and capacity to compete with Westerners. Add these conditions to the initial poor education of these immigrants in Western terms, and Oriental students experienced growing rates of failure. Later, this led the government to establish special routes for Oriental students, fixing their disadvantaged position (Swirski, 1990, 90–102).

For illustration, in 1961, only about 35 percent of the Oriental Israeli-born completed nine to twelve years of schooling compared to 65 percent of Western Israeli-born. A similar gap existed between the parents of these youngsters, so gaps were transmitted from the immigrants to their children (Ben-Porath, 1986a, 159). Further, in the 1970s, more than 40 percent of the pupils in elementary schools (mostly Orientals) were categorized as "disadvantaged" (Eisenstadt, 1985, 262; Swirski, 1990, 97).

Consequently, Oriental immigrants were relegated to, and fixed within, the secondary labor market that grew due to their entrance, primarily in peripheral areas. They found work as manual laborers, partially seasonal, in agriculture, construction, and manufacturing, in many cases replacing Western workers who moved into the newly created bureaucracies. Moreover, this growth of a mass labor force had the impact of lowering blue-collar workers' income. At the same time, the bureaucratic class was generally closed to Oriental immigrants, as better-educated Westerners took advantage of the professional opportunities afforded by the bureaucracy.

The upshot was that the exploitation of Oriental immigrants as cheap labor in the 1950s and 1960s triggered the growth in the Israeli economy, especially in construction and manufacturing, while the main beneficiaries were Westerners. Industrialization increased from 1954 on when agriculture, still the main economic sector, proved unable to serve the state's goals of full employment. Economic growth was fueled not only by the availability of a mass, cheap labor force, but also by liberal trends inherent in the elimination of the austerity policy and, after 1953, German reparations for the loss of Jewish life and property in the Holocaust. Part of the sum—3.5 billion marks— streamed directly into government coffers for economic development. The state then could actively promote industrialization beginning in 1954 by encouraging private entrepreneurs. In practice, the government provided entrepreneurs loans at low interest rates, financed the development of infrastructure, financed exports, protected against competing imports, and more, in addition to its social policies permitting the exploitation of low-paid Orientals. Consequently, by 1959, manufacturing employed 25 percent of the total manpower compared to a few percent during the early 1950s (on industrialization, see Beilin, 1987, 125–126; Schweitzer, 1984, 99–124; Swirski, 1989, 13–14).

Developing towns then became reservoirs of perpetually low-paid Orientals dependent, more than in any other area, on a limited number of employers. The government's policy was to collaborate with business entrepreneurs in directing capital to those areas as a means of promoting industrialization (Swirski, 1981, 64–69). Accumulation of capital then became contingent on the security mission encouraging the settlement of remote border towns.

Similar to former waves of immigration, Orientals pushed Western manual workers into the middle class. Veteran Westerners, and gradually, Western immigrants as well, staffed the bureaucratic professions that developed following the economic growth and the creation of statist executive agencies. As in former periods, war preparation nurtured bureaucracy expansion, a powerful army (see below), and mechanisms for taxation and the monitoring of production (see Barnett, 1992, 161–169). The Histadrut and other public bureaucracies gradually comprised about 50 percent of the total labor force. Many others of this collective constituted the rising business-managerial elite. The state also distributed lands to the Westerner-dominated agricultural sector, which comprised about 5 percent of the whole population, and to private business entrepreneurs; a great deal of this land had been confiscated from Palestinians, both refugees from the 1948 War and citizens.

Moreover, the Histadrut deliberately supported demands put forward in the mid-1950s by organized workers, mostly Westerners, to eliminate the principle of equality of income, a legacy of the pioneering Yishuv society. This move, in conjunction with the other effects stemming from the reconstruction of the labor market, helped shape an inequitable ethno-class structure based on Westerners' class dominance, nourished by, and therefore also dependent on, the maintenance of the Orientals' peripheral position.

To illustrate long-term outcomes, in 1972 only about 10 percent of the Orientals were occupied in professional, white-collar occupations relative to about 30 percent of Westerners (Swirski, 1981, 58–60). During the same period (1969), the income of Western Israeli-born males was 62 percent higher than that of Oriental Israeli-born males. In 1976 the figure was 77 percent (Fishelson et al., 1980, 265). Gaps widened further, especially in the second generation, as a consequence of the fixation of the labor market's structure during the early 1950s.

The Oriental immigrants' exploitation as cheap labor was made possible by several factors. First, Orientals were manipulated as mass-unorganized immigrants, culturally estranged in an economy suffering from unemployment that stood at a rate of more than 10 percent during the state's first years. In contrast, Westerners came to Palestine in former waves of immigration enjoying social-political networks already formed in their countries of origin. Second, unlike former waves of immigration, inequality in schooling was pronounced for the reasons mentioned above. Westerners took advantage of the economic boom of the state's first years to seize the dominant positions, most critically in the state bureaucracy, thus effectively curtailing the Orientals' mobility, a trend that became even more pronounced as public service became increasingly professionalized (see Shapiro, 1984a, 134–135). Third, the Orientals' mobility was further checked because of their ethno-cultural distinctiveness which, as I will show, helped entrench their low social position and also harbored the potential to trigger interethnic conflict.

Fourth, the Histadrut did not really represent low-paid Oriental immigrants. It was the patron of the organized workforce of the veteran Yishuv on which it drew its political support. As for the Orientals, they could be enlisted in support of the political establishment. As long as they were dependent on both the state's and Histadrut's services (first and foremost employment and medical services) and unorganized, the Histadrut was not particularly motivated to organize them. On the contrary, the Histadrut's economic sector, *Hevrat Ha'Ovdim*, was a holding company that directly benefited from exploitation of low-wage Oriental workers. By administering these policies, the Histadrut legitimized the segmentation of the labor market and as such was instrumental in producing the inequitable ethno-class division of labor. Finally, the state played a key role in legitimizing exploitation as we will see later. In sum, unlike the pre-state society, the immigrant group that arrived last was rendered immobile and relegated to a fixed, peripheral social position.

In contrast to Orientals, European immigrants who came in the second half of the immigration (some of them Holocaust survivors) were treated similarly to their Western predecessors in the Yishuv period. They were absorbed into, and supported by, the long-established Western social networks. In many cases the government deliberately settled them in veteran neighborhoods or, relying on their social networks, they were more successful than Orientals in moving from peripheral towns to the center; state agencies did not attempt to settle these European immigrants against their will, as they did the Orientals. Western immigrants were also more successful in moving from blue- to white-collar jobs and protesting against poor housing or employment conditions (Swirski, 1981, 62–64). So, the political establishment was more sensitive to these immigrants' preferences. Consequently, as the figures above indicate, peripheral towns or neighborhoods became almost homogeneously Oriental enclaves (on the creation of social structure in the Jewish community, see Bernstein and Swirski, 1982; Rosenfeld and Carmi, 1976; Peled, 1991; Shalev, 1992, 186–226; Shapiro, 1984a, 128–136; Smooha, 1984a; Swirski, 1981, 1989).

The urgency to ensure unquestioned full employment for low-wage Jewish workers, mainly Oriental immigrants, constrained Israel's approach to the Palestinians. Cheap Palestinian labor could jeopardize, through competition, full employment of the Orientals as long as the two groups competed in the secondary sectors of the labor market. Unemployment among Oriental immigrants, however, could have sparked protests against their peripheral status. Exclusion of Palestinian workers from the Jewish labor market thus became one of the main devices through which the state regulated the labor market. Similar policies were formulated under identical conditions by the Jewish elites during the pre-state era.

Two war-based mechanisms were instrumental in excluding the Palestinian labor force. First, the Military Administration was imposed on the Israeli Palestinian population. Conceived and formally legitimized as a means of controlling a potentially hostile population, the Military Administration isolated the Palestinian towns from the Jewish ones and regulated the flow of Palestinian labor into the Jewish labor market according to the rate of unemployment among Jewish laborers and the demand for low-paid workers in the secondary labor market that could not be supplied by Jewish workers.

A second mechanism was to block access for Palestinian refugees to the Israeli labor market, by sealing the state's borders and combating infiltrations. Some of the territory acquired by Israel in the 1948 War had previously been inhabited by Palestinians. They had fled from their villages and towns during the fighting, in some cases encouraged to do so by Israeli army commanders and political leaders for perceived security reasons (Morris, 1988). The end of the war found about 700,000 refugees in temporary camps along Israel's borders, awaiting a permanent solution. They tried to infiltrate into Israel primarily for economic reasons. A new unmarked and unnatural border, cutting off the refugees from their former homes, fueled this phenomenon (Morris, 1993, 34–54). Israel, for its part, attempted to prevent the refugees' entrance, triggering border frictions during the 1950s (see chapter 3).

Furthermore, exclusion undercut refugees' power not only as laborers but also as property owners. When the state was established, it also confiscated land from Palestinians, refugees and citizens alike, and appropriated the abandoned houses left by Palestinian refugees. In sum, it gradually controlled six times the land it had acquired in the pre-state period (Carmi and Rosenfeld, 1993, 290). Importantly, if the government could settle immigrants in the newly abandoned land and houses, there was no need to reallocate resources between immigrants and veterans (see Segev, 1986, 74–88). Reallocation might have significantly slashed the Western middle class's standard of living.

Besides, discrimination in resource allocation practically obstructed the creation of an economic infrastructure and intelligentsia among the Palestinian minority. At the same time, strategies of co-optation were employed, beginning in the mid-1950s, through penetration by the Histadrut and political parties, supplying services and cultivating local elites loyal to the state in return for electoral support. Such policies constructed a low-cost annexation relative to alternative policies based on violent repression, without granting citizenship and other rights (see Lustick, 1980; Shalev. M, 1989; Smooha, 1985; Peled, 1992; Rosenhek, 1996, 80–122).

In sum, unlike the policies toward Orientals, Palestinians were overtly discriminated against their ethnic (national) origin. The reality of conflict with the Arab states was invoked to legitimize policy that affected the construction of an inequitable social structure. Furthermore, conditions had been created, precluding cooperation between the groups now composing the working class in Israel, namely, Palestinians and Orientals. Once the Palestinians were excluded as a potential "fifth column," Oriental-Palestinian cooperation would have contradicted the Orientals' national identity as Israelis by which they were striving to gain a "pass-key" into a new society.[2]

Although Israel's approach was directly driven by security and demographic considerations, this policy indirectly correlated with and backed its domestic policies: It seems logical to assume that had the state adopted one of the alternative models of absorption or if Oriental immigration had not risen, then Jewish employers' tendency to exploit the Palestinian workforce, both local (citizens) and external (refugees), would have increased. From those employers' perspective, exploitation of Palestinian laborers would be crucial or available: It would be crucial in the case of egalitarian absorption, by means of which labor cost in the secondary labor market would increase; it would be simply available in the case of market-oriented absorption, by which pressures toward full employment within the Jewish society would lose much of their value. Possible exploitation might have led to demands that the government display more flexibility toward border-crossing as a counterbalance to those considerations which accounted for the policy of exclusion. A similar situation had been created during the Yishuv period, when pressures of this kind generated an exploitation of the Palestinian labor force despite the prevailing ethos of "Jewish Labor," that is, a separation between the two ethnic labor markets (see Shalev, 1992, 39–44; Shapira, 1986, 94–100).

To recall, the state not only played a pivotal role in the construction of the ethno-class structure but also in legitimizing its products through *universalization* of the state's action.[3]

MAMLACHTIYUT

State legitimation of social inequality took shape in two ways. First, the state employed intensive methods of a typical welfare state encompassing the Jewish sector exclusively: policies oriented toward full employment with state subsidies (policies in which the exclusion of the Palestinian labor force from the Jewish labor market played a key role, as it will be recalled); all-inclusive medical services; social security; obligatory and free elementary schooling; and the subsidizing of basic foodstuffs and public transportation (see Shalev, 1992, 104–105, 205–206). To some degree welfare policies partly mitigated the effects of policies of absorption. Second, and most important, the state, in practice, universalized its particularist action through the *Mamlachtiyut* (statism).

State-directed absorption was part of a process that placed the state at the center of the new social-political order, a disposition that was ideologically supported by the Mamlachtiyut—the state ideology. Mamlachtiyut was formulated, mainly, by David Ben-Gurion, the first prime minister and defense minister. Mamlachtiyut raised the state to a supreme symbol as the embodiment of Zionism, supplanting any particularist conception incompatible with state-directed goals. It inculcated the notion that the state possesses a legitimacy that does not depend on any domestic political force. This contrasted with the concept propounded by the Left, especially Mapam (United Workers Party), according to which the state's legitimacy depended on its ideological substance and the political groups staffing its institutions (see Cohen, 1987, 213–219; Horowitz and Lissak, 1989, 91; Sprinzak, 1986, 77–92).

Still, Mamlachtiyut was not merely a Ben–Gurion-tailored political formula, nor was it a voluntarily ideological preference as it has been portrayed by some writers (see, for example, Carmi and Rosenfeld, 1993, 284–299; Cohen, 1987, 228–259; Keren, 1983; Kese, 1986). These writers focused on Mapai's intentions and ideology while neglecting the role played by Mamlachtiyut in structuring power relations. They have also overlooked the alternative trajectories of absorption, and hence have failed to explain how and why this ideology prevailed beyond the initial entrepreneurial action. These issues are the subject of the rest of the chapter substantiating the argument that the universalist ethos of Mamlachtiyut was realized by placing the state above the powerful pre-state power centers. By and large, this process heavily relied on the militarization of Israeli society.

In practical terms, the realization of Mamlachtiyut involved state internal expansion by which the state assumed roles that had been carried out by the pre-state power centers in the Yishuv period. Assuming roles was not, per se, excessive as compared historically to bureaucracies in other states, new states in particular. Moreover, the state leaders simply took advantage of the change of power relations between the Jewish Agency, and Mapai and the Histadrut since the new state bureaucracy had not only inherited the Jewish Agency's powers but also those of the British Mandatory government. However, state expansion targeted notably Mapai's roles through its main apparatus, the Histadrut.

Mapai garnered huge political power during the pre-state period due to its combined control of the Histadrut and the Jewish Agency. The Histadrut controlled workers by means of the infrastructure it had established consisting of economic enterprises and social services covering employment, education, health, and other areas. These services were financed by the Jewish Agency. Through its control of the Histadrut, Mapai mustered the political support of the population, constituting the majority of the Yishuv, that used, and hence was dependent on, the Histadrut's services. And through its ability to enlist the support of the main population, Mapai controlled the Jewish Agency through which it monitored the flow of resources from both external and internal sources. This meant mainly raising Jewish capital to underwrite the Histadrut's enterprises, i.e., Mapai's political control. Thus, Mapai's control of each institution nurtured its control of the other. Through its control of the organizational mechanisms and its identification with the prevailing ideology of the Yishuv, Mapai achieved political dominance that was successfully reproduced in the transition from pre-state to state (Shapiro, 1977).

Consequently, the young state's bureaucracy depended on the Mapai-ruled power centers at several levels. First, they functioned as quasi-statist agencies in significant areas of typical statist activity, for instance, educational and employment services. Second, the party machine mobilized political support for its emissaries in state institutions, a heritage of the pre-state period (Shapiro, 1977, 98–102, 187–188). As long as the dialogue between the state and its citizens was mediated by the social networks affiliated with the parties (the press, schools, trade unions, etc.; see Galnoor, 1982; Shapiro, 1996) the position of the leadership heavily depended on the support the party could muster through its own channels. Because of this, the party was in a position to demarcate the bounds of its emissaries' activity in state institutions (as the case of the abolition of the austerity policy has shown). Third, the Histadrut provided "services" in the form of political mobilization, legitimation of the split structure of the labor market, and restraining potential militancy of the organized labor force—services that shaped the unique character of corporatist arrangements between the state and trade unions in Israel (see Grinberg, 1993a, 53–55; Shalev, 1992, 103–115, 186–226).

The state's appropriation of part of the party-based centers' roles involved several major moves in addition to taking control of immigration: (1) the dismantling of the underground organizations associated with the parties (see below); (2) the establishment of a Government Employment Service instead of the Histadrut-controlled labor exchanges; (3) the establishment of a statist educational system that took over the schools founded by the parties; (4) the establishment of a statist civil service that gradually shaped achievement-oriented criteria for promotion instead of ones based on party affiliation; (5) the use of the military for settlement purposes via the Nahal ("Fighting Pioneer Youth" units) and for managing the camps of new immigrants in 1950; and (6) the state's displacement of the Jewish Agency as the internal distributor of funds originating from foreign sources—both American aid beginning immediately after Israel's independence and, from 1953 on, German reparations to Israel that were partly channeled directly by the government.

Further, the state's appropriation of pre-state institutional functions meant that the only way an individual or a group could realize collective needs was through the bureaucracy, while volunteers were replaced by salaried employees tied to the state bureaucracy (Shapiro, 1977, 159–161). A cyclical process was then set in motion: Veteran Western social groups, particularly youngsters, reacted with a weary apathy to the state's penetration, displaying little inclination for political participation (of an active kind, as distinguished from voting and media consumption) or volunteering (see Badi, 1963, 134; Eisenstadt, 1958; Horowitz, 1960; Kreitler and Kreitler, 1964; Lissak, 1953). Then, the decline of voluntarism was cited by state agencies as a reason for the state to further assume civilian activities. For example, the state intensified its role in settling the frontiers using the military beginning in 1953, inasmuch as the agricultural movements' motivation to do so appeared insufficient (see Sraya, 1954, 17–26). In sum, the partial autonomy that the post-Yishuv civil society had enjoyed was gradually eradicated in the state period, helping the state achieve sturdy domination over political space.

In consequence, the pre-state power centers, mainly the Histadrut and indirectly Mapai as well, were dramatically weakened. They were eventually at the state's mercy. For example, the Histadrut's control over the workforce placed within the state-regulated secondary labor market (Palestinians and Orientals)—that was also translated into Mapai's electoral gains—was conditional on state regimentation. At another level, the Histadrut relied on the state for its very existence, to underwrite its powerful institutions, such as its Sick Fund (*Kupat Holim*), pension funds, and the Hevrat Ha'Ovdim holding company (on state relations with the party-based centers, see Barnett, 1992, 161–165; Cohen, 1987, 228–249; Horowitz and Lissak, 1989, 151–164; Kimmerling, 1993a; Migdal, 1989; Shalev, 1992, 103–107; Sprinzak, 1986, 77–92).

It follows that contrary to what I call "Mapai-centered approaches" a distinction needs to be drawn between the state and the party. According to

Mapai-centered approaches, the political parties were the most important organizations in Israeli politics because of their historical role in shaping the society. Israel, after all, has often been called a "parties state." Conceptually, this approach suggests that Mapai controlled the state machinery as long as its emissaries staffed the main positions in the state agencies (see, for example, Grinberg, 1993a; Shapiro, 1976, 1977, 1980, 1984a, 1996). This approach to explaining state–party relations is arguably not plausible. True, Mapai controlled through its emissaries most of the state agencies, but in practice, once an institution was transferred from party to state control, the party machine lost much of its control over this institution. Although party emissaries managed the institution, decisions were gradually made in statist forums rather than party councils. Further, moves were more and more directed by universalist considerations, not partisan ones, as a natural requirement from a statist institution to satisfy groups outside the party's constituency. Hence, as a part of the state bureaucracy's pursuit of functioning autonomously, conditions were formed for separation between the party machine and the party's emissaries in the various state agencies, so that they could operate without relying significantly on the party. Put differently, this separation meant that party emissaries gradually developed a "schizophrenic," autonomous pattern of behavior vis-à-vis the party, arising from raisons d'état rather than from a rationale of party. To some degree this separation resembles similar distinctions between state agencies and the groups from which those agencies draw.[4]

By bolstering its supremacy vis-à-vis the pre-1948 party power centers, the state enhanced its relative autonomy as its dependence on these centers decreased, and hence their ability to limit the state's capacity to implement its policies declined. And, more important, conditions were laid down to universalize state action by manifesting its diminishing dependence on particularist party-based institutions. The state's universalism then rests on its image as an embodiment of the society's unity transcending factional schisms and not favoring any specific power group (see Gold et al., 1975, 40, at the theoretical level).

Pushing the argument further, the universalist Mamlachtiyut impacted directly on interethnic relations. It was, first and foremost, the military that played a pivotal role in administering universalist policies, central to which was the *ethos of egalitarianism* within the military.

THE MILITARY ASPECT OF MAMLACHTIYUT

The IDF (Israel Defence Forces) was the successor of the pre-state military organization, Haganah. Inspired in 1946/47 by the image of the British army, Ben-Gurion inculcated in the Haganah elements of a standing, professional, and disciplined military, eroding its militia profile. This also involved

mass semivoluntary conscription even before the state was formally established (see Gelber, 1989). The IDF was formally created at the state's establishment. During the 1948 War the pre-state military underground organizations
were dismantled and at the end of the war the "Defense Service Law" (1949)
took effect, shaping the new military.

Basically, the IDF was a small regular military, the ranks of which were
staffed by imposing universalist, compulsory military service of two years
(later extended to thirty months) on all Israelis at the age of eighteen. Career
personnel filled the officer corps and part of the professional echelon. A large,
well-organized reserve army was considered to be on "permanent leave," and
was capable of swift mobilization. The regular army, according to this model,
functions as the "manufactory" of the reserve army as well as the initial forces
assigned to curb an enemy's attack until mobilization of the reserves can be
completed. This model was opted for by Ben-Gurion and his associates over
alternative models. One model was the creation of large standing military without trained reserves as some generals preferred. Leftist Mapam, on the other
hand, took an opposite stand. It was inspired by the Palmach, the elitist pre-state
underground movement—many of its activists came from the Kibbutz
Movement identified with Mapam. Accordingly, it advocated an elite army
closely related to the labor movement and one that would supply protection
against perceived, potential violent challenge by the right wing.

Several considerations led to the opted organization, balancing between
conflicting requirements (see Barnett, 1992, 161, 169–176; Ben-Gurion, 1971,
31–43; Horowitz, 1987; Neeman, 1985; Segev, 1986, 267–273; Teveth, 1971,
367–369). First and foremost, the chosen model facilitated a maximum extraction of manpower as a means of bridging over Israel's inferiority vis-à-vis the
Arab countries—perceived as threatening Israel's existence—in both territorial
and demographic terms, but without overburdening the civilian sectors.
Moreover, this model facilitates abbreviation of a war's length because of the
high level of readiness of the reserves, who can move quickly to the offensive
following a brief defensive stage (see more in chapter 3).

Second, adoption of each of the alternative models would have strengthened the military and could have led to too much autonomy over the political
level. Moreover, Ben-Gurion, representing the rationale of Mapai, was politically motivated by a fear of Mapam's growing strength as a leftist alternative to
Mapai's centrism and its desire to loosen Mapai's hold on the army by utilizing
its influence on the Palmach. He even feared that young discharged soldiers,
primarily Palmach veterans, would join forces with Mapam to violently undermine Mapai's rule. If so, a mass military, amenable to the mobility of thousands
of new recruits, including officers, would diminish the influence of the Palmach
on the IDF.[5] Third, this and other fears that the army's empowerment might
bring about its active intervention in politics interwoven with diversion of

resources from security to absorption of immigration underlay Ben-Gurion's rationale for discharging the majority of the 1948 conscripts and further shrinking the regular army at the beginning of the 1950s. Israel's defensive military doctrine prevailing at this period simultaneously fueled and was fueled by this move.

But as a by-product of the IDF's main mission, the army assumed the role of an interethnic "melting pot," as *only* in the mass military could all Israeli Jews meet on equal terms, without social barriers. The military thus enjoyed the image of the "People Army" (see Ben-Gurion, 1971, 42–43). Universal, mass conscription then galvanized the egalitarian ethos by being applied to both women and men, veterans and new immigrants alike, even though it excluded the Palestinians (see more below) and some individuals from distressed areas who had not completed a certain level of education, and exempted ultra-orthodox Jews—under their rabbis' pressures to let the youngsters study in yeshivas instead of serving in the military. That ethos was also seen in the army reserves, service that was imposed on men up to the age of forty-nine, who were called up several times a year for training in order to maintain their combat readiness (ibid., 72).

The ethos of egalitarianism had additional, concrete manifestations. Significant was the uniform service induction for both soldiers and officers. Unlike most other armies (including the British army, which had left a powerful imprint on the IDF's founders), which separated officers from enlisted men through military academies, Israeli officers spring from the mass of ordinary soldiers and receive special training only after a period of basic training. This practice, together with the functional, plain uniforms, emphasizes the equal position of all inductees. This effect is furthered by the IDF's mode of command: The doctrine of "After me," which typifies the Israeli officer's conduct in the battlefield, reflects the commander's personal involvement in the performance of his soldiers, without compartmentalization according to ranks, as occurs in Western armies (Schild, 1973). Most important, the ethos of egalitarianism was reflected in the selection system, based on the uniform, objective, quantitative rules determining eligibility for promotion (see Bar-Haim, 1987; Gal, 1986, 83). Individuals were not measured against attributive traits per se, but in relation to their ability to fulfill missions in the service of the military.

Notwithstanding the prominence of the declared ethos, an inegalitarian ethno-functional division of labor was shaped within the military, the counterpart to the civilian ethnic division of labor. Inevitably, the IDF's creation as a modern, Western-style military meant that the ostensibly rational, objective criteria determining an individual soldier's position were, in fact, geared more toward the education, values, and primary skills of the Western draftees. These were less compatible with the background of the Oriental immigrants who lacked a Western education, a deficiency aggravated by the inferior education available in the areas where the Orientals lived, compared to those where the Western population lived (see Amir, 1967; Amir et al., 1975; Ben-Rafael, 1982, 188–193; Hurewitz, 1969, 431–432; Roumani, 1979, 70–86; 1991; Smooha, 1984b; Yinon and Freedman, 1977).[6]

The result was that the military granted dominance to Western soldiers while perpetuating the peripheral position of the Orientals. David Ben-Gurion addressed this issue in late 1953: "From the very outset, I was afraid that our military would be divided into two races: the commanders would all be Ashkenazis, while their subordinates would for the most part come from the Oriental communities" (1981, 10). In his survey of the military's ethnic makeup, Ben-Gurion found about 200 officers from the Oriental communities out of some 4,000 officers in the conscript and career armies (ibid.). This stratification seemed justified, at least in the IDF's first years. As Ben-Gurion explained, "The new recruits who are inducted from among the Oriental new immigrants took psychotechnical tests and they will not succeed in becoming commanders. . . . Although in time we shall also educate Yemenite and Moroccan new immigrants to be physicians, engineers, and teachers—we cannot wait" (1971, 142–143). Ben-Gurion also doubted whether the Oriental soldiers could show a fighting spirit on a par with that of the Westerners (1981, 9). Such dicta reflected the essence of the Mamlachtiyut, which identified the veteran (Western) community with qualities enabling it to take the lead in building a new society. The Oriental immigrants, in contrast, were regarded as *joiners* of the society, whose Western qualities they had to assimilate; until that process (i.e., modernization) had run its course, they could not be real members of the society but just contribute at the *quantitative* level.

At the same time, the ethno-functional division of labor that developed in the military was perceived as a legitimate structure by the agents involved. The underlying perception was that this structure existed precisely in a mass, seemingly egalitarian military, inculcating its personnel with the idea that their status was determined by objective criteria of achievement inherent in the military's needs, and not by the ascriptive criteria of ethnic affiliation. In fact, the modern, Western norms on which the military was founded provided the seemingly egalitarian criteria and thus also the legitimation for Westerners' dominance. Thus, during the 1950s, the inequality in the IDF was considered to be a temporary phenomenon, conflicting with the declared social goals of the military as they were articulated by Ben-Gurion himself. Because the immigrants believed the official ideology that military service constituted an entry ticket to the society, their very induction, rather than their status in the organization, became a symbolic resource in itself, motivating them to accept what was perceived as a temporary preference enjoyed by the Westerners.[7]

Surely, the denial of military service to the Israeli Palestinians buttressed the national-social meaning of military service, and underscored the social position of those having access to that service, especially from the Orientals' point of view. As mentioned above, the universality of the military was an exclusively Jewish perception. True, the Palestinian minority that became part of Israel after the 1948 War was formally granted full civil rights and was officially liable for military service. In practice, however, the Palestinians were exempted and excluded from army service, although there is evidence that many youngsters wanted to serve during the 1950s (Benziman and Mansour, 1992, 116–118). In part, this policy originated in the government's unwillingness to mobilize an ethnic group that was part of the Arab nation with which Israel was engaged in a violent conflict.

Consequently, the Israeli political community was shaped as an ethno-republican community in which Jewish ethnic affiliation was a necessary condition for belonging and that membership defined one's civil status (Peled, 1992). Participation in military service, while exempting the Palestinians from the duty to serve, embodied also a participation in defining society's "common good." This deprivation, by invoking the Arab-Israeli conflict, meant that the Palestinians could be set apart from the Jewish community in a subtle, quasi-consensual manner; hence also that they could be denied the rewards available to discharged soldiers (see Cohen, 1989; Horowitz and Kimmerling, 1974; Kimmerling, 1979). By the same token, the fact that the Druze—some ten thousand citizens who had been annexed to Israel after the 1948 War—did military service allowed for their differentiation from the Arab community (see Ben-Dor, 1973).

At the bottom line, the IDF's ethos of egalitarianism both compounded the inequality within the military by reinforcing the effects of the unequal conditions of entry and, simultaneously, legitimized that inequality.

Pushing the argument further, with their dominant position in the IDF legitimated, Westerners could parlay their dominance within the military into social status outside the military, further legitimizing their social dominance over Orientals to avert an eruption of interethnic clashes. This was at the root of how the military worked to legitimize the unequal interethnic power relations outside its ranks. Legitimate parlaying relied, to a large extent, on the symbolism of Mamlachtiyut and that of the "fighter." Instead of Chalutziyut (pioneering), the dominant symbolic status in the pre-state society previously used for evaluating social action (personal and collective), Mamlachtiyut laid down a new status identified with the state's bureaucrat groups. It gave priority to an individual or group placing themselves in the service of the state, forming a new ethos known as *state pioneering*. By so doing it embodied the new society's code of civic virtue defining the criteria by which one could become an active member of the society, and engineered a distinction not only between Jews and Palestinians (see Peled, 1992), but also among social groups within the Jewish communities.

This dovetailed with the appearance of a new set of values associated with management and efficiency, namely *bitzuism* ("getting things done without letting moral scruples get in the way"). It took the place of the traditional ideological tenets and the pioneering values (Kalderon, 1984, 14; Yatziv, 1986, 145–148), although the bureaucratic ethos had already been raised in the Yishuv (Shapiro, 1984a, 128–136). Naturally, Orientals' move into the working class was accompanied by the decline of the status of "Jewish worker," previously part of the vanishing "pioneer," in favor of the rise of a "working-class intelligentsia"—Western professionals who were mobilized to take their part in state-building (Keren, 1989b).[8]

The gradual displacement of the "pioneer" status with the rise of new instrumentalist values also paved the way for the emergence of the "fighter" (see Gertz, 1985/86, 269; 1988, 280–281; Kimmerling, 1971; Shapira, 1992, 365–370). A further militarization of Israeli society relative to the pre-state period simultaneously nurtured and was nurtured by this process. Militarization meant that preparation for war was regarded as normal social activity (partially in Mann's terms, 1987, 35) on which the society organized and social criteria were established. From the outset, Mamlachtiyut emphasized the state's violent mission and its historical responsibility for ensuring the community's existence in the light of the Arabs' threat in an eternal war of the "few against many" (Gertz, 1995, 13–34). Mamlachtiyut was regarded in this context as a kind of "civil religion," in the sense that its adherents perceived the state as the earthly embodiment of the Jewish people's rebirth with substitution of secular for religious symbols, or their admixture (Liebman and Don-Yehiya, 1983, 83–98). Further, the military's social functions, its complete divorce from the political arena, and the moral halo it was awarded by Ben-Gurion and his coterie blurred the distinction between ideals and power (Keren, 1983, 81–85).

By ascribing the birth of the state to the potency of military force, no longer was social action considered to be motivated by the voluntary will of the individual, but by means of the military and a strong leadership. Groups associated with the new state apparatuses, who carried on the political discourse, began downplaying the contribution of the Yishuv elites—with the "pioneer" in the center—to the state's establishment and emphasized instead the role of the military organizations revolving around the "fighter" (Gertz, 1985/86, 269; 1988, 280–281). Further, although military service was obligatory, it was shrouded in a voluntary, pioneering-like ethos. Witness the language of the mobilization order (albeit at a later period): "The draftees are called up to the colors by law, but they come as volunteers." The fact that conscripts received only token salaries further encouraged this ethos. Add to this the IDF's unique role as an interethnic integrator, and pioneering now meant military service, while "fighter" displaced "pioneer."

Discursive militarization was an outcome of the prolonged violent conflict from which the state was born. However, already during the 1940s, youngsters belonging to the native-born generation had invoked military-oriented symbols to legitimize their self-proclaimed social position vis-à-vis the older generation and other groups, thus contributing to the militarization of the political discourse (Ben-Eliezer, 1995, 115–133). As this competition heightened in the state's first years, taking the form of a struggle between statist and prestatist groups (see below), instrumentalist symbols of this kind gained further prominence. Still, the "fighter" celebrated its triumph over the "pioneer" only in the mid-1950s, following the Sinai Campaign in 1956 (see chapter 3).

In sum, whereas in the Yishuv discourse the right to use violence was presented as a cardinal instrument of policy implementation backing diplomatic means, with the Arab-Israeli conflict taken as given (Ben-Eliezer, 1995; Shapira, 1988, 46–54), now the use of force was transformed, taking on *symbolic*, not just *instrumental*, value and overshadowing political means.

Due to the inegalitarian ethno-functional division of labor within the IDF, the central "fighter" status was achievable mainly by Westerners, who had established the military and dominated it, whereas the Orientals, who had joined a military controlled by the Westerners, had only limited access to the new status.[9] The Orientals' military contribution was perceived in quantitative terms whereas the Westerners were perceived as providing a qualitative contribution (Smooha, 1984b).

Practically, the victory in the 1948 War waged by the state on its establishment was credited to the young Western generation, afterward called the "1948 Generation" or the "Native-Born Generation," those youngsters who had manned the pre-state, elitist underground organization and occupied prominent positions in the IDF during the 1948 War. Among the war's participants and victims, however, were also youngsters from the small existing Oriental community and the new immigrants who poured into the country. That stratification was solidified by the ritual commemorating those killed in battle. Such commemoration focused on elite groups among young Westerners, while the fallen among the Oriental immigrants and those recruited abroad were given limited commemoration in relation to their losses (Sivan, 1991, 55–101). Commemorative projects were initiated voluntarily by the groups who could exploit their material resources and access to the means of communication to heighten the impact of their participation in the war. Thus, Western groups honored the military achievements of casualties drawn from their own social networks. And, as Aronoff (1993, 53) has put it, "while the funerals for the fallen are their final rites of passage, for the groups that claim them, their annual memorial ceremonies are an ongoing source of legitimacy." Owing much to this process, the "1948 Generation" seized control over the highest social strata in Israeli society (Ben-Eliezer, 1984, 29–30; Shapiro, 1977, 163–165).

Another manifestation of the interrelation between military participation and the accumulation of social power was the status enjoyed by the

Kibbutz Movement, the communal agricultural settlements that were largely Western. Kibbutz youngsters played a central role in the military, disproportionate to their numbers in the Jewish population. For many years that role justified the large material resources channeled by the state to the kibbutz settlers, enabling them to constantly upgrade their standard of living (see Eisenstadt, 1985, 249–250, on other areas of the kibbutz's prominence with implications for accumulation of resources).

To the extent that the ethno-functional division of labor in the military was deemed legitimate, the ensuing rewards were widely perceived by the main social groups as legitimate, too. After all, the status of "fighter" seemed equally attainable by both ethnic groups as it was based on an equal obligation to do military service and the egalitarian ethos of the IDF. By contrast, the status of "pioneer" had been available exclusively to the Western groups in the pre-state era. The ascendancy of the "fighter" thus lent credibility to the notion that social status in Israeli society accrued through objective criteria based on achievement regardless of the fact that, in practice, the same dominant groups had access to social status both in the pre-state and state eras.

These military symbols, together with the civilian symbols of Mamlachtiyut, jointly worked to legitimize Westerners' dominance. Three components are relevant, central to which is the state-created political-ideological barriers to Orientals' political action demanding all-encompassing reallocation of the societal resources. First, Mamlachtiyut imbued the Orientals with the idea that their social position depended solely on their contribution to the state. Accordingly, they were expected to enter the society through "contributory" social activity; but, until they could do so, they had to accept their inferiority vis-à-vis the Westerners, whose contribution (certainly their historical contribution) was portrayed as greater than that of the Orientals. This dovetailed with the depiction of the absorption of the Orientals as a process of integration into or even "joining" a full-fledged "society" that antedated their arrival and was associated with Western traits: modernity, technological know-how, manufacturing, and sophistication (see Swirski, 1981, 50–55).

Civilian semantics were also invoked to underscore the distinction between the two ethnic groups: The newly arrived Orientals were sometimes called *mehagrim* (immigrants), whereas the Westerners who had immigrated during the Yishuv period were known as *olim* ("those who ascend"; see Eisenstadt, 1948). The same symbolic effect was achieved by periodizing the Yishuv era through its "waves of immigration" ("First *Aliyah*," "Second *Aliyah*," and so on). Each period had its unique, even heroic, archetypical characters. However, periodization in these terms came to an abrupt end with the influx of Oriental immigrants.

So, the more a group is portrayed as shouldering the glamorous burden of national redemption, the less other groups are able to blame it for its social well-being. Conditions are then created for legitimizing this social dominance by ruling out, at least for the short term, social protest. The state, therefore, indirectly made asymmetrical power resources available within a framework of social participation possessing an egalitarian image. The result was that the statist criterion reinforced Western dominance, albeit covertly, and the Orientals, for whom the new statuses were out of reach, were actually restrained from developing the self-awareness by which they could battle against their deprivation. Mamlachtiyut, from this angle, became a kind of mechanism mediating between individuals and social rewards.[10]

As for the second component of Mamlachtiyut, the Mamlachtiyut-informed symbols of unity extended to the emphasizing of Israeli society's essence as an interethnic (Jewish) "melting pot." This meant delegitimization, and hence obstruction, of ethnic-based political organizing (as well as other expressions of distinct Oriental culture). Westerners' organizing was portrayed as universalistic, but similar attempts by the Orientals were branded as "ethnic," conflicting with the ethos of the "ingathering of the exiles" (Herzog, 1985).

Finally, the state wrapped its policies in national-military symbols, by which it accomplished a low-cost mobilization of the Orientals to take their part in state-building. So, for example, to settle remote villages meant fixing the new borders beyond a routine policy of housing that eventually created a reservoir of low-paid laborers. This worked to reduce the costs of absorption and employment without resorting to the level of income and social services that otherwise would have been required under Orientals' demands. Oriental settlers came to perceive themselves as pioneers, serving their new state rather than as victims of the state's inequitable policies (see more in chapter 3).

To close the cycle, the IDF's contribution to legitimizing interethnic power relations was dependent on two intersecting elements. First, the IDF was a socially prestigious institution that both motivated social groups to demonstrate their military achievements and enabled them to convert those achievements into social rewards, albeit in a differential manner. Otherwise, social groups' status within the military would have been unvalued in civilian terms. As the following chapters show, the IDF's status was conditional on its engagement in belligerence.

Second, and most important, was the IDF's preserving its egalitarian image. Here we ought to bring into play another factor that worked to further solidify the IDF's egalitarian image, that is, the very constitution of the IDF as a universalistic military rather than an elitist politically oriented entity. Dovetailing with the fundamental trends of Mamlachtiyut, the IDF's establishment was accompanied by the severing of political party affiliation with military forces. This was achieved by two moves. In the first move, the underground organizations—Palmach, the IZL (the rightist National Military Organization), and the LHI (Fighters of Israel's Freedom)—were dismantled and absorbed into the IDF. This move involved clashes between the state and the organizations affiliated with political parties but ended with the government's triumph. In the second move, the IDF became subject to Ben-Gurion's personal oversight. This was markedly different from the system of control over the pre-state Haganah, which had been based on party channels. Yet the process by which the labor parties withdrew from their exclusive control over the Haganah via the Histadrut had already been taking place since the 1930s (see Pail, 1979). Now, however, Ben-Gurion's aims were to ensure the military's compliance with statist political authority in addition to neutralizing Mapam's attempts to intervene by preventing access of political parties to security issues via the cabinet and the Knesset (Peri, 1983, 49–69; Perlmutter, 1969, 54–68). Consequently, the State of Israel stood the typical test, common to other "new states," of gaining monopoly control over the means of violence extremely well. These arrangements of political control were challenged and then bolstered during the 1950s, as we shall see in chapter 3.

An egalitarian, universalistic image was crucial for cementing the IDF's ability to fill its formal and actual roles in the interethnic domain. It seems safe to assume that had the IDF adopted ethnic-oriented criteria for conscription and promotion or been constituted on party-oriented rather than Mamlachtiyut elements, its universalistic image would have been impaired. It then would not have been able to legitimize its part in perpetuating the ethno-class division of labor. In that case, its action would have been interpreted as supportive of the dominant social groups that staffed and commanded its units and, as such, could have inflamed the kind of interethnic tension common to many ethnically divided societies (see Enloe, 1980; Goodwin and Skocpol, 1989). Similarly, a politically oriented military would have likely drawn political criticism and as such been depleted of much of its potential prestige. As I will elaborate in later chapters, had the IDF both lacked social prestige and not maintained a seeming egalitarianism, Orientals would not have grasped their military participation as a symbolic resource, more accessible than other symbolic and material resources that had been unattainable for them in the civilian society.

In sum, the political-military elite, committed to the idea of the military as a "melting pot," did not engage in conscious, deliberate activity to achieve these structural ends. But its system of ethnic images, its invocation of modern, professional, Western norms, with the political and professional calculations underlying the specific model of military organization, *unintentionally* brought this structure about. So, notwithstanding the approach of the dominant school in Israeli sociology, the military did not serve as an agent of modernization helping promote social equality.[11] Rather, the IDF was a chief ingredient in legitimizing inequality.

Thus, inequitable ethno-class relations grew, resting on three war-based pillars: (1) state-led differential gains from the very state of war by the different ethno-class groups: To a larger extent than their Oriental counterparts, Western groups gained from confiscated lands and houses from war-driven expansion of bureaucracy, and from military-based social prestige; Orientals gained not only from Palestinian property but also from the monitoring of the Palestinian labor force; (2) Western groups' exploitation of Orientals within the labor market, based on government socio-policies and backed by nationally invoked mechanisms featuring remote settlements; (3) legitimization of inequality by universalizing state action through Mamlachtiyut and the IDF and by administering full employment

Universalism was thus grounded in the popular perception of Mamlachtiyut as a neutral, objective ideology in relation to social power even if, in practice, it supported a particular social class. The products of the state action in the social domain could therefore be seen as objective phenomena, divorced from the Westerners staffing the state institutions. Conversely, it seems safe to assume that had the state overtly remained dependent on the old Western partisan agencies that were associated with particularistic interests, its universalistic image would have been impaired and it would not have been able to legitimize its action in perpetuating the ethno-class division of labor. In that case, state interventionism would have been interpreted as supportive of the dominant social groups that staffed and managed its institutions and, as such, would have been perceived as illegitimate. Delegitimizing and, hence, obstructing Orientals' organizing while justifying both Orientals' sacrifice as such and Westerners' sacrifice as a source of social rewards were the practical reflections of Mamlachtiyut. Nonetheless, it is worth emphasizing that social reproduction in itself cannot be positively proven, since it explains *what has not occurred*, that is, the alteration of the social structure.

Paradoxically, the result was the creation of a structural interdependence between the state's ability to play its part in legitimizing the ethno-class division of labor and the diminution of the political power held by Western political elites. To put it differently, the preservation of the Westerners' social dominance compelled the reinforcement of the state which, in turn, required the state to impose its authority and weaken its dependence on the pre-state power centers identified with the elites of the same ethnic class. Conditions were then created to shape *structural relations of exchange*, whereby the Westerners practically maintained their position as the dominant social class in exchange for two unconscious concessions: their readiness to accept the state's internal expansion at the expense of their party-based power centers and their readiness to carry out the war burden, with implications for the IDF's position and the state policies toward the bordering countries (see more in chapter 3). Practically, the state acquired the ability to act in a manner that contradicted the short-term interests of the dominant groups in return for the part taken by the state in reproducing the social structure, which is the long-term interest of those groups (see, at the theoretical level, Poulantzas, 1978). The state's universalism and autonomy became interrelated as autonomy affected universalism.[12] Indeed, Mamlachtiyut faced a critical challenge from Mapai, the main "victim" of state empowerment.

THE STATE–MAPAI CLASH

As state expansion ran its course, Mapai's leaders, associated with the party machine and the Histadrut, opposed the state's internal expansion at the expense of their power. They claimed to preserve the party's (and the whole labor movement's) unique missions despite the establishment of a state. From their perspective, the party had an existence in its own right rather than just as a statist instrument as it was espoused by Ben-Gurion and his allies. The state, Mapai's leaders stipulated, should protect, not dismantle, the party's strongholds. Ben-Gurion and his group, for their part—who were associated with Mapai's young guard, military officers, and young bureaucrats—endeavored to undo the traditional party-centered pattern. Their efforts went beyond the Mamlachtiyut. They were accompanied by the fruitless attempt to change the electoral system from a national (in which people vote for party lists while the whole country is one region) to a regional mode similar to the British model. This, it was thought, would ensure a Mapai majority and also weaken the dependence of state agencies on the ruling party for enlisting support and reduce the strength of the party apparatus by creating direct channels between the party constituency and elected representatives. On top of this, Ben-Gurion tried to circumvent the party by organizing extraparty mass political movements while he was temporarily retired in 1954/55 (Goldberg, 1991).

Mapai's leaders opposed Ben-Gurion's moves. Beyond torpedoing any change in the electoral system, they objected to beefing up the military with manpower earmarked for the agricultural settlements associated with the labor movement. They were even convinced that Ben-Gurion was planning a putsch, perhaps with the connivance of the army, an apprehension that intensified insofar as the IDF manifestly assumed purely civil roles such as the management of camps for new immigrants, paving roads, and establishing new settlements (Beilin, 1984, 14; Sharett, 1978, 171; Teveth, 1992, 231–253). So, Mapai's leaders displayed resentment toward the flourishing of the military establishment. Still, the basic move of dismantling the Palmach and constituting a universalist army was accepted by the party.

Another confrontation took shape between Ben-Gurion and the Kibbutz Movement. Ben-Gurion, seeking to portray the state and its symbols as the successors to pioneering, downplayed the national mission of the kibbutz, the traditional epitome of pioneering (see Tzahor, 1994, 195–210). This argument was in conjunction with another controversy raging between General Moshe Dayan, the military's third chief of staff and a prominent ally of Ben-Gurion, and the leaders of the agricultural sector. The argument revolved around whether officers from the kibbutz should remain in the career army following the completion of their compulsory military service. Dayan claimed that military service was an expression of pioneering; the Kibbutz Movement countered that land settlement alone was the concrete articulation of pioneering (Dayan, 1976, 180–181, 195). So, central to these debates was the confrontation between the "pioneer" and the "fighter."

Similar objections were voiced in 1953 by some party leaders to the state takeover of the Histadrut's education system in order to create a statist system (Bar-Zohar, 1975, 951). These politicians were more successful in blocking attempts made by Ben-Gurion to nationalize the Histadrut-controlled Sick Fund that served the majority of the country's population (Grinberg, 1993a, 80–81) and to establish compulsory "labor brigades," composed of unemployed immigrants, to carry out national missions (Segev, 1986, 152–154). At another level, the collapse of the austerity policy in 1951, following Western middle-class pressure mediated by Mapai, also exposed the state's dependence on the party (see also Cohen, 1987, 249–253).

Theoretically, this dispute over the foundations for the political division of labor between ruling party and state did not go beyond the expected historical conflict between a state and power centers that antedated its establishment (see, for example, Badie and Birnbaum, 1983, 55–59; Mann, 1985; Migdal, 1988). Structurally, the state then faced a two-level problem. On the surface, the Mapai groups challenged the state's capacity to function autonomously. To look beneath the surface, those groups in practice questioned the underlying relations of exchange. The state's capacity to legitimize the ethno-class structure was affected as long as its universalism could be called into question—particularly once its dependence on, and its orientation toward, the Western community became apparent. This created the potential for the Orientals to accumulate social power as the reality of social inequality became more apparent in the absence of a mechanism of legitimization. Overall, then, the Western political elites, by challenging the relations of exchange, also demonstrated an innate tension between the social interests motivating them: They unconsciously adhered to their short-term interests, expressed in the immediate accumulation of political and material resources at the expense of their constituency's long-term interest, namely, the reproducing of their social dominance through the empowerment of the state.

The state, through its bellicose policy, unintentionally reconstructed these interests and thus not only cemented the relations of exchange but also deepened them. This will be dealt with in the next chapter.

CONCLUSIONS

Theoretically, "once institutions are in place they can assume a life of their own, extracting civil societal resources, socializing individuals, and even altering the basic nature of civil society itself. . . . Once a critical choice has been made it cannot been taken back" (Krasner, 1984, 240). Indeed, once the Western groups opposed the austerity policy, they in fact shaped a centralized state involved with both interclass regulation and an external violent conflict. Table 2.1 suggests a tentative evaluation of the alternative trajectories of state-building derived from the model of absorption along four key dimensions—labor market, state extraction, profile of militarism, and relations between the state and dominant groups—and their ultimate effect on the potential intensity of the Arab-Israeli conflict (needless to say, intervals are neglected but still reasonable).

Table 2.1
Alternative Trajectories of State-Building

	Structure of Labor Market	State Extraction	Profile of Militarism	State-Group Relations	Potential of War
Egalitarianism	Jews' unemployment	low	middle	coercion	middle
Market-Oriented	Jews' unemployment	low	low	partial exchange	middle
State-Directed	Jews' full employment Jews-Palestinians separation	high	high	exchange	high

Had the state adopted each of the alternative models of absorption, state-building would have taken another course and with it, the implications of the potential of war. The egalitarian model could have created conditions by which state-imposed equal incomes within the Jewish labor force would have inclined employers to rely on Palestinians, both locals and refugees. Confiscated Palestinian lands would have been utilized but Palestinians' partial commuting to Israeli territory as low-wage laborers might have practically decreased the scope of confiscation and, hence, the interests oriented toward the perpetuation of the post-1948 political status quo. With fewer lands and workplaces, unemployment within the Jewish sector would have increased. Moreover, it seems likely that the Histadrut would have embraced a more militant trade-unionist posture derived from equal orientation toward the two ethnic groups.

At the same time, the state would have enjoyed less capacity to extract resources, aside from its interventionist position, because of the restricted accumulation of capital. It even seems less likely that the United States of that period would have demonstrated largess toward a socialist project. The state's universalism would be a reality, not only an image, in the civilian domain as long as it actually worked to promote social equality. But the IDF would have taken a position as an institution engaging in interethnic integration *among* other institutions. Hence, the IDF's semiprestigious status. Mamlachtiyut, moreover, possibly might have seen fit to mix more traditional social-democratic rhetoric with its technocratic elements. This might have affected power relations between the state and the party-based centers and the weight of militarism may have seemed less appealing insofar as the gains from the post-1948 status quo were less instrumental to the stabilization of social order.

Consequently, relations of coercion rather than exchange would more likely have formed between the state and Western groups as an outcome of state interventionism. All of that would have possibly worked to downscale an external conflict, at least in the short run. Low-level border friction (due to partial incorporation of refugees within the labor market), together with a low-extractive state, decreased militarism, and coerced Westerners with low motivation for combat, might have restricted bellicose tendencies. Still, an army under these conditions might have been alienated and hence more inclined to be active in domestic affairs or to propel state belligerence in the long run.

A similar picture could have been created had the state adopted market-oriented policies with selective immigration. It then would have shaped a similar labor market with a reduced degree of Palestinian-Israeli friction as long as the lack of statist pressures toward full employment in the Jewish sector paved the way for utilizing Palestinian cheap labor. With the speedy rise of an upper class (unrestricted by a welfare system) with a limited reliance on the state (as long as it played a limited role, relative to the model of Mamlachtiyut, in regulating social tensions), the state would have possibly also been hindered in its efforts to extract internal resources. Low-level relations of exchange between the state and the middle class (similar to the European model) might have been the result.

In a similar fashion, it seems safe to assume that a flourishing capitalist ethos would have had two discursive effects. First, the demanding tone of Mamlachtiyut would have been decreased. Second, the capitalist ethos would possibly have made the IDF an ordinary institution competing with other civilian institutions for both resources and employees. With consumerism enjoying a prominent status and limited gaining from the fruits of the 1948 War, moreover, militarism (and battlefield achievements with it) would not have played a focal role in shaping social criteria. Taken together, the state would have met difficulties in employing strategies of war preparation with its implications for the potential for war. Still, had an elitist, selective-based army been adopted, even if overtly discriminating against Orientals (as a possible suboption of this trajectory), it could have enjoyed, at least for the short run, a great deal of social prestige among the Western communities. But, for the long run, an army further restricted from external action would more likely have been shaped, but as an alienated one, with similar implications in regard to the model of egalitarianism; furthermore, with a high probability of interethnic conflicts, the IDF would have been more prone to intervene in domestic politics. As chapter 6 demonstrates, Israel's embarking on a market-oriented trajectory from the 1970s on has generated a similar pattern, bringing about de-escalation of the conflict.

On the contrary, the chosen model, the state-directed trajectory, was conditional upon the creation of full employment in the Jewish sector. Monitoring the Palestinian labor force and capitalizing on confiscated Palestinian lands and houses to fuel economic growth were key ingredients of this strategy. Concurrently, the state acquired a high capacity for resource extraction that could be channeled to military buildup due to the capacity to exploit the cheap labor force (by the state and employers alike) and the flow of external revenues to it under the guise of the Zionist mission (see Barnett, 1992, 161–165).

Alternative practices to those prescribed by the opted-for model—for example, an overtly inequitable army, inclusion of the Palestinian labor force, market-oriented settlement projects—became less likely to emerge. At the same time, this trajectory gradually habituated a new reality that worked to construct new war-oriented interests that could not have been structured within any of the alternative trajectories. The accepted model was in the interests of those dominant groups who were satisfied with the inequitable social structure resulting from the state's domestic policies and legitimized by the state of war via an interventionist state. The policies toward Palestinians, the national meaning of labor exploited in remote settlements, and a prestigious military working to ensure social peace were among the war-incited mechanisms playing a key role in creating satisfaction and, hence, fueling militarization of Israeli society. State-building was thus characterized by trial-and-error methods that state agencies, together with Western groups, employed.

Structural relations of exchange between the state and the Western middle class then paved the way for internal state expansion which dovetailed with the military burden; the Westerners gradually accepted this control and burden in return for the confirmation of their social dominance but without necessarily identifying the linkage between social gains and the war-driven state empowerment. Construction of new interests was at work. Overall, concerted removal of Palestinians, combined with a high-extractive state, high-profile militarism, and state-dependent Westerner communities created conditions to intensify violent frictions between Israeli Jews and Palestinians. In turn, this war-driven trajectory of state-building augmented the inegalitarian social order from which this trajectory was elicited. The 1950s' border wars dynamically fashioned this trajectory.

Informed by scientific-realist concepts, the state's internal expansion was dialectically and simultaneously both the major medium and the outcome of political discourse.[13] Its emergence as a centralistic institution increased the major groups' inclination and capacity to relate to the state as a discursive object (see, at the comparative level, Mann, 1993, 221–222; Skocpol, 1985, 21–25; Tarrow, 1994, 62–78; Tilly, 1992, 99). This took two shapes. First, groups *bargained* with the state mainly via party channels and the everyday interaction between the state bureaucracy and individuals and groups. Groups, however, confined their interests-prescribed demands to state-controlled resources, aimed first and foremost at the elimination of state-directed egalitarianism and a portion of its revenues. As it will be recalled, this phenomenon brought about "statization" of the political discourse accompanied the decline of a traditional, ideological discursive pattern (see also note 8). Second, demands *invoking* the state, primarily in the symbolic domain, were raised by several groups attempting to represent their own interests. They were those staffing the state's new bureaucracy as a part of their struggle vis-à-vis partisan groups, the military officer corps via the "fighter" versus the "pioneer," Westerners taking advantage of their contribution to state-building to legitimize their position over Orientals, and more. Again, statization was the outcome. All in all, the state became, similar to its Western counterparts, "the ensemble of fields that are the site of struggles [over the construction and imposition of] universal and universally applicable . . . common set of coercive norms" (Bourdieu in Bourdieu and Wacquant, 1992, 111–112).

Only partially aware of the full meaning of their interest-driven activity, these groups, in fact, produced through legitimization a new structure based on a centralist state with its social criteria. The state, for its part, produced power by legitimately eroding the autonomy of those very groups but gave them an alternative asset in the social realm.

State agencies customarily prone to internal empowerment by means of bureaucratic penetration, dovetailed with statist, nationalist ideology. More important, however, are the conditions under which that empowerment takes place. If so, notwithstanding the romantic, voluntarily preferred elements and national symbols implicit within Mamlachtiyut and tailored by Ben-Gurion and his associates (Carmi and Rosenfeld, 1993, 284–299; Cohen, 1987, 228–259; Keren, 1983; Kese, 1986; Liebman and Don-Yehiya, 1983), the very implantation of this ideology might be attributable to social interests carried by the participants in the Mamlachtiyut discourse. Had these agents encountered unsatisfying results—that is, had state-directed absorption impeded the social mobility of the Westerner-dominated middle class—groups would have been more likely to reshape their stand, and cling to alternative trajectories of state-making. That is what they indeed did regarding the austerity policy, and, as we shall see, would do at later periods. It is this conceptualization of state action that guides the empirical discussion in the following chapters.

The consequences of Mamlachtiyut that went beyond its architects' intentions nurtured Israel's bellicose policy during the early 1950s. By itself, this occurrence helped complete the "unfinished business" of the state's internal expansion. Bellicose policy is the subject of the next chapter.

CHAPTER 3

Bellicose Policy Drives
Internal State Expansion
and Vice Versa (1951–56)

This chapter deals with the bellicose policy employed by Israel during the 1951–56 period, starting with reprisal raids against bordering Arab states and culminating with the Sinai Campaign (1956). What explains Israel's choosing such a policy over more moderate ones? What made this policy possible in light of internal hindrances to its execution?

Arguably, an *internally originating* hardening of bellicose tendencies dominated sociopolitical processes during the early 1950s since domestic interests—agrarian, demographic, and material—actually limited the scope of methods from which Israel could choose to combat infiltrations into its territory from Jordan and Egypt. Especially so, as the state was previously furnished with the Mamlachtiyut-stimulated capacity to extract resources for war preparation. Israel then became trapped within a cycle of escalation and counterescalation, losing the flexibility to reverse its moves. Concurrently, moreover, an internal, not only external, overlapping cyclical motion evolved in which bellicose moves allowed the main social and political Jewish groups to gain from the outcomes of bellicose policies and from their very participation while carrying out those policies. Domestically, gaining not only motivated the main groups to work for or to accept the bellicose policy despite previous opposition; gaining also made it too costly to revert to more moderate policies, aggravating the typical failure to deal with the external security dilemma. Construction and execution of the bellicose approach dialectically intersected. Figure 3.1 sums the mutli-phase process.

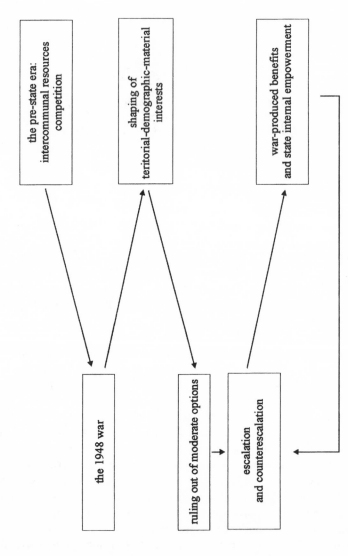

INTERNAL

EXTERNAL

the pre-state era:
intercommunal resources
competition

shaping of
teritorial-demographic-material
interests

war-produced benefits
and state internal empowerment

the 1948 war

ruling out of moderate options

escalation
and counterescalation

Figure 3.1
The Reciprocal Effects of Internal and External State Action, 1951–56

THE FOUNDATIONS OF VIOLENT CONFLICT

Chapter 2 showed the interconnectedness between state-making and war-making in the Israeli context. To recall, the Arab-Israeli conflict evolved from competition between indigenous Palestinians and Jewish immigrants in the labor market of Palestine under the British Mandate. Inspired by their "imported" material interests, Jewish immigrants competed against Palestinians and engendered a violent conflict (Shafir, 1989). Seen in our terms (see chapter 1, figure 1.2), social groups *evaluated* external assets (labor market strongholds) and made them their material interest. With the establishment of the Histadrut and labor parties a pre-state was created based on segregation between the two economic sectors. Through pre-state-building the settlers' material interests were actually *universalized* into interests of the entire Jewish community (the settlers fought for "Jewish Labor," not for material interests). Now those interests took the shape of communal demographic and territorial interests for which the two communities—Jewish and Palestinian—were mobilized (Kimmerling, 1976). Directly, those and other social groups benefited from full employment shielded by economic segregation; indirectly and dynamically, they also benefited from the conflict due to the pre-statist capacity to erect bureaucracies in which laborers enjoyed mobility (Shapiro, 1984a, 28–50). This was the first and most crucial phase in shaping war-prone interests in the Jewish state then coming into being.

The State of Israel, therefore, was born into a conflict over material resources that constituted its collective identities and the meanings ascribed to Arab behaviors. Nevertheless, the extent to which the state's military policies issued from, or at least were affected by, former preferences is overlooked by IR scholars, who naturally focus on the state, rather than pre-state, unit of analysis.

Evolving from the Israeli-Palestinian intercommunal conflict, the interstate conflict took the form of the 1948 War fought by the newly founded State of Israel mainly against the armies of Egypt, Jordan, Syria, and Lebanon, which were joined by Palestinian forces. The direct background was the opposition of the Arab states to the UN resolution of November 1947 partitioning Palestine into two states, Jewish and Palestinian. Utilizing its advantages over Arab armies (see Amitzur, 1995), Israel expanded its boundaries beyond those designated for the Jewish state by the UN and retained some of these territories after the war under the terms of the armistice agreements signed in 1949. Most important, Israel took advantage of the fighting and expelled or encouraged to leave most of the Palestinian population residing in the conquered areas and those originally allotted by the UN to Israel. Initially, the military rationale of removing a hostile population directly drove Israeli commanders (Morris, 1988). Taking this together with Egypt's introduction of a military administration in the Gaza Strip and Jordan's annexation of the West Bank in 1950 (as a part of a tacit cooperation with Israel against the Palestinians, see Shlaim, 1990), the establishment of a Palestinian state was averted.

In the absence of a Palestinian state, about 600,000 to 750,000 Palestinian refugees settled in temporary camps along Israel's borders with Egypt (the Gaza Strip) and Jordan (the West Bank and Jordan Valley), awaiting a permanent solution. It was these refugees who triggered the border frictions during the 1950s. Refugees tried to infiltrate into Israel primarily for economic reasons (about 90 percent)—to recover their land, smuggle goods, steal, visit relatives and the like. Most infiltrations were independent initiatives on the part of individuals. Only a few organized, primarily by Palestinian organizations, were violent or aimed at collecting intelligence. A new border, unmarked and unnatural, cut off the refugees from their former homes and stimulated this phenomenon (Morris, 1993, 34–54).

Israel, for its part, perceived the infiltrations as a threat to its sovereignty, as an element of the hostility displayed by the Arab states. Against this background, Prime Minister Ben-Gurion and his political allies endeavored to seal the borders by settling them. Backing up the territorial status quo was the main target, making irreversible the expulsion of Palestinians and the confiscation of their abandoned resources. To recall, the government moved swiftly at the end of the 1948 War to settle newcomers in the recently abandoned Palestinian villages, the most available space at the time. By opting for this approach, Israel practically ruled out pacifist options to de-escalate or even terminate the Arab-Israeli conflict. Indeed, this period saw the establishment of channels for negotiations between Israel and its neighbors to achieve political settlements in place of the armistice arrangements, which were military in nature. The Lausanne Conference was convened in 1949, in the aftermath of the 1948 War, with Israel and the Arab states participating. The sides agreed on a protocol based on the Arabs' acceptance of the principle of partition in Palestine, implying recognition of Israel. Nevertheless, Israel, inspired by its newly defined security interests, signed the document but impeded its translation into a political agreement. Instead, according to Pappe (1992, 206–213), the Israeli side took advantage of the discord among the Arab delegation in regard to the outcomes of the 1948 War. Pappe argues that, at bottom, Israel preferred the political status quo over a quest for peace (see also Flapan, 1987, 15–53).

Efforts to perpetuate the status quo were also apparent in Israel's secret political negotiations with the Arab states in the early 1950s, as described by Itamar Rabinovich (1991). According to Rabinovich, the Arabs put forward territorial demands based on the (agreed) temporary status of the armistice accords, but these were rejected by Israel. Examples are David Ben-Gurion's refusal to meet with Syrian ruler Za'im for fear he would demand border rectifications in the Kinneret–Jordan River area; a similar refusal to meet with King Abdullah of Jordan and rejection of Jordan's proposal to annex the southern Negev and give that country an outlet to the Mediterranean; Israel's refusal to agree to territorial adjustments in the Negev; and Israel's refusal to permit part of the Palestinian refugees to return. Rabinovich concludes that the question of which side missed the opportunity for peace, the Arabs or Israel, is moot. Such a summation is a challenge to the official Israeli position, which is internalized deeply within the country's political discourse, the more so because it comes from a historian who is in the mainstream of the Israeli academy (and was Israel's ambassador to Washington during the 1993–96 period) (see also Morris, 1993, 8–25; Segev, 1986, 15–42).

Israel, then, stood at a crossroads. It could have defined its security interests, namely, its secured survival in the region, in political terms by means of exhausting the potential for achieving peace/de-escalation in the region—even at the price of territorial concessions and readiness to reabsorb some of the Palestinian refugees (two concessions that had been partially accepted by Foreign Minister Moshe Sharett as Pappe indicates; see also Segev, 1986, 32–33). Israel could have employed tactics of de-escalation along with communicating nonoffensive intentions to test the Arabs' willingness to make peace and even to bring about a change of attitudes.

Risks of an arms race, moreover, were still low at that period because both sides were restrained by the 1950 Tripartite Declaration (America, France, and Britain)—the Powers' attempt to slow down the flow of weapons to the region as a means of sustaining the balance of power (Barnett, 1992, 165–166). At the same time, the Soviet Union did not yet intensely engage in Middle East affairs. Insofar as this factor could have strengthened Israel's sense of confidence, especially when it displayed impressive military supremacy in the concluding moves of the 1948 War, Israeli strategists could have read the prevailing regional reality as an opportunity for peace/de-escalation. At greater risk than its adversaries, small (and still poor) Israel was adverse to an arms race. To a large extent, precisely the level of vulnerability innate in its territorial inferiority might have induced Israel to rely on political arrangements rather than military power with the high likelihood of war. Losses were intolerable from Israel's perspective. In short, by paying a territorial price Israel could have laid the foundations for avoiding a prolonged, heavy, and risky military burden. We, however, cannot judge whether Israel could really have advanced the peace process in this period. Nor can we evaluate the Arab side's reaction. We can only question Israel's avoidance of fully exhausting the potential for furthering the process. Achieving peace was not Israel's (as much as the Arab state's) strategic goal. To a large extent, Israel took an active part in shaping the region as a threatening environment; it did not only react passively.

In terms borrowed from contingent realism (Glaser, 1994/95, 60, see chapter 1, note 19), Israel might have been concerned about the high risks of future competition and the low risks of present regional cooperation. But the low risks of present competition and the potential high risks of future cooperation affected it more. The scale was tipped in favor of the bellicose path. The Israeli leadership's inclination to take a hard line toward Arab states was directly nurtured by the embedded "zero-sum game" nature of the Arab-Israeli conflict. This had evolved from the Jewish-Palestinian conflict and was aggravated by Arab countries' hostility during the 1948 War and their reluctance to recognize Israel's existence afterwards. Possibly, the Holocaust of European Jewry further fed existential concerns.

Guided by self-help principles under conditions of perceived existential threat posed by unreliable regimes, Israel was determined to expand its security margins. Bridging over its perceived power inferiority vis-à-vis the Arab countries in both territorial and demographic terms by retaining the territorial-demographic gains of the 1948 War was Israel's strategic design. Israel accordingly was reluctant to take the risks entailed in meeting the Arabs' demands for territorial concessions or to allow the return of Palestinian refugees. This force-oriented agenda, however, could not have been shaped unless Israel was from the outset furnished with high statist capabilities, particularly the ability to extract resources and mobilize a mass army. With this advantage Israel could downplay the military risks that the retaining of status quo entailed.

We may infer from Israel's preferences that the "Arab threat" is not an objective vision based solely on the manner in which Arab countries communicated their intentions. Threat is translated according to leaders' power, perceptions, and interests rather than by scientific methods. Hence, weak Arab states' pragmatism in the early 1950s could be perceived as a threat.

Security interests, however, actually reflected, and hence were also filtered through, domestic interests as well within the underlying trajectory of state-building. We remember, as chapter 2 has implied, that ensuring unquestioned full employment for low-wage Jewish workers within the secondary labor market played an indirect role in constraining Israel's approach to dealing with the refugee-infiltrators. Also, confiscation of Palestinian refugees' abandoned houses and lands rescued the young state from reallocation of material resources between veterans and immigrants. Reallocation might have jeopardized the Western middle class's material achievements. Likewise, remote, isolated border towns also functioned as reservoirs of cheap labor. Expanded borders, which conditioned the isolation of these settlements, thus became a sort of gain for those groups who exploited that labor force. Though these civilian considerations did not serve as a *direct, intentional driving force* behind hardline policies, the very concert of groups benefiting from the territorial status quo may explain why civilian groups did not counterbalance military considerations. They let the military mind-set govern statecraft with minor impediments confined mainly to the execution (as we will later see), not the very formulation, of security interests. With vested groups benefiting from this policy's outcomes, Sharett and his allies were in a disadvantaged position. On the contrary, as we will later see, changes in Israeli society gradually habituated a new reality, its main foundations grounded on the perpetuation of the status quo with future implications for the hardening of foreign-military policies.

Putting security interests in practical terms, Israel, convinced that the bordering Arab states would attempt to undermine the newly created status quo, was bent on preventing the Arabs from jeopardizing its defined security interests and valuable assets. Jeopardy could take the shape of a "second round" of war to be launched by Arab countries subsequent to the 1948 War. Another threat could be infiltrations that also precluded definitive demarcation of the boundaries and hence undermined state sovereignty over territory. Accordingly, Israel was determined to retain its military superiority over the Arab states through retaliation, deterrence, and defense. Communicating offensive motives was part of this trend: Advocacy of territorial expansion to the West Bank and Jordan was sporadically broached by IDF officers and hawkish politicians (Morris, 1993, 10–13). Still, Israel realized that notwithstanding its military superiority it could militarily triumph over Arab states but could not impose a political settlement. This was the Israeli version of achieving "relative gains" in the regional arena. A powerful response to the infiltrations was thus deemed militarily necessary to cement the state's borders (on Israel's strategic doctrine from the IR perspective see Aronson and Horowitz, 1971; Evron, 1989; Handel, 1973, 21–36; 1994; Horowitz, 1979, 1985; Shimshoni, 1988, 34–122).

To sum up, two different sets of national interests were practically considered, rather than a single rational approach inspired by self-help principles that would have unavoidably led to a particular choice. The latter is implicit in arguments raised by Israeli IR scholars inspired by broader theoretical perspectives. Hence, the international system does not provide a sole determinant of Israel's preference. We need to address the alternative calculations, the values on which each route was grounded, and the role played by domestic considerations in decreasing the state's freedom in the global arena by setting the bellicose policy against *countervailing* pressures. In short, the historical processes should be read as a *history of alternatives* (Pappe, 1993, 108). We turn now to describe Israel's actual military policies and we will problematize them afterwards.

THE EVOLUTION OF BORDER WAR

Combating border-crossings was the most immediate target. Israel's initial mode for coping with the infiltrations was to set up about 350 settlements during 1948–53. Most of them were agricultural *moshavim* (cooperative farm communities); many of them were located along or near the borders, in many cases built on the ruins of abandoned Palestinian villages. In addition, most of the newly erected development towns were also located near the borders. The purpose of this policy was to fortify Israel's hold along the borders and ensure that refugees did not return to their former, no-longer-abandoned villages (Morris, 1993, 121–123). In addition, during 1948–50 Israel expelled Palestinian population, some of them refugees, residing in villages and towns located along the borders within Israel's territory (ibid., 138–143).

As it will be recalled, the new settlements were populated mainly (about 70 percent) by Oriental immigrants, the most mobile population in the Jewish community of this period. Further, data reveal that about 50 percent of the new Oriental-populated moshavim were built in peripheral areas relative to about 10 percent of the Western-populated moshavim (Swirski, 1981, 22). Remote moshavim were built as concentrated settlements with little space between houses as a means of sealing the borders (Morris, 1993, 123). However, this allocated less land relative to other settlements, veteran and new alike, a fact that worked to perpetuate the Orientals' disadvantaged position (Swirski, 1981, 22–24). Add to this the isolation-produced poverty in developing towns, and differential gains were legitimized in military terms.

Once a new settlement was built on the site of an abandoned Palestinian village, it became a magnet for infiltration regardless of its distance from the border. As the following sections show, the evolution of the bellicose policy was cyclical: By establishing border settlements as a means of coping with infiltration and fixing the state borders, the state exposed the settlers to existential danger. Yet it concurrently took measures to repulse that danger, mainly in the form of reprisal raids in which Israel escalated the military frictions by its reactions to the infiltrations; those reactions made the infiltrators and the neighboring states more hostile and willing to translate their hostility into active violence, aggravating the potential danger to Israel. Then, in a counterreaction, Israel raised the level of violence another notch, justified by citing the danger to Israel—a danger itself fueled by Israel's reprisal policy. In sum, not only Arab images and domestic interests constrained military policies but also the cyclical nature of Israel's policies which worked to rule out more moderate strategies to deal with the problem, a typical failure to cope with the security dilemma.

The First Reprisal Raids

In addition to settlements, Israel employed violence against nonviolent infiltrations. Initially, the leadership perceived the problem as one for the police rather than the military and it was, therefore, dealt with by the Border Corps. As such, the main Israeli effort was directed toward preventing penetrations rather than executing reprisals, a trend that fit with the overall defensive posture prevailing in that period (see Tal, 1990, 18–22). Nevertheless, in light of the infiltrations' costs particularly in the realm of the state control over its new land, pressures, primarily from civilian institutions such as the Jewish Agency and the Jewish National Fund, prompted Prime Minister Ben-Gurion to react harshly (Morris, 1993, 32–34, 116–119). Soldiers deployed along the border shot at would-be infiltrators and even at Arabs passing near the border on the other side, while some border settlements mined their access roads. These measures culminated in between 2,700 and 5,000 Arab fatalities from 1949 to 1956, the majority in the 1949–51 period (ibid., 124–135, 416). Rhetorically, from the outset, the Israeli leadership injected into the country's public discourse the idea that the border-crossers (even the nonviolent refugees at the beginning of the period) were "infiltrators." The term "infiltrators" (*mistanenim*) connoted criminal trespassers who posed a threat to Israel and therefore deserved a violent response (Laor, 1993, 10); the state constructed boundaries between "enemy" and "friend."[1]

Israel's violent response was even more pronounced when taken against the background of the armistice agreements with its neighbors that prevailed in those years. Under these agreements, direct and routine bilateral talks were held with Syria, Egypt, and Jordan. Israel used these meetings to complain about the infiltrations and to hold the respective Arab governments responsible. The latter undertook to deal with the matter. Accordingly, they deployed more army units along the border, punished infiltrators, and tried to move refugee camps away from the border area. Indeed, the number of infiltrations declined but the problem was not completely solved (Morris, 1993, 70–92; Tal, 1990, 41–53). It is noteworthy that the Arab side—notwithstanding their perception of the armistice boundaries as temporary, with the permanent solution to be decided in the future (ibid., 11–13)—sought to apply the authority of the state, through the military, to the new borders with the new refugee population (Morris, 1993, 70–92; Tal, 1990, 41–53). To recall, both sides were restrained by the 1950 Tripartite Declaration.

Beginning in 1951, after the defensive violent approach had failed to staunch the flow of infiltrators, Israel escalated the border frictions. The IDF began carrying out reprisal raids against villages across the borders with Egypt and Jordan suspected of assisting the infiltrators. In addition, Jewish settlers occasionally executed their own retaliatory raids, crossing the border and inflicting damage on Arab property. At this stage reprisals were intended to induce Egypt and Jordan to act, as the Israeli leadership felt that the Arab governments were not doing enough to put a stop to the infiltrations. Israel also continued to discuss the issue within the framework of the armistice commissions. The joint effort by Israel and the Arab governments went some way toward reducing the scale of the phenomenon (Morris, 1993, 70–92, 138–166; Tal, 1990, 27–34)

In their first stage the reprisal raids were usually executed by small forces, generally of company size, although some operations involved light artillery fire or limited air attacks. The operations were carried out at the army's initiative and with the approval of Prime Minister and Defense Minister Ben-Gurion without causing serious political controversy. These attacks, executed by untrained troops from the IDF, frequently failed to fulfill their mission (see Dayan, 1976, 111–112; Yaniv, 1994, 105–106).

The violent Israeli reaction not only failed to treat the problem but actually aggravated it, as the infiltrators responded in kind. They armed themselves, organized in squads to evade the IDF units that patrolled the border, and launched violent raids deep inside Israel (Morris, 1993, 131, 411–414; Yaniv, 1994, 67–70). Israel then stood again at a crossroads. It could either intensify its response or opt for de-escalation, which would entail one of two approaches. (1) Israel could deal with the infiltrations by exhausting the channel of the armistice commissions and appealing to the international community. By doing so, Israel could ensure both the support of the Western powers and the stability of the armistice agreement as a means of preventing war. Moshe Sharett, the foreign minister of the period, posited this alternative, challenging Ben-Gurion and the IDF's hawkish stance (Morris, 1993, 231–234; Sheffer, 1988; Shlaim, 1983). Or (2) Israel could bolster its defensive means, such as fencing the borders and deploying forces along the borders, an alternative put forward by the Foreign Ministry, some IDF officers, and a few politicians, insofar as the raids had proven ineffectual and decreased the prospect of regional stability (Morris, 1993, 216–219; Shalom, 1996, 99–111).

Israel took the hard-line road. The new approach was carried out by a new, but temporary, Israeli leadership. At the end of 1953 Ben-Gurion withdrew from the cabinet and settled in Kibbutz Sde Boker in the Negev. Foreign Minister Moshe Sharett was named prime minister and Pinhas Lavon defense minister. On the eve of his retirement Ben-Gurion also selected General Moshe Dayan as the new chief of staff. It was this leadership—not a harmonious trio—that devised the reorientation of the Israeli stand. Noting that civilian considerations played an indirect part in propelling military policies, while the IDF was pushed to deal with the infiltrations by politicians, the IDF now became involved in steering these policies. Its military mind-set, centered on offense and retaliation rather than defense and restraint, left a powerful imprint on civilian statecraft.

Israel's new approach was strikingly exemplified in the well-known reprisal raid of October 1953 against the Jordanian village of Qibya. The direct background to the operation was the murder of a mother and her two children in Yahud, an immigrant town in the center of the country, by infiltrators from Jordan, the latest in a series of violent attacks. Ben-Gurion, still premier but on leave, decided on the operation apparently without the knowledge of Sharett, then the acting prime minister, even though Jordan had made unusual efforts to apprehend the perpetrators (Sharett, 1978, 34–41). The Qibya raid was the first large-scale effort carried out by Unit 101, an elite unit mainly composed of draftees from the veteran agricultural settlements, created to execute raids under the command of Ariel Sharon. The Israeli force blew up a large number of houses with their occupants inside, killing dozens of civilians (Benziman, 1985, 28–58).

Both intellectuals and politicians, including Sharett, widely criticized the operation. Amitai Etzioni, for example, wrote at the time that the Qibya raid had shown Israel to be a normal society, since it had acted in accordance with the norms of the British in Kenya and the Americans in Japan rather than according to the Jewish norms that had characterized Israel until then (Etzioni, 1954). Taken aback by the criticism and fearing sharp international condemnation, Ben-Gurion stated that the raid had been perpetrated by border settlers who were fed up with the infiltrations and that the IDF had not been involved (Teveth, 1971, 395). Nevertheless, the Qibya raid heralded a further escalation of the cross-border infiltrations that displayed a violent rather than economic profile (Morris, 1993, 292–300).

Qibya, then, demonstrated acutely the shift in the IDF's reprisal policy, especially as it had been carried out by a special force. This was one element in the sea-change wrought by General Moshe Dayan. Essentially, the change involved the inculcation of operational principles in the army and the beginning of reorientation from a defensive to an offensive posture. A three-year plan prepared by the army at Ben-Gurion's behest heralded a major upgrading of the combat forces and included the formation of eighteen brigades and squadrons of jet fighters and helicopters from French sources. Accordingly, the compulsory military service was increased at the end of 1952 from two to two-and-a-half years (Dayan, 1976, 109–110). Nothing better illustrated the new attitude than Dayan's pronouncement that a commander could abort an ongoing mission only if half the unit's personnel had been killed or wounded (ibid., 113–115, 145; Teveth, 1971, 387–388).

These moves fit in well with warnings by the political leadership about a "second round" against the Arab states. This perceived threat increased following the "Free Officers" coup in Egypt in July 1952, which deposed King Farouq and brought to power a junta of officers led by General Muhammed Neguib and Colonel Gamal Abdel Nasser. Their Pan-Arabist tendencies, vigorous demand that the British evacuate their Suez Canal bases, and the prolonged closure of the Straits of Tiran (in the Red Sea) to Israeli navigation from 1951—by itself causing economic damage—added to the anxiety of the Israeli leadership (see Avnery, 1968, 90–101, Hebrew language edition). Further, the Israeli activism of those years was stimulated also by Israel's relations with the West. Beginning in 1953, and following its failure in the Korean War, the United States revised its attitude toward Israel as part of its effort to establish an anti-communist front of Arab states, which bore partial fruit in 1955 with the Baghdad Pact. As it increased its involvement in the region,

Washington demanded that Israel curb its militancy, viewed by Western states as a threat to their status in the Middle East because this militancy would increase the radicalization of Arab regimes. An extreme line was taken by U.S. Assistant Secretary of State Henry Byroade, who called for limitations to be placed on Jewish immigration to Israel in order to allay Arab fears of Israeli expansion. So, it is not surprising that Prime Minister Sharett was reported in 1954 by his aide (Teddy Kolek) to have said that the army's leadership "is consumed with passion for war" (Sharett, 1978, 246), while militant ideas to expand the country's borders were often raised (ibid., 229–230, 347–377).

There were other spheres as well in which Israeli activism expressed itself.

(1) The border with Syria. On the Syrian border, notwithstanding the failure to achieve peace and as distinct from the Egyptian and Jordanian arenas, no acute refugee-infiltrators problem developed. However, in contrast to the territorial status quo that prevailed in the other arenas, a different problem arose. It involved the demarcation of the border and the division of the area's water resources (the Jordan River and Lake Kinneret) between Israel and Syria. At the core of the dispute lay the demilitarized zone (DMZ), set up within the framework of the Israeli-Syrian armistice agreement to defer a decision on permanent borders. Situated in the northeast of Lake Kinneret, the DMZ was declared an area in which state sovereignty was not finally defined; as such, agreement was reached on barring the entry of armed forces into the zone. This amorphous situation was a virtual recipe for generating friction between Israel and Syria, as each attempted to create areas of civilian influence within the DMZ. Most striking was Israel's drive to seize land on a massive scale and expel the Arab population, followed in the early 1950s by the establishment of new settlements. Disputes were aired in the Mixed Armistice Commission. Beginning in 1951, Israel's inclination reached its height in the attempt to take control of the project to drain the Huleh Valley at the expense of Arab-owned land. Syria opposed the project and shot at Israeli workers. Talks held within the framework of the Armistice Commission and via other channels failed to produce agreement on dividing the DMZ. However, de facto Israeli agreement was obtained to carry out the drainage works only on the west bank of the Jordan River, and thus avoid infringing on Arab land. Quiet prevailed until 1954. Arye Shalev, whose report on the events is that of an eyewitness (he was the Israeli liaison officer to the Armistice Commission), claims that Israel could have avoided the tension with Syria from the outset by not employing earthmoving equipment on land belonging to Arabs (Shalev. A, 1989, 1–253; and see pp. 180–182 for his assessment).

At the end of 1953 Israel also began diverting the waters of the Jordan to generate electrical power. This was a unilateral act that was not clearly mandated by the armistice accord and as such produced Israeli-Syrian friction over exploitation of the countries' common water sources. Syria demonstrated its displeasure by firing at Israeli boats in Lake Kinneret. The United States sent a mediator, Eric Johnston, to work out an arrangement for dividing the waters of the Jordan (ibid., 261–285).

(2) The "Essek Bish" ("Mishap"). In 1954, a special Israeli intelligence unit carried out an operation designed to dissuade Britain from evacuating its Suez Canal bases. Its method: perpetration of terrorist incidents against Western targets in Egypt in order to create the impression in the West of Egyptian instability. The operation failed and the unit's members were apprehended. Since the operation was not authorized by the prime minister or the cabinet, nor did the defense minister and the IDF take responsibility for its approval, Prime Minister Sharett set up a secret commission of inquiry to discover who had ordered the operation. However, the commission was unable to determine responsibility and the upshot was Lavon's resignation as defense minister (Elam, 1990, 71–92; Eshed, 1979; Sharett, 1978, 618–736).

Interestingly, no substantive debate took place within the Israeli leadership about the operation's underlying political conception. But it was a controversial issue and several Foreign Ministry officials questioned its wisdom. They argued that Egypt's nationalization of the Suez Canal was the realization of a historic aspiration and that Cairo would now be able to turn to negotiating peace with Israel (Rafael, 1981, 42; see also Handel, 1994, 557). Thus, Elam (1990) maintains that the question of formal responsibility for the order was irrelevant; the important point was that the operation derived from a particular mood and conception that emerged in that period and shaped Israeli policies.

Lavon's withdrawal paved the way for Ben-Gurion's return in February 1955 as a defense minister in the Sharett government. This milestone, as we shall see, signaled the formal collapse of Sharett's somewhat dovish lead.

Challenging Security Interests

At this point, we may infer from the above description that the state's selection of the response to infiltrations was characterized by a "trial-and-error" method rather than a prior, intentional choice. That is, Israel exercised other options as well—de-escalation under the Lausanne Conference and a diplomatic-defensive approach in the early 1950s—before embarking on the opted route. But once Israel defined its interests in retaining the political-territorial status quo, it was inclined to select aggressive methods to combat border-crossings. And once it chose those methods, the underlying cyclical nature dominating Israel's response practically worked to rule out more moderate strategies for dealing with the problem.

Nevertheless, Israel's scope of freedom in the external arena was still considerably broad; it could still have accomplished its goals by reverting to one of these neglected alternatives, particularly the diplomatic-defensive one.

After all, moderate alternatives were broached, albeit half-heartedly and within the confines of the force-oriented paradigm, by Moshe Sharett, a senior member in the political elite, the adoption of which could have led to de-escalation (for illustration of Sharett's vision, see Sharett, 1978, 54–55). Simply said, the very fact that Sharett challenged the existing policies attests to Israel's refraining from exploiting the potential for de-escalation. Further, by selecting a more moderate approach as a means of communicating nonoffensive/nonviolent intentions to the Arab side, Israel could have solved the security dilemma presented by the ineffectiveness and spiral effects of the raids, by de-escalation rather than escalation. The absence of a regional arms race still kept this option alive. A security dilemma by itself is just a dilemma, not a causal force, the way states confront it merits problematization (see Wendt, 1995, 77).

Likewise, by adhering to cooperation with the bordering states within the framework of the armistice agreements, the parties could have internalized new patterns of dialogue, as a means of coping with Israel's anxieties nurtured by the rise of military regimes in Arab countries. Instead, Israel eased its anxieties by aggravating Egypt's sense of uncertainty with the "Mishap" and the other military policies. So, it is clear that politicians read the regional reality through the military prism by which self-help-guided principles were ascendent. We, therefore, ought to further scrutinize the driving force that was powerful enough to set the bellicose policy at that stage against counteroptions.

The more so, as external alternatives coincided with internal challenges. Notwithstanding the preference for harsh response, at about this milestone of 1953/54, the steering of the bellicose policy encountered three main internal objections—be they to the policies themselves or to the cost that they entailed—propounded after the execution of the first raids. Each of them could have generated a reverse course toward one of the moderate strategies. All three originated from the Western-dominated, growing middle class from which the state drew its military capabilities and for which it utilized those capabilities.

To begin, the leadership of Mapai, inspired by its traditional concepts, espoused a moderate military approach and rejected an impulsive response to the infiltrations. For that reason, Mapai ministers often supported the approach of Foreign Minister/Prime Minister Moshe Sharett, who had been partially successful in his attempts to restrain some of Ben-Gurion's and the IDF's militant initiatives in 1953–55 (see Aronson and Horowitz, 1971; Shapiro, 1991, 153–154; Sharett, 1978, 419, 949–950, 99–100). Still, Mapai's support of Sharett was also inspired by intraparty considerations germane to the machine's attempts to clinch its position in the light of Ben-Gurion and his allies' empowerment as chapter 2 illustrates and as will be discussed below (ibid., 119; Teveth, 1971, 418–420).

A second source of opposition came from the agricultural sector. This sector possessed huge power based on its economic centrality at the time and its being the most traditional (Western) constituency of Mapai and the other labor parties. Against this background, the political-military leadership moved to establish an independent military unit to serve the agricultural sector's needs, namely, the *Nahal* (an acronym for "Fighting Pioneer Youth"). The arrangement, which came into effect upon the creation of the army in 1949, obliged all conscripts to serve one year—out of two years of compulsory service—in the Nahal. An additional element of those close relations with the state was the Territorial Defense Organization. It relied—as a heritage of the pre-state defense conception—on the veteran border agricultural settlements as forward outposts. The agricultural sector was thus able to retain its control over a large part of the draftees at the expense of the professional, regular military.

In the early 1950s, as security needs increased due to the escalation of the reprisals, the reorientation of the IDF from a defensive to an offensive approach involved the diversion of manpower from the Nahal and the Territorial Defense Organization to combat units (Bar-On, 1992, 93–95, 101–103; Dayan, 1976, 160–161, 195). Finally, in 1953, the year of service in the Nahal was effectively abolished as an obligation. This move ran concomitantly with the extension of compulsory military service from twenty-four to thirty months (Ben-Gurion, 1971, 71–72, 93, 175–178), partially annulling the effects of the 1949 demobilization. Interestingly, these moves were legitimized by invoking the incompatibility of Oriental draftees with the IDF's growing needs (ibid., 175–178).

Military buildup inflamed the opposition of the agriculture movement's leadership supported by some Mapai leaders (as part of the state–party dispute), who, in fact, opposed the buildup of the army at the expense of their power (see Dayan, 1976, 180–181, 195; Sharett, 1978, 171). This controversy took place in the shadow of Ben-Gurion's confrontation with the Kibbutz Movement over a similar issue but at the symbolic level (see chapter 2).

A third impediment to the execution of the bellicose approach stemmed from Western youngsters. In the early 1950s the IDF's combat units were manned increasingly by draftees from the Oriental collective. While about 40 percent of the recruits were Orientals, the Westerners either staffed rear headquarters or served in the Nahal. This lopsided situation was in part the result of the demographic shift, but it also derived from the frame of mind of the Western youngsters. They were fed up following the 1948 War and unwilling to serve in frontline units (see Teveth, 1971, 355–356, 364–365, 375–376). Orientals, in contrast, perceived military service as a necessary "entry station" to the society and were therefore eager to serve (see, for example, Milstein, 1974, 173). The situation was particularly acute among the young generation of the kibbutz, which had just played a central role in the Palmach. The disbanding of the Palmach triggered a mass resignation of kibbutz members from the army and also paved the way for the IDF to emulate the rigid discipline of the British army which stood in contrast to the Palmach's (and also the kibbutz) spirit

(Gelber, 1989, 247–254; see also evidence in Weizmann, 1975, 78–80).

As it will be recalled, the 1951–53 period was marked by the execution of the first reprisal raids, which revealed the low standard of the combat units. Their inadequate professionalism was attributed by their commanders to the high percentage of unskilled Oriental inductees (Rabin, 1979, 88). Of these units, General Moshe Dayan said—reflecting the ethnic images that increasingly prevailed—that their members were hashish smokers, criminals, and thieves (Dayan, 1976, 111, and see also chapter 2 for other statements made against a similar background by Ben-Gurion). Clearly, from the IDF commanders' point of view, it was essential to make an attempt to lure Western youngsters back into combat units to meet the growing IDF needs; otherwise, the IDF could not fulfill its bellicose missions.

In short, not only had alternatives been available to the chosen policy, but this policy itself also stimulated disapproval by the groups who were expected to carry it out. War preparation was challenged both in the realm of political support (Mapai) and at the material level (military buildup). Realization of the initial demographic-territorial-material interests that stimulated bellicose moves mattered and so the Mamlachtiyut-oriented structure built on this realization. But the agents in the evaluation of interests within the initial phase who benefited directly from the war's gains and those involved in the implementation did not necessarily overlap, although both groups were embraced within the Westerner-dominated middle class. Particularly so, as the fruits enjoyed from land, exclusion of Palestinians, and remote settlements were not fully sensed at this period. This raises the question of what made Israel's policy internally possible.

State agencies had to overcome internal resistance (in part originating within the government circle itself) by injecting their perception of military-informed security interests as a means of mobilizing internal support for the bellicose agenda with the resources for military buildup that it entailed. As such, supply of security in light of perceived threats is not sufficient to mobilize social groups for a war effort. Moreover, these instances suggest that the IDF did not possess at that time a dominant status furnishing it with the capacity to exert its military mind-set over civilian statecraft. Here, again, important are the distinctions to be made between objective facts and the way agents reach an understanding of them. That is what is absent in the neorealist analysis, which confines itself to presumably objective realities alone.

If so, the *construction* of security interests interlock with the *execution* of those interests because deficient execution indispensably entails redefinition of policies, that is, a reversal toward more moderate policies. It is therefore incumbent upon us to tackle the process by which the dominance of the bellicose-oriented, winning formula came about as an *internal* political process (see the theoretical critique of neorealist scholars by Andrews, 1975, 1984). This process ran within the confines of the decision-making system but the hawkish group's success could not have commanded Israel's policies without support drawn from outside this circle. To accept, like the Israeli IR students cited above (who mirror their American neorealist counterparts), the self-help-informed winning formula as a point of departure to explain Israel's behavior is therefore inadequate. So is the acceptance of the IDF's buildup as a starting point for analysis (see the theoretical critique by Barnett, 1990, 529–535).

The next section proceeds with a description of the escalation. I will argue in the following section that the escalation nurtured itself through its unintended consequences: production of gains for an array of groups.

Escalation and Counterescalation

Ben-Gurion's return to the cabinet as a defense minister fortified the hawkish segment within Israel's political leadership, but, at the same time, also amplified a disagreement between Sharett and the defense establishment. Contrary to Sharett, Ben-Gurion, like senior commanders of the IDF and former defense minister Pinhas Lavon, believed that Israel's isolated position required it to demonstrate an independent policy. As he declared when he addressed an IDF parade in April 1955, "Our future depends not on what the goyim [gentiles] say but on what the Jews do" (Sharett, 1978, 966–967). Hence, he advocated a rigorous response to infiltrations.

The next level of escalation, subsequent to several raids executed by Unit 101 and the Paratroop Brigade (within which the unit was assimilated), was the Gaza raid (February 1955). Aimed at the Egyptian army stationed in Gaza, it resulted in about forty Egyptian fatalities. This was also a case of disproportionate escalation, as the attacks that triggered the response had not significantly exceeded the profile of other frictions during that period (Morris, 1993, 324). Gaza was the first major operation carried out against a military, not civilian, target—a development that should also be seen within the context of the criticism of Israel following the Qibya raid. In response, the circle of animosity broadened.

Following the Gaza raid, clashes between the IDF and the Egyptian army and Jordan's Arab Legion became more frequent (ibid., 306–314). Concurrently, Egypt embarked on a large-scale military buildup, culminating in the signing of the Egyptian-Czech arms deal in May 1955, the first significant alliance between the Eastern bloc and an Arab state. (Subsequently, a second, small deal was signed between the Soviets and Syria in early 1956; ibid., 285, note 100.) Possibly, the Gaza raid, concurrently with the "Mishap," caused President Nasser of Egypt to lose his interest in the possibility of reaching a political settlement with Israel. This occurred after three years of a relatively moderate approach in which Nasser's main concern was economic growth and maintaining the political status quo along the border with Israel rather than military buildup (ibid., 270–273; Slater, 1994, 191). The arms deal ensured Egypt a massive supply of modern weapons. The situation looked even grimmer from the Israeli standpoint in October 1955 when Egypt signed a defense treaty with Syria (Morris, 1993, 364).

The arms deal thus dramatized the failure of the American strategy to achieve hegemony in the Middle East. Possibly, Israel made the Soviet encroachment easier by gradually adopting a pro-American stance, rebuffing, for example, overtures from China to establish diplomatic relations (Bar-Zohar, 1975, 1135–1136). Other occurrences were also potentially threatening from Israel's perspective: the possibility arose of military intervention by the British in the form of aid to their ally, Jordan; destabilization of Arab states as a result of agitation by Palestinian refugees; and radicalization of the Arab world, reflected in Nasser's evolving nationalist agenda and in the diminished British influence in the Arab Legion (the organized and battle-ready army force in Jordan) (see Morris, 1993, 263–265, 324, 386–390).

More immediately, Cairo responded to the Gaza raid by strengthening the *Fedayeen*, Egyptian army units manned by Palestinian refugees. Their mission was to carry out attacks in the Israeli heartland, and they were able to inflict large numbers of casualties. Still, for Egypt it was a means of regulating the growing unrest among Palestinians in the Gaza Strip following the raid (see Love, 1969, 83–84). The upshot was that the infiltrations, which in the beginning had been unorganized, sporadic, and restrained by the Egyptian government, became deliberately organized by the Egyptian state. Finally, escalation also took the form of tightening of the Egyptian blockade in the Straits of Tiran (Morris, 1993, 351–354).

Manifestly, the Israeli retaliation policy *decreased* again its security, a typical failure of coping with the security dilemma: What had been confined to the realm of routine security now became a more significant threat to the state's security by aggravating the sense of threat in the Arab side. "Second Round" became a real, no longer theoretical, threat backed up by an arms race. Israel failed in constructing Egypt's moderation; conversely, it took an active role in shaping regional politics as a threatening environment. Self-help efforts proved their self-fulfilling nature.

Indeed, the heightened security danger again paved the way to over-escalation, justified by citing the threat to Israel—a threat which was itself inflamed by Israel's reprisal policy. In practice, the escalation demonstrated in the Arab response confirmed the tendency of the Israeli leadership, led by Prime Minister (again from November 1955) and Defense Minister David Ben-Gurion and Chief of Staff Moshe Dayan, to intentionally deteriorate the situation at the borders as a step in the initiation of war. The war aimed to prevent Egypt from realizing any military superiority acquired by the Czech arms deal, especially in air power and artillery (Bar-On, 1992, 64–65; Morris, 1993, 278–282).

Institutionalization of Israel's shift from defensive to offensive doctrine was then at work. In the state's first years, the IDF was organized according to a defensive conception that had been formulated by David Ben-Gurion and General Yigael Yadin, Israel's second chief of staff. Its main tenet was that Israel should not initiate a war. Should war erupt, the standing army would act to curb the enemy until the mobilization of the reserves, when the fighting would be carried into the enemy's territory. The war must be kept short owing to the state's economic and political constraints (Wallach, 1987). So, if a defensive posture prevailed during the state's first years, guided by Israel's lack of resources in the face of similarly deficient Arab armies, an aggravated threat, compounded by the emergence of militant regimes in Egypt and other Arab states, led Israel to adopt an offensive thrust. In doing so, an Israel-initiated war would take the form of a preemptive strike or a preventive war but, at least at the declarative level, this would be aimed at retaining the status quo.

This agenda was substantiated by massive military buildup involving a change in the composition of the army from infantry-based to armor-based owing to a massive acquisition of weapons from France, including tanks and jet fighters. By this acquisition, the IDF became a modern military especially in air force and armor while its defensive systems drastically shrank (Bar-On, 1992, 93–95, 101–103; Naor, 1988, 225–226; Weizmann, 1975, 163–139). Further, an additional cornerstone in Israel's strategic doctrine was crafted: making efforts to ally with one of the Western powers to ensure political support and a supply of weapons. Since Israel's pursuit of an agreement with the United States and Britain had failed, it concentrated on France. Also the France–Israel agreement involved assistance to build a nuclear reactor (see chapter 4). France, for its part, attempted to remove Nasser as long as it blamed him for backing the Algerian independence movement (Golan, 1982, 41–54). France could thus be assisted by Israel as long as Israel's initial military capabilities had proven effectual. Power entailed further empowerment.

So, by adopting an offensive posture, the strategic doctrine was also adapted to the state's limits of power, both externally (a quantitative territorial-demographic inferiority vis-à-vis the Arab countries) and internally (the ability to mobilize resources in the domestic arena). Drawing from IR scholars (see, mainly, Handel, 1973, 21–36; Horowitz, 1979, 1985; Inbar and Sandler, 1995; Yaniv, 1994), the advantages of offensive doctrine, given Israel's limitations, were clear: to neutralize the effects of uncertainty in the face of the perceived Arab threat; to transfer the war into enemy territory as a means of making it remote from concentrations of civilians in a country without much territory; and to better utilize Israel's qualitative advantages in manpower and tactics relative to the Arab armies.

Most important, an offensive doctrine employing a preemptive strike or a preventive war eliminates the time-consuming process entailed by a protracted defense posture until reserve forces can be mobilized and reach the front to mount an offensive. The war is thus potentially concluded more quickly and is consequently of shorter duration (see Levite, 1988, 65–66). This necessarily created conditions to lighten the burden of war mainly imposed on reservists. Moreover, the state drew on conscripts, rather than reserves, for the growing needs of manpower, either by drastic downsizing of noncombat missions (as, for instance, establishing agricultural settlements) or by extending the compulsory military service from twenty-four to thirty months (Ben-Gurion, 1971, 71–72, 93, 175–178). Concurrently, the Territorial Defense Organization was sharply downgraded. Thus, preparations for war and war participation were appropriated from the civilian population by the professional army. Together with civilian arrangements that ensured a rapid shift to a war footing by the civilian sector, the offensive doctrine permitted Israel to move swiftly from the routine to a war situation and vice versa, thereby also reducing the social costs of managing the war (see Kimmerling, 1985a).

Rhetoric was invoked to mobilize internal support for the coming war. The militarization of the political discourse went beyond the initial foundations laid down within the Mamlachtiyut. This was tellingly articulated by Chief of Staff Moshe Dayan in his famous eulogy for Ro'i Rutenberg, a kibbutz member who was killed by infiltrators from Gaza in April 1956, shortly before the Sinai Campaign. "It is our generation's fate," said Dayan, "it is our choice in life to be ready and armed, strong and unflinching, lest the sword slip from our grasp and our lives be cut off" (quoted in Benn, 1988, 46–49). Dayan thus conferred eternal, perhaps metaphysical, meaning on the use of force, and in fact subordinated the very existence of Israel to the use of force. Moreover, the fact that he was a professional soldier contributed to the introduction of a force-oriented thrust into the political discourse as a routine subject. Thus, no wonder that the new discourse focused on the force-oriented implementation of a given activist approach, subordinating diplomacy to military means.

Another discursive expression was the extension of the idea of security into salient civilian areas such as immigration, settlement, technology, education, and more (Ben-Eliezer, 1994, 57). Activity in those spheres was often determined by military needs, though this was camouflaged by the habitual use of the term "security" rather than "military." On top of that, a Defense Fund was established in late 1955 by the government to raise money from the public for arms purchases following the Czech arms deal. Quasi-voluntary in character, the fund was really an instrument of mass mobilization, since the state could have better achieved the same goal through taxation. At a later stage, as part of the army's deployment for the war, a broad volunteer campaign to fortify the border settlements was launched; at its height, about 100,000 people were involved in the project (Bar-On, 1992, 23–29, 96–97).

To escalate the border frictions toward war, Israel paralyzed the work of the Israeli-Egyptian Armistice Commission (Sharett, 1978, 902–922, 1018–1021; Tal, 1990, 55–57). Practically, Israel rejected Nasser's proposal to demilitarize the border (Love, 1969, 91–95). Further, Israel intensified the reprisal policy, the raid in August 1955 against the town of Khan Yunis in the Gaza Strip being one example. Provoking an Egyptian response, which would hand Israel a pretext to seize parts of the Gaza Strip, was the main objective. Escalation also involved erection of Israeli settlements in the DMZ along the Israel–Egypt border, besides attacking the Egyptian army stationed there. Raids then were converted from a mechanism of combating infiltrations combined with deterrence to that of anti-deterrence, provoking a preventive war (Evron, 1989; Morris, 1993, 175–183; Yaniv, 1994, 64–72, 111). This happened even though the French arms procured by Israel were sufficient to maintain the military balance with Egypt after the Czech arms deal (Be'er, 1966, 226–230; Bar-On, 1992, 375–378). Israel's moves, however, were aimed at altering the post-1948 territorial-political status quo accounted for the border clashes (ibid., 376–382). But the Egyptians did not play the role assigned by Israel, limiting their official responses while escalating raids by the Fedayeen (Morris, 1993, 280–281, 349–351, 357–361).

In March 1955, Ben-Gurion (still defense minister under Sharett) proposed to the cabinet that Israel should conquer the Gaza Strip and subsequently, in November 1955, this time as premier too, that Israel capture the Straits of Tiran and open the waterway to Israeli navigation. Both proposals were blocked by a coalition of ministers led by Sharett (Bar-On, 1992, 72–75; Sharett, 1978, 864–867; Tal, 1990, 103–104). Nevertheless, Ben-Gurion in December 1955 initiated the Kinneret raid, a brigade-level attack on Syrian positions above Lake Kinneret as a part of border frictions revolving around the control over the DMZ and fishing in the Kinneret. The Kinneret raid claimed the lives of some fifty Syrian soldiers. The scale of the operation was excessive but Ben-Gurion wanted to mollify the army following the cancellation of the Tiran Straits plan (Bar-On, 1992, 76–85) and to drag Egypt into a war in the light of an Egyptian-Syrian military cooperation agreement (Morris, 1993, 364). General Uzi Narkiss, then a senior general staff officer, also claimed that the scale of the attack went well beyond operational needs (Narkiss, 1991, 164–167). Sharett, who personally investigated the circumstances of the attack during a visit to the Kinneret region, found that an Israeli police boat on the lake had "drawn fire" from the Syrians, and that Israeli civilian fishing vessels had not been fired on, as had been claimed to justify the operation. Indeed, the fishing area was a protected zone and a military attack had not been called for (Sharett, 1978, 1346–1347). The Kinneret raid did not elicit an Egyptian counterattack.

The following months of early 1956 were devoted to a final effort at negotiations with Egypt. The talks were held at the mediation of the American emissary Robert Anderson. Anderson reported that Nasser was ready to make peace if the Palestinian refugees were permitted to choose between receiving compensation and returning to Israel, and if a territorial link between Egypt and Jordan were created in the Negev. Ben-Gurion and Sharett rejected these ideas and demanded direct negotiations with Nasser. The Anderson mission failed (Bar-Zohar, 1975, 1161–1166; Morris, 1993, 286–288).

Ben-Gurion, stymied by the Sharett-led opposition, demanded the foreign minister's resignation. Sharett acceded to what amounted to an ultimatum and was replaced in June 1956 by Minister of Labor Golda Meir in the face of objections by Mapai leaders to a move that strengthened Ben-Gurion's activist approach (Bar-Zohar, 1975, 1190–1197; Sharett, 1978, 1413–1452). Now with the large number of Israeli soldiers killed in the operations, questions were raised about the efficacy of the reprisal raids. The assessment of the defense establishment was that the operations had run their course and were no longer effective, and therefore the time had come for a full-scale campaign (Bar-Zohar, 1975, 1224–1226; Teveth, 1971, 439–440). This was the prevailing conception even though the Arab states, and Egypt in particular, had not "cooperated" with Israel in its effort to engender a clear casus belli.

The Israel-initiated Sinai Campaign (or the Suez War) of October 1956 was launched following intensive secret talks between Israel and France beginning that June. The plan was for Israel to conquer the Straits of Tiran and confront the Egyptian forces in Sinai, while France and Britain would seize the Suez Canal. Both France and Britain had a vested interest in the operation. France had a prolonged resentment toward Nasser in light of its efforts to oppress the Algerian rebels, while the British were outraged at Nasser's decision to nationalize the Suez Canal, which they perceived as a British asset. However, the fact that Britain was Jordan's ally ruled out any possibility of extending the campaign to that country. The cabinet approved the plan, although the ministers were not apprised of the triple alliance until almost the final stage of the preparations.

At the end of the war Israel occupied both the Sinai Peninsula and the Gaza Strip, but was forced to withdraw from both regions within a few months under Soviet and American pressure. Moscow threatened to attack Israel and feigned the entry of a Soviet naval force into the region. In the light of this, and an announcement by Washington that it would not assist Israel, Ben-Gurion decided in November to withdraw. Political opposition to the decision was limited, but did include Chief of Staff Dayan (Bar-Zohar, 1975, 1277–1285).

Calm prevailed in the region for some years following the Sinai Campaign. Infiltrations by Palestinians from Gaza declined drastically. In Jordan, though, the same outcome was achieved by the Israeli reprisal raids and Amman's beefing up of the Arab Legion along the border (see Evron, 1989). Besides, Israel's withdrawal was accompanied by tacit agreement under the auspices of the Powers that the Sinai Peninsula remain demilitarized, with UN forces buffering between the two armies. Israel's borders with Egypt and Jordan were de facto fixed.

What, then, accounts for the domination of the approach of the hawkish group, which ruled out more pacifist options, interlocking with the state's success in implementing its bellicose agenda by overcoming domestic opposition?

THE STATE'S INTERNAL DOMAINS: THE UNINTENDED CONSEQUENCES OF THE BELLICOSE POLICY

It is time to further link the external level of the bellicose moves with the internal one. Arguably, the escalation, by itself intentionally and rationally conceived to deal with the perceived Arab threat, had *unintended consequences* that made military policies possible and in turn, further fueled the bellicose thrust. This went beyond the intended consequences centering on the retention of confiscated Palestinian property.

To illustrate concrete effects, I analyze the processes by which the state's supremacy over the labor parties was enhanced; how the Westerners' dominance in the military was consolidated interwoven with the state's further capacity to regulate interethnic tensions; and how political restraint of the IDF was accomplished. Later, I will analyze the impacts of these processes on the hardening of the bellicose approach.

Enhancing State Supremacy over the Labor Parties

Mamlachtiyut became further identified with violence owing to the bellicose policy. This worked to imbue the state with supremacy relative to the party-based power centers that had constituted the state. The more the state "sold" protection, the more it was held to be exclusively responsible for assuring the very existence of its inhabitants, unlike the other centers whose activity was not identified with existential missions. This worked to weaken the labor parties and the Histadrut.

In practical terms, although the Mapai leadership took a moderate military approach with respect to the reprisal raids, it was aware that the public, primarily the border settlers, longed for security and expected the military to provide it. To put it differently, Mapai's moderation was incompatible with the construction of the Arab-Israeli enmity through military action. Therefore, as the escalation along the border ran its course, Mapai, bit by bit, supported via its cabinet emissaries operations that not only served military needs but also tried to meet the public's wishes and thus increase electoral support for the party (see, for evidence, Aronson and Horowitz, 1971; Barzilai and Russett, 1990; Morris, 1993, 179–180; Shapiro, 1991, 153–154; Sharett, 1978, 949–950, 673, 999–1001).

The dilemma in which the party leadership found itself—having to choose between a moderate political approach and an activist military orientation—was resolved by two steps. The first was the "Mishap," which exhibited Sharett's weakness as the party's leader. Concerned about the party's position, the machine leaders called Ben-Gurion to return to office as defense minister (Bar-Zohar, 1975, 1038–1039; Sharett, 1978, 709–711). This move that preceded Ben-Gurion's reappointment as the party's candidate for the premiership in 1955 (when Sharett was still prime minister) augmented the hawkish front in the cabinet. The second step came with the results of the elections to the Israeli Knesset held in July 1955 (two months after the Egyptian-Czech arms deal). The moderate parties, with Mapai at the center, lost seats, whereas the hawkish ones did better (the right-wing Herut Party even doubled its number of seats). Mapai's decline extended even to its traditional supporters among the veteran Western population (see Badi, 1963, 138–142; Berger, 1955, Raanan, 1955; albeit these are not electoral research works per se). Possibly, this outcome, caused by other factors in addition to security, induced the party leaders to decide in favor of Ben-Gurion's approach by enabling him to overthrow Sharett in June 1956, over their original objections. By this they lifted the most significant internal political obstacles for stepping up the raids up to the Sinai Campaign. Simply put, Mapai paved the road to the empowerment of the military paradigm.

This background suggests that the dispute between Moshe Sharett and Ben-Gurion was one aspect of the conflict between Ben-Gurion, the architect of Mamlachtiyut, and the party, rather than only a disagreement over the thrust of foreign policy or an intergroup conflict. The underlying issue was the status of the party with regard to the political division of labor in the state era, a part of the ongoing clash already explained in chapter 2. Mapai leaders, for their own reasons, resented the flourishing of the military establishment following their basic attempts to curtail the state empowerment inwardly. The group around Ben-Gurion, for its part, adhered to its statist orientation backed by a bellicose agenda.

The raids thus fueled the enduring dispute, but at the same time, also marked a decision—taking the form of Sharett's removal from the cabinet—in favor of the state's ascendancy over Mapai. Mapai, for its part, benefited at several levels. The first was ensuring electoral dominance drawn from state-supplied security, which, moreover, increased political stability by decreasing disquiet among the frontier settlers. This meant that Mapai grasped the link between force-oriented reaction to external problems and electoral gains but was hence at the mercy of the state as the source of this gain. Indeed, the elections held in 1959, after the glorious Sinai Campaign, affirmed the renewal of Mapai's unquestioned electoral dominance by getting the votes of 40 percent of the electorate.

Second, Mapai through its powerful agricultural sector benefited from abandoned Palestinian land and land that Israel attempted to seize in the DMZ along the border with Syria. Both gains were conditional on the entrenchment of the conflict as a means of delegitimizing the Palestinians' claims to lands and erecting obstacles to Israel–Syria dialogue. Only from the mid-1950s onward did these lands, which had been appropriated in practice earlier, allow for the growth of the Israeli economy from which this sector benefited (Shalev, 1992, 203–204). Hence, the part played by this process in mitigating previous opposition. Third, the Sinai Campaign marked an ultimate demarcation of Israel's borders, including their being sealed against Palestinian infiltrations and the cheap, unorganized labor force that they represented. Mapai's control via the Histadrut over the labor market was thus cemented. Moreover, the bellicose policy's contribution to the entrenchment of the Arab-Israeli conflict meant also entrenchment of the Military Administration over Israeli Palestinians. This, at that stage, went beyond monitoring the labor market insofar as Mapai via the Histadrut effectively translated its control over this population into electoral gains (Shalev, 1992, 52–57). Finally, the raids imbued the youngsters of the agricultural sector with prestige (see below). It is noteworthy that we do not have evidence suggesting that Mapai groups consciously grasped the linkage between bellicose moves and gains. But it is clear that the more groups were satisfied by those policies, the less likely that a dovish front could be crystallized to resist Ben-Gurion's moves. Indeed, when frustration displaced satisfaction, those groups reversed their orientation, as chapter 4 tells.

Mapai's gains, however, were exchanged for its neglect of prominent political status vis-à-vis the young state. On the contrary, Mapai's and the Histadrut's gains attest to their growing dependence on the state for realizing their interests, so the state gradually reconstructed their interests in empowerment of the state that entwined with militarization. This move, moreover, signaled the ascendancy of the military mind-set over civilian statecraft. Several levels are relevant. First, the state enhanced for the short term its autonomy to steer military policies with less dependence on Mapai, albeit with more dependence, for the long term, on those groups who benefited from the state of war (see more below). Second, the bureaucratic group that emerged as a result of the army's expansion was not beholden to the parties, with General Dayan and Shimon Peres, the general director of the Defense Ministry, in the center. Third, security became a tangible resource allocated by the state to its citizens, again bypassing party mechanisms, especially those of the Histadrut. For example, Ben-Gurion declared that the reprisals were aimed also to fill the Oriental settlers (viewed as a potential constituency of the hawkish parties) with pride, and to prove to them that the state was not abandoning them to the mercy of infiltrators—in contrast to the humiliations which, he claimed, they had suffered in the Arab states (Bar-Zohar, 1975, 1139). Further, the state's ascendancy was also apparent in its ability to autonomously confer social status. It became the source of such status, whereas in the Yishuv era, with its pioneer ethos, social prestige had flowed from the political organizations identified with the labor parties. Consequently, it made the formerly dominant group dependent on the state to enjoy access to the new resource.[2]

Fourth, the bellicose policy served Ben-Gurion and his allies in their effort to reduce the state's dependence on the party for enlisting political support by enhancing the military as an extra-party mechanism. The buildup of the army created a channel for direct dialogue between the state and its citizens through an organization that was a meeting point for most Jewish youngsters. The interaction between the IDF and Israeli society had been structured along "fragmented boundaries" (in Luckham's 1971 term): Civilian values highly penetrate the military, and vice versa, along several conjunctions partly due to the civilian roles taken by the IDF. This structure inspired the image of Israeli society as a "nation-in-arms" (Ben-Eliezer, 1994; Horowitz, 1982; Lissak, 1984b). Consequently, citizens were affected by state-controlled channels of political communication supplanting the pre-state party-controlled social networks (see Galnoor, 1982). A channel of this kind was visible in the mobilization of mass support that accompanied the escalation of the reprisals.[3]

Furthermore, inclusion of most Jewish youngsters within the military meant that the military could deal with inculcation of social discipline among youngsters by using its disciplinary mechanisms. Habituation to military discipline could be converted into social discipline, routinizing the youngsters' awareness as subjects of the fledgling state. The more the military was constituted on mass elements, the more effective its performance as a disciplinary mechanism.[4]

A fifth gain of the state relative to the labor parties was that the escalation along the borders gave security needs priority over those of the agricultural settlements and helped delegitimize the demand by the agricultural sector to receive preference over the army in manpower. To put it differently, implementation of the military buildup was conditional on military escalation by which the state dynamically invoked the external arena as a means of overcoming internal difficulties. The result was that the state cemented its autonomous status by forcing a policy on a power center (the agricultural sector) that conflicted with the latter's consciously defined, short-term material interest. Organizational change in the military, moreover, enabled the state to gain direct control of its draftees, without resorting to the mediation of a sectorial power center, such as the agricultural sector (see, at the comparative level, Thomson, 1994, on the linkage between sovereignty and direct control over conscription).

Finally, the large military buildup was among other factors triggering a massive industrialization of the Israeli economy from the mid-1950s under the state's aegis (see chapter 2). Industrialization involved the erection of an enormous military industry, notably controlled by the state, to meet the growing needs of the modernizing military. Indirectly, military industry prompted civilian industries as well, such as metal, chemical, machinery, and electronics. These years saw in particular the erection of Israel Aircraft Industries (IAI) in collaboration with France and an electronics industry, mainly the Histadrut-owned Tadiran. Also, the foundations were laid to develop nuclear weapons (see chapter 4).

Several consequences originated from military industrialization pertinent to the state's internal empowerment (on the case of Israel, see Barnett, 1992, 165–169, 182–184; Shalev, 1992, 213–214; for a similar process in the United States, see Hooks, 1990; Hooks and McLauchlan, 1992; and in Europe, Porter, 1994, 155–156).[5] First, industrialization worked to increase the state's economic power relative to the Histadrut because industrialization intersected with military buildup raised a new economic sector directed by the state—that is, inasmuch as the state could channel required resources for industry either directly (for example, by using foreign aid to promote industries according to military needs) or indirectly as the main client of many industries, especially the military ones. Further, a reliance of the Histadrut-controlled Hevrat Ha'Ovdim (the business sector) on the state insofar as it was involved with military industry was created. Second, and by the same token, the middle class's dependence on the state, its roots in the formation of ethno-class division of labor, solidified and became a more concrete, direct reliance. This had the potential, for the long run, to downgrade this class's linkage to the Histadrut in favor of the state. Finally, industrialization brought about full employment in the Jewish sector by the early 1960s, a syndrome that was one of the foundations on which the state legitimized its domestic policies. Clearly, mass military participation entails effective welfare systems by which political-social consensus is attained and an obstacle to uninterrupted participation of peripheral groups in the military is lifted (see Shaw, 1987, at the comparative level).

On the long-term plane, the overall move accelerated Mapai's decline, paradoxically in tandem with entrenchment of its constituency's (the Western collective) social dominance. These effects were beyond the party leadership's consciousness—they would grasp the real meaning of their decline only in the aftermath of the Sinai Campaign (see chapter 4).

Neutralization was the fate of Mapam, the left-wing opposition to Mapai. A series of measures taken by the state—dismantling the Palmach, which was closely associated with Mapam, curtailing the activity of trade unions in which the party wielded influence, and other steps—debilitated the party. At the same time, the party, as an economic and bureaucratic machine similar to Mapai, heavily relied on the state, especially when it allocated confiscated Palestinian land to Mapam' Kibbutz Movements (*Ha'Kibbutz Ha'Artzi*) and the party was a part of, and hence also benefited from, the Histadrut's machine. Pressures then built up within the party for greater moderation, for moving toward the center of the political map. This was among the factors triggering mounting tension among the party's factions, which were split over Mapam's place as an opposition alternative to Mapai. In 1954, a schism occurred, with Ahdut Ha'Avodah (Unity of Labor), a centrist though hawkish group, breaking away from the left-wing Mapam. Still, both parties joined the ruling government coalition in 1955. However, the long-term consequences were far-reaching. With the Mapam splinters situating themselves at the political center, the Israeli Left lost its ability to present a viable alternative to the Mamlachtiyut (see Carmi and Rosenfeld, 1993).

The implications became fully apparent in the Sinai Campaign, when Mapai was able to drag in its activist wake even post-schism Mapam. The latter party, although espousing a dovish orientation in foreign policy, took a pragmatic stand on the reprisal raids and the Sinai Campaign. This, too, meant Mapam was sucked into the political consensus of which Mapai was at the center (see Amitay, 1988, 67–81; Barzilai, 1992, 59–82; Bar-Zohar, 1975, 1282–1285). The enfeeblement of the Left was also felt in the contribution made by the force-oriented Mamlachtiyut discourse to the growing delegitimation of pacifist outlooks, which were linked to a shirking of the security burden. As a result, no effective peace movements positing at least dovish alternatives to bellicose policies sprang up (until the late 1970s) despite the centrality of the conflict with the Arabs in the Israeli experience (see Hermann, 1989, 204–213).

The depth of militarization was strikingly felt in the election campaign for the Third Knesset in 1955 about a year before the Sinai Campaign. The heart of the campaign was a debate among the parties as to which political movement had contributed most to the state's establishment in the military domain. No such debate took place in earlier or later elections (until 1981). Thus, for example, Herut, the right-wing party that had been organized on the foundation of the pre-state underground IZL, emphasized its part in the conquest of the Arab city of Jaffa, adjacent to Tel Aviv. The left-wing parties, for their part, underlined the contribution made by their military and agricultural organizations. Mapam went so far as to invoke the participation of its members in the Warsaw Ghetto Uprising during World War II (data drawn from the press of the period). The debate showed how widely Mamlachtiyut, with the status of the "fighter" at its center, had taken hold; the parties presented their contribution to the state as the central criterion for which they deserved political support, even more than their vision for building the state and the society. They turned their back on the present in favor of the heroic past and emphasized their military contribution over their accomplishments in other spheres.[6] In sum, the state constructed the parties' interest in militarization as a political asset.

Consolidating the Westerners' Dominance in the IDF and Regulating Interethnic Tensions

The escalation of the border clashes was instrumental to the state action to legitimize the interethnic power relations in both the military and civilian spheres.

Border clashes served the IDF's attempt to reconstruct the ethnic composition of the military. The seeds of the campaign were laid in 1950–52, when Western high school graduates were assigned to combat units over their protests. Nahal units, where many of the Western elite served, were also gradually cut as part of the shift from defensive to offensive doctrine (Teveth, 1971, 364–365, 375–376). Instrumental to this effort was the transformation in the character of military activity due to the escalation of the reprisal raids. The turning point came in 1953, with the establishment of the elite Unit 101 to execute reprisals. The operations carried out by the unit under the command of Ariel Sharon, beginning with the Qibya raid (1953), vastly enhanced the IDF's prestige, especially as the unit was absorbed into the Paratroop Brigade and passed its spirit to other units (Dayan, 1976, 119). For example, Ben-Gurion considered the Gaza raid a heroic action. He visited the unit that had carried out the attack, termed the paratroopers "path-breakers" [*rishonim*], and wrote them a letter he signed "With fondness and admiration" (Bar-Zohar, 1975, 1127–1130).

Consequently, young people, particularly from the agricultural sector, began to be attracted to these units and to view service in them as a challenge (Benziman, 1985, 55–62). The escalation of the reprisals, up to the Sinai Campaign, restored the army's status as a magnet for Western youngsters. Through the IDF, they could reacquire the prestige denied them during the state's first years. IDF's failures in the struggle against the infiltrators and its other current preoccupation, considered dull and dreary when compared with the heroic myth of the 1948 War, were among the ways in which military service rendered prestige in the early 1950s. Now no longer alienated from the military, Westerners became more amenable to volunteering for combat units and joining the career army (see Dayan, 1976,130, 360–361). At the same time, the raids even further motivated Orientals' effort to find a place in the army as a necessary channel of mobility into the absorbing society. Nor did it matter that, in practice, the Orientals failed in the contest for advancement at that stage. Still, had the IDF not previously been wrapped with the Mamlachtiyut-produced prestige (especially relative to what may have been created had the Western elites opted for one of the alternative trajectories of state-building), its commanders' capacity to fascinate the Western youngsters might have been significantly more complex.

Structurally, the result was the entrenchment of Westerners' dominance in the army which, to recall, was converted to social dominance outside the military; or, from a different perspective, elimination of any possibility that the Orientals might attain a significant quantitative advantage in the combat units, at least for the short term. Had the raids not worked to recompose the IDF, this outcome would not have been achieved nor would the conversion of military status into civilian status been so straightforward.

The bellicose moves impacted the domestic structure even more profoundly. With conspicuous militarization of the political discourse and prestigious raids, supply of security possessed higher value, which worked to fortify the "fighter" status. To put it differently, the military had taken part in aggravating the external threat and concomitantly acquired prestige by repulsing this very threat. Self-creation of symbolic resource was at work. Indeed, it can be argued that the "fighter" now triumphed over the "pioneer" as part of the competition between statist and pre-statist groups under the guise of the Mamlachtiyut. All that took root in the absence of other channels through which the young generation could acquire untapped symbolic status. State-originated symbolic status, "pioneer" and "fighter" alike, was still the main resource.

At the same time, the "fighter" status actually compensated the agricultural groups for the loss of the "pioneer" that had been historically embodied by this sector. Therein lay the state's capacity to reconstruct these groups' interest from fulfilling direct material interests by means of preferring productive, agriculture activity over military service, to appropriate military service. No wonder that this sector invoked thereafter its military participation to legitimize its unique social status relative to other sectors. Consequently, the force-oriented discourse expanded as long as new groups became interested in spreading military-oriented ideas. I suggest, therefore, that the emergence of the "fighter" was linked to, and driven by, social interests, rather than being a product of a cultural process per se.

Israel's worsening security situation thus served to underscore the Westerners' superiority, compared to the Orientals' inferiority as combatants. By the same token, the IDF's system of objective, achievement-based criteria for promotion—which underlay the army's ability to play its role in the domain of interethnic reproduction—was revalidated. This situation made it unnecessary, from the Westerners' point of view, to impose the kind of overt institutional limitations on the mobility of Orientals that dominant ethnic groups in other ethnically divided societies used. The latter is aimed at excluding peripheral ethnic groups from the military or impeding their promotion within it (Enloe, 1980, 12–21). In the Israeli case, however, Western dominance was rooted in supposedly objective, hence legitimate, criteria. Yet these very criteria hampered the accretion of power by Orientals unaware of their implications, while they legitimized Westerners' social dominance. A *materialist militarism* grew, characterized by a strong link between discourse and material interests. Unlike other historical forms, this pattern was shaped by dominant groups as a means of legitimizing their status, not by peripheral groups trying to justify their social claims (see, for example, Mann, 1987) or by the military establishment alone attempting to confirm its social centrality (see, for example, Vagts, 1959).

At another level, the escalation of the reprisal raids brought home the danger facing the country's citizens and made it more legitimate for the state to extract the resources—including manpower—needed to maintain security. This had a further effect of limiting the ability of Western youngsters to avoid military service with the support of their social networks such as the agricultural movements. Taking this process with the neutralization of pre-state power centers and the other steps by which the state's control over the political space was taken, the state demonstrated its capacity to discipline the Western middle class. Its internal penetration was completed. This process mirrors the formation of some European states in which the state functioned like a mechanism of protection (in Tilly's terms, 1985b), convincing its citizens (consumers) to increase their demand for security and to purchase it at higher "price," thus promoting the state's capacity to extract its citizens' resources (Lake, 1992).[7]

It is worth emphasizing that this story does not suggest a conspiracy. The military elite tried to improve the operational ability of combat units by beefing them up with Western soldiers, believing that they were best suited to military activity. Ultimately, Western youngsters accepted being disciplined by the state as a response to the perceived security danger, but later exchanged their acceptance for achieving social prestige. Still, the implementation of this policy affected, unintentionally, interethnic power relations, as the Westerners maintained their dominance within the army.

Also significant was another impact of the border clashes. Arguably, the more valuable protection became, the less likely Orientals and Westerners alike would make demands for other than existential goods, especially when the state leaders' calls for sacrifice invoked military needs (as with the Defense Fund, see above). Still, the state's protection-oriented action was further significant to many Orientals. It signaled their joining of the society which, for the first time, granted them protection as a collective group. So, given that the reprisals were aimed also to fill the Orientals living in the border settlements with pride, according to Ben-Gurion's declaration, the bellicose policy possibly worked to delay Orientals' protests against their deprivation.

Not only Orientals were politically neutralized. Neutralization extended to the working class as a whole since the Israeli-Palestinian conflict in conjunction with the exclusionary policy toward the Israeli Palestinians fixed the internal split within the working class. This made interethnic cooperation between peripheral groups, Orientals and Israeli Palestinians, less likely to materialize.

Political Restraint of the IDF

The bellicose policy had two ostensibly contradictory impacts on the IDF. It worked to increase the political power of the military and concomitantly to institutionalize its subordination to civilian political supervision. Consequently, political restraint of the military was achieved.

Though the principle of the army's subordination to the civilian authorities was already firmly rooted in Israeli political culture as a heritage of the Yishuv (see Ben-Eliezer, 1995; Pail, 1979), politicians during the state's first years were fearful that the army's empowerment might bring about its active intervention in politics (see Segev, 1986, 150–151, 268–271; Teveth, 1971, 368–369). To recall, this already underlay Ben-Gurion's rationale for discharging the majority of the 1948 conscripts and further shrinking the regular army at the beginning of the 1950s. In addition, fears emerged concerning Ben-Gurion's possible putsch, as mentioned above. Nevertheless, state civilian agencies stood successfully in the primary test, namely, demobilization of the majority of the 1948 conscripts and regimentation of the military afterwards. Emerging political control was, paradoxically, no more blatant than in the nature of arguments between the two institutions: In 1952 and 1953, two successive chiefs of staff—Yigael Yadin and Mordechai Makleff—resigned over disputes with Prime Minister and Defense Minister Ben-Gurion concerning the division of powers between the Ministry of Defense and the IDF (see Peri, 1983, 194–197; Teveth, 1971, 368–369).

To recall, the IDF of the first years was engaged with "grey" missions, with its main resources being diverted to civilian missions; politicians pushed its involvement with the infiltrations, displacing the police-like Border Corps. In light of state-created unsolved problems along the borders, the IDF's engagement empowered the organization. General Moshe Dayan's appointment as chief of staff in late 1953 signaled Ben-Gurion's new expectations for the IDF with his selection of a well-known militant officer.

Indeed, frictions between politicians and generals reached their peak when the IDF carried out the raids. The army tended to act independently in defiance of Defense Minister Pinhas Lavon, who himself displayed disloyalty toward Prime Minister Sharett during 1954/55. The IDF virtually dictated to the political level a series of operations, or exceeded the politicians' framework of approval, and in some cases did not even report its cross-border activity to the prime minister (see, for example, Dayan, 1976, 150–152; Morris, 1993, 300–303; Sharett, 1978, 34–41, 446–447, 514–526, 670–680). The most notorious case was the telling "Mishap" in 1954 involving military activity in Egypt without clear approval from the political level (Eshed, 1979).[8]

Faced with this situation, the civilian leadership considered it imperative to upgrade political supervision over the army. To begin with, Prime Minister

Sharett introduced a formal procedure whereby reprisal raids would need the approval of a small ministerial forum (Sharett, 1978, 53). Ben-Gurion, after his return to office in 1955, instituted a more stringent method in the wake of the dispute triggered by the Kinneret raid: The complete plan of every reprisal raid required his personal approval (Teveth, 1971, 428). At the same time, the division of power between the IDF and the Ministry of Defense was consolidated in a manner that diminished the former's authority in the realms of budget and procurement and made the latter unequivocally responsible for areas not directly connected with the management of operational military activity (Greenberg, 1993). On top of this, Ben-Gurion could order the army to withdraw from the Sinai Peninsula when the Suez War concluded over the army's objection.

Paradoxically, the militarization of Israeli statecraft, interwoven with the political debates over the IDF's status and resources, played a crucial role in this process. Debates (such as between the military and the agricultural sector) demonstrated the IDF's growing dependence on the politicians for mobilizing the needed resources and legitimacy to energize military activity. Consequently, as "soldiers . . . became ever-more dependent on their civilian supporters for the wherewithal of war . . . the autonomy and personal power of the [military] men [was decreased]" (Tilly, 1985a, 78, at the theoretical level). Had the military been funded by an external power or had the country not suffered from a scarcity of resources, the competition over resources between the IDF and civilian sectors that produced that dependency might have been deflected.[9]

Arguably, beyond meeting the IDF's needs, the state civilian agencies resolidified structural relations of exchange with the army following the arrangements created in the pre-state period (see Ben-Eliezer, 1984; 1995, 227–279, 309–310, on the relations between the Palmach/young IDF and the Yishuv/state elite in 1948/49): The politicians acknowledged military thought, with the involved allocation of material resources, as the preferred mode for dealing with the Arab-Israeli conflict in exchange for ensuring the IDF's loyalty. For example, when the raids were being conceived and planned, Prime Minister Sharett maintained that opposition to the army's moves might encourage officers to reject the government's authority, like the "breakaway" underground organizations—the IZL and LHI—in the Yishuv period (Sharett, 1978, 1205). Boldly put, however, needs pertinent to political control over the military were not the driving force (as claimed by Ben-Eliezer), but were among the considerations impinging on doctrinary annulment and were a by-product of the bellicose policy and, moreover, could downplay the Mapai leaders' call to block the military empowerment with the internal expansion of the state that it entailed. Indeed, the IDF was targeted less and less by the party-oriented groups.

The army, for its part, accepted the politicians' unquestioned authority in exchange for several gains. First, the IDF benefited from huge material and human resources, allowing it to maintain a massive, long-term buildup and significantly upgrade its combat fitness, beyond the direct needs of the early 1950s. But militarization spelled out new gains serving as engines of political control beyond material dependency: By accepting its political subordination, the army showed itself to be without political interests or inclinations, acting universalistically on behalf of the entire Jewish political community. It could then produce net prestige from its warfare activity. Conversely, had the IDF intervened openly in politics (similar to many of its Third World counterparts in the same period) and, doing so, become a target of open political criticism, it would have lost part of its social prestige, being portrayed as one corporation among others. So, alternative channels for attainment of prestige worked to reduce the officers' motivation to act hyperautonomously. Building on its growing prestige, the IDF's third gain was the acquiring of capacity to leave a powerful impact on civilian statecraft, in fact forming relations of partnership with, rather than instrumental obedience to, the political institutions without resorting to overt intervention (Peri, 1983). Militarization of the political discourse and the prestige with which it imbued the military therefore also helped create the conditions to restrain the military.[10]

Universalization of the IDF, moreover, went beyond the organizational domain. As the raids solidified the IDF's universalist status, it was further able to play its part in legitimizing interethnic relations. Otherwise, the IDF would have lost its attractiveness in the eyes of some groups when its political agenda was revealed. The "People Army" must be portrayed as divorced from politics.

Taking together the unintended consequences that bellicose policies produced, the main Jewish groups through their very participation in carrying out the raids earned gains categorized into three types:

First, some gains were produced directly through the bellicose action in the domains of security, material resources, social prestige, political stability, electoral dominance, and more.

Second, going back to our discussion on the Mamlachtiyut, the entrenchment of the Arab-Israeli conflict produced gains, and hence constructed interests, in the domains of retaining confiscated lands and property and keeping local and external Palestinians distant from the Jewish labor market. This also embraced interests of statist agents themselves, centering on building a centralist state, due to the war, by which they acquired more leverage in allocating resources (such as lands, abandoned Palestinian property, jobs, etc.).

Third, warfare activity legitimized the state's supremacy and universalized its image via the Mamlachtiyut, through which its ability to legitimize social inequalities was bolstered. Full employment, the social roles of the IDF, the weakening of particularist party-based centers, the national image of remote settlements that enabled low-cost exploitation of Oriental labor, and so on, were among the war-incited effects. Western groups, for their part, could then not only gain more than their Oriental counterparts and retain their dominance in the labor market; they could also convert assets directly attained by means of war participation, as social prestige, into long-term gains taking the form of social dominance. By the same token, Orientals were kept from accumulating power, or their potential for doing so was greatly reduced. Part of it was due to the realization of their interests via the border clashes, namely, security and employment. Had this development not occurred, it would have practically raised the costs of maintaining the ethno-class division of labor. Interethnic reproduction and the war's entrenchment became interrelated more than ever.

Indeed, the year 1954 marked the beginning of a long cycle of economic growth, the main engines of which were capital inflow, a growing level of employment among the low-wage workforce drawn from the Oriental immigration, and confiscation of Palestinians' lands (Shalev, 1992, 203–204). At least the last two factors were directly produced by the Arab-Israeli conflict but had not been felt earlier. As such, their potential beneficiaries were more concerned with the costs of war than enjoying the fruits of it; hence, the early impediments to the bellicose thrust.

To the extent that groups gained from the reality of war, their inclination, through (re)construction of interests, to work for or at least accept the bellicose approach was high. Previous opposition grounded on ideological considerations or the reluctance to pay the costs vanished. The very nature of the problem of the border frictions, and the very nature of the escalation of these frictions, created conditions by which the state successfully lifted the main obstacles to its force-oriented thrust. With the IDF universalized by means of political control, the state could mobilize both political support and material resources, enabling a military buildup to take its course at the expense of the civilian sectors. Reverse motion was not necessary.

Satisfied with the newly created war-based reality, social groups' openness to receiving force-oriented signals transmitted by the military command was greater than their openness to hearing moderate calls voiced even half-heartedly in Arab countries. This is especially so since ordinary citizens were deprived of information mainly about these signals and the alternative military doctrines considered by the political elite. Satisfaction, by nature, dictates low demand for information. A public discourse that allowed for two or more alternative avenues to deal with the regional threat with the costs, risks, and relative advantages that each option entailed was averted. Nor was the Ben-Gurion-Sharett debate voiced publicly.

State agencies could thereby inject their previously constructed military concepts into the political discourse—especially with their interpretation of

the term "security interest," which was informed by the perceived Arab threat—
by translating security interests into vested actual interests of an array of social
groups. This structure allowed a link to be created between identities, ideas, and
images on the one hand and political action on the other. True, state agencies
worked to "convince" the public to support the force-oriented response, but this
discussion uncovers the dynamics hidden behind the process. Domestic groups
filtered security risks through the lenses of their interests, allowing militarization to flow across the country. In short, the definition of national interest
might entail (re)construction of groups' interests. *Legitimization* of state strategies of taxation, production, and conscription for war are no less significant
than the strategies themselves (as the latter are outlined by Barnett, 1992).

An asymmetric balance between a military command eager to employ
hard-line policies and civilian groups—benefiting by military means, infused
with militarism, and politically passive—let the ascendancy of the military
establishment take place at the expense of the diplomatic school of thought.
Relatively dovish forces lost the capacity to leave their imprint on the formation
of foreign-military policies.

By contrast, if the impact of the military operations had been different—if, for example, Orientals, not Westerners, had gained social prestige
from massive participation in the raids, by which they could demand bettering of their peripheral social position, or if the policy's human and material
costs had been intolerable—then Mapai, certain social groups, and even some
state agencies might have tried to restrain the defense establishment's
activism and more carefully consider external moderate signals. The same
groups had already challenged the state and brought about the elimination of
the austerity when they found that it conflicted with their material expectations from the state. Relations of exchange between the state and social
groups had tangible effects.

Theoretically, the state does not simply "reconstruct." In practice, it takes
advantage of the situation in which agents are split between conflicting interests.
At the same time, it both channels resources and uses its coercive power to direct
agents' behavior. If it succeeds, social interests are reconstructed. It is worth
emphasizing that I deal with *invisible, unconscious interests*. Remember our conceptualization of "exchange" in chapter 1: Agents shifted their behavior following
their reading of a new reality and their own situation within it, rather than formulating the direct linkage between the entrenched conflict and multiple rewards. To
put it differently, agents did not rationally calculate several alternatives in terms of
losses and gains; at least for the long term they possibly could have partly satisfied
their interests even had the state selected a more pacifist policy. Rather, agents reconciled their interests to the new created reality that satisfied them *relative* to a past
reality, not necessarily to a tentative one. By generating agents' passive or active
cooperation with the state agencies, the state corrected agents' "error" of chal-

lenging the bellicose agenda with the state empowerment that it entailed and from which those agents drew their social status.

The immediate results were pronounced in the Sinai Campaign. It was managed as an "elite war." Conceived and planned in complete secrecy by Prime Minister Ben-Gurion and a few advisers, it was not brought to the cabinet for approval until almost the eleventh hour. The upgrading of the army's offensive capability in the years preceding the war enabled a lightning operation to be mounted, with most of the burden falling on the standing army. Casualties were negligible—230, or 0.01 percent of the total population (Sussman, 1984, 14)—and the civilian rear was unharmed. The government was therefore in a position to bow to the pressure of the superpowers and order a speedy withdrawal from the Sinai Peninsula without arousing significant domestic opposition.

However, the effects of the mobilization of support and resources went beyond the execution of the policy itself and worked to propel the state's internal expansion (the third domain of state action). The very process by which support was mobilized for the war effort also stimulated the creation of civilian, bureaucratic mechanisms to deal with the war at the expense of the pre-state power centers, such as military buildup, military industry, information channels, and the like. Consequently, new reservoirs of state-controlled resources were created based on the war's gains. Some of those gains were channeled to ensure social peace beyond what had been needed for the war effort: security, full employment, and prestigious military service to Orientals; economic growth, social prestige, and legitimation of social dominance to the Westerners. The remainder became the state's "fee," taking the form of state empowerment, as long as the production and allocation of gains were mediated by the state (see Wolfe, 1974, at the theoretical level).

The state's internal empowerment was beyond the involved agents' conscious awareness. They supported the bellicose moves for their own dynamically constructed interests but, in fact, paved the road for state empowerment, sometimes in a manner that partially conflicted with their interests, particularly the Mapai-affiliated groups. There again, following my argument with respect to the dialectical nature of Mamlachtiyut, though agents work to realize their self-interests they, at the same time, set in motion a new structure, taking the form of a centralist state. It disempowered the constitutive groups themselves in the political realm in return for an alternative asset in the social realm. The "unfinished business" of state-building was completed. In short, acceptance of the state of war entailed acceptance of the state's internal expansion.

Structurally, the relations of exchange between the state and Western groups then were recemented: The Westerners accepted, through the military-driven empowerment of the state, the burden of the war and a downgraded political status via the enfeeblement of Mapai. This was in return for the upgrading of their material-symbolic status under the auspices of a centralist state. The state actually eradicated the party mediation between the state and social groups by which the former could reward the latter. The innate tension between conflicting interests was mitigated, but at the same time, mutual commitments were further tightened.

Pushing the argument further, the very execution of security interests also affected their construction by hardening the war-oriented motives. We move from passive support to an active "push and pull."

HARDENING THE FORCE-ORIENTED THRUST

Hardening of bellicose tendencies dominated sociopolitical processes during the early 1950s, beginning with the selected trajectory of state-building and the demographic-territorial interests that it entailed, proceeding with the ensuing opted-for methods to combat infiltrations, and ending with gains-production through bellicose action. Hardening followed several courses, central to which is the internally originating loss of the state's flexibility in the external arena.

Externally, the failure to deal with the security dilemma under the ascendancy of a militaristic worldview generated escalation as a counterreaction to Arab moves and so forth. But this motion was domestically fueled as well.

State-crafted domestic, sociopolitical arrangements circumscribed the range of alternative options available for decision-makers, even though Israel could have accomplished its strictly, external security goals by reverting to more moderate, less internally burdensome, diplomatic-defensive, alternatives. Critical were the constraining effects of the newly habituated reality revolving around the perpetuation of the post-1948 demographic-territorial status quo. What was the reality grasped by decision-makers? It was settlers who had seized previously held Palestinian houses and lands and who were uncompetitively employed as blue-collar workers in a business run by a governmental or Western entrepreneur in a remote town which prestigious soldiers protected.

'Habituation' refers to the new, "common knowledge" political actors deploy and grasp that comes to seem an inevitable, though not necessarily conscious, component of decision-making. Decision-making is usually bound to a narrow range of alternative options, narrower than their actual scope, from which agents select their preferred moves. Rather than maximization, satisfaction with outcomes falling within an acceptable zone is the customary model of decision-making (see Simon, 1976, 38–41, 80–84, 272–273), in which habituated structures become the main term of reference.

In grasping the new reality, moreover, crucial is the role played by the politicians' inherent reluctance to incite sharp political fluctuations by reallocating resources. That goes beyond the lack of knowledge and know-how among political leaders that affect decision-making, as Simon has established.

Though we cannot find clear testimony, for instance, that the prime minister was concerned with the domestic implications of making peace more than with security, it is safe to assume that with a deeply habituated reality, decision-makers even unconsciously directed their attention to less complicated, less costly options, i.e., war.

Had the Israeli leadership selected a more pacifist option, it would have had to pay a greater cost for maintaining social peace and political stability. Reversal of hard-line policies meant, for example, that reabsorption of Palestinian refugees would entail reallocation of lands. Peace-incited down-grading of the IDF's social prestige meant diminishing of social status of those groups who staffed the army's front-line units and commands as much as deval-uating the army's role as an interethnic integrator of the new immigrants. Treating Israeli Palestinians as equal citizens (without the limitations of con-flict) meant unemployment, hence, social unrest, in the Orientals' sector.

To sum up, the state was trapped within two cyclical motions, external and internal. Their conjuncture left a limited space for the state to do anything other than adhere to its force-oriented policies. So, though the state increased its autonomy to wage war, relative to the party-based power centers, this autonomy was gradually converted into a loss of autonomy to de-escalate war relative to those groups benefiting from the war. (But unlike the state's dependence on the party-based centers, the newly created dependence was less overt and thus less enfeebling of state universalism.)

In structural terms, noting that the state's selection of the response to infiltration was characterized by a "trial-and-error" method, in each stage the state lost flexibility in the external arena. Central to the relatively moderate moves in 1953/54 were the asymmetric relations between the burden the state imposed over the three "impeding groups" and the degree of return. No wonder that errors the state committed in its military policies (in the sense that its com-bat methods seemed ineffectual) stimulated internal opposition. Paradoxically, only by embarking on stiff escalation could the state create sources to benefit groups who, in return, backed harsh, not moderate, policies. Realization of the state's and domestic groups' interest in perpetuating the political-territorial sta-tus quo, moreover, in fact, was conditional on a constant escalation of the mil-itary tension between the two sides. The alternative was to try to bring quiet to the borders, thus bringing pressure on Israel to make concessions in the spirit of the UN partition resolution.

This created structure, moreover, had also a discursive dimension, taking the form of the interests-incited militarization of the political discourse. Reaching its zenith in the 1955 election campaign, discourse indirectly impacted on Mapai's losses by crafting force-oriented expectations. We remember how it effected Mapai's shift toward giving the military more leverage for administering its offensive policies. Discourse, then, was among the hardening mechanisms.

Through self-creation of gains, agents in practice augmented state empowerment with the military buildup that it entailed, revealing a third course of hardening. Manifestly, the more the state's ability to carry out the policy was enhanced owing to its capacity to mobilize support and resources (by means of rewarding domestic groups and attracting French aid owing to Israel's demonstration of military effectiveness), the more militant groups within the government and the IDF became motivated to act aggressively. Now their view seemed implementable. Consequently, a shift from the initial defensive posture to a dynamically shaped offensive one was prompted with the ascendancy of the military mind-set over the diplomatic school of thought. Theoretically, offensive ability in this situation is more likely to be translated into operative action (see Posen, 1988, 16–23), and state agencies might be more easily directed by rigid, inertial organizational routines divorced from political calculations (see Allison, 1969; Levy, 1986). To illustrate, Prime Minister Sharett was reported in 1954 by his aide (Teddy Kolek) to have said that the army's leadership "is consumed with passion for war" (Sharett, 1978, 246), when militant ideas to expand the country's borders were often raised (Morris, 1993, 10–13; Sharett, 1978, 229–230, 347–377). Kolek's diagnosis came about in tandem with the military buildup. Thus, statist agents dynamically adapted the construction of "security interest" to the repertoire of both opportunities and capacities created by the interaction with social groups; Israel's security was not an objective given. Under other domestic conditions, such as those that prevailed before 1953, the IDF could have selected a less ambitious course, as its founding commanders did before becoming embroiled in the border war.

As for the fourth course of hardening, the more the IDF's ability to gain from the state of war took the form of the prestigious "fighter" symbol, material resources, warfare experience, and political influence, the more its officers corps was motivated to entrench the state of war. I have already addressed the meaning of new relations of exchange between the state civilian agencies and the IDF. As Handel argues, moreover, military intelligence rejected a number of peace signals transmitted from Arab states. This arose from the "IDF's desire to monopolize all major national security decisions, for emphasis on diplomacy and peace would by definition have relegated the IDF and its commanders to a secondary role" (Handel, 1994, 556–557).

Finally, by placing many Orientals in border settlements the state's hands were actually tied to act other than in a rigorous fashion. Animosity was created between a great deal of the Oriental community and the Palestinians, put in competition over the same assets—abandoned houses and lands. Some Israeli scholars have attributed the Orientals' hawkish orientation, which was to appear at a later stage, to their hostile encounters with the Arabs in their countries of origin (see, for example, Shamir and Arian, 1982). Nonetheless, the case in point demonstrates that the "imported" orientation, whether hostile or not, manufactured enmity through the very nature of state action. Oriental settlers were then mobilized by the state for the war effort directly by constructing an interest in protection. The hawkish front was augmented.

More important, precisely by placing Orientals along the borders, the state was further compelled to provide protection. That is because the leadership felt that Oriental immigrants would be unable to persevere in the face of the infiltrations, in sharp contrast to the staying power manifested by the Westerner-populated border settlements in the pre-state period (Tal, 1990, 15). Indeed, the recurring infiltrations led many Orientals to abandon their homes and move to the center of the country (Morris, 1993, 108–115). Bellicose action then played a double role: It combated infiltrations, but concurrently also "combated" Orientals' exodus from border settlements. Possible abandonment of settlements was at odds with the government's policy of making irreversible the expelling of Palestinians. At the same time, retaining Orientals in the border settlements at the periphery of the country was instrumental to the fixation of interethnic relations of power, as I claimed in chapter 2. Nonetheless, this value did not play any direct role in military considerations. Through this double-targeted policy, state agencies' degree of freedom to steer their external policies was further reduced.

Once again, construction and execution of the bellicose approach dialectically intersected.

CONCLUSIONS

To recall, the spotlight in this chapter has been focused on two questions: What explains Israel's policy and what made this policy possible? This chapter has problematized these issues by highlighting the alternative doctrines available to Israel during the period. Later it became evident that internal groups could have led to the adoption of those alternatives through their very attempts to impede the bellicose moves. Since the external events could not adduce a sole answer, we have addressed the role played by domestic groups.

In practice, domestic groups played a double interest-driven role. Initially they took part in stimulating, generally in an indirect manner, the very crystallization of the Arab-Israeli conflict dovetailed with state-making up to 1948. This reality elicited harsh military policies for the struggle with border-crossing and accounted for the downplaying of peace options. Subsequently, since the outcomes of the initial bellicose orientation allowed groups to gain materially, politically, and symbolically, they accepted, even hardened, the force-oriented posture.

As this case reveals, the internal arena affected the decision-makers more profoundly, albeit less consciously, than the external arena, because Israel's scope of freedom in the external arena was gradually reduced due to the internal interests, pressures, and structures. Hypothetically however, had Arab leaders and the Powers, particularly France, defined their strategic goals in terms of terminating the conflict, Israel could not have adhered to its bellicose orientation. So, external war-prone vectors conjoined with internal ones to overbalance their peace-prone counterparts presented by seeds of Arab pragmatism and declining labor party moderation.

This domestic interest-centered analytical method has several advantages over the existing IR and statist scholarship, especially as it offers integration of existing theories (incorporation of the IR-focused Domain I into a three-domain analysis) rather than substitution of one by the other.

To begin, I have not neglected the change in the regional distribution of material capabilities (central to which are radicalization, the Pan-Arab orientation of Arab states, and the Soviet intervention) which nurtured Israel's existential anxieties. Domain I of state action has largely embraced this dimension of statecraft. While this serves as a point of departure for neorealists, this study shows that:

(1) Israel's concerns were both grounded on previously created intercommunal competition and aggravated by moves which Israel's very policies also fueled. Provided that Israel took part in shaping the Middle East as a threatening environment, its leadership's images should be considered not only as as a *cause* but also as a *consequence*: they also resulted from self-created events, not only drove them. Incredible, therefore, is the acceptance of the leadership-imbued images about the Arab threat backed by the Soviet hostility and amplified by the ineffectiveness of the United Nations as a point of departure, an autonomous stimulus to the brushing aside of more moderate options (as done by Brecher, 1974, 225–317). Further, even if we put aside the manner in which the leaders themselves constructed their images, the opposition to the hard-line approach necessitates examining how these previously constructed images became publicly installed, that is, accepted by those groups who had earlier resisted their inculcation or implementation.

(2) At several crossroads, Israel could have exhausted more moderate alternatives. Not only images of external threat but also the domestic dimensions of a greatly routinized conflict (gains earned from lands, property, full employment, etc.) reduced leadership flexibility.

(3) External threat as such is an insufficient motivating force for policies unless concurred with, and joined by, the interests of domestic groups on which the carrying out of policies is shouldered. Mobilization of those groups, however, is not a static event, i.e., state agencies do not simply mobilize support for a previously designed policies. Rather, it is a very dynamic process through

which mobilization runs in tandem to, and mutually enhances, construction and execution of policies. War preparation, which also encompasses the making of legitimacy, thus, simultaneously affects and is affected by the actual policies. The capacity to maintain a state of war might be, then, the very source for gains that energize the war, and even hardens war-prone policies. As it will be recalled, statist theories have overlooked this causal linkage, the turn from state features to actual performance.

(4) Real assets were at the heart of the border wars rather than state existence in a threatening environment as such. So, my argument might also fill one of the theoretical gaps innate in constructivist scholarship (see mainly Wendt, 1992). This study calls us to look at the explication of the constructivism-informed process of "state socialization" through the terrains of domestic, interest-driven filters and their impact on the creation of intersubjective meanings generated by structural distributions of power *inwardly*, not only at the interstate level. By asking "who benefits?" we have addressed the internal structure facilitating, fueling, and hardening state action in the external arena.

In sum, while rational strategic calculation, an assumption in which IR students have had a great stake, describes the *actual*, the problematic claimed above requires us to look at the *possible* as well (see Wendt's distinction between actual and possible, 1987, 362–365). The *possible* has been suggested by factoring in the other domains (II and III) of state action.

The advantages of this analytical method still holds true even if we dissolve the state-as-actor unit of analysis, as it is perceived by the neorealist school, into its constitutive agencies (following the critique made by Wagner, 1974). Agencies of this kind might be the military establishment (see Peri, 1983; and also Mills, 1956, on the case of the United States), individual actors such as Ben-Gurion and Sharett (Sheffer, 1988; Shlaim, 1983), and the political parties, with Mapai in the center (see Shapiro, 1977). In the case of the military, it is incumbent on us to offer an in-depth explanation which exposes the structural conditions giving rise to the IDF's capacity to achieve dominance over other agencies and groups. This outlook puts at stake the relations between the state and leading groups, through which the IDF gained its preferred status. The same process holds true regarding Mapai, beside the critique of a Mapai-centered approach presented in chapter 2. A similar rationale might convince us to reject explanations centered on individual actors. Further, a plausible explanation ought to address the structural limitations impacting on leaders' moves. At another level, the internal political process indicates that ideology by itself did not drive Israel's preference inasmuch as debates were taking place within the boundaries of the political elite whose members had shared basic ideological ideas. The main pillars on which Zionism was grounded permitted agents to select each of the underlined alternative avenues to deal with the external challenge.

As much as the state-constructed social order created the background for the border frictions in the 1950s, the arrangements erected due to these frictions—with IDF empowerment at the center—played a key role in the lead-up to the Six-Day War (1967) and its aftermath. That process is addressed in the next chapter.

CHAPTER 4

The Six-Day War (1967):
Expanding the War-Prone Circle

An inequitable social structure regulated by a centralist, extractive state energized a military-oriented posture and vice versa—a bellicose thrust energized the legitimized ascendancy of the Westerner-dominated middle class. During the late 1950s to early 1960s, these pillars were simultaneously solidified and eroded, affecting Israel's military policies. Solidification, which had taken the shape of a leadership reshuffling and a schism in Mapai, fueled the military-dominated lead-up to the Six-Day War due to the decline of Mapai-based antagonism toward the military mind-set. Erosion, which had taken the form of economic recession and the beginnings of Oriental protest, fueled the entrenchment of the war's political-military outcomes, that is, an occupation of a huge territory. Central to this process was the creation of new state-controlled reservoirs of material and symbolic resources by which the state could improve the ethno-class groups' standard of living without altering the basic social structure. In turn, those social gains further hardened the state's posture aimed at retaining the occupation.

THE LEADERSHIP RESHUFFLING

As will be recalled, the Sinai Campaign, the lead-up to it, and its conduct as an "elite war" had made manifest the state's empowerment vis-à-vis Mapai, the Histadrut, and other sectors. Casualties were not only negligible—230, about 0.01 percent of the total population (Sussman, 1984, 14)—but the war was not followed by a sharp increase in defense expenditures (Berglas, 1986, 176). This was sufficient to avoid political organizing by burdened groups against their sacrifice, but not to stifle a sense of loss by Mapai's groups identifying with the pre-state power centers—the Histadrut, the Mapai machine, and the other labor parties. Their direct goal was to contain Ben-Gurion's inclination to promote the young generation in Mapai at the expense of the traditional party leadership. Younger Mapai members had cut their teeth in the state bureaucracy, particularly the military-security apparatus, and were led by General Moshe Dayan, now minister of agriculture, and Shimon Peres, now deputy defense minister, both of them architects of the Sinai Campaign.

As we have seen, Ben-Gurion had pursued this policy since the 1950s, constantly looking for channels through which to bypass the party and bolster the state bureaucracy. During the 1960s the idea of overthrowing the traditional political leaders by a military putsch was again in the air. This time, however, it was not only a rumor but a real idea raised by two of Ben-Gurion's allies and it sounded threatening against the background of Ben-Gurion's renewed efforts to alter the electoral system (see Grinberg, 1993a, 73–77; Teveth, 1992, 273–286). Mapai's youngsters, moreover, attempted to exploit the success of the Sinai Campaign to empower the group at the expense of the Mapai leadership by calling to make the state more autonomous in the socioeconomic realm with the Histadrut as a prime target. To the young activists it was an impediment to the state's ability to conduct an autonomous socioeconomic policy. They sought limitations on the operation of the trade unions (establishing compulsory arbitration in labor conflicts was a case in point), the transfer of more functions (health services especially) from the Histadrut to the state, and even unemployment to increase economic efficiency (Cohen, 1987, 252–257; Medding, 1972, 252–259; Shapiro and Grinberg, 1988, 13–16).

On the surface, this was an intergroup struggle with an intergenerational dimension over power within Mapai. Viewed from a broader perspective, however, the Mapai leadership actually worked to contain Mamlachtiyut and prevent the state from becoming stronger at the expense of the party and its affiliated institutions (see chapters 2–3 for the conceptual critique of a Mapai-centered approaches). The Lavon Affair of the early 1960s provided an opening for Ben-Gurion's opponents to step up their criticism of his so-called etatist approach. The affair was the political backlash of the famous "Mishap"—who had given the order for Israeli agents to sabotage Western targets in Egypt in 1954 in the hope of delaying the British evacuation from the Suez Canal? Pinhas Lavon, the defense minister at the time of the events, had been forced to resign. A decade later, during his tenure as the secretary general of the Histadrut, he demanded that he be officially exonerated—after evidence came to light that the army had forged certain documents. Lavon's demand sparked a bitter confrontation between Ben-Gurion and his supporters on one side and the Mapai leadership on the other. At issue was how to determine where responsibility for the debacle lay. Ben-Gurion demanded the appointment of a committee by the Supreme Court—authority, in other words, should reside with the state—whereas his adversaries in Mapai thought the party institutions were the appropriate forum. Various questions of principle arose during the clarification of the issue, particularly, whether the party's institutions had supremacy over the state's activities through its emissaries. Moreover, Lavon's demand for exoneration questioned the IDF's integrity and thus further fueled the dispute (Yanai, 1982, 139–140).

A group of liberal intellectuals who supported Mapai took part in this debate, calling themselves *Min Hayesod* ("From the Foundation"). They rejected the Mamclachtiyut-produced eradication of civil society and the identification of Mamlachtiyut with force and violence, as it had been through the initiation of the Sinai Campaign. By criticizing the social value of the "fighter," they called for a reassessment of the state's national destiny (on this group, see Gertz, 1983, 58–59; Keren, 1986, 22; 1989a, 54–57; Shapiro, 1996, 104–106; Yanai, 1969, 29–31; 1982, 139–140).

After years of debate, the party leadership decided against Ben-Gurion, refusing to appoint a judicial committee, not least as a means of curtailing the power of Ben-Gurion and his young allies. Ben-Gurion resigned as prime minister and minister of defense in 1963, to be replaced by Finance Minister Levi Eshkol, one of the prominent leaders of the Mapai machine. Within two years, the Ben-Gurion group left Mapai and its formal positions (those held by Dayan and Peres among them), establishing a new party named Rafi (List of Israel's Workers). Rafi ran independently in the 1965 elections and did poorly. It was shocked by the power of the Mapai machine bolstered by the establishment of "the Alignment" in 1965 composed of Mapai and Ahdut Ha'avodah aimed at blocking both Rafi and militant workers (see more below).

Seemingly, the state–Mapai dispute was decided in favor of Mapai. Indeed, the notions of democratization and liberalization often have been evoked to describe the period, especially the change marked by Prime Minister Ben-Gurion's resignation that was backed by the security calm achieved after the Sinai Campaign (see, for example, Galnoor, 1982, 363–366; Keren, 1986; Medding, 1990, 226–229). Liberalization and democratization found expression at several levels beyond the legitimate appearance of Min Hayesod: (1) greater public supervision of the army was accomplished through the releasing of military censorship on the press (Negbi, 1985, 35–36); (2) interest groups arose that for the first time gave expression to private rather than public interests and were not necessarily affiliated with parties (Yishai, 1987, 66–69); (3) the state encouraged literature, the arts, and higher education (Keren, 1986), coinciding with the individualization of the political culture at the expense of Mamlachtiyut (see Gertz, 1983, 55–59, 66–67; Miron, 1985/86, 118–125); (4) the state Broadcasting Authority was converted from a government agency into a public association to which a greater number of political groups enjoyed access (Mishal, 1978); (5) the number of strikes significantly grew (see below);

(6) the Military Administration imposed on Israeli Palestinian citizens was abolished (see below); (7) liberalization was reflected strikingly in the legitimation that was bestowed on the right wing's political action in contrast to the situation that prevailed during the early years of the state. Practically, political cooperation developed between Mapai/the Alignment and *Gachal*, inspired by the crisis in Mapai. The latter was a political bloc established in 1965 between the rightist Herut Party and the Liberal Party (Goldberg, 1986, 160–163).

Notwithstanding these trends, scholars have overlooked the military buildup that ran in parallel, despite, or even owing to liberalization, generating the Six-Day War. The state was further empowered more than the society was liberalized, as we shall see now.

THE LEAD-UP TO THE SIX-DAY WAR

Furnished with internal power within a social-political order legitimizing the military-oriented posture, the state could uninterruptedly proceed in its military empowerment. The lead-up to the Six-Day War illuminates the new heights this autonomous power reached.

Military Buildup

A massive military buildup was the main pillar on which the lead-up to the Six-Day War was grounded. To begin, Israel's military capabilities were backed by nuclear armaments, utilizing the secret reactor that had been established in the southern town of Dimona following a French-Israeli agreement in 1957. By itself, this agreement was linked to the global cooperation between the countries, which was highly pronounced during the Suez War (Aronson, 1992, 41–60; Golan, 1982, 71–75). Nevertheless, military doctrine continued to be based on conventional weapons despite the stand taken by Ben-Gurion, Dayan, and Peres but in accordance with that of the left-wing labor parties in the government coalition, Ahdut Ha'Avodah and Mapam (on the debate, see Aronson, 1992, 83–111; Evron, 1987, 17–21). Israel then adopted a "doctrine of opacity." Its purpose was to keep the country's nuclear status deliberately vague to avoid paying political costs in the international arena that would have been entailed by Israel's formal adoption of an overt, nuclear deterrence. Costs of this kind might have taken the shape of superpower pressure to restrain Israel's power, or the triggering of Arab countries to acquire nuclear arms to balance Israel's power. Arguably, by the same logic, the state avoided paying costs in the internal arena as well that an open debate on armament would have entailed. In practice, although nuclear weapons apparently began to be developed and became available in 1969, a massive, conventional military buildup also took place (see Aronson, 1992, 83–111; Dowty, 1975; van Creveld, 1993, 97–100).

Most significant was the institutionalization of Israel's offensive doctrine. It was now based on a rigid casus belli for an Israel-initiated war in the case of the entry of a foreign army into Jordan, or the entry of Egyptian forces into the Sinai, or an attack on the nuclear reactor in Dimona (see Horowitz, 1973). Formulation of casus belli aimed at deterring the Arabs, shortening a future war, and confronting regional uncertainty in light of the perceived Arab threat. To ensure the efficacy of this plan, the IDF's offensive capability was improved, involving mainly the regular army and enabling Israel to strike at Arab airfields by extending the capability of armor, paratroops, and air forces—part of it based, for the first time, on American supply. The purpose was to permit Israel to launch independently a preventive war without the aid of a foreign power—in contrast to the situation that prevailed at the time of the Sinai Campaign, in which Israel's alliance with France and Britain conditioned the initiation of the war (Aronson, 1974, 109–118; Rabin, 1979, 130–131). National investment in security increased accordingly from about 8 percent of the GNP in 1955–61 to about 10 percent in 1962–66 (Berglas, 1986, 176).

Manifestly, Israel gradually established a strategic alliance with the United States, after years of American coolness. With the Cold War at its height, Washington perceived the Soviet presence in the Middle East as a threat to global stability; hence its inclination to strengthen Israel as a counterbalance. Washington's decision to assist Israel was also stimulated by the fear that Israel would draw on its nuclear arsenal if it felt threatened. By upgrading Israel's conventional armaments, the United States sought to squelch such ideas among the Israeli leadership (Yaniv, 1994, 167–173). Indeed, Eshkol's government (contrary to Ben-Gurion's approach) accepted a limited American inspection in Dimona and agreed to slow down its nuclear projects in return for a massive American supply of arms (Aronson, 1992, 83–111).

Practically, by adopting an offensive posture, Israel embarked on an irreversible path because the vast expenditures for arms procurement left few resources for the acquisition of defensive armaments such as American Hawk anti-aircraft missiles (eventually a limited purchase was made mainly to defend the reactor in Dimona against Egyptian attack) or building a line of fortifications on the border with Egypt. Both options were available in the 1960s but rejected by the IDF (Yaniv, 1994, 179–184).

The upshot of these developments, beginning with the shift to an offensive military doctrine in the mid-1950s, was that the state could manage external conflict with greater autonomy, internally and externally. The increased offensive power, particularly of the regular army, lowered the costs entailed by the conflict's maintenance by reducing the state's dependence on the reserves. Israel, moreover, was gradually unleashed from reliance on a foreign power that might have restrained its offensive posture. In addition, the fact that inflexible causes were set for launching a war lowered the threshold of a future war and created conditions for shortening its duration, hence further reducing the internal costs of such a war.

However, the price was that civilian politics were ultimately subordinated to military thought within the state apparatus. Rigid casus belli limited the state's leverage for autonomous political, not military, action in a situation of crisis, whether the state leadership sought an alternative action or not (see, by comparison, the case of Schlieffen Plan, Levy, 1986). The nature of political discourse, albeit within the limited boundaries of the political elite, illustrates the new position of civilian politics. Fragmented discussion, revolving around the question of what might constitute a casus belli and confined to the technical-military realm, characterized the new pattern (Horowitz, 1973; see also Bar-Or, 1989). Planners avoided consideration of the political implications. Issues that were the subject of the debate between the Ben-Gurion and Sharett schools of thought in the 1950s were decided definitively and vanished from the discursive repertoire. Furnished with both political support and material resources and backed up by nuclear capabilities, the IDF could more autonomously adhere to its rigid routine as the escalation of border frictions indicates. Military thought prevailed but politicians, guided by their own implanted force-oriented worldview, let it happen (see at the theoretical level Miliband, 1969, 136–137). I elaborate below the political sources of this process.

Escalating Border Friction

In the 1960s, the focus of military activity was on the Syrian rather than the Egyptian or Jordanian fronts. Incidents on the Israel–Syria border were sparked by two unresolved problems that had produced friction between the countries in the early 1950s: sovereignty in the demilitarized zone (DMZ) and the exploitation of the Jordan River waters. Israel's inclination to assert its sovereignty in the DMZ and apply the same principle to the exploitation of the Jordan waters generated sporadic violence with the Syrians until American-mediated agreements were reached in the 1950s. Then, following several years of quiet, the sovereignty issue arose again in 1964 when Israel activated its National Water Carrier by utilizing the Jordan waters according to its interpretation of the bilateral arrangements. In reaction, Syria tried to scuttle the water project by diverting the Jordan in areas where it flowed outside Israeli territory. The Arab states also moved to support political and military organizing by the Palestinians by establishing the Palestine Liberation Organization (PLO) under Egyptian auspices and the Fatah Organization under Syrian patronage (Yaniv, 1994, 184–187). This development triggered military escalation in the region in the fall and winter of 1964/65.

In the view of the Israeli leadership, Syrian diversion attempts had to be prevented at any price. Of crucial importance was the conception echoing the hard-line heritage of the 1950s that the preferred response to Arab behavior along the borders was military action. This mind-set now reasserted itself. It was shown in the tendency to use force and generate escalation that brought about counterreactions by the Arabs, ruling out possible options to settle the crisis other than by war. This perception stemmed from two sources. First, Israel perceived the Arabs' actions as threatening in character even if this was not necessarily the case, even though Israel could have afforded a moderate reaction given its clear military superiority as the Six-Day War eventually showed. Second, Israel was jealous of its deterrence; hence, the IDF devised "flexible retaliation," geared to deter the Syrians or, alternatively, induce them to react by escalating the frictions and then giving Israel cause to launch a full-scale attack. Deterrence of this kind was perceived as necessary, particularly when taken against Israel's preference to refrain from drawing its deterrence from overt nuclear means (Aronson, 1992, 100–101). Israel, then, became trapped in its own formula of deterrence (see Yaniv, 1994, 192). As in the past, security interests prevailed and were subjectively defined, adapted to the repertoire of state-created capacities in the realms of material means, nuclear capabilities, and legitimation. Under other conditions, the IDF's commander would have possibly displayed more self-restraint.

Practically, in response to Syrian fire, Israeli armor went into action against the Syrians' earthmoving equipment. The long-range tank and artillery duels that resulted went beyond the level of the routine friction that had prevailed until then between Israel and its neighbors (Rabin, 1979, 124–125). When the use of armor failed to stimulate the Syrians to react, Israel's modern jet fighter planes struck massively against Syrian positions on the Golan Heights. Prime Minister and Defense Minister Levi Eshkol gave the go-ahead at the request of Chief of Staff Yitzhak Rabin. General Ezer Weizmann, then the head of operations and the former commander of the air force, points out that this was the first time the government had approved air strikes other than in a war situation (Weizmann, 1975, 237). Finally, the Syrians were forced to desist from their attempts to divert the Jordan headwaters (on Israel's escalatory approach, see Yaniv, 1994, 187–193; Yaniv and Maoz, 1984).[1]

Concurrently, between 1963 and 1966, the IDF introduced a provocative policy that was designed to let Israel seize control of the DMZ. To further that purpose, Israel built roads, conducted forward patrols, tried to capture territory in no-man's land, escalated firefights, and so forth (Benziman, 1985, 93–97; see also the testimony by one of the Foreign Ministry's senior officials, *Ha'aretz*, June 16, 1995, 15). The next stage of escalation occurred on the Jordanian front. Following a series of Palestinian infiltrations from Jordan, Israel decided to carry out a large-scale raid in reprisal. In sharp contrast to the raids of the 1950s, the attack on the Jordanian village of Samua in November 1966 was the first one executed in broad daylight, making use of both armor and air power

(Weizmann, 1975, 253–254). This raid torpedoed the secret dialogue transacted between Israel and Jordan during the period and was among the factors that pushed King Hussein of Jordan to make a military covenant with Cairo (Zak, 1994, 6).

Military escalation reached new heights in 1967 when the Syrians resumed their diversion project on the Jordan River and Palestinian organizations launched attacks from Syrian territory. Israel sent the air force into action again. In one encounter (April 1967), Israel's air force chased Syrian jets all the way to Damascus and shot down six of them (Bartov, 1978, 106–120; Weizmann, 1975, 254). Chief of Staff Rabin then declared that Israel's purpose was to topple the Ba'th regime in Syria. This was an extraordinary statement, first because it emanated from a military man and second because it contradicted Israel's consistent military justifications for its activity on the northern front. Rabin was reprimanded by Eshkol (Haber, 1987, 146).

Confronted with the escalation and Rabin's declaration, Syria asked Egypt for help in curbing Israeli aggression, invoking their 1964 defense pact (Weizmann, 1987). Thus, in May 1967, just a few weeks after the major incident in the north, Egyptian President Nasser sent a large force into the Sinai Peninsula. This was a violation of a bilateral, tacit arrangement that Sinai would remain demilitarized, a violation that looked to Israel like a clear casus belli (Horowitz, 1985, 71). The situation then snowballed. Israel called up its reserves and asked the Powers to bring about Egypt's withdrawal from Sinai. Egypt exacerbated the crisis by causing the removal of the UN forces that were stationed in Sinai and by blocking again the Straits of Tiran to Israeli navigation at the end of May. In response, Israel continued to mobilize, finally calling up the entire army.

During the "waiting period" for war, the differences between the military command and the political leadership became more pronounced than in the Sinai Campaign. The IDF, with Rabin in the lead, had concluded immediately upon the Egyptians' entry into Sinai that war was inevitable and claimed therefore an Israeli initiative (Haber, 1987, 194–198, 210–212). General Weizmann even reported that IDF commanders were eager to seize the opportunity to strike at the Arab armies (Weizmann, 1975, 260–264), a natural approach given the contribution of massive military buildup in imbuing self-confidence among the generals. The Eshkol government, for its part, displayed indecisiveness. Still, its considerations were confined to the calculation of a military response (timing and scale) rather than to a wider range of political alternatives (Geist, 1975).

Such a military stand virtually ruled out pursuit of a political resolution of the crisis that could have been attainable, particularly since Nasser did not necessarily intend to attack. At least initially he preferred to preserve the status quo (Mor, 1991). His purpose was, as the dominant Arab leader, to deter Israel from acting against Syria and he had long sought a pretext for removing his army from a protracted and costly war in Yemen (Yaniv, 1994, 205). But it is also possible that he was provoked by the Dimona project (Cohen, 1996) and even wanted to initiate war before Israel would become nuclear (Aronson, 1992, 109). Further, during the crisis Nasser considered political options to restore the status quo, although he was prompted by his military commanders to take the attack initiative. Then, he consented to resume the Joint Israeli-Egyptian Armistice Commission to negotiate on some unsolved bilateral problems. Significant was his declaration during the crisis: Egypt would start a war *if* Israel began hostilities, and then Egypt would aim to destroy Israel. This declaration terrified the Israelis precisely because only the second part was emphasized by the media and politicians (Avnery, 1968, 31–32 [Hebrew language edition]; Love, 1969, 684; Rodinson, 1982, 176–182). It seems logical to assume that Nasser could have removed his forces while gaining prestige as the leader of the Arab nations, at the same time ending Egypt's involvement in Yemen (Aronson, 1992, 109).

Indeed, Rabin was criticized for the army's role in the deterioration into war. Moshe Dayan, as an ordinary member of the Knesset, had criticized the IDF for taking injudicious action, such as overflying Damascus and attacking Samua in daylight (Rabin, 1979, 137). Moshe Shapira, the leader of the National Religious Party (the most important coalitional partner of the Alignment), assailed Eshkol and Rabin for taking actions "bordering on madness" (ibid., 156–158). Even Menachem Begin, the right-wing leader who would become prime minister a decade later, claimed that the Six-Day War was a "war of choice"—even if his purpose at the time was to justify the Lebanon War of 1982—as the IDF could have refrained from taking the initiative and it is possible that the crisis could have been ended without an immediate war (see Yariv, 1985, 19–21). Still, the most important reaction was that of Ben-Gurion. Rabin, he said, had been wrong to call up the reserves, as this placed Israel in military and political distress and left no choice but to launch a preemptive strike (Rabin, 1979, 150). Ben-Gurion called on the Israeli leadership to defuse the situation and seek a political resolution as long as Israel's bellicose action would not be supported by the Powers as in the scenario of 1956 (Yaniv, 1994, 207). The former prime minister recalled his response to a similar situation that had arisen in February 1960. At that time, Israel had reacted to the entry of Egyptian forces into Sinai by executing a secret, limited call-up of the reserves and conducting clandestine, indirect talks with Cairo that had brought about a solution without war (ibid., 155–156). Since the critics were elite members, it is safe to assume that Israel did refrain from exhausting political means for diffusing the crisis before taking the irreversible step of a general mobilization. And, further, a less prepared and powerful army would have been inclined to interpret Egypt's moves otherwise.

The political-military spirit coincided with, and possibly—by employing an overt, full call-up—even fueled public anxiety and criticism of the government for its inaction while the reserves were mobilized and the economy was paralyzed. Consequently, calls for a cabinet reshuffling were voiced loudly. Such an attempt at intervention by extra-elite groups in the extremely sensitive national-security sphere was remarkably unusual within the Israeli political culture of the period. Therein lay the inner weakness latent in the Israeli military doctrine: Not only was the government's reaction bound to force-oriented action by formulating a rigid casus belli, but further, although an offensive doctrine was formulated, the government in practice reacted within the limits of a defensive posture, keeping reservists on a full war footing but idle for a lengthy period. Moreover, the political costs could have greatly increased had the reservists been discharged without seeing action. So, once the state formulated a rigid casus belli that relied on a call-up of reservists, its hands were tied in dealing with the crisis other than by vigorous military means, particularly as it deliberately refrained from acquiring defensive capabilities.

Indeed, the combined pressures brought about the appointment of Moshe Dayan, then a leading member of the Rafi group, as defense minister on June 1, 1967. At the same time, the government coalition was expanded to include, for the first time, the right-wing Gachal to demonstrate political unity in the face of a perceived existential danger. These moves tipped the scales in favor of a war initiative within four days, after five weeks of a "waiting period."[2] On June 5 Israel launched a surprise preemptive strike on Egyptian airfields together with a ground thrust across the Sinai that was soon extended to the Jordanian and Syrian fronts. The war ended in six days with a massive Israeli victory: the destruction of the fighting Arab armies and the conquest of large territories, namely, the Sinai Peninsula, the Golan Heights, East Jerusalem, the Jordan Valley, the West Bank, and the Gaza Strip.

The ascendancy of military thought was demonstrated again as the war resulted not just in the destruction of the Arab armies and the minimal occupation needed for defense, but in the occupation of the Sinai Peninsula and other areas. Moderate goals, as implicitly defined by Prime Minister Eshkol and Defense Minister Dayan, were expanded under the pressure of army commanders, leaders of the agricultural sector, and Minister Yigal Allon (leader of Ahdut Ha'avodah and ex-commander of the Palmach), while Jordanian and Syrian moderate fire on Israeli civilian targets provided a pretext (Aronson, 1992, 118–120; Benjamini, 1984). This demonstrates the extent to which the military mind-set gained domination, leading to the conquest of territories that in the years to come would interfere with political processes, in particular the capture of the Suez Canal and the occupation of the West Bank and the Gaza Strip, with their one million Palestinians.

We can draw some conclusions from the analysis regarding the two relevant levels: the military doctrine's formulation and its execution in the crisis. The regional system offered again a repertoire of strategic options composed of escalation-prone vectors (growing Arab enmity from the mid-1960s) equal to de-escalation-prone vectors. The latter took the form of formal and informal security institutions prevailing in the region that could have been used by Israel to retain the status quo: the clandestine dialogue with King Hussein of Jordan; Egypt's preference for the status quo under the Powers' auspices and the restraining influence of the Soviet involvement (as its efforts to calm the May–June crisis reveal; see Love, 1969, 684); and even tacit arrangements between Israel and Syria regarding the sovereignty in the DMZ and the exploitation of the Jordan waters. Trapped in typical failures of a security dilemma, the military mind-set, backed by the material capability to wage war, made the state disinclined to struggle with the built-in regional threat by establishing tacit cooperation with the bordering states. The pursuit of peace, with the internal costs that it entailed, was not at issue; Israel could have prolonged the new status quo, with the benefits it involved relative to the existential risks that preemptive strike entailed had the Egyptian military taken the initiative or the Jordanian and Syrian militaries attacked Israel in reaction to its attack on Egypt.

Indeed, the issue of mobilizing support and resources to back the military domination is of great importance. Unlike the case of the lead-up to the Sinai Campaign, the military was not activated by the political level to protect civilian assets directly and crystallize state internal domination indirectly. Rather, the IDF was guided by its post-1956 modus operandi but greatly shielded by political support. Within the state boundaries, it is difficult to identify a government decision on the principles on which the military doctrine was built in the absence of a new version of the Ben-Gurion–Sharett debate. Rather, bureaucratic practices constructed policy that was backed by civil-political decisions diverting resources to the military at the expense of investments in civilian sectors. As for the level of state–groups relations, despite, or maybe owing to, the partial liberalization, the state still enjoyed great autonomy in formulating security policy mainly via the IDF. The public was left out and decisions were made by a coterie—although this group had grown somewhat following Ben-Gurion's resignation. Evidently, political groups did not challenge the lead-up to war, although it was a long process. Naturally, only middle-class groups could have demanded more access to strategic decision-making. But, having benefited from the state of war under the social arrangements worked out in the 1950s and from the fruits of liberalization, those groups preferred to focus their demands on their gains rather than on the very reality of war preparation. Oriental groups were still silent while hawkish moves were basically endorsed by this community particularly insofar as their grip in the IDF constantly grew. Only during the "waiting period" was discontent voiced but it was mainly war-prone. As in earlier occurrences, escalation constructed public opinion.

Arguably, the leadership reshuffling and the schism in Mapai paradoxically bolstered the state's capacity to steer its military policies autonomously. On the surface, Prime Minster Eshkol was propelled by militant figures, mainly the Ahdut Ha'Avoda group with whom General Yitzhak Rabin was associated. This group was more authoritative than Eshkol in military issues (see Aronson, 1974). Still, personnel changes do not fully account for the overall move since the case of the 1950s suggests that civilian politics were eroded under Ben-Gurion, not despite, but due to, his leadership. More significant was the structural dimension of the leadership reshuffling: Since the party-oriented group took power over state agencies, including the military, they could run the state agencies with low-level opposition from the party machine. Indeed, Min Hayesod was satisfied by Ben-Gurion's dismissal and then muted its critique and supported its ally Eshkol's leadership, which eventually led to war. Eshkol, for his part, when he became premier, acted as a statist, not a partisan agent. Hence, his effort to strengthen the IDF.

Of prime importance, moreover, was the tendency toward greater political supervision of the army. The Lavon Affair, with its acute questions of operative command over the defense establishment, exposed a breakdown in control of the political institutions over the military and within the defense establishment itself. Consequently, both politicians and the press demanded greater access to information about military affairs and did not recoil from going outside the party channels (especially Lavon). The Min Hayesod group's activity, the unprecedented discussions held by the Knesset's Foreign Affairs and Defense Committee on the Lavon Affair, and the space devoted to the issue by the press—marking its growing independence from the fetters of military censorship—showed which way the wind was blowing (see Bar-On, 1981, 81–142; Negbi, 1985, 35–36). No longer were the prime minister and the ruling party permitted to retain exclusive control.

Liberalism and democracy were not the only products. Also, further divorced from the substantive question of the legitimacy of the state as a violent apparatus, political discourse turned into an operative discussion of how to optimize formal control over the military organization (see, at the theoretical level, Levy, 1995). A case in point is the behavior of the government's critics regarding the "Mishap." They showed no interest in what the debacle implied about Israel's foreign policy: the opposition to regional decolonization and the preference for cooperation with the Western powers over a possible alliance with the Arab liberation movements. The same pattern—a reluctance to address underlying foreign policy questions and a presupposition of basic general agreement—showed itself in the absence of debate over the Franco-Israeli cooperation, which increased just as France was suppressing the Algerian revolt and in 1967 vanished when Algeria won independence (see Avnery, 1968, 90–107, Hebrew language edition). Furthermore, the less the narrow Mapai circle solely supervised the IDF, the more the latter's universalist image increased. In sum, the tightening of political control over the IDF paradoxically contributed to the amplification of military thought. Again militarization and political control marched together (see chapter 3, note 10).

Military industries also played a significant role in dampening political action. They were rapidly expanded in the 1960s owing to the state's growing investment. In addition to the development of the huge Israel Aircraft Industry (IAI), Israel began manufacturing guns, missiles, and artillery shells (Reiser, 1989, 52–77). Military industrialization was considered at that period a lever for overall growth as military needs propelled modernization of civilian manufacturing. Weapons gradually even became export products (Barnett, 1992, 184). This suggests that a complex of interests was constructed around the military buildup, including not only the IDF, but also the growing business-managerial elite, Hevrat Ha'Ovdim-owned industries (which, as it will be recalled, involved military production), and even trade unions. Hence, the process gained legitimation, or at least did not stimulate political criticism. On the contrary, the post-1956 discourse lionized technological values. Less importance was attached to the human operator of the technology or whether it was beneficial—or harmful (Keren and Goldberg, 1980). By itself, technological discourse was the product of the state's internal expansion: Industrialization combined with the growth of the middle class, reinforcing the instrumental aspects of the discourse by which it bettered its social position (like the intelligentsia; see Keren, 1989b). It was a suitable background to incubate a frame of mind of "exterminism" in which the arms race is propelled by technological systems taking on a life of their own, not guided exclusively by a political rationale (see Thompson, 1984; Suchman and Eyre, 1992). Technology, not just politics, stimulated the constant renewal of military doctrines (see, at the theoretical level, Posen, 1988, 55–57). It was no more blatant than in the plan conceived in the IDF from the 1950s to attack Arab airfields in preemptive strikes.

In sum, neither ethical nor political obstacles blocked the military empowerment and its reflection on the battlefield. A similar scenario repeated itself in the aftermath of the war.

THE AFTERMATH OF THE WAR: THE CREATION OF NEW GAINS

As the guns fell silent on June 10, 1967, a four-level process was unfolding, impacting on, and being impacted by, the domination of a military mind-set (in part, each level reflects a different stage). Figure 4.1 shows the process.

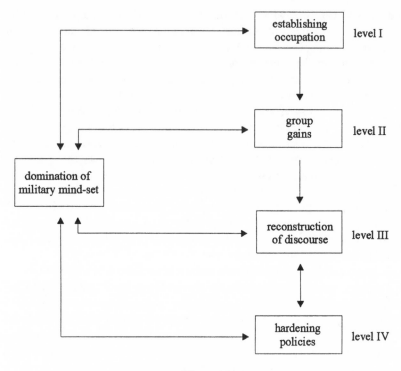

Figure 4.1
Entrenching the Occupation

First, a military-oriented approach automatically worked to establish Israel's occupation. However, at the second level, this policy had unintended consequences in the internal arena, central to which was the capacity of social agents to gain from the occupation in particular and from the perpetuation of the state of war in general. Social interests were accordingly (re)constructed and mirrored, at the third level, by the postwar political discourse. Consequently, at the fourth level, the state not only acquired more ability to maintain its bellicose policies, but the internal arena also further hardened military policies, evidenced by missing more peaceable options. Reformulation of military doctrine was thus administered bit by bit.

Level I: Military Posture as an Inertial Process

The newly conquered territories were immediately placed under the Military Administration, which is inherently temporary. This was all-encompassing in the West Bank and the Gaza Strip, while East Jerusalem was reunited by force with the city's western section. Immediately after the war, most of the territories were considered a bargaining chip toward peace agreements, witness the cabinet's endorsement of withdrawal to the armistice lines in return for peace, though the resolution did not encompass the Gaza Strip, which Israel sought to annex, and did not mention the fate of the West Bank. However, this resolution was quickly switched to a more rigid stand in a few weeks, concurrent with the erection of a few new civilian settlements in the territories (Pedhatzur, 1996, 47–93). Furthermore, there is uncertainty whether Israel's initial, moderate stand was delivered to the Arabs as an official proposal (*Ha'aretz*, May 19, 1995, 13). At any rate, the Arabs publicly rejected the peace option at the Khartoum Summit Conference held in September 1967.

At this juncture, Israel had to choose between two avenues: to adhere to its initial, declared targets, namely, to bargain on full withdrawal for peace, awaiting, even attempting to shape Arab orientation toward moderation; or to capitalize on the Arabs' rigidity, utilize the territories at the economic and symbolic levels, and thus rigidify the territorial-political status quo. Israel opted for the second road.

Israel, intentionally and gradually reformulated its military doctrine based on the underlying paradigm as it had been crafted during the 1950s. Central to this version was the insistence on holding part of the occupied territories, even after any future political solution, to ensure total security against the perceived Arab threat, which now was reinforced owing to the Khartoum Summit Conference (Yaniv, 1994, 241–245). These territories furnished Israel with strategic depth, distancing the border (and the enemy) from the main population centers. By expanding the "security margins," Israel was able to absorb an Arab attack without endangering the civilian population. Grasping the lesson of the "waiting period," no longer was it necessary to define rigid "red lines" and cling to the idea of the preemptive strike, as became clear in October 1973, when Israel absorbed an Egyptian-Syrian attack and only afterward contained it. "Defensible borders" displaced "preemptive strike" (Horowitz, 1985, 72–73). To a large extent, the existence of nuclear capabilities backed up this status quo-based military doctrine, even though Israel shrouded its nuclear deterrence capability in opacity. However, the Americans were monitoring nuclear projects less and Israel retained its monopoly due to the Soviet reluctance to supply Egypt with bombs (Aronson, 1992, 123–137).

Accordingly, Israel demanded the annexation of areas viewed as crucial to ensure defensible borders: East Jerusalem, the Golan Heights, Sharm e-Sheikh, the Jordan Rift Valley, Judea Hills, and a part of North Sinai. In practice, Jewish settlements were established in areas demanded by Israel, a kind of de facto "creeping annexation" of the territories without paying external and internal costs entailed in formal enactment of sovereignty. (In parallel, the Military Administration itself was institutionalized at the levels of law, administration, taxation, etc.) Some settlements were built in unsettled areas, such as the Jordan Rift Valley, others in areas of dense Palestinian population, such as East Jerusalem and the city of Hebron. The agricultural sector and religious groups played a key role in prompting the government to allow the erection of new settlements (see Kimmerling, 1985b, 90–91). The settlements, together with the army's deployment on forward defensive lines (notwithstanding the striving for strategic depth but in accord with rigid military thought), kept friction with the Arabs at a high level. The major areas of confrontation were with the Egyptians along the Suez Canal, where the War of Attrition was fought from 1969 to 1970 (see below), and with the Palestinians. Not only the West Bank and the Gaza Strip became arenas of clashes with Palestinians; since 1967 Israel has paid the price of controlling a huge Palestinian population when a low-intensity conflict manifested in growing attacks by Palestinian organizations against Israeli civilian targets in Israel and abroad, mostly in Europe.

Strategic considerations were backed, even driven, by the excessive "self-confidence" implanted within the dominant military mind-set in the wake of the impressive military victory. This frame of mind, which guided "civilian" politicians as well, encouraged the country's leaders to opt for political maneuverability and to frequently state that "time works in favor of Israel." The victory lessened Israel's concerns about its very existence in favor of a tendency to ensure "total security." Also it seems safe to assume that an inertial trajectory accounted for the IDF's and Defense Minister Dayan's moves to anchor the new holdings, similar to the IDF's eagerness to dynamically expand the war's goals a few months earlier. For example, the "open bridges" policy, permitting the flow of goods from Jordan into the territories, was introduced by the army (and approved by Dayan at a later stage) immediately after the occupation (Narkiss, 1991, 351–353). "Open bridges" were instrumental to the smooth incorporation of the West Bank into the Israeli economy by which, as we shall see, a set of domestic interests was shaped. However, with their prominent status, the military and the defense minister easily infused their force-oriented perspective into political discourse.

Critical to these frame of mind and behavior was the tightening of the United States-Israel alliance following the Israeli victory in 1967. This confirmed Israel's usefulness to the United States, particularly as America displayed weakness in another anti-Soviet front, the Vietnam War (Shlaim, 1994, 41–47). Beyond granting generous military and financial aid (see below), Washington also showed itself ready to accept Israel's occupation of the territories, even its settlement drive, without bringing pressure to bear for a withdrawal as in the wake of the Sinai Campaign.

Still, since Israel swiftly shifted from a status quo approach when the war ended into an expansionist orientation in a few months (balance of power in the regional system remained stable during that time), we ought to further uncover domestic obstacles to reversal moves. Moreover, while a sense of military inferiority during the 1950s and 1960s had propelled Israel to take bellicose initiatives, the bellicose agenda was now nurtured by a sense of superiority. Relative power, as such, is not a sufficient explanatory factor.

By locking in the occupation, arguably, new structural orders were shaped pertinent to the social domain by which social groups benefited from the new reality. In turn, the military thrust was politically legitimized and even further nourished.

Level II: Reconstruction of the Social Structure

The 1967 War unintentionally increased the state's capacity to legitimize the unequal social structure and thus to defer an emergence of interethnic conflicts within the Jewish sector and even a Jewish-Palestinian conflict within Israeli polity. Central to this process was the creation of new state-controlled reservoirs of material and symbolic resources due to the entrenchment of the outcomes of the 1967 War. Building on this policy, the state could improve the ethno-class groups' standard of living without altering the basic social structure. In terms of its economic effects the war assisted the state in short-term coping, through a structural shift in the Israeli economy, with the difficulties that had been engendered a few years earlier by the economic recession.

The effects of extensive industrialization that began to be felt in the mid-1950s went beyond the creation of an inequitable social structure as described in chapter 2. Industrialization also generated full employment, which reached its peak in 1964. This situation derived directly from the growth of the economy and was instrumental to the state's efforts to legitimize its action. By guaranteeing full employment, the state could defer the emergence of social conflicts relating to the distribution of resources (see at the theoretical level, Offe, 1975, and for the Israeli case, Shalev, 1984, 9–13). Arguably, full employment was not divorced from the structure whereby the state met the basic needs of its population in return for their being mobilized for the war effort, as long as full employment was primarily crucial to the new immigrants who staffed the growing military units (see at the theoretical level, Shaw, 1988).

At the same time, a situation of full employment gave many groups of workers leverage vis-à-vis the Histadrut. In this situation workers could struggle for higher wages without being disciplined by the Histadrut as a provider, directly and indirectly (via Hevrat Ha'Ovdim), of employment. Hence, the proportion of strikes lacking Histadrut approval rose from 25 percent in 1960 to an average of 60 percent during the years of full employment. Further, powerful, new middle-class-based trade unions (teachers, academics, and engineers, among others) threatened to bolt the Histadrut, and there were even cases of ethnic unrest (see below). In short, the dialectical nature of the state's relations of exchange with the main social groups manifested itself: By realizing several groups' material interests, the state in practice strengthened their position to demand more, revealing a tension between short-term and long-term interests motivating the Westerner-dominated middle-class groups. These groups, through their very demands, not only challenged the institutional functioning of the state but also, albeit unintentionally, the state's capacity to confirm their social dominance. Given that the state's resources were limited, widening of the interethnic gaps by meeting those demands could have catalyzed interethnic conflicts over the distribution of resources.

The state, moreover, faced a fiscal crisis in the 1960s. Several factors accounted for this crisis: Foreign capital inflow, part of it aid from America and Germany, began to dry up; the trade deficit doubled to 30 percent in 1964; wages increased owing to full employment and Orientals drifting out of the secondary labor market; profits in manufacturing declined due to the above factors and built-in inefficiency; and more. As a consequence, the state could no longer sustain growth and respond to material demands as a mechanism of ensuring social calm (on the economic crisis, see Grinberg, 1993a, 113–130; Shalev, 1992, 208–214). Possibly, the increase in the state's investment in security from 6–7 percent in the 1950s to about 10 percent in the 1960s as a proportion of the GNP (Sussman, 1984, 22) also kept the state from investing resources in growth and improving the standard of living. In sum, the crisis was not divorced from the same socioeconomic arrangements structured by the state during the 1950s that accounted for its military empowerment.

To struggle with the crisis, the state intentionally and drastically adopted a strategy of recession in 1966/67. As investments and capital subsidies were deliberately cut, temporary workers were fired and unemployment became rampant, going from 4 percent to 12.5 percent, with Orientals and Palestinians suffering the most. In this situation, the Histadrut could resume its corporatist capacity to discipline the labor force: Witness the sharp reduction in the number of strikes and the militancy of trade unions—70 percent of strikes were authorized by the Histadrut relative to 20 percent in the mid-1960s. Restraint of workers, moreover, also benefited the Histadrut's business, Hevrat Ha'Ovdim, and hence its enthusiasm for cooperating with the government. Similarly, the state was better able to bring capital forces under its thumb by reducing both the scale of capital substitution and, as a direct result of budget cuts and unemployment, domestic demand (Shalev, 1992, 215–226, 233 note 44; Rosenhek, 1996, 122–145). By restraining both labor and capital, this strategy increased the state's autonomy. Structurally, the Histadrut's dependence on the state was now more pronounced than ever because the state, not the Histadrut, disciplined unions that had displayed autonomy vis-à-vis their umbrella organization. Mapai therefore accepted this state strategy despite its previous objection to initiation of unemployment.

At the same time, the Military Administration imposed on Israeli Palestinian citizens since 1948 was abolished in 1966. Like other actions of the period, this was not just a liberal gesture. As Orientals had moved from blue-collar to white-collar jobs, a shortage of low-paid workers in the Jewish sector was created, leading the government, already beginning in the mid-1950s, to allow Palestinians entrance into the Jewish labor market without jeopardizing Jews' employment. Remembering that the state-controlled Palestinian labor force did not enjoy the Hisatdrut's support and that it was viewed as a potential "fifth column," it was not treated as an ordinary labor force; war-oriented mechanisms neutralized market-oriented ones. This mode of control thereby increased Jewish employers' gains, evidenced by gaps in earnings between Jews and Palestinians. Still, not only Jews benefited but Palestinians as well as long as their entry into the Jewish labor market worked to increase wages (Ben-Porath, 1986a, 165–166). The abolition of the Military Administration dovetailed with a parallel moderation of the state's control over the Palestinians to counter the attraction of the Communist Party among them (see Shalev, 1989, 109–114). Importantly, the years 1966/67 saw a very short period in history in which Israel was a *full democracy* in the sense that it did not militarily control an indigenous population.

Still, the mixture of recession with a moderate stream of Palestinians into the Jewish labor market signified no more than a temporary solution. The absence of a structural solution to the inherited problems in full employment generated the crisis of the 1960s, first and foremost the strengthening of labor relative to capital. Long-lived unemployment, moreover, could have generated delegitimization of the ethno-class division of labor. Indeed, the need to ensure legitimacy was not an abstract one.

In 1959, disquiet erupted in riots by Oriental immigrants, notably discharged soldiers, in the Wadi Salib neighborhood of Haifa. The unrest spread to other areas as well. This was a protest against the harsh conditions in the neighborhood compared with the Western neighborhoods of the city (Galnoor, 1982, 356–367). Still, with the state's guarantee of full employment owing to the state-led economic boom, the exclusion of the Palestinian labor force, and the constitution of a welfare system, Orientals could struggle to seek a higher standard of living. This was the first protest of its kind made by Orientals—nearly a decade after their immigration—and the government moved quickly to calm the unrest. Even the IDF was used when Ben-Gurion sent General Moshe Dayan, still chief of staff, to meet with representatives of the protestors (Grinberg, 1991a, 102). At the same time, Ariel Sharon, then a senior officer in the IDF, convinced Ben-Gurion to step up officer training for soldiers from the Moroccan community. Such officers would bring pride to their community and, at the same time, dissipate interethnic tensions (Karpel, 1993).

This was a striking demonstration of how the IDF contributed to the universalization of the state. While the protestors became increasingly aware of the built-in inequality created by civilian institutions (witness their targeting of the Histadrut's and Mapai's bureaus), the IDF, underscoring the ethos of equality, had gained the confidence of Orientals, witness their testimonies in the judicial commission of inquiry who investigated the event (Swirski, 1995, 107). Nonetheless, the involvement of recently discharged soldiers in the Wadi Salib riots pointed out that, in the long term, military action in the social domain might encounter difficulties. After all, implicit in the Orientals' demand for the righting of social inequality was a protest against the asymmetry between the seeming opportunity for equal participation in the military—the Sinai Campaign was a case in point—and the inequality in the allocation of other rewards (see Idan, 1983). So, the more military service set the criteria for real membership in Israeli society, by which the inequitable social structure was legitimized, the more likely that Orientals would invoke these very criteria to legitimize their social demands insofar as their grip in the IDF constantly expanded.

To sum up, the prolongation of the recession could have delegitimized the state-constructed social structure. Owing to the 1967 War, the factors generating the recession now were turned on their head and several new arrangements took shape.

(a) Military buildup. Following the war the state's investment in security increased from about 10 percent in the period preceding the war to about 21 percent as a proportion of the GNP, but only about 14 percent of the GDP if we subtract the American and other external resources (Berglas, 1986, 176; Trop, 1989, 52). This energized a massive military buildup. Now the size and armament of the IDF were adapted to the new situation of Israel's presence in extensive territories and the needs of deterrence, as the Arab states continued to brandish the military option for securing return of the territories. In contrast to the pre-1967 offensive orientation, the IDF was organized in line with a conception that was simultaneously offensive and defensive. This required a major expansion of armor, artillery, and air force, particularly of the regular army (see Wald, 1987, 233–240). In the absence of rigid casus belli and with the upgrading of the regular army, the state was less dependent on mobilizing civilian reservists. The state's weakness, which had been so blatant in the "waiting period," was thus rectified.

Military buildup generated a complex of industries and services that supported the military and, simultaneously, were fed by it. After France had imposed a weapons embargo on the Middle East with the breakout of the war, military industry also aimed at furnishing Israel with independent weapons production. The military industry, moreover, became a major channel to ensure growth and employment—at the peak (1982/83), about 25 percent of all industrial employees were employed in this sector (Mintz, 1985, 14; see also Kleiman, 1986, 94; Mintz, 1987). In addition to former projects, missiles, tanks, and jet warplanes were now produced. Beyond further reliance on the existing state/Histadrut-owned large companies, the government financially encouraged the incorporation of private firms within military production, mainly to increase efficiency. The growth of firms such as El-BIT and EL-OP exemplified this trend (Barnett, 1992, 196–202, 235–236). At the same time, the dispute at the highest levels of the defense establishment, which had been taken place a few years earlier, over whether it was more practical to set up a military industry or make purchases abroad was effectively resolved in favor of production at home (Peri and Neubach, 1984). Furthermore, export of military production became a major economic factor. Israel's policy of arms exports was broadly supported politically, while critical questions concerning the economy's reliance on an export of this kind and the countries to which Israel exported—in many cases governed by authoritarian regimes—was ruled out, in both the cabinet and the public sphere (Peri and Neubach, 1984, 63–64).

Ultimately, the main beneficiaries from military buildup and industrialization were the IDF itself (with the constituting groups as we see below), managerial groups, business entrepreneurs, and organized workers. A military-industrial complex was created, composed of military officers and senior executives, with a high number of officers drifting from the IDF to industry (see Mintz, 1985, 19–23; Peri and Neubach, 1984).

Military industrialization was financed largely by American foreign aid, which became massive following the war, rising from $77 million in 1968 to about $950 million in 1973 and $1,250 million in each of the years 1974–80 (Berglas, 1986, 183). America also replaced France as the main weapons supplier.

With the military buildup subsidized by the United States, there was no need for the state to pay for it by slashing the standard of living (see Sussman, 1984); real wages increased (see below). In other words, the arms buildup produced no immediate social or political costs that might have constructed new interests associated with a different policy—territorial concessions as a means of terminating the high-cost conflict, for example. On the contrary, American aid hardened social group interests in favor of the entrenchment of the conflict. To a large extent, American aid was generously given not *despite* the Israeli occupation but to a large extent *due* to the occupation, as long as Israel was viewed as an effective block against the Soviet regional presence. Speculatively, had Israel embarked on a peace-oriented track, this aid was more likely to be decreased. If so, our analysis ought to consider the American aid as an *endogenous* factor indirectly regulated by Israel.

(b) The reshaping of the labor market. The war produced a cheap, mass labor force by speedy incorporation of the occupied West Bank and the Gaza Strip into the Israeli economy. Gradually, about 60,000 Palestinians (in 1973) streamed to Israel as cheap labor directed mainly to construction, agriculture, and manufacturing, thus overcoming the pre-1967 deficiencies of low-paid manpower in the secondary labor market. Palestinians accounted for 5 percent of the labor force of Israel and 30 percent of the labor force of the occupied territories (Semyonov and Lewin-Epstein, 1987, 10). In 1969, the income of unskilled Palestinian workers was about 43 percent of Jewish workers' income (ibid., 89). Interestingly, this stream effectively nullified the arrangements of the 1950s, when the exogenous Palestinian workforce was excluded as a means of combating infiltrations. Changing needs, however, made the (potential) infiltrators of the 1950s part of the labor force from 1967 on.

Taking advantage of the cheap Palestinian workforce and American aid, the state stepped up its intervention in the economy by renewing the injection of capital, primarily to reinvigorate public construction. Increased state budgets, moreover, energized an expansion of the public sector. Health and education in particular about doubled in 1968–78 in real terms (Ofer, 1986).

Overall, the entry of the Palestinians into the Israeli labor market affected the ethnic groups differentially. By and large, the economic boom dramatically decreased unemployment, which mainly struck Orientals, from about 10 percent in 1967 to about 3.5 percent in 1970. At the same time, in 1968–73 real wages increased about 19 percent while GNP rose 12 percent from 1967 to 1970 (Ben-Porath, 1986b, 11, 20). Many Orientals improved their lot by moving up from peripheral professions—mostly blue-collar jobs, now taken by the Palestinians—into the bureaucratic machinery, where more manpower was needed as a result of the postwar economic boom. Consequently, in 1977 about 13 percent of the Orientals occupied white-collar professions, up from the percentage in the state's first years (relative to about 35 percent of the Westerners; Swirski, 1981, 59). Effectively, the Palestinians' entry into the Israeli labor market was a kind of "immigration" which, like earlier Jewish waves of immigration, "pushed" the peripheral social group toward the center and gave it greater mobility. In sum, during the period from 1969 to 1982 the mean occupational status of the main Israeli groups (including Palestinian citizens) improved by approximately 10 percent (Semyonov and Lewin-Epstein, 1987, 51).

With growing public budgets, the state could reward preferred groups. The Westerner-dominated upper middle class and business corporations (including state/Histadrut-owned) were able to accumulate greater capital by exploiting the new workers. Mobile Orientals incorporated into the middle class of veteran Westerners. Among these middle-class groups were those who had displayed militancy during the years of full employment. These groups occupied professions like academics, teachers, civil servants, and military officers, or they staffed state-owned corporations. They were well organized and well protected by the Histadrut. Since Palestinians' access to these sectors was denied, competition between Jewish and low-paid Palestinian laborers was averted (see Grinberg, 1991b, 66–71, 75–97; Swirski, 1990, 190–193).

Nevertheless, many other Oriental workers remained in the secondary labor market and were even pushed down into the underclass. They received poorer wages than the organized workers in other sectors because the entrance of the Palestinian labor force worked to decrease wages and the direct competition they faced from the Palestinians gave them less leverage to fight for better pay. This was apparent in sectors in which Palestinians gained access, mainly construction, agriculture, and industrial sectors not involved with military production or high-tech manufacturing. In these sectors, the Histadrut's power to restrain workers' militancy was deeply felt (see Farjoun, 1983; Grinberg, 1991b, 66–71, 75–97; Kimmerling, 1989, 273–274, 277–278; Shalev, 1992, 261–262).

Ironically, the economic growth benefited the Israeli Palestinians as well. Their being state-disciplined was further pronounced during the Six-Day War, including the "waiting period," when Israel's fate was ostensibly questioned but Israeli Palestinians remained idle. Increasingly trusted by Jews, Israeli Palestinians could take advantage of the new postwar economic opportunities. Those opportunities coincided with the earlier elimination of the Military Administration and the Israeli Palestinians' reestablished interaction with the Palestinian population in the West Bank and the Gaza Strip. Similar to their Oriental counterparts, Israeli Palestinians were partially replaced by laborers from the occupied territories, thereby being "pushed" into the middle class. Many Israeli Palestinians then turned to small business and subcontracting, mainly in construction, while their value as mediators between Israeli systems and the occupied Palestinians grew. Concomitantly, the growth of an Israeli Palestinian middle class was reflected in the significant expansion of the education system: the establishment of new high schools, and the growing number of students. The war thus created conditions for Palestinians' mobility that also accounted, alongside other mechanisms described in chapter 2, for the state's enduring, low-cost disciplining of a previously hostile minority. But at the same time, mobility also enhanced Palestinians' national consciousness, reflected in autonomous, political organizing revolving around the Israeli Communist Party and other organs. This trend grew following the "Day of the Land" in March 1976, during which Israeli police killed six Israeli Palestinians in a demonstration against confiscation of land in the Galilee (see Ben-Porath, 1986a, 165–166; Bishara, 1993, 13–15; Semyonov and Lewin-Epstein, 1987, 51; Swirski, 1990, 159–171).

Conjoining with the state's socioeconomic policies and previously patterned interethnic gaps, the entry of the Palestinian labor force reshaped the ethno-class stratification of Israeli society. In general, gaps within the Oriental community were widened, and hence the gaps between the Jewish social classes in general.

Most significant were the gaps in schooling, which originated in the structure of absorption in the 1950s. Gaps in secondary schooling were basically closed in the 1970s, but the channeling of Orientals into technical and agricultural schools from the 1960s made them less likely to be promoted in the IDF and to enter universities. Thus, the "inflation" of secondary schooling devalued this level of education in the labor market, affecting mainly the Orientals for whom this level became mostly the highest they attained. Taking this process together with differential material capabilities, no wonder that interethnic gaps in higher education remained wide.[3]

It follows that whenever the Orientals were successful in narrowing the gap with the Westerners, this gap was reopened by the establishment of new criteria for promotion. While they stem purely from the professionalization and modernization undergone by the Israeli economy, the new criteria were actually more adapted to the Westerners' improved skills. Many Orientals (and Israeli Palestinians) were thereby effectively blocked once again (Nahon, 1993a, 39–44; Swirski, 1990, 95–102, 199–200; see also Kraus and Hodge, 1990).

Consequently, while gaps between the foreign-born generation of each ethnic group in terms of presence in white-collar occupations were narrowed, gaps between the Israeli-born generation of each ethnic group increased about 10 percent in 1961–81, accounted for mainly by schooling (Nahon, 1993b, 61–62). And, the more the return for education increased and worked to widen gaps between blue-collar and white-collar workers in general and among women in particular (Amir, 1986), the more gaps in wages between the Israeli-born generation of each ethnic group were widened (those who were potentially competing in the professional labor market). True, in crude terms, the gap in monthly earnings between Orientals and Westerners declined from 37 percent in 1957/58 to 26 percent in 1968/69 (Ben-Porath, 1986a, 166), while real wages of both ethnic groups increased an average of about 15 percent during this period (Ben-Porath, 1986b, 11). But if we go beyond crude data to differentiate between foreign-born and Israeli-born groups, we discover that in 1969, the income of Western Israeli-born males was 62 percent higher than that of Oriental Israeli-born males. In 1976 the figure was 77 percent (Fishelson et al., 1980, 265).

Turning from crude data to segmentation of the Oriental communities, data suggest that three Oriental segments were molded: mobile, materially mobile, and nonmobile. The mobile segment enjoyed mobility both culturally and materially. It comprised in the early 1980s about 20 percent of the

Orientals, mainly those residing in the big cities who entered white-collar sectors of the labor market, compared to about 10 percent in the early 1970s (see Nahon, 1993a, 44; Swirski, 1981, 57–60). Most of the members of this segment also acquired academic/para-academic education, as the data above suggest. Many of them adopted elements of Westernized Israeli culture, particularly its materialism and competitiveness, and at the same time, became more politically involved. Most of these Orientals Westernized and were assimilated almost completely into the middle class. Not only did their social interests overlap, but the mobile Orientals also worked to blur interethnic distinctions (on change of attitudes, see Ben-Rafael, 1982, 156–177).

The materially mobile segment, which consisted of about 40 percent of the Oriental community, acquired only secondary-school education. However, its members compensated for this disadvantage by turning to alternative channels of mobility, primarily in lucrative small businesses, thus narrowing the material gap with the Western middle class. Still, the disparity in social status, which was nurtured by the Western symbols of Mamlachtiyut, remained wide, and as such fueled frustration (see Nahon, 1993b).

The nonmobile, poorer segment of the Oriental population did not enjoy the same social mobility. This was particularly so in the Moroccan community concentrated in the peripheral development towns, where competition with the Palestinian labor force in the secondary labor market was felt. The towns comprised about one-fifth of the total Jewish population and one-third of the Oriental population, while the Orientals comprised 70 percent of the residents in these towns (Ben-Zadok, 1993, 96–100). Data from 1983 reveal that 53 percent of the workforce in these towns was employed in low-paying industries relative to 43 percent in the country as a whole, including the Israeli Palestinian sector. Socioeconomic indicators placed this sector below 70 percent of the entire population (Peled, 1991, 8–9; on the interethnic structure in general, see Farjoun, 1983; Grinberg, 1991b, 66–71, 75–97; Nahon, 1987; Smooha, 1993).

The state's strategies toward the Orientals were thus practically changed, turning from legitimization of inequality alone to combined strategies of both mobility and splitting the Oriental collective. Splitting, moreover, also applied to the working class as a whole since the Oriental-dominated working class was situated in competition with the Palestinian workers, Israelis and residents of the territories alike. Hence, structural obstacles to broad cooperation between these segments were erected.

These processes were reflected in the reshaped ethno-class structure: In the mid-1980s the class of blue-collar workers who made up the secondary labor market consisted mainly of Israeli Palestinians and about half of the Orientals. This class accounted for about 40 percent of the total population (about 40 percent of this segment is categorized as poor population; the remainder is low-wage workers). The middle class was mixed, with Western preponderance (about 45 percent of the whole population), while the upper middle and upper classes were predominantly Western (about 15 percent) (Smooha, 1993, 175–176).

It follows that the Histadrut benefited from the occupation both as an employer and as the umbrella organization of the workers in Israel. Its economic sector, Hevrat Ha'Ovdim, dramatically recovered from the recession by exploiting cheap labor in construction and military production and by entering into the Palestinian market. As a trade union the Histadrut benefited from the creation of a Jewish-Palestinian split labor market by increasing its power to restrain workers. Militant organizing by labor, particularly in the secondary market, was thus virtually ruled out. Simultaneously, workers in this segment became more dependent on the Histadrut as a mechanism that guaranteed employment and better wages under conditions of Jewish-Palestinian competition. The Histadrut, in turn, took advantage of the situation to broaden its control over various groups in the workforce. At the same time, the Histadrut's reliance on the state became more pronounced, for it was the state, as the conduit for the workforce, that indirectly enabled the Histadrut to gain. In the final analysis, the state was able to activate the Histadrut more effectively at the corporatist level, as a mechanism through which to restrain the labor force (see Grinberg, 1991b, 53–55, 64–71; 1993a, 176–182; 1993b; Shalev, 1992, 289).[4] With the rise of the defense industry, moreover, trade unions turned into a lobby advocating the IDF's buildup to increase its acquisition from the local military industry (Grinberg, 1993a, 181–182). Overall, the workers' organizations –singly tied to the state, losing some of the autonomy they had enjoyed during the prewar crisis.[5] In sum, the state constructed the interest of the Histadrut toward perpetuation of the Arab-Israeli conflict as a means of entrenching the occupation. In exchange, the Histadrut accepted the reempowerment of the state.

(c) The Palestinian market. New opportunities were opened for marketing goods in the territories and using them as a jumping point to other Arab markets (Kanovsky, 1970, 62–64).[6] Three policies worked to make these opportunities obtainable. One was the "open bridges" policy mentioned above (Saleh, 1990, 43). Second, despite ministerial decisions, no capital was invested in the territories to encourage the development of local means of production (Gazit, 1985, 147–150). Third, Israel restricted export of local products to its territory (Farsoun and Landis, 1990, 23). Consequently, both a stream of Palestinians from the territories into Israel in search of work was ensured and competition between the two economies was averted up to the point of the creation of dependency of the Palestinian economy on Israel. To illustrate a long-term result, in 1986 the West Bank and Gaza Strip imported $780 million worth of Israeli goods constituting about 90 percent of their total import (ibid.). At the same time, by allowing a stream of workers and open bridges, Israel reduced the price of the occupation on the Palestinian side, so Israel could control without resorting to employment of massive force.

(d) Housing. The main Jewish groups were rewarded by being given the opportunity to buy cheap, state-subsidized housing in the new settlements established on confiscated land in the territories. Settlement projects had existed from the beginning but until 1977 were confined to areas viewed as crucial to ensure defensible borders, while after 1977 (the change of government; see chapter 5) settlements were expanded to areas of dense Palestinian population in the West Bank and Gaza Strip. At the institutional level, this project initially benefited the traditional agricultural movements, mainly associated with the labor parties, who took the settlement initiative. For them, it was a renewal of the pioneering tradition through which they had gained prestige prior to the state's establishment.

(e) Reconstructing the ethno-functional division of labor in the IDF. Military service also differentially bettered the Jewish ethnic groups' social position. The growing Oriental participation in military service during the 1960s (particularly by the second generation of immigrants) enabled them to share the credit for the victory. Indeed, the Oriental soldiers were praised for their fighting ability whereas before the war senior officers had expressed uncertainty about their professional skills (Roumani, 1991, 70; Smooha, 1984b, 16). Moreover, Orientals indirectly benefited from the importance ascribed to military symbols in the postwar political discourse (see below), as they were perceived to have taken part in the major social action symbolized within the new discourse.

This development could have enhanced the Orientals' position to attain or demand substantive equality within the army and to convert their military participation into political and social resources. The higher living standard that some Orientals achieved due to their professional mobility also raised their potential for political participation, as their material dependence on the state diminished.

Such potential notwithstanding, several factors worked to block the mobility of Orientals and impede their capacity to turn to effective collective action. First, it seems safe to argue that the post-1967 process dulled the Orientals' consciousness of their peripheral social standing. This came about because they grasped the prestige that was ascribed to their military service as a symbolic asset that, in fact, they were granted in place of material resources. It was historically similar to other peripheral groups' behavior.[7] Consequently, conditions were created for moderating Orientals' claims on such resources and concentrating their demands within the military sphere alone.

Second, the political-military discourse worked to moderate preoccupation with social issues as compared with the 1960s and subordinated social goals to security missions beyond the instrumentalism that already marked the discourse. It is instructive in this connection to recall the controversy that raged in the early 1970s between Finance Minister Pinhas Sapir and Defense Minister Moshe Dayan. Its crux was whether Israel could afford to improve social welfare while also maintaining its high-profile defense posture. The dispute was an offshoot of the notion that the people should be content with a modest standard of living as long as the country faced an existential threat. That demand, however, was directed primarily at the weaker sectors, which were asking the state for resources while the middle-class groups improved their position, as illustrated above. This attitude was yet another example of how the state's engagement in violence made security an acceptable substitute for material resources.[8]

As for the third and most important factor, the war produced no more than a insignificant change in the asymmetry between the Orientals' more intensive military participation and their peripheral positions within the military hierarchy. Crucial was the expansion of command centers and technocratic units at the expense of the combat level (see Wald, 1987, 72–79, 143–156). This shift, which in itself resulted from the army's self-perceived needs, mostly reinforced the dominance of Westerners in three interrelated ways. It affected promotions, the value of their acquired positions, and the conversion of military positions into civilian ones.

First, Westerners obtained the senior staff positions, while many Orientals were relegated to peripheral assignments in the new formations and thus reblocked. The new criteria were better suited to the skills and premilitary educational level of the Westerners. At the same time, the military build up slightly increased promotion of Orientals.

Data reveal that in the 1970s about 67 percent of the conscripts and squad commanders were Orientals, but Orientals accounted for only about 30 percent of the junior officers and 10 to 17 percent of the senior officers (Smooha, 1984b, 19).[9] In the civil sector, about 50 percent of blue-collar workers were Orientals (the rest were, notably, Palestinians), while Orientals accounted for only about 12 percent of white-collar professionals in 1977 (Swirski, 1981, 59–60). Although the proportional rates of Westerners' and Orientals' mobility seem equal in both sectors, the Orientals' route through the military was of greater significance as military occupation accrued social prestige.

The growing numbers of Oriental officers was felt mainly in the mobile segment. Naturally, the materially mobile and nonmobile segments enjoyed less mobility, due to the combination of alienation and lack of motivation with ineligibility for promotion. The military status of many of them was portrayed as "hewers of wood and drawers of water" (Gordon, 1992, 36). Many others, especially those situated in the nonmobile segment, were not drafted at all, while nonparticipation among women was higher than among men for reasons of poor schooling, religion, and marriage. Thus, less mobile Orientals sat on the fence, preferring either a strategy of entering the middle class through the military or neglecting the military route (see testimonies in Swirski, 1981, 296; 1989, 130, relating to the mid-1970s).

With the growing professionalization within the military and promotion increasingly based on quantifiable achievements, the Orientals' slow promotion once again was made to seem legitimate. Together with the minor promotion of Orientals, these criteria worked against the Orientals' ability to grasp the fact of their peripheral status. The IDF's image as a universalist military remained unquestioned, which, by itself, hindered Orientals' political action. So, the state's strategy of mobility toward the Orientals was further conditioned on the entrenchment of the Arab-Israeli conflict by which military buildup could be energized and attain social prestige.

Second, in addition to blocking the promotion of Orientals, the military reorganization resulted in the devaluation of the status of some of those who had already been promoted. Although the Orientals could more readily serve in front-line combat units, the post-1967 shift entwined with the economic boom gradually gave rise to the status of the "military manager" and technical occupations. Both were associated with the Westerners' new occupations, while the status of the "fighter," now more achievable by relatively educated Orientals, saw some devaluation. Devaluation was also amplified inasmuch as officers were gradually less disposed to view their service as a "calling" and more as a career (see Popper and Ronen, 1989, 156–168). To a large extent, this was due to the establishment of a "dual career": officers, beginning in 1957, were compelled to retire at age forty-five, after which they embarked on a second, civilian career (Peri and Lissak, 1976).

Third, this asymmetric positioning in the military was extended in the conversion from a military position into a civilian career. Military service effectively prepared nonmobile Oriental soldiers to find jobs primarily in the secondary labor market, that is, in blue-collar jobs. In this as in other ways, the army helped perpetuate the Orientals' peripheral status, even when it tried to give a "second chance" to conscripts from distressed population groups (Roumani, 1979, 70–86; Smooha, 1984b). At the same time, the training of Westerners as military managers and technological experts provided them with even better tools to succeed in the modernizing, civilian market following their release (see Radom, 1968). The ability (or failure) to translate skills learned in the military to the civilian labor market had an even stronger negative effect on Orientals' mobility under two new conditions. A military-industrial complex emerged, networks of "high society" (Eisenstadt, 1985, 242–247) with which Westerners could capitalize more effectively than Orientals.[10] Second, as noted above, the Israeli economy underwent processes of professionalization and modernization.

These developments dovetailed with the rise of the business entrepreneur. A new social status that emerged during the 1960s, it was accessible primarily to upper-middle-class Westerners (see Shapiro, 1977, 161–163). The increased cooperation between the business management and security realms endowed the entrepreneur with a neutral, objective image rooted in defense needs and thus produced commensurate social rewards. Overall, Westerners were more successful than their Oriental counterparts in converting the direct gains from military participation into social, civilian improvements.

It follows that Orientals' mobility within the military did not account, by itself, for social mobility. The "assets" attained by each ethnic group during military service mattered but only in terms of relative social prestige and labor market value. Orientals' mobility, however, occurred side by side with the erosion of the social value of this mobility (a point overlooked by sociologists—like Lissak [1984a]—who claimed the IDF was a channel of social mobility. Hence, they were not in a position to achieve real mobility nor were they able to challenge the Westerner-dominated ideological symbols that played a key role in legitimizing inequality. The shift from a military that established objective criteria, which placed Orientals in a peripheral position, to a military that promoted Orientals to devalued positions was set in motion. Orientals were ascending a descending escalator.[11] By taking part in the extensive state action that split Orientals into mobile and nonmobile segments, the IDF, albeit unintentionally, played a large role in perpetuating inequality rather than acting as an interethnic integrator.

Nevertheless, as the case of Wadi Salib suggests, the inherent tension between ostensibly universalistic criteria and inequality bore the potential to ignite Oriental protest. A growing burden without quid pro quos and the uncovering of biases implicit in the criteria might both be triggers for such protest. Chapter 5 will illustrate both entwined outcomes, reproduction and protest.

To conclude the social dimension of occupation, Shalev (1992, 270–271) argues, against the background of the post-1967 socioeconomic process, that "Israel's failure to distance itself economically from the occupied territories . . . reflected the vested interests of the occupation's economic beneficiaries . . . in Israel." Withdrawal, it was thought, would trigger the kind of social unrest that had characterized the 1960s. Still, interests embraced the social domain as well. And, more important, interests were not only realized by the occupation but also constructed and even reconstructed: The dominant Western groups— mainly the business-managerial elite groups and organized workers—(re)constructed their interests in a force-oriented posture as they equated the occupation with their own well-being. Soon the whole middle class abandoned their previous liberal-dovish stance, as we will see. The arrangements that derived from the occupation, moreover, gradually constructed the Orientals' interest in the conflict's perpetuation, too; they took on a hawkish orientation, as this ostensibly improved their social standing at the material and symbolic levels alike (see chapter 5).

Manifestly, the war rescued the dominant Jewish groups from the necessity of reallocating the societal resources that otherwise would have been required to ensure social stability in the face of seeds of unrest by Orientals and deep unemployment. It may be inferred, moreover, from the fact that the occupation benefited both Jewish ethnic groups and Israeli Palestinians, albeit differentially, that the linkage between its perpetuation and the reproduction of the social structure was reconfirmed. We find that the occupation worked mainly to sustain the state strategies of legitimation (full employment, welfare systems, universalist army), mobility, and splitting toward Orientals and the entire working class. The net effect was that the foundations of the social order, which had somehow cracked in the 1960s, were patched up by the outcome of the war. Still, the potential for crisis existed, as shown by the contradictory impacts of the war on Orientals and Palestinians, and it would become even more acute.

Level III: Reconstructing the Political Discourse

The perpetuation of the war's results was blatantly internalized in political discourse. The "state of siege" in which Israel found itself became accepted as though forced on Israel and as a reality that could not be changed. With reference to the optimal political settlements, concepts such as "defensible borders" and "strategic depth" were the buzz words of both the Left and the Right (Shapiro, 1991, 151–159). Israel's doctrine thus showed the subordination of political ends to military goals, as the military logic of "worst-case analysis" overshadowed the political logic of taking risks in return for convertible political assets (Kimmerling, 1993b, 136; Wald, 1987, 202–206).

Military domination was well illustrated in the character of the peace plans that were put forward. The best-known of them was the Allon Plan, drawn up by Deputy Prime Minister and retired General Yigal Allon. Considered relatively moderate (it advocated a partial annexation alone), the Allon Plan was nevertheless based on military rather than political principles (Allon, 1989, 16, 43). Similarly, even the symbols that distinguished the right wing from the left wing were based on a security approach toward the continued occupation of the territories. An overview of the social order was distinctly lacking (Arian and Shamir, 1983). No wonder then that the military style—authoritative, decisive, and simplistic—dominated the civilian culture (Gertz, 1985/86, 275–276).

Political discourse then became a military discourse in every respect, becoming more narrow than ever. The prewar political discourse conferred *dominance* on the use of violence to cope with political problems, but in the post-1967 discourse military thought achieved *exclusivity*. The 1950s dispute between the diplomatic and military schools of thought (within the boundaries of an essentially activist approach) was displaced by disputes *within* the military school between doves and hawks.

Gradually military discourse was wrapped in a messianic worldview, supplanting the seed of universal humanism that appeared during the 1960s and challenging the strict military rationale regarding the fate of the territories. The idea of the Jewish nation's return to its heartland with sites sacred to Judaism, such as Jerusalem's Walled City and Hebron, the elimination of the Green Line from maps, and the use of the biblical notion of "Judaea and Samria" instead of "West Bank" indicate the new rhetoric (Gertz, 1988, 281; Keren, 1989a, 59–76; Lustick, 1993, 357–361). This worked to "reshape the cognitive map of Israeli to conform with an image of the country which included the territories as no different from other regions of the state" (ibid., 361). Former trends expedited the infusion of new discursive frames. Among them was the implementation of "Jewish consciousness" studies in schools from the early 1960s, thus clouding the secular portrait of Mamlachtiyut (Cohen, 1987, 246–249). Another expression from the 1960s was the mystification of the use of violence within the public discourse as a backlash to the Holocaust (Zweig, 1969, 201–212). However, it is worth emphasizing that the awakening of religious, historical sentiments did not play a key role in that period as long as the pragmatist Alignment and its allies in the IDF formulated the military doctrine. Still, the minority opposition Gachal Party (from 1970) gradually invoked religious argumentation that, at a later stage, the security-oriented entrenchment of the occupation paved the road to their dominance (see chapter 5). At the bottom, a dispute between two schools of political thought took place, each claiming to represent Israel's raison d'etre. One, associated with the right wing and religious groups, advocated expansion and force culminating in annexation of the occupied territories; the other, associated with the Center-Left (the Alignment and the more leftist parties), urged demographic homogeneity entailing withdrawal from the Palestinian-populated territories but not from territories deemed as security assets (Kimmerling, 1993a; on the cultural dimension of the shift, see also Kimmerling, 1985c; Liebman and Don-Yehiya, 1983).

Four occupation-inspired political mechanisms played a leading role in molding the force-oriented discourse. One mechanism was the entry of retired senior officers into politics. Insofar as the political discourse reflected the crushing military victory, many civilian groups put their trust in retired generals regarding decisions about national security affairs. As those generals also became electoral drawing cards, the major parties made efforts to recruit them. Several generals even occupied ministerial positions, such as Moshe Dayan, Yitzhak Rabin, Ezer Weizmann, Ariel Sharon, and others. As for the officers, they converted their growing prestige into political status through which they could inject their worldview into civilian policy-making (Peri, 1983, 111–114).

Although the autonomous character of civilian politics was undermined as military thought prevailed, greater political supervision over the army was institutionalized thanks to the same very process: Politicians, some of them former senior officers (or assisted by such), sharpened their scrutiny of the army although they paid the price of greater penetration of military thought into the political sphere. This was accompanied by institutionalization of regulations regarding the initiation of military operations. The end result was that the army was no longer able to initiate military activity with the same independence that had been so pronounced in the lead-up to the Six-Day War, especially under Defense Minister Moshe Dayan (see Ben Meir, 1995, 101–102, 128; Handel, 1994, 554–555; Horowitz, 1982). The IDF, for its part, practically exchanged the officers' ability to convert their military prestige into political status after their retirement for self-restraint vis-à-vis the political level. Beyond the other effects pertinent to the pattern of exchange, open intervention in politics would have also created difficulties in gaining the support of politicians whose stand affected the officers' political promotion (see Peri, 1983, 137–138, on the case of Israel; Mills, 1956, 285, on the American experience; Vagts, 1959, 308–309, on European militarism; Harries-Jenkins, 1973, on the case of Victorian Britain). A clear linkage then was created between the officers' potential civilian occupations and the social prestige conferred on the army (see, by comparison, Feld, 1968). Conversion of social prestige into political status at the individual level thus added a new dimension to the relations of exchange between the state civilian institutions and the military. Militarization, by which the military profession became an electoral asset, thus worked again to increase political control as well.

No wonder that the second mechanism involved with inculcation of military discourse was the IDF itself. Generals' active participation in shaping public opinion was expanded following the war, which made them notable figures and enhanced their partnership with politicians in shaping postwar military policies. Shielded by its political subordination, military professionalism could be portrayed as "above politics," to use Mills' dictum (1956, 200); the military could influence discourse while not being a target of political criticism by which military values might have been questioned.

A third mechanism was the political union that was effected in 1968 among Mapai, Ahdut Ha'Avodah, and Rafi. The latter was led by Moshe Dayan and Shimon Peres. Ben-Gurion did not join his two protégés, opting instead to form an independent party that garnered little support; in 1970 he retired from political life. Together, the three groups constituted themselves as the Labor

Party which, with Mapam (now a small party), formed the Alignment (distinguished from the former Alignment between Mapai and Ahdut Ha'Avoda).

Rafi's return to a common political framework with Mapai reflected the leading role of statism in the 1967 victory. Much of the credit for the victory went to the group that had been identified with statism, had been drummed out of the party in 1965, and had then been called to lead the country, with Dayan as defense minister, when Mapai had vacillated on the eve of the war. In other words, the statist thrust again overrode the party-oriented tendencies that had been expressed by Mapai and the Histadrut during the 1960s. In practice, although Mapai's decline accelerated following the war, it benefited by being unleashed from the challenge by Rafi and by enjoying Dayan's huge popularity; both carrots could have been converted into sticks in a case of intraparty crisis. In return, ex-Mapai members let Rafi gradually dominate the unified party. In other words, Mapai was sucked into the hawkish paradigm molded by its partner and gradually lost its pragmatist tone even though part of it rejected the force-oriented approach (see Beilin, 1985). Owing to Rafi's domination, the Labor Party did not erect obstacles to the state's reempowerment. Taking together the first and third mechanisms with the Histadrut's benefits from the occupation, the state again constructed the old Mapai interest in augmenting militarism, materially and discursively alike, as a political asset by which the state concluded its triumph over the parties and the Histadrut.

A fourth mechanism nurturing the discourse was the institutionalization of the national unity coalition following the elections of 1969. Its major components were the Alignment and the right-wing Gachal. The cooperation between these former bitter rivals solidified the embedded force-oriented discourse and focused it on short-term, instrumental points of biparty consent, the political-territorial status quo. Moreover, the relatively dovish Liberal Party, which had joined forces with Herut in 1965 through the Gachal bloc to challenge the labor parties' socioeconomic policies while territorial issues were dormant, now lost its uniqueness as a moderate party. It was completely sucked into the hawkish stance formulated by Herut.

Notwithstanding the prominence of these mechanisms and the interest of the agents involved in designing a force-oriented discourse, we still may ask what accounted for their success. The political discourse, allegedly, did not reflect ideological stands per se. It was first and foremost a state production through the state's entrenchment of the occupation. After all, the ideological debate over the country's borders was silenced up to 1967 after the failure to expand them in the Sinai Campaign; even the right-wing Herut Party reconciled itself to the reality of fixed borders, evidenced by its alliance with the dovish Liberal Party. And unlike the post-1948 reality, the occupation of 1967 was deemed temporary by the majority of Israeli citizens. Moving one step further, as much as Israel could have opted for a peace/de-escalation route, social groups in light of this new reality could have adopted more pacifistic discursive frameworks, or even clung to the prewar relatively liberal and dovish frames. External occurrences could then have been translated by certain groups into opportunities for peace rather than justifications for retaining territorial holds. That is so especially when taken against the impressive victory that might have led to concessions driven by self-confidence.

Nevertheless, gaining from the new reality that was gradually routinized and the new opportunities that were created and that satisfied their everyday needs, agents were more inclined to collect force-oriented signals transmitted by political entrepreneurs rather than signals that might have altered the relatively convenient situation. Ears were not attuned to the moderate signals transmitted from the Arab world (see below) and echoed by some leftist figures (see, for example, Avnery, 1968). Under these conditions, the question of whether Israel could have achieved identical gains by embarking on a peace-oriented road is irrelevant. A u-turn might have entailed the forsaking, or at least risking, of immediate gains with which the Israelis felt confident for an uncertain, vague future and a frustrated recent past. A new economic recession with telling effects on political stability, downsizing of the IDF as a result of a de-escalated conflict, and even a decrease in American aid were all intolerable costs that might have caused political dissatisfaction by the new gainers. Discursive changes in fact reflected (re)construction of social interests as outlined above.

No wonder, then, that this trend captivated not only state agencies but also military-oriented intellectuals, journalists, and other shapers of public opinion. Indeed, a glance at the evolution of the political discourse reveals that while immediately after the end of the Six-Day War a broad consensus existed, advocating the temporary nature of the new reality of occupation, political views began hardening (Barzilai, 1992, 123–131; Beilin, 1985). A new version of materialist militarism then evolved.

In contrast, had the war's outcomes been domestically different—if, for example, the military buildup had to be entirely financed by Israel's citizens, or had the Palestinians resisted the occupation and economic exploitation, making the status quo costly—then many groups possibly would have tried to restrain the defense establishment's activism. After all, a series of episodic military crises was not at issue but, rather, a long-lived political process running under relative security calm. So, agents could at each stage have reassessed their position toward the conflict relative to their gains. Hawks and doves were therefore socially constructed; hence, my focus on sociopolitical processes rather than the discursive outcomes alone studied by proponents of political culture (such as Gertz, Arian, Shamir, Keren, and Lustick, cited above).

Moving from the third to fourth level (see figure 4.1), political discourse played its part in hardening the foreign military policies and in reempowering the state.

Level IV: Hardening Political-Military Policies

Cyclically and dialectically, by nurturing the military-oriented discourse, leaders lost the autonomy to reverse the foreign-military policies at a low cost. As public opinion was patterned by hard-line formulas, reversal gradually also meant an electoral risk. Reversal might also affect the integration of the Labor Party (the relations with Rafi in particular) and the government coalition insofar as political groups gradually entrenched their stand (see Lustick, 1993, 362–366; Sella and Yishai, 1986, 127–186). Consequently, the military agenda was shaped, and hardened, by discursive means. Similar to past occurrences, changes in Israeli society habituated a new reality that limited the scope of alternatives from which decision-makers could select their preferred policies (see my argument in chapter 3 on the scope of decision-making).

An asymmetric situation was then apparent: The IDF, with huge resources, political power, and social prestige, was, more than any other institution, interested in the entrenchment of the conflict. This interest extended to "military" politicians, those retired generals whose political status was determined by the extent to which military values prevailed. Those politicians and the IDF worked together to entrench the territorial status quo, as evidenced by the arrangements they structured in the territories, their stand regarding interim agreements, and the strategic air bombing during the War of Attrition (see below). Apparently, military intelligence, which is the dominant intelligence agency, confined its job to collecting war, not peace, signals from the Arab world.

These war-prone forces expanded to become a vast coalition. The IDF and "military" politicians were conjoined with the Histadrut, settlers, business entrepreneurs, mobile Orientals, and others who gained, doves and hawks alike. The military mind-set, backed by religious hawks, tipped the scale in favor of the status quo. "Civilian" politicians—doves affiliated with Mapai and Mapam among them—reacted passively. Satisfied with the status quo, they were disinclined to challenge the military domination; on the contrary, they furnished the IDF with huge capacity by means of military buildup.

The American generosity that facilitated the military buildup and enabled Israel to avoid domestic constraints added to these processes. But though there was no pressure on Israel to withdraw, the decision to maintain the political-territorial status quo was an autonomous Israeli decision. America *allowed* but did not *coerce* Israel into taking that road. Still, Washington's toleration toward Israel's approach worked to harden the hawkish trends within the Israeli establishment.

Reempowerment of the state completed the amplification of the military agenda. Similar to former occurrences, a dialectical pattern was set in motion. Through agents' discursive reaction to the new beneficial military-political situation, they revalidated state practices, meaning violence management, rather than the preoccupations of civil society, which had seen moderate revival in the years preceding the war. However, because these agents were not fully aware of the implications of their approach, their very actions increased the dominance of the state. The latter, in turn, again deprived agents of their potential for civil autonomy (see, at the theoretical level, Isaac, 1987a, 56–58; Wendt, 1987, 355–361). Structurally speaking, the state redominated the political space by discursively underscoring the existential danger and the state's need to cope with it. It again effectively convinced its citizens to more carefully incorporate collective security interests within their calculations, and then to consume protection at a high price (see Lake, 1992; Tilly, 1985b, for the theoretical concepts).

Costly consumption and deprivation meant legitimizing the entrenchment of the conflict, supplanting previous liberal-humanistic-pacific orientations. But in return, the state benefited the agents in the social-economy realm. Military discourse, moreover, universalized particularist interests by assimilating them within security interests. In this discourse, for example, industrialists did not exploit Palestinian workers; a "benevolent occupation" (permitting flow of workers to Israel) worked to ensure "strategic depth"; and new settlements on confiscated land did not struggle with the Israeli agricultural sector's scarcity of land but were "security settlements."

To illustrate the dialectical pattern illuminated above, the prewar liberal trends were reversed at several levels. First, several groups that arose during the 1960s now restrained themselves. There was a fall-off in militant labor organizing; a sharp decline in expressions of social protest, which had reached their peak in 1966 (76 cases) to about 45 cases in the years 1967–69 (Lehman-Wilzig, 1990, 34); the curbing of the political Left, which began to put forward pragmatic, moderate ideas for resolving the conflict (see Hermann, 1989, 260–297); renewed restrictions of the press, which showed itself ready to accept those restrictions commensurate with the security situation (Kahana and Cnaan, 1973; Negbi, 1990, 87–88); and the suspension of the prewar efforts to repeal the Defense (Emergency) Regulations, a vestige of the British Mandate that gave the government extraordinary powers (ibid., 154–155). So, with prewar liberal trends annulled, internal, potential obstacles to maintain a durable occupation were lifted.

Second, revalidation of the statist criteria for evaluating social action was apparent. It was triggered by the young generation, which seized on its military service to refute accusations by the founding generation that the youth's national contribution was inadequate (Keren, 1989a, 80–82). As in former processes, collective political passivity accompanied the accretion of social prestige. Symptomatic was *Fighters' Talk* (Kibbutz Movement, 1967), a compendium of responses to the war by the elite among the soldiers—the young generation of the Kibbutz Movement. They referred to the political leadership with some bitterness, but were not truly critical. They agonized over the morality of their behavior in the war, which had frequently contradicted their civilian principles, yet they drew no conclusions about the political order that had produced this situation. One critic of the book said its participants displayed a "shooting and crying" syndrome—striving for moral expiation without taking real responsibility. In the final analysis, that generation subjected itself to the ideological order and forsook its autonomy (Pitovsky, 1990). The same pattern was repeated in the conformity displayed by students (Shapira and Etzioni-Halevy, 1973, 27–36). This pattern indicates the extent to which values of compliance and obedience had taken root among Israeli youngsters, imbued, in no small measure, by military experience (see Ben-Eliezer, 1993). Manifestly, the military agenda did not meet with resistance from the young generation.

Furnished with internal, political legitimation, material capabilities, and American support, the country's leaders could neglect long-term implications of the territorial-political status quo and avoid having to exploit the war's gains for external political goals, even limited in scope, which *would not* have jeopardized the war's socioeconomic gains. Leaders' moves were unimpeded by political opposition. We now look at the practical expression of the military-dominated foreign policies to further substantiate the overall argument.

The Consequence: Missed Opportunities
for Peace/De-escalation

Israel obstructed progress toward a peaceful solution through the political dialogues that were held with Arab states through UN and American mediation. Israel, like the bordering Arab states, formally endorsed UN Resolution 242 of November 1967 calling for a peace settlement based on Israel's withdrawal, a resolution that signified Egypt's annulment of the Khartoum stand. For all practical purposes, however, Israel interpreted this resolution in accord with its new territorial interests, objecting to withdrawal to the prewar lines (Touval, 1980, 72).

The political vacuum in the regional arena was filled with warfare. Initiated by Egypt and fought along the Suez Canal from 1969 to 1970, the War of Attrition was the direct result of Israel's hold of the East Bank of the Suez Canal as a rigid defensive line. Defense Minister Moshe Dayan had not wanted to take the canal in the first place, but could only grant its capture ex post facto approval. If the canal had remained open to civilian shipping, the Egyptians would have had an incentive to keep calm. Against this background, Egypt launched the new round in order to alter the status quo. This war ended with a cease-fire mediated by the United States (see Bar-Siman-Tov, 1988; Yariv, 1985, 21–23; see more in chapter 5). The war demonstrated the manner in which Israel unsuccessfully dealt with the security dilemma: In reaction to Egyptian shelling of IDF outposts along the canal in 1969, Israeli ground troops carried out fruitless raids inside Egypt. The next step of escalation came in 1970. Encouraged by the United States (as it had been interpreted by Israeli ambassador, General Yitzhak Rabin, see Bar-Or, 1994, 39–41), Israel employed strategic air bombing. The Israelis did not even flinch from initiating dogfights with Egyptian planes flown by Soviet pilots. Finally in July 1970 both parties agreed to an American-mediated cease-fire, but the Soviet Union supplied Egypt with anti-aircraft missiles that seriously cut into the air superiority that Israel had enjoyed in the region (Yaniv, 1994, 250–258). Not for the first time, Israeli escalation exacerbated the military threat to Israel, resulting from its boundless aggravated threat on the Arab side. Here again, political considera-tion was dominated by military assessment and left no space for calculation of political alternatives or to how terminate the War of Attrition by political means (Bar-Or, 1994). At the bottom line, this war exacted a heavy toll in Israeli casualties—about 260—while the total casualties from the end of the Six-Day War to the end of the War of Attrition were more than 500 (Barzilai, 1992, 142–143).

In April 1970, during the War of Attrition, Prime Minister Golda Meir, who succeeded Eshkol after his death in 1968, refused to approve a meeting between Nahum Goldmann, the president of the World Zionist Congress, and Egyptian President Nasser, at the latter's request. Israel insisted on formal channels for negotiations as much as it was afraid of being under pressures leading to political concessions.

Subsequent to the war a similar scenario of missed opportunities to settle the conflict by political means repeated itself in 1970/71. Now the postwar social structure was already constructed and thus hardened external moves. At that time both Israel and Egypt approved U.S. Secretary of State William Rogers' and the UN mediator Gunar Jarring's initiatives to terminate the con-flict (for Israel the immediate political price was the Gachal's exit from the national unity government). But Israel's reluctance to undertake full with-drawal hindered on narrowing the gap between the sides; that reluctance was only solidified when in September 1970 Egypt violated the cease-fire agree-ment that terminated the War of Attrition along the Suez Canal. Egypt, for its part, advocated a peace treaty in return for full withdrawal (Shlaim, 1994, 46; Touval, 1980, 71–77).

Having rejected full withdrawal for peace, Israel could only advance interim agreements. Nonetheless, the next crucial case of missed political opportunities was the failure in 1971/72 to achieve an interim settlement with Egypt. Such an agreement would have entailed the IDF's withdrawal from the Suez Canal area so that the waterway could be reopened to civil navigation. The whole move was advanced by the United States but with Soviet cooperation as a part of détente and the other Soviet efforts to restrain Egypt (see Aronson, 1992, 136–137).

Whereas President Sadat of Egypt (Nasser's successor after his death in 1970) announced his willingness to make peace with Israel, Israel adhered to its rigid stand centered on retaining part of the territories in any future agreement. Nor did Israel agree to execute a pullback deep into Sinai, which entailed the canal-crossing of a small Egyptian military force for defence needs. (In the interim agreement that was eventually signed with Egypt in 1975, Israel made greater concessions for similar returns.) Dayan, who had initially opposed the IDF's occupation of the canal, supported the effort to reach an interim agreement with Egypt, at a high price, to solidify security calm. However, he was in a minority in the cabinet and was not even supported by the army, which invoked a purely military rationale to dismiss the initiative (Sella and Yishai, 1986, 20–21). And even when Israel reluctantly softened its position, it allowed the American diplomacy to let slip the opportunity to move toward peace. In retrospect, it is possible that if an interim settlement had been achieved in 1971/72, the October War (1973) would have been averted (see Gazit, 1984, 148–153; Rabin, 1979, 338–368; Touval, 1980, 77–80; Yaacobi, 1989).[12]

In parallel, Israel missed opportunities to advance political settlements with Jordan. In March 1972 King Hussein of Jordan proposed to establish a federation between the West Bank and the East Bank under the Hashemite Kingdom, but Israel rejected his proposal. Nor did Israel accept proposals offered by local Palestinian leaders in the occupied territories. Prime Minister Golda Meir even denied the existence of the Palestinians as a distinct nation. Still, tacit security arrangements were established between Israel and Jordan inspired by the traditional enmity toward Palestinians (see Shlaim, 1990). Jordan intensively struggled with Palestinian forces in September 1970, leading to the transfer of the Palestinian commands from Jordan to Lebanon. In this struggle Jordan was protected by Israel against an expected Syrian intervention. In a similar fashion, Jordan refrained from joining Egypt and Syria in the October War that they initiated (Kleiman, 1995).

Again, we do not have any indication regarding the Arab leaders' real intentions. But Israel declined to employ tactics of de-escalation to test the Arabs' willingness for peace. Advantages entailed in cooperation strategies—decreasing of uncertainty, downscaling of the arms race with the costs that it involved, changing of the other's attitudes through the very dynamics of de-escalation, and more—were not exploited again. Nor was achieving peace Israel's strategic goal in that period.

Back to the general argument, the episodes in the Egyptian and even in the Jordanian sectors confirm that, unlike the period from the late 1970s to the 1990s, reversal was still possible at relatively low political costs. At least the case of the interim agreement with Egypt shows that ex-Mapai leaders could have joined forces with Defense Minister Dayan to prevail over the IDF's opposition without taking domestic political risks (after all, the political level, as in former and later periods, overpowered the military command). The interim agreement, moreover, could have not jeopardized the worthy control over the Palestinian-populated territories.

But the war's political and socioeconomic effects—by augmenting the military domination—triumphed over political flexibility and worked to decrease this flexibility. Simply put, the more groups and state agencies gained from the state of war, the less autonomy the state possessed to reverse its move at a low cost. State–group relations rather than the seemingly ideological split between hawks and doves was the crucial factor.[13]

CONCLUSIONS

Similar to past conjunctions, the regional system offered a repertoire of strategic options composed of equally war-prone and peace-prone vectors. Israel opted for a force-oriented, self-help approach rather than struggle with the regional threat by means of establishing cooperative security regimes.

War-prone internal forces, in conjunction with war-prone external ones, counterbalanced their peace/cooperation-prone counterparts in a two-phase move: The empowerment of the military establishment lent preference to an escalation in response to border frictions during the mid-1960s. It was leading to a war with expanded goals ending with a fixed hold on a huge territory. Relatively moderate internal forces with Mapai in the center remained mute following the leadership reshuffling, letting the IDF implement its bellicose agenda autonomously. The military mind-set was trapped within a vicious cycle of escalation and counterescalation, accounting for Israel's moves.

At the second phase, the war-prone forces expanded to a vast coalition of those who gained from the occupation, encompassing doves and hawks alike. Furthermore, in both periods American aid played its role as an external war-prone vector in allowing Israeli initiatives. Also remember that the Khartoum Summit's resolutions, and nonsignificant peace-prone forces—taking the form of the extremist Left in Israel and murmurs of moderation in the Arab world—could not counterbalance their war-prone counterparts. In sum, given that Israel faced a crossroads in the external arena, the internal arena was the more crucial factor reducing the scope of decision-making. "Trial and error" prevailed again as a relatively moderate posture during the first months after June 1967 was gradually "corrected" by hawkish policy driven by new benefits stemming from the occupation.

By utilizing the freedom allowed by the external arena, the state could construct/reconstruct the main social agents' interests in congruence with the entrenchment of the occupation by which these groups benefited. It mitigated the tension between social interests, so that groups could realize short-term interests in the material and symbolic domains while neglecting former strategies that effectively could have eroded the state's dominance and, eventually, their own social dominance as well. Structurally, the underlying relations of exchange were dressed in a new form: Each of the Jewish groups exchanged its support for the occupation for realization of social interests. Unintentionally, agents, particularly those drawn from the Western elites, again worked to reempower the state and to increase its capacity to regulate interethnic relations. The fact that smooth reconstruction was at work questions the dominant perception among Israeli sociologists of the war as a "break," its origins exogenous to the Israeli system, impeding the country's development as a "normal," liberal society (see the critique by Levy and Peled, 1994, on Horowitz and Lissak, 1989; Kimmerling, 1989; Medding, 1990). Liberal and force-oriented postures were exchangeable strategies of dominant groups rather than implanted beliefs.

State empowerment, externally and internally alike, dialectically bore within it the seeds of its own decline. That decline became a lead-up to de-escalation, as the following chapters show.

CHAPTER 5

The Watershed Years (1968–81)

The wars that followed the 1967 War marked a new era: state–middle-class relations of exchange declined following the prolonged Israeli occupation. Overproduction of gains set external and internal limitations on bellicose policies. External Arab moves—in response to the occupation—inflicted losses on Israel beginning with the October War (1973). This coincided with the American shift from status-quo-oriented policies to the restraining of Israel's bellicosity, utilizing Israel's dependence on the United States. Paradoxically, however, growing sacrifice (which confrontation with the United States might have aggravated) was not in harmony with the rise of the expanded, Westerner-dominated consumerist middle class in the post-1967 War economic boom, cracking materialist militarism. Exit from, hence breakdown of, the war-based social structure was occurring.

Dominant groups then reconstructed their interests from war-prone to peace-prone. Through multiple forms of political action, middle-class groups bolstered externally originating restraints on using force and amplified the war-produced costs and losses. Together with echoing the more attractive opportunities innate in the post–Cold War international system relative to the decline of war-produced internal gains (mainly following the Intifada), this class narrowed the scope of policies available to the state other than de-escalation. A two-way negative movement from reconstruction of group interests (which generated the state's internal withdrawal) via failure in state mobilization to the state diminishment in its external arena (see chapter 1, figure 1.2) is at the root of chapters 5–6. This chapter focuses on the period between 1967 and 1981 in which the state zigzagged between a hard line and a soft line. The following chapter deals with the shift from the Lebanon War (1982) to the de-escalation of the 1990s.

MILITARY DEFICIENCIES AND MILITARY BURDEN: THE WAR OF ATTRITION AND THE OCTOBER WAR

The wars subsequent to the Six-Day War signified the decline of Israel's military capabilities and showed the limitations of Israel's use of military power. Israel not only faced difficulties in converting military achievements into political gains, but also in accomplishing its military objectives.

To begin, the lengthy War of Attrition, fought along the Suez Canal from 1969 to 1970, signaled the beginning of Israel's military decline, even though it was successful in retaining the territorial status quo (see chapter 4). The war exacted a heavy toll in Israeli casualties (about 260). Further, Egypt launched the war in order to get the Suez Canal reopened to civilian shipping. Israel, for its part, had short-term, military ends revolving around maintaining the status quo, ruling out political options (Bar-Or, 1994; Wald, 1987, 195). Israel's deterrent, based on strict military superiority, could not therefore deal with the political rationale of an effort to break a political status quo at the price of a military failure. Since, for the first time, a war ended without a clear decision, Israel's deficiency of deterrence on which it staked so much was apparent (Horowitz, 1985, 90–92). This diminishing of the Israeli deterrent was not only a factor exogenous to Israel's military. Rather, a force-oriented stance informed by domestic social interests hardened the offensive doctrine to the point of an obsolete perception relative to the reality shaped by the Six-Day War.

Equally if not more significant, for the first time in Israel's history the necessity of war was questioned by various groups. Most striking was the "Letter of the High-School Seniors." Sent to Prime Minister Golda Meir by a group of students on the eve of their draft, the letter called on the government to follow through on the peace process in order to justify their future military service. It was written in the direct aftermath of Meir's refusal to approve a meeting between Nahum Goldmann, the president of the World Zionist Congress, and Egyptian President Nasser, at the latter's request. The "Letter of the High-School Seniors" sparked a public furor because its authors were part of the core of the social elite and because its style was unconventional in terms of protest expected from the young generation in the era's prevailing political culture, in that it made military service contingent on a moral justification instead of unquestioned obedience (on the letter, see Yaacobi, 1989, 20). Potential soldiers demonstrated their ability to invoke military service to legitimize political action, an expression of the deeply embedded military patterns in the political discourse.

Indeed, even less legitimate was another protest, the provocative musical satire *Queen of the Bathtub*, a pioneering attempt to question the necessity of the protracted conflict. It voiced youngsters' protest against the fruitless sacrifices of the war, a far cry from the "rules of discourse" (see Alexander, 1985,

143–149). Ultimately, wide public protest forced the theater to close the show. Political considerations with regard to military policies therefore figured in the growing public sensitivity to human losses in wars (see Bar-Or 1994, 35–36). Still, it is hard to evaluate their ultimate impact on Israel's decision to accept the U.S.-initiated cease-fire.

The entrenchment of the occupation and missed opportunities to obtain a comprehensive or interim agreement with Egypt were the sparks that ignited the October War (or the Yom Kippur War) of 1973. It began with a surprise attack executed simultaneously by Egypt and Syria, violating the cease-fire arrangements, in an effort to break the political status quo. Despite a series of intelligence warnings, the IDF was not deployed properly to meet the Arab offensive. The misreading of the situation came to be known as the "Blunder" [*Ha'mechdal*]. To no small degree it was the fruit of the ascendancy of military thought in the wake of the Six-Day War. The essence of the intelligence blunder was the mistaken conception that the Arab states, despite their leaders' bellicose rhetoric and territorial interests, would not go to war as long as Israel retained air superiority. Again, the Arabs' political rationale clashed with Israel's military rationale, resulting in a deficient deterrent. The intelligence chiefs also overestimated the amount of time that Israel would have at its disposal to prepare for an Arab attack. Nor was their appraisal of Israel's battlefield superiority wholly realistic (Lanir, 1983, 18–30, 54–75). The reliance on the doctrine of "defensible borders" was also reflected in the absence of a clear definition of casus belli. This lack prevented the leadership from ordering the IDF to make a preemptive strike even though the Egyptian-Syrian plan had become known some hours before the projected start of hostilities (see Posen, 1988, 27–29). Israel failed in coping successfully with the security dilemma: By increasing its security at the expense of its neighbors' sovereignty, the latter were compelled to take countermeasures. As those measures were more effective than ever (motivation, coordination, new weapons systems, etc.), they aggravated the threat to Israel's security.

Social factors, moreover, also played their role in producing the "Blunder." Israel's refraining from launching a preemptive attack was highly stimulated by American pressures, whose effectiveness stemmed from Israel's dependence on the United States not only for arms but for maintaining the social order as well. Further, grasping the multiple price of the call-up in the "waiting period" for the Six-Day War, the War of Attrition, and in May 1973 (when Israel mobilized part of the reserves in a war alarm), the politicians were reluctant to allow a full call-up on the eve of the October War despite the IDF's demand (Yaniv, 1994, 270–272). As Yaniv (ibid.) notes, moreover, Israel's government responded to social pressures (the Oriental Black Panthers' protest was part of it; see below) to divert resources from defense to welfare. Hence, the drastic cut on the eve of the October War of the defense budget and the basic decision to cut compulsory service. So, the byproducts of the post-1967 economic boom—multidimensional dependence on the United States and social pressures—aggravated the military deficiency.

Yet despite the adverse opening conditions, the reserves were mobilized rapidly and the IDF was able to contain the offensives on both fronts and seize Arab territory it had not held before the war began. But again, Israel accepted American pressures for cease-fire before completing its victory.

Cyclically, the military deficiency that resulted from this process further increased the general defense burden on Israeli society. This growing burden was felt at several levels. First, the total casualties of Israel from the end of the Six-Day War to 1974 were about 3,500, more than 0.1 percent of the total Jewish population. Second, a considerable extension of military service ran up during the years: Compulsory service for males was extended from thirty to thirty-six months during the War of Attrition; the expansion and altered nature of reserve duty, with routine security assignments on a large scale, added to the original exclusive function of preparing for war. In general, this burden became 60 percent to 100 percent higher than the levels of the 1960s (measured by the yearly crude length of reserve duty), leading some to emigrate from Israel (Cohen, 1988). Third, the defense budget rose to about 28 percent of the GNP or 16 percent of the GDP if we subtract the American and other external resources, compared with about 21 percent and 14 percent, respectively, in 1968–73 (Berglas, 1986, 176; Trop, 1989, 52). Direct taxation of the GNP rose from 12 percent in 1967 to 24 percent in 1976 (Barnett, 1992, 229). Fourth, the state suffered from a fiscal crisis, particularly the increase in the national debt from about $980 million in 1965 to more than $9 billion in 1978, mainly attributable to military costs and the growth and sustenance of a high level of standard of living (Ben-Porath, 1986b, 20–21). The growing American aid covered only about 40 percent of the defense budget (Trop, 1989, 52). Concurrently, real wages declined about 3 percent in 1973–76 (Ben-Porath, 1986b, 11), while the rate of per capita income grew by 0.8 percent annually in 1972–82, in contrast to about 5 percent annually between 1922 and 1972 (Ben-Porath, 1986c, 28–29; data refer to the Jewish economy in Palestine until 1947 and in Israel after 1950).

Nevertheless, unlike in former wars, the military burden was not offset by social prestige conferred on the army and its constitutive groups. Despite its objective achievements, the army was perceived to have failed in its primary mission. The heights of its triumph in the aftermath of the Six-Day War were matched by the depths of the public disappointment that were manifested six years later. This was compounded by a well-publicized "war of the generals," centering on who bore responsibility for the circumstances of the war's outbreak and for the tactics that were employed in some of its stages (Ben-Dor, 1977; Lanir, 1983, 56). The upshot was that the army's image, not only as an effective organization but also as one that was united and separate from politics, suffered. Criticism of the army, particularly in the press, was in part a reaction to the uncritical approach that had prevailed until October 1973, and which may itself have been partly to blame for the "Blunder" (see Goren, 1977; Schiff, 1974, 238–245).

The economic burden, moreover, was also inequitably imposed since gains were inequitably earned. Drawing from Shalev (1992, 236–306), instead of promoting economic growth and working to decrease social disparities, the state pumped its resources, including U.S. aid, into the rewarding of preferred groups and business corporations. First, the state subsidized costly military industries (private, state-, and Histadrut-owned alike) over and above what it would have cost to purchase weapons from the United States. More than ever weapons became an export product, rising from $50 million to $2.5 billion after the October War (Yaniv, 1994, 288). Second, under the state's auspices, concentration of capital was set in the hands of a few giant corporations, mainly, the three biggest banks that controlled industrial conglomerates (such as *Clal* and *Koor*). These power centers enjoyed significantly larger direct and indirect state subsidies than in the 1960s, raising their profits disproportionately to their real output and level of taxation.

Third, some trade unions were greatly empowered. This stemmed from the growth of business corporations and the public sector conjoined with the Histadrut bias toward middle-class-based trade unions. Remember, the Histadrut drew its power from those unions. Consequently, the state's capacity to restrain the wages of preferred groups became more difficult. Moreover, those unions even took part in lobbying for their firms' interests (see also Grinberg, 1991b, 64–97). Fourth, the nature of the occupation (the exploitation of both labor and markets) had the effect of reinforcing the "backward" sectors of Israel's economy, again under the state's auspices and subsidies. Thus, the state's traditional inclination toward capital, upper middle-class groups, and middle-class-based trade unions empowered these forces to the point that they could stand by themselves vis-à-vis the state.[1] Consequently, the state's available resources for meeting various internal demands were reduced.

Nonetheless, to assure social stability, real wages increased again from 1976 mostly under the Likud-led government that took power in 1977 (see below). Per capita consumption then increased about 35 percent during the years 1972–82, while production per capita rose no more than 8 percent (Ben-Porath, 1986c, 34). Two key policies were instrumental: the self-styled "economic liberalization" policy aimed at lessening controls on foreign currency and the allowing of manipulation of the value of stocks in banks utilized to increase profits of investors. These policies, accompanied by a growing national debt, brought about a spiraling inflation beginning in the mid-1970s. In 1985 inflation stood at an annual rate of about 400 percent.

Clearly, unable to function autonomously in the face of conflicting political demands—mainly capital growth, military buildup, and retaining of welfare systems—the state's dependence on the U.S. aid increased. This aid helped Israel escape a sharp increase in taxation and a diversion of resources from civilian expenditures (net taxes actually declined in 1974–80). American aid, moreover, helped Israel deal with the national debt and compensate for both the war's losses and the growing costs of energy following the Arab oil boycott after the October War (Barnett, 1992, 231–233; Berglas, 1986, 186–188). This dependence meant, beyond supply of weapons, reliance on aid to maintain the standard of living with a flow of external revenues. Had the Americans withdrawn or drastically diminished the aid, the Israeli social order could have been destabilized if subsidies had to be cut to business corporations and greater taxation had to be imposed on middle-class groups. Equally significant, mobility of Orientals and Israeli Palestinians could have been interrupted as well with implications for social stability. Notwithstanding this dependence, the scale was not tipped from war to peace due to the appearance of counterbalancing internal demands.

NEW FORMS OF COLLECTIVE ACTION

A growing inequitable burden sponsored only in part by America marked the beginning of a new era when for many groups militarism no longer drove material well-being, but, rather, hindered its advance. For other groups militarism might replace unattainable material gains. As for the state, it lost a portion of its autonomy relative to capital power centers and those groups who might practically claim that their relations of exchange with the state had been undermined.

Similar to past experience in Europe and America, the state created through the wars a *political opportunity structure* for collective action embracing four processes (see, at the theoretical level, Tarrow, 1994, 62–99).[2] First, the more military participation was extended without symmetric quid pro quos, the more groups could invoke their military contribution in order to make multiple demands pertinent to military policies (similar to the high school students during the War of Attrition). Chapter 1 (see mainly note 12) has addressed this pattern by drawing from the European and American experience. As for the second process propelling collective action, the more the boundaries of political discourse were extended following the perpetuation of the occupation and the more the traditional boundaries between Left and Right became blurred as a result, the more new groups could take part in shaping this discourse. Third, the rise in the standard of living brought higher levels of education, greater exposure to the media, and more leisure time—elements that tend to heighten public awareness and stimulate political involvement (see Sella and Yishai, 1986, 49). Finally, the more the internal expansion of the state took its course, the more the role of the party-based social networks as mediators between groups and the state waned. So, autonomization of social groups was at work. The efficient "gatekeepers," that is, the parties and the Histadrut, declined following the reconstruction of state–party–group relations (see also notes 5–7 below; on the concept of "gatekeepers," see Easton, 1965, 122–123). State autonomy to conduct the external conflict was affected by these processes as we shall now see by sketching the main appearances of collective action.

The Orientals' Political Action

The Orientals' political awakening was rooted in the state-directed persistence of social disparity between the two Jewish ethnic groups (see chapter 4). However, its rapid spread was due to a large extent on the ability of both Oriental activists and rightist parties to take advantage of the underlying political opportunity. Increasing military participation and the reconstruction of political discourse played a key role.

The reemergence of Orientals' protest, following the fiasco of Wadi Salib, began in 1971 with the organization of the Black Panthers by young Moroccan Jews concentrated in Jerusalem—nonmobile Orientals, in our terms. They were appalled by the huge social gaps that existed between the second generation of Oriental immigrants and the veteran Western population, which became apparent following the post-1967 economic boom and particularly when the War of Attrition ended and social issues gained more attention (Stone, 1982, 291).

One of their major demands was to be drafted. At the time, the IDF did not draft individuals from distressed areas who had not completed a certain level of schooling. In so doing, the Panthers acknowledged the legitimacy of the "rules of the game" in Israeli society, including military service as the supreme criterion for the allocation of rewards (Etzioni-Halevi, 1975, 505; Yishai, 1987, 61). Equally significant, this was the first time that a protest movement had specifically linked social rewards with military service. With the importance ascribed to military symbols in the post-1967 political discourse, for many Orientals it was army service as such that mattered, for they perceived that service (in both practice and potential) as a central channel of social mobility. However, they were less concerned about their status within the IDF. In essence, they were challenging the particularist inclinations of a central mechanism of reproduction, but in a roundabout, muted manner that did not imply direct criticism of the IDF. The army's ethos of egalitarianism remained unquestioned. Similar to the Wadi Salib group, this case suggests that the tension between the military service-based universalist criteria for real membership in Israeli society and social inequality bore the potential for Orientals' protest. The Black Panthers were overtly political and their struggle won much sympathy, albeit short-lived, from various political camps. The government, in any event, responded by expanding conscription among nonmobile Orientals. A special track of service was created for them, which did not necessarily coincide with the army's real professional needs (Kimmerling, 1979, 30–32). In addition, the government adopted a few measures in the realm of welfare policy. The political cost of quelling the Black Panthers' protest amounted to no more than that. The Black Panthers, however, as much as the Wadi Salib group, epitomized a social rather than an ethnic protest, as the groups underscored social demands against the background of material deprivation, rather than cultural demands to struggle against ethnic marginalization. Social protest shifted to ethnic-oriented political action after the 1973 October War.

The Orientals' consciousness of the linkage between army service and the allocation of resources was heightened following the post-1967 wars, in which many soldiers from the Oriental communities participated and died (either as combatants or as servicemen in auxiliary professions; again, the overall trend of Orientals' contribution has to be estimated in the absence of formal data). This period also saw the emergence of popular senior officers of Oriental origin (notably the generals Avigdor Kahalani, Yitzhak Mordechai, Yekutiel Adam, and Moshe Levy, the last serving as chief of staff from 1983 to 1987). Orientals showed a greater willingness to volunteer for combat units—even compared to kibbutz youngsters (Zamir, 1987). In addition, the social exposure to Western soldiers improved the Oriental draftees' self-image, as later data revealed (Schwartzwald and Amir, 1994). Finally, many disadvantaged Oriental youngsters were drafted under the policy of giving a "second chance" to the young who had been neglected by the civilian educational system—one of the Black Panthers' demands (see Eitan, 1985, 168–172).[3]

Such developments stimulated expectations among the less mobile Orientals—materially mobile and nonmobile—for increased social status in return for their military contribution. Basic material gains originating in the post-1967 economic boom and the supply of protection was no longer sufficient to reproduce the relations of exchange between the state and Orientals; on the contrary, they gave rise to more demands. To some degree, these expectations fueled the construction of a hawkish identity and stimulated protest among Orientals. Collective action was inevitable.

Orientals then began to ask themselves why the interethnic equality that prevailed on the battlefield was not replicated in civil society. As one of their activists put it,

I felt that even before I got to the army they already didn't want me. Was I unfit or something? . . . In the army I proved that I was a good soldier [in an elite infantry brigade]. It was a kind of stage in growing up, *that caused a break between the house and the outside.* . . . I discovered how many obligations we had [in the army] and what rights we received [outside] (quoted in Michael, 1984, 121, my emphasis).

This description was typical of an Oriental youngster's attempt to find his niche in the army, though well aware of the barriers. His success as a soldier released him from psychological shackles originating in childhood experiences of ethnic deprivation. At the same time, he saw for himself the asymmetry in the allocation of rewards in the society. This stimulated him to take social action.

Another activist claimed (although after the Lebanon War): "Ethnicity was defeated on the battlefield. . . . The euphoria of the fraternal spirit among soldiers and on the home front [must be] exploited in peacetime as well" (quoted in Smooha, 1984b, 24). Another explained: "It was precisely in the Lebanon War that a gross disparity revealed itself between the equality in victims and comradeship in battle, and the inequality in the society between the Oriental class and the Ashkenazi [Western] class" (Idan, 1983, 41). Growing social awareness was also furthered due to the weakness displayed by the IDF in these wars, exposing the Westerner-dominated high command's incapacity and thereby stimulating Orientals to take a more critical stand toward the Westerner-dominated establishment (ibid.).[4]

The linkage between the Orientals' participation in war and their political action is further seen in the contrast between the approaches of the Black Panthers of the 1970s and the Oriental activists of the 1980s. Whereas the former concentrated their demands on being allowed to serve in the army as a lever for attaining material rewards, the latter concentrated on the return for actually expending service. Implicitly, from their point of view, it appeared less relevant that the jobs assigned to Orientals in the army still reflected an unequal ethno-functional division of labor. Being alienated from the dominant culture, Orientals emphasized their genuine contribution in the national-military sphere, contrasting it with their cultural marginalization, rather than only their material deprivation by the state under the leadership of the Alignment Party. As one of the activists put it:

Today I'm an officer, and when I go to the army [for reserve duty] they look at me, they can't tell whether I'm Ashkenazi or Sephardi or Moroccan. "What, you're Moroccan?" and they raise their eyebrows. Or I pass through a group of soldiers and hear them say: "What? He's a Moroccan?" They find it hard to believe that a Moroccan could reach such a rank (quoted in Swirski, 1989, 69, the monologue documented in the late 1970s).

Possibly, this frustration was furthered by the statement of Chief of Staff General Mordechai Gur in 1978. He compared the Oriental soldiers to the Arabs and declared that "Many years will pass before Oriental[s] . . . will succeed in competing with the mentality . . . of the West" (quoted in Roumani, 1991, 71).

This frame of mind coincided with Orientals' increasing hostility toward the Histadrut, the organization that epitomized the Alignment, for its quasi-statist role in restraining workers in the secondary labor market.[5] But, with their decreasing material dependence on the Histadrut (in the situation of full employment that prevailed after 1967), they could act more autonomously in the political domain. By enjoying less leverage to exchange services for political support mainly in the socially peripheral sectors (Orientals and Israeli Palestinians), the Histadrut declined as a mechanism of political mobilization working for the Alignment (see Shalev, 1992, 268–275, 286–290).

A clear expression of Orientals' political awakening appeared in the elections of 1977 when the Labor Party–Mapam Alignment was dramatically weakened in the Oriental constituencies in favor of the victorious Likud Party. Most of the Orientals (at the peak, about 60 percent), especially of the second generation, were attracted to the hawkish Likud Party relative to 30 to 50 percent in former elections, although this party had been led by Westerners. The Likud Party, led by Menachem Begin and composed of Gachal and several small right-wing parties, then joined forces with the National Religious Party (NRP) and the middle-class-dominated Democratic Movement for Change (DMC), to oust the Alignment from power after more than forty-five years of dominance (see Arian, 1975, 1977).[6] This trend deepened in the 1981 election campaign, which was labeled an ethnic campaign: The veteran Western population tended to support the Alignment bloc and to favor a dovish solution to the Arab-Israeli conflict, whereas the Orientals backed the Likud and took a decidedly hawkish stance (Shamir and Arian, 1982).

Unlike the Westerner-dominated Alignment, the Likud offered the Orientals a different vision of Israeli society. Rejecting the secular, Mamlachtiyut-era myths, the Likud offered partnership focused on the Jewish underpinnings of Israeli society, while taking advantage of the occupation, which made symbolically significant sites accessible again to the Israeli Jewish community, such as the Old City of Jerusalem and Hebron. For many groups it was a stimulus to reassert their identification with Jewish tradition. Symptomatic was the use of the religious concept *Eretz Israel* (Land of Israel) rather than *Medinat Israel* (State of Israel), the term prevalent in the rhetoric of Mamlachtiyut until the 1970s. The redefinition of geographic borders evoked ancient symbols and associations that often supplanted those prevailing in the civil realm. Traditional Judaism, which invoked the primordial in the building of the Israeli Jewish community, began to demarcate the boundaries of Israeli society and challenged the notion of "Israeliness."

Traditionalism attracted nonmobile Orientals who were alienated from the dominant Western-secular culture identified with Israeliness. The rise of traditionalism, therefore, gave Orientals a sense of belonging to the society as equal partners, without blurring their ethnic distinctiveness. Moreover, this status was not conditional on contributing to the state—primarily through military service—as required by the Labor movement-crafted Mamlachtiyut. Equally, if not more significant, this redemarcation distinguished the Orientals from the Israeli Palestinians, and hence underscored their preferential position within Israeli society (on the cultural change, see Fischer, 1991; Kimmerling, 1985c; Liebman, 1989; Peled, 1991; Shapiro, 1991, 164–172).

The Likud even hammered home the point that the country's national-military achievements could not have been attained without the Orientals. The party's leader, Prime Minister Menachem Begin, concentrated on that theme in his speeches at mass outdoor rallies in the 1981 election campaign. With his rhetorical skills, Begin gave the Orientals flocking to his rallies from development towns and distressed urban neighborhoods the feeling that they themselves had participated in the army's heroic exploits (Gertz, 1983). Begin could thus highlight the joint contribution of both ethnic communities to the national struggle and deflect the ridicule heaped on him by a popular entertainer working for the Alignment during the campaign, who charged that Alignment supporters had served in front-line combat units, while the Orientals had been posted to rear-guard service units (Eisenstadt, 1985, 498–499).

Hawkish political identity thus did not derive only from Orientals' hostile encounters with Arabs in their countries of origin (Shamir and Arian, 1982) or from their competition in the Israeli labor market (Peled, 1990). Orientals' hawkish orientation can also be construed as a defense of their gains, going from property and lands left by Palestinian refugees in the 1950s, to the 1967 War-incited prestige, social mobility, and symbolic assets. It was the Orientals' satisfaction with these gains that worked to shape the hawkish identity of many of them. Hawkish identity was to a large extent even a counterreaction to the Western Left seeking to devalue Orientals' gains by criticizing the IDF and advocating the termination of the conflict (see below; see Ariely, 1983, 158, and also the comparative discussions on the conscription of peripheral groups, which support this line of interpretation, in chapter 4, note 7). Shaping of ethnic-political identity signified the unique route of nonmobile Orientals' social mobility.

Using the Likud model of political mobilization along ethnic lines, which included the promotion of Oriental politicians, the selection by Orientals of an ethnic-based action, rather than class-based, from the repertoire of options for collective action was more likely: The Orientals' hawkish orientation implicitly epitomized a demand to take part in steering national security and to remove decisions from the exclusive institutional framework of the Westerner-dominated traditional party elites (see Nagel, 1995, on resource competition).

The interethnic struggle thus focused on indirect control of the army. In this struggle, explicit criticism of the army for its part in structuring disparity was *removed* from the discursive repertoire. Unlike ethnic groups in other countries (for comparison, see Enloe, 1980), Orientals did not question the military's ethos of egalitarianism nor did they denounce the Westerners' dominance within the army—a stark contrast to their trenchant criticisms of other prestigious institutions such as the courts and the kibbutz.

Clearly, the deep-seated legitimacy of the ethos of egalitarianism conjoined with the centrality of security in Israeli experience channeled the Orientals' social protest into indirect strategies, even when many of them became aware of the illusory nature of the ethos. In the words of one Oriental activist: "The rejection of Orientalness is found *even* in the army, which is considered a *true* melting pot" (Yemini, 1986, 98, my emphasis). Furthermore, promoted, exposed to Western influence, and awarded symbolic rewards they saw as a pass-key to Israeli society, Orientals were inclined to shield the ethos of egalitarianism. It could be invoked in the struggle to improve their status in the army, to demand that they be drafted, and, primarily, to enhance the social value of their military contribution as a means of legitimizing their extramilitary demands. Orientals, therefore, tended to refrain from devaluing their accomplishments, in practice and potential, by questioning that ethos.

Nevertheless, by their very activity Orientals unintentionally worked to reproduce the social structure within which they functioned and which placed them in a peripheral position as long as that very ethos partially legitimized their actual lesser status. And to the extent that the Orientals conducted a political struggle within the realm of the Arab-Israeli conflict, they neglected ethnic class action aimed at drastic change in interethnic power relations; an alienated group such as the Black Panthers might have put forward demands of this kind. Interestingly, an essentially proletarian segment was more attracted by a right-wing party's ethnic-cultural formula than by the social egalitarian approach. In consequence, Orientals, in practice, protested against the ideological trappings of the inequitable social structure, the Mamlachtiyut, while neglecting the underpinnings of that structure itself. So, it was Mamlachtiyut as *a strategy of de-ethnization* that was enfeebled by the emergence of the Orientals' challenge (Herzog, 1985); however, the mixture of the Orientals' war-created gains with the deeply rooted paradigm of Mamlachtiyut within the IDF accounted for the very essence of their protest—the channeling of a class struggle to the political-ethnic arena. Mamlachtiyut as a tacit *strategy reproducing interclass relations* then celebrated its success (see, at the comparative level, Thompson, 1989, 98–100, on the case of African Americans).[7]

It was not only Orientals who took advantage of the post-1967 structural opportunity. We turn now to examine how the Westerner-dominated middle class achieved the same effect.

The Middle-class Challenge:
Discharged Soldiers, Gush Emunim, and Peace Now

The post-1967 wars left their imprint in the significant broadening of challenging political participation. Almost as soon as the guns fell silent in October 1973, vociferous protest movements sprang up in Israel demanding the government's resignation for its mishandling of the war. These protests were notably initiated by reservists who had fought in outposts along the Suez Canal, infantrymen who had experienced the most horrible events. Remembering the structural opportunity created for collective action by war, innate tensions within the military doctrine played an important role.

Since the 1950s, two trends in military doctrine had been unintentionally instrumental in reducing war's political costs, or, to put it differently, minimizing the opportunity structure. The first trend was to decrease the military burden on civilian reservists, be it by both using conscripts and shortening the duration of war by means of offensive doctrine. A second trend was to alter the composition of the army from infantry-based to technology-based. The nature of infantry combat is such that the soldier engages in direct contact with the enemy. Soldiers who have experienced face-to-face combat are more likely to develop the potential for political participation after the war, since they become aware of the human meaning of war for victims and victimizers alike. The increase in armor, artillery, and air capabilities meant relying on weapons that create distance, hence alienation, of combatant from victim. The resulting desensitization to human meaning reduces the likelihood that military participation will be converted into political action.[8] Yet, since the state after 1967 refrained from a clear-cut decision between offensive and defensive postures by which a versatile, costly military was formed (Wald, 1987, 233–240), reserve duty was expanded. Add to this the reliance on rigid, infantry-based defensive lines, and the initial trends were set back, placing a heavy burden on reserve infantry units.

The immediate political effect was the heavy losses suffered by the Alignment in the elections held two months after the war. Its dominance, however, did not end until four years later. Concurrently, a judicial commission of inquiry was appointed, the Agranat Commission. The commission's findings and political protests induced the resignation, in 1974, of Golda Meir and Moshe Dayan as prime minister and defense minister; they were replaced by Yitzhak Rabin, the architect of the Six-Day War, and Shimon Peres, one of the architects of the Sinai Campaign.

Nonetheless, the primary challenge to state institutions came from Gush Emunim ("Bloc of the Faithful"), founded in 1973. Central to the appearance of this movement was the renewal of the political debate over the state's borders in the aftermath of the 1967 War. To recall, this debate took place within the military-dominated political discourse that legitimized partial annexation. That controversy grew more intense as Israel seemed determined to hold the territories permanently and not to decide the question by political methods. Further, a debate over the territorial borders expanded into a debate over the substantive borders of the Israeli political community, which had been blurred by the de facto incorporation of the territories and their Palestinian population (Evron, 1988, 345–346; Kimmerling, 1985c, 1989). As Lustick (1993, 386–395) put it, the occupation marked the breakdown of the Green Line (the 1949 armistice borders) as the hegemonic conception of the territorial composition of the state. This was a crisis of Mamlachtiyut that signified the dominance of the Zionist secular school of thought over the religious one, namely, the adherence to establishing a Jewish state as a goal in itself while abandoning the religious-messianic idea of the "Whole Land of Israel." Nevertheless, the existence of a Palestinian majority in the West Bank and the Gaza Strip and the internal controversy over the territories' fate blocked a hegemonic construction based on the "Whole Land of Israel." Beyond empowering the Likud, the underlying breakdown legitimized the entry of new groups into the political arena. The Orientals' action via the Likud was one expression; religious youngsters, who had not played a meaningful role in the pre-1967 political discourse, signified another expression embodied by Gush Emunim.

Gush Emunim was established by young, observant Westerners demanding the application of Israeli law in the West Bank and the establishment there of Jewish settlements. Gush Emunim staged protest demonstrations that included illegal settlement in the occupied territories, violent attacks on local Palestinians, and, subsequently, resistance to the two-stage peace moves with Egypt made by the Rabin and Begin governments (see below). Central to those activities was the movement's capacity to both draw organizationally from the National Religious Party and prompt it to take advantage of the party's membership in the government coalition to advance the Gush's demands (Lustick, 1988, 42–71). Viewed from a broader perspective, Gush Emunim challenged the state's legitimation system by its refusal to recognize the state as the primary object of its loyalty. The movement professed allegiance to a entity that was exogenous to the state: the metaphysical idea of the "Whole Land of Israel." Some of its leaders even supported the establishment of a theocracy. Gush Emunim denied that the state possessed the authority to withdraw from the occupied territories and rejected the military logic for retaining the territories in favor of a religious motive. Therefore its activists did not hesitate to clash with soldiers who tried to prevent them from establishing settlements in the territories without the government's authorization. The movement thus tried to put forward an alternative source to secular legitimation, whereas the young generation of secular Westerners accepted the state's authority passively (on the comparison, see Oz, 1983, 131–133; on the Gush's ideology, see Lustick, 1988, 72–90; Miron, 1987; Moskovitch, 1992, 82–85).

The emergence of Gush Emunim as a group saliently distinct from the secular youngsters is also attributable to the difficulties its members encountered when trying to incorporate into the secular-dominated middle class. The very identification of the IDF—a pivotal mechanism of mobility into the middle class—with secularism stimulated the appearance of the group. Secularism was embodied in the dominant figures who personified the army, the rational-secular character of any modern army, and the identification of the military gains with the Labor Movement. An Israel Television personality, who grew up in a religious family, explained: "In the 1960s, we who were members of the religious [young] generation felt inferior to the secular youngsters. They went to Unit 101 and to the [ultra-elite] reconnaissance patrols, while we tailed along behind them" (Israel Segal, Israel Television, April 4, 1994). It was against this background that Gush Emunim tried to exploit its military contribution, which stood out in the Six-Day War and afterward, as a lever for substantive political involvement. As an alternative to the basic value of army service, the Gush put forward the idea of settlement in the territories. In effect, as was often noted in public discourse, Gush Emunim tried to resurrect the "pioneer" ethos that had been displaced by the symbol of the "fighter." This argument gains credence from the fact that, as already mentioned, Gush Emunim activists did not recoil from clashing physically with the army, an event without precedent in the history of relations between the IDF and civilian groups.[9]

The roots of Gush Emunim explain why it made no effort to enlist the support of the Orientals, who were also hawkish in their political outlook. Yet the different social origins of each group produced a different type of hawkishness. Gush Emunim was firmly ensconced in the country's dominant social class, even if it was culturally peripheral. And the Orientals found little to attract them in a movement that emphasized its members' participation in the military effort as part of the overall Westerner contribution. Orientals gave their support to movements, such as the Likud, which expanded the concept of Israeliness into areas of expression in which Westerner dominance was not blatant. As hawkish (like dovish) stands were socially constructed, ideology per se could not provide a common ground for cooperation.

Thus, notwithstanding its grassroots image stemming from its singular political claim, Gush Emunim was a state-incubated movement owing to the latter's durable hold on the territories. A decade before the Six-Day War, the capture of the Sinai Peninsula had also given rise to messianic visions, encapsulated in Ben-Gurion's pronouncement about the establishment of "The Third Kingdom of Israel." But, unlike the case of the 1970s, that mood was dashed immediately upon the IDF's withdrawal from the peninsula.

Peace Now, an extraparliamentary mass movement founded in 1978 by retired officers, was in some ways the mirror image of Gush Emunim. It urged the government to show greater flexibility in order to expedite the peace process, which had taken a dramatic turn following the visit to Israel by President Sadat in November 1977. Left-wing groups then felt that a historic opportunity was slipping away because of the Begin government's rigid stand.

Peace Now was a movement of the social elite, drawing its support from the upper middle class and in particular from academe and the professions. The movement's leaders liked to emphasize their impressive military record primarily as officers. By adhering to the "rules of discourse," Peace Now became a legitimate movement although it was the first time in the state's history that discharged soldiers in practice endeavored to impact on matters of national security outside of the traditional party elites.

The appearance of this group was directly triggered by the fact that young, middle-class Westerners felt estranged from the new social-political group that held the reins of power in the Begin regime. Peace Now, however, was preceded by several peace movements (see Hermann, 1989); its unprecedented success in enlisting mass support is attributable not only to the change of government but also to the tension implicit in the combination of a heavy military burden with a growing standard of living. This burden became more and more incongruent with the materialist values with which Israeli society was infused from the late 1970s. Materialism was expressed in the trend that "[the traditionally prevailing] socialist ideology has lost support for two of its classical foci: The requisite of a state-owned and state-regulated economy (the production aspect), and the priority of individual welfare over national strength and economic growth (the humanitarian aspect)" (Gottlieb and Yuchtman-Yaar, 1985, 408; see also Talmud, 1985). To put it differently, this trend, accompanied by the right wing's taking on Mamlachtiyut, signaled the initial demise of this ideology's dominance.

Thus, the security burden became heavier in *proportional* rather than absolute terms. To put it differently, gains and costs of external occurrences were always appreciated by multiple social agents rather than high strategic thinkers alone. And the more costs were not compensated by new gains, and the more people had more attractive options for their time and their money than participation in war, and the more Israel's very existence was seen stable, then the less the wars' costs became tolerable. Thus, paradoxically, as the state worked to raise the standard of living as a means of legitimizing its rule and the military burden, it increased social groups' expectations. Materialism and militarism gradually became competing, not mutually supporting, values within the framework of materialist militarism. Peace Now's supporters, moreover, were mainly from professions a far cry from those groups that had mostly benefited from the occupation (business corporations, military industry, entrepreneurs utilizing the Palestinian labor force and market, and powerful trade unions). The burden was proportionally affected by differential benefits. Hence, Peace Now's constituency was open to the political alternatives to the military-dominated foreign policy as posited by the group. As this book points out, more than once Israel refrained from exploiting opportunities to de-escalate the conflict. Nonetheless, these events had not stimulated public protest meditated by efficient entrepreneurs such as Peace Now until *internal* processes created the suitable opportunity.

More speculatively, with the blow that the army's prestige had suffered in the October War—a prestige on which this group's social status was based— and the increased presence of Orientals in the army, no longer an exclusive Westerner stronghold, Western youngsters could take a more autonomous stand. Thus, unlike their past tendency to favor a bellicose approach, as that was a contributing factor to the group's social dominance, Peace Now's supporters took a critical position, downgrading the symbolic assets that military service conferred. Middle-class groups then actually begun to reconstruct their social interests. By "reconstruction" I mean that groups' interests have remained fixed for the long term (to ensure social dominance) but their instrumental focus shifted from entrenchment of the conflict to de-escalation.

This interpretation is lent support from the stand taken by Peace Now toward the Orientals. Although Peace Now tried to enlist the Orientals' support, the two groups were mutually alienated. Peace Now explained, to no avail, that peace was in the interest of the Orientals, for they would benefit by the cessation of the massive diversion of resources to the maintaining of the occupation. Still, Peace Now concentrated its efforts on downscaling the conflict and did not become involved in social issues, particularly as it relied on the upper middle class (on Peace Now, see Bar-On, 1985, 13–21, 89–91, 146–159).

Unlike Gush Emunim, Peace Now was a conservative movement, refraining from challenging the state's legitimation system, obeying the law, and rejecting conscientious objection. Its conservatism may have derived from the fact that it represented the "sated half" of Israeli society (Kalderon, 1984, 22)—the segment that benefited from the state, maintained relations of dependence with it, and was socialized by its agencies, particularly the army (see Ben-Eliezer, 1993). Still, endeavoring to affect directly government policies, Peace Now accumulated power by prompting the Alignment to side with dovish stands in situations in which the latter displayed indecisiveness.

Peace Now and Gush Emunim had much in common. Both movements emphasized their followers' contribution to the military effort. Their efforts to convert military participation into political involvement demonstrated how discharged soldiers could acquire power. Structurally speaking, moreover, for these groups, the relations of exchange with the state had proven deficient inasmuch as the state, although granting the middle class social dominance, had also tightened its grip over it by increasing its military obligations without a symmetric return. But whereas social dominance and its attendant material gains mattered for the groups from which Peace Now drew, the unattainability of gains of this kind prompted the hawkish groups to embark on the cultural route.

Peace Now and Gush Emunim also took advantage of the state penetration that had neutered the parties to the point where they had virtually lost the allegiance of their traditional supporters. Still, the movements relied on the organizational infrastructure of established parties—Gush Emunim on the National Religious Party (Sprinzak, 1981), and Peace Now on the parties of the Left, including the opposition Alignment. Notwithstanding their reliance, both were extraparliamentary groups, seeking alternative channels such as a direct dialogue with the state. By circumventing the party system, both movements gave expression to the yearning for a substantive change in the political division of labor. They called into question the state's authority to conduct political and military moves without the political participation of the social groups that bore the burden of the conflict and were able to enlist mass support toward that end. The state thus lost much of its autonomy in the management (toward escalation and de-escalation alike) of the Arab-Israeli conflict. Although it continued to enjoy a large measure of independence in the realm of foreign policy, it had to take into account the conflicting preferences of the two movements if it wished to avoid a head-on clash with them.

In sum, the war-prone coalition was augmented with the conjoining of Gush Emunim and hawkish Orientals. Not just hardening of the Labor-led government was at work; a new political expression became apparent. This was the change of government of 1977 and the shift undergone by the National Religious Party from a dovish to a hawkish stand as long as it drew support from both Oriental and Gush Emunim constituencies. At the same time, the dovish coalition saw empowerment as well, not a quantitative but a qualitative one through the rise of Peace Now. Discursive boundaries then expanded from debates between doves and hawks within the political elite to an active discussion encompassing social groups.

The October War thus marked a watershed, a transition from state empowerment to a situation in which the state seemed to be in a deep crisis (see literature dealing with several aspects of the "crisis syndrome": Barnett, 1992, 228–243; Grinberg, 1991b, 75–97; Horowitz and Lissak, 1989; Kimmerling, 1993a; Levy and Peled, 1994; Lustick, 1993, 386–395; Shalev, 1992, 283–314; Shapiro, 1991). As this discussion shows, this seeming crisis stemmed dialectically from the state-directed entrenchment of the occupation, the proportional burden that it entailed, the rise in the standard of living, the construction of an inequitable social structure, and the disempowerment of the "gate-keepers."[10] The state's weakness extended to its capacity to carry out the conflict.[11]

THE EGYPT–ISRAEL PEACE ACCORD

With growing conflicting internal pressures intersecting with military deficiency, growing security burden, and growing dependence on the United States, the state's moves subsequent to the October War were a series of zigzags. In practice, Israeli governments devised two rational options. The first was to reach a comprehensive agreement with the neighboring Arab countries and the Palestinians by fully withdrawing from the occupied territories. In fact, as long as many groups gained from a low-cost occupation, nothing challenged military-dominated political thought. Conversely, reassessment of the military doctrine toward termination of the occupation might have had domestic costs, particularly when taken against the empowerment of the war-prone coalition. Moreover, American pressures were focused mainly on the Egyptian sector to convert Israel's concessions into a regaining of American holdings in Egypt at the expense of the Soviet Union. So, the comprehensive peace option was ruled out.

Alternatively, reducing the conflict's costs through removal of the dominant Arab state, Egypt, from the conflict became the target. Hence, Israel was ready, despite previous resentment, to grant territorial concessions in the Sinai Peninsula in return for political agreements with Egypt. Furthermore, although the concept of "defensible borders" still prevailed, a notable lesson inferred from the October War was the necessity of creating security regimes. They were to be based on UN-monitored, demilitarized, buffer zones combined with arms-limited zones. This seemed to provide downscaling of military frictions, prevention of an Arab surprise attack due to the creation of distance between the armies (Bar-Siman-Tov, 1995, 39–45), and immediate decrease in routine security missions as a means of diverting resources to resume military buildup.

Accordingly, following a disengagement agreement established subsequent to the end of the October War between Israel and Egypt, an interim accord was signed in September 1975 by Rabin's government and the government of Egypt led by President Anwar el-Sadat. U.S. Secretary of State Henry Kissinger played a key role in the mediation (see Golan, 1976). A similar, albeit purely military, agreement was established in the Syrian sector in June 1974 at the cost of Israel's withdrawal from the city of Kuneitra. This agreement generated calm along the border in the Golan Heights from 1974 until the time of this writing. Nevertheless, in the spirit of the countervailing pressures, Prime Minister Rabin refused in 1974 for domestic political reasons to discuss an American proposal for an interim settlement with Jordan entailing Israel's withdrawal from the city of Jericho. The Israelis balked even though the price was not exorbitant and a settlement would have strengthened King Hussein of Jordan vis-à-vis the less moderate Palestinian forces. Indeed, a few weeks later, in the inter-Arab Rabat Conference, Jordan lost its representation of the Palestinian issue in favor of the PLO (ibid., 221–222). Subsequently, the new hawkish front prompted the Rabin government to establish new settlements in the occupied territories including, for the first time, the West Bank.

The IDF's shift from advocating a rigid, territorial status quo to accepting military-political arrangements was clear in Chief of Staff Mordechai Gur's support for the interim agreement with Egypt (Rabin, 1979, 461–462). Two factors worked to shift the army's stand. First, the IDF entirely cooperated with the political level as part of the underlying relations of exchange by which the military gained resources and prestige for accepting political supervision. Economic crisis, interwoven with growing public criticism of the IDF, made this structure more relevant than ever. As a second factor, the IDF had a clear interest in downscaling the conflict to renew a military buildup.

By establishing interim agreements, external and internal de-escalation-prone pressures had mutual impacts: Israel's weakness in the opening moves of the October War and its inability to complete its victory enhanced Egypt's self-confidence. Military arrangements of disengagement, which resulted from this change, helped the two sides internalize new norms of cooperation and confidence that could almost smoothly lead to more advanced agreements (see Bar-Siman-Tov, 1995). With that structure dovetailed the significant moderation of public opinion in Israel that resulted from the costly October War (Kiess, 1978). Foreign Minister Moshe Dayan (who served on a personal, nonpartisan basis in the Likud government in 1977–79) apparently then could agree in secret moves to fully withdraw from the Sinai Peninsula as a continuation of the interim agreement. Through this understanding, the dramatic visit to Jerusalem of President Anwar el-Sadat of Egypt became possible in November 1977. And, reciprocally, Sadat's visit and the negotiations that followed it further moderated public opinion in Israel whether directly (Arian, 1995a, 95–96) or indirectly through Peace Now's activities and their impact on the Alignment's moderation. So, de-escalation had its own dynamic.

Consequently, in 1979 Israel, led by the hawk Menachem Begin, signed the peace agreement with Egypt, Israel's first peace treaty with an Arab state. Under the terms of the agreement, the Israeli army agreed to withdraw from the Sinai Peninsula by 1982, despite the reluctance to make such a move for equal return prior to the October War, as mentioned in chapter 4. As in the interim agreements, the IDF played a critical role in formulating the peace agreement, and subsequently, in executing the withdrawal and the evacuation of Jewish settlements in North Sinai over the settlers' resistance (on the peace process, see also Dayan, 1981; Weizmann, 1981).

Strategically, by creating a new regional institution that would reduce the perceived Arab threat, resources could be diverted to forcefully realize other security interests in sectors where regional institutions were viewed as both unattainable and costly. This was without resorting to greater burdens that otherwise would have been required; but, on the other hand, the peace was not utilized to decrease the military burden. From this point of view, the peace process does not reflect a renewed domination of civilian thinking over a military mind-set. It shows, rather, how the military mind-set adapted itself to changing conditions.

Practically, beyond lessening American pressures for making concessions in other sectors, the peace accord paved the way for a massive military buildup supported by America. The armored forces were increased fourfold, the number of tanks was tripled, the air force was expanded by 60 percent in terms of warplanes, the regular army doubled in size, and the number of available reservists grew by 60 percent by increasing the rate of call-up among discharged soldiers (Wald, 1987, 143). Paradoxically, however, the more the state increased its military power relative to the Arab forces by means of military buildup, the more it reduced its autonomy to use this power due to its growing dependence on the United States for financing and supplying the buildup.

Concurrent with its peace agenda, the Likud-led government also launched a massive project of settlement in the West Bank and Gaza. This went on despite the government's pledge in the peace treaty with Egypt to hold talks on granting autonomy to the Palestinians in the territories as an interim arrangement. Ultimately a permanent settlement would determine the final status of the occupied territories. While the talks proceeded, Israel launched a major drive to settle tens of thousands of Jews in the areas that were to receive autonomy. Furthermore, the Begin government removed the Alignment-led government's restrictions on Jewish settlement by endeavoring to erect settlements in areas of concentrated Palestinian settlement. Massive colonization was depicted as an attempt to create "facts on the ground" and thus to reduce the possibility of restoring the territories to Arab sovereignty.

Indeed, the presence of more than 100,000 settlers, who had been partially armed under the auspices of the IDF for "self-defense" and who had shown their willingness to violate the law and to use violence against local Palestinians, shaped a new reality. Many Israelis came to acknowledge that any attempt to evacuate Jewish settlers to establish political agreement with the Palestinians or Jordan might threaten the integrity of the political system by causing violent clashes within the Israeli polity (Lustick, 1993, 366–373). Begin's government thus further bolstered the hawkish front. This approach led to the resignation of the moderate ministers who had been the architects of the peace treaty with Egypt: Moshe Dayan (in 1979) and Ezer Weizmann (in 1980) (Dayan, 1981, 243–249; Weizmann, 1981, 363–370). Weizmann was replaced by retired General Ariel Sharon in 1981.

The enactment of the "Golan Heights Law" revealed a similar logic at work. In December 1981 the government rammed legislation through the Knesset that applied "Israeli law, jurisdiction, and administration" to the Golan

Heights. The government's purpose was to ensure that the Golan Heights, unlike the Sinai Peninsula, would not be returned to Syria in future peace negotiations. Similarly, in 1980 the government passed a law officially declaring united Jerusalem Israel's capital. Thus, a discussion on future repartition of Jerusalem between Israel and any Arab entity was ruled out. Finally, as part of restoring its deterrent, Israel insisted on retaining its regional monopoly on nuclear weapons. Hence, Iraq's efforts to build a nuclear reactor with French assistance ceased in June 1981 when Israel's air force destroyed the construction site. A few months later, the attempt to restore Israel's deterrent was more pronounced in the Lebanon War (see below; on the reformulated doctrine, see, Aronson, 1992, 178–187; Lanir, 1985, 143–148; Yaniv, 1994, 316).

By employing a mélange of de-escalation and escalation moves, the state was also able to partially satisfy the three main social-political groups as a means of mobilizing support. Peace Now was placated by the signing of the peace treaty with Egypt. Gush Emunim was co-opted by the massive project of settlement and gradually neutralized politically when the state undertook the funding and building of the settlements. Gush Emunim's neo-pioneer veneer vanished. And when Gush Emunim set up institutions to manage the project, it became a bureaucracy that was dependent on the state's favors and functioned as an interest group (see Goldberg, 1993; Moskovitch, 1992, 91–92).

At the same time, the state created an autonomous instrument by which to reward the lower-middle-class groups, mainly the Likud's Oriental electorate, by granting subsidized, cheap housing in the West Bank (Levy and Peled, 1994, 223). Going back to our discussion on alternative models of absorption (see table 2.1), with the rise of consumerism, market-oriented methods governed the settling of the new frontiers, a far cry from the pioneering-like methods of the 1950s. Hence, the ensuing economic price that played a decisive role in triggering reservations by some groups. Projects of settlement, then, dovetailed with the overall effort to better the standard of living of the country's Jewish residents (Preuss, 1984, 83–90), in this case, residents of the country's center who had encountered difficulties buying housing in those areas when the post-1967 economic boom increased the prices of housing. The state could thus satisfy, hence neutralize, hawkish Orientals as well. And because Orientals enjoyed political mobility under the auspices of the Likud, their hawkish stand derived from their social position, and the moves of de-escalation did not imperil their other gains; this collective offered its passive support. Indeed, Orientals, as such, did not take part in resisting the Egypt–Israel peace moves (see Sella and Yishai, 1986, 80–96).

Still, judging whether the state-created hawkish front drove these policies, particularly the colonization project, or just encouraged the military-incited moves (architected by Minister Sharon and Chief of Staff General Rafael Eitan) is problematic. Suffice it to say that notwithstanding these and other generals' part in settling the West Bank, the right-religious discourse now legitimized the use of military force for national-religious purposes beyond goals of a strict security nature (Kimmerling, 1993b, 137). If so, while in the past the military rationale paved the road to gains-production from the occupation, the latter now overshadowed the initial logic and became a driving force in and of itself.

In sum, the state's moderate moves were supported by the major social groups. Coinciding with the IDF's interests and American pressure, these moves became irresistible, even for the hawkish Likud-led government that partially balanced its peace moves by employing hard-line policies elsewhere. However, in a situation where two bickering internal forces favored de-escalation and war/status quo, only a dramatic change involving external intervention could mark the beginning of decision. The escalation of the Israeli-Palestinian conflict played this role.

CHAPTER 6

From Escalation to De-Escalation (1982–96)

With the removal of the main threatening enemy, Egypt, Israel could intensify its combat against the Palestinians. A military failure in Lebanon further escalated the conflict, culminating in the Intifada (1987). Now Israel's military failure paved the way to de-escalation with the 1993–95 Israel–PLO agreements. The next section focuses on the military policies; the sociopolitical level will be analyzed in the following sections.

THE ISRAELI-PALESTINIAN CONFLICT
The Lebanon War (1982–85)

The external origins of the war are traceable to the PLO's making Lebanon its new center from September 1970 when Jordan, to a large extent guided by fear of Israeli retaliation, evicted the Palestinian command from its territory. Insofar as a Palestinian mini-state was appearing, Israel intensified its efforts to neutralize the Palestinians' power and to curtail their endeavors to initiate attacks against Israeli targets. For Israel, the struggle with the Palestinians in Lebanon was linked to the general interest in sustaining a low-cost occupation in the West Bank and the Gaza Strip with the symbolic and economic advantages involved. This was also conditional on filibustering the talks on Palestinian autonomy. For the political-military establishment, moreover, the PLO was an enemy with which it was impossible to conduct a political dialogue based on compromise. Israel then turned to a military mode of action in order to minimize the potential damage this perceived enemy could cause, rather than pursuing a political settlement or accepting the status quo.

Through this prism of a "zero-sum game," Israel worked to back the Palestinians' opponents, be they King Hussein of Jordan in September 1970 or the Maronite Christians in Lebanon from the mid-1970s. Accordingly, Israel intervened in the civil war in Lebanon that broke out in 1975 between the Palestinians and the dominant Christians by proffering military aid to the Christians. Nor did Israel object when Syria invaded Lebanon in 1976 at the Christians' invitation.

Israeli aid was stepped up considerably following the change of government in 1977. In March 1978 Israel launched the Litany Operation following a terrorist attack on a civilian bus near Tel Aviv. The operation ended with Israel in control of a strip of territory between ten and fifteen kilometers wide in South Lebanon. Most of that area was handed over to an Israeli-backed Christian force. In the meantime, the civil war had become more intense while Syria and the Lebanese Christians were now adversaries. Israel increased its military support for the Christians. In the summer of 1979 Israel escalated its activity and began to initiate operations, primarily aerial bombing raids on PLO bases deep in Lebanon. Israel's aim was to prevent the emergence of a PLO-controlled Palestinian "state within a state" in South Lebanon.

As these events unfolded, Israeli leaders held secret talks with the Lebanese Christians. Pressured by the Christians, Israel pledged to come to their defense if they were attacked from the air by Syria. Israel fulfilled its commitment in April 1981. After the Syrians overran a Christian position on Mount Lebanon, the Israeli air force shot down two Syrian helicopters. Damascus responded by moving anti-aircraft missile batteries into the Lebanese Biqa' Valley, a move that terminated a tacit agreement between Syria and Israel: Syria would not interfere with Israeli air activity over Lebanon and Israel would do likewise regarding Syrian actions in northern Lebanon. Diplomatic efforts to get the Syrian missiles removed were futile, but Israel, under intense American pressure, did not attack them.

In July 1981, the PLO launched an impressive artillery barrage against northern Israel that was unprecedented in its ferocity. This was the PLO's reaction to the Israel-initiated operations—an abrupt about-face by the organization, which until then had shown relative restraint. Even Israeli sources acknowledged that the PLO had not been the initiator of the deteriorating military situation (Shiffer, 1984, 57). Ten days of artillery duels and Israeli bombing raids followed, until a cease-fire agreement was established between Israel and the PLO worked out by the United States. Importantly, for the first time in the country's history, during this mini-war of attrition hundreds of Israeli inhabitants abandoned their homes along the northern border and moved to the center of the country to wait for a cease-fire (Yaniv, 1994, 316).

A familiar pattern thus repeated itself in Lebanon: Israeli reprisal raids escalated until the reaction of the Arab side made a full-scale military operation a virtual necessity. The state's agencies preferred escalation to acceptance of the political status quo—in this case, the emergence of a Palestinian quasi-state in

South Lebanon, with which Israel could come to terms. The availability of that option was demonstrated during the year that followed the cease-fire: The PLO meticulously upheld the cease-fire, while Israel sought a pretext to violate it. There again Israel took part in shaping the regional system rather than just reacting to an exogenous reality.

Indeed, from that stage the Lebanon War became inevitable because the outcome of the military clashes strengthened the Palestinians' quasi-state base in Lebanon. At the same time, the enactment of the legislation applying Israeli law to the Golan Heights increased the likelihood of another war with Syria.

Against this background, the IDF drew up a plan for an operation that would eradicate the Palestinian infrastructure in Lebanon. The plan was expanded with the appointment of retired General Ariel Sharon as defense minister after the 1981 elections. The revised conception called for the conquest of South Lebanon, the occupation of West Beirut (the Muslim sector of the city), and the deployment of forces to block possible Syrian intervention from the Biqa' Valley. All of that would be ended by linking up with the Christians in Beirut, helping them establish a Christian state and impose a "new political order" in Lebanon. Further, it is a safe assumption (even if it cannot be supported empirically) that the stigma of 1973 prompted the IDF to try to restore its prestige and reinstate its social status by launching a war under conditions of military superiority. It is also possible that this rationale inspired the IDF's support for the pacific moves with Egypt to allow diversion of resources into the northern sector.

For the first five months of 1982 the army sought a pretext for going to war. Several attempts were made to obtain the cabinet's go-ahead because a majority of the cabinet members opposed Sharon's stand. Indeed, on more than one occasion Israeli troops were moved to the border region even before a decision was made. In early June, Palestinian gunmen (not from the PLO) made an assassination attempt on the Israeli ambassador in London. Israel took advantage of the event to bomb PLO bases in Lebanon, breaking the cease-fire. When the PLO retaliated with an artillery attack on northern Israel, the Israeli government—apparently with implicit American permission (Kimche, 1991, 145)—gave the IDF the green light to launch a limited operation (the survey of events is based on Horowitz, 1983; Khalidi, 1986; Oren, 1983; Schiff and Yaari, 1984, 11–124; Shiffer, 1984).

Manifestly, execution of the subjectively defined security interests matters, since the state was able to set in motion a lengthy lead-up to war without generating political opposition, even after the founding of Peace Now. Several factors accounted for this expression of the state's autonomy in the military arena. First, the massive military buildup—focusing on the regular component of the military—enabled the government to launch a large-scale military offensive without calling up reserve forces. The regular army is by nature obedient and politically uninvolved; consequently, potential protest from reservists was virtually precluded. In the apt phrase of Avishai Margalit, a peace activist at the time, a "gigantic symposium" of reservists on the impending war, like the great debate that characterized the "waiting period" before the Six-Day War, was averted. As a result, Margalit concludes, Peace Now was rendered ineffectual on the eve of the war (cited in Edelist and Maiberg, 1986, 324–325). Naturally, this gain would have been lost had the peace with Egypt not come about, for then Israel would have had to prepare for a military reaction from Egypt to the war in Lebanon.

Second, opposition was also muted by the impact of the technologization of armaments on military-political thinking. The lead-up to the Lebanon War involved the use of the air force and artillery to strike at Palestinian civilian targets. In each episode the IDF's activity produced heavy Arab civilian casualties. Yet this was not perceived as controversial because the improved technology of the 1980s ensured the combatants' remoteness from the victims. So soldiers were unlikely to turn to protest after their discharge and there was no documentation of events liable to shock political and public opinion.

A third factor was the role of political discourse. To recall, in the 1970s, the discourse about the Arab-Israeli conflict was dominated in part by metaphysical concepts of the right-religious wing, somewhat displacing the strict military rationale (Kimmerling, 1993b, 137). Even the Center-Left adopted some Orthodox Jewish myths to humanize the war (Gertz, 1995, 99–117), while symbols related to the Jewish Holocaust were often borrowed to demonize Arabs as a means of legitimating Israel's aggression (Segev, 1993, 396–404). With this in mind, Prime Minister Menachem Begin could wrap the assistance to the Christians in a moral justification: "We have a moral commitment to the Christians," Begin said. "We cannot sit idly by while a religious or national minority is destroyed. We [ourselves] are a majority in our own country but a small minority in the Middle East" (quoted in Shiffer, 1984, 28).

Finally, as in former instances, militarization coincided with tightening of political control over the IDF. In 1976, the "The Basic Law: The Army" was enacted. Seeking to put an end to the formal ambiguity that had become flagrantly obvious before the October War, the law asserted that the army was subordinate to the elected government. It also laid down the procedure for appointing the chief of staff. Thus, as in earlier situations, increased political supervision of the army created conditions that bolstered the army's image as a universalist organization wholly subordinate to the state's authority. Concomitantly and paradoxically, the sharp increase of public criticism of the IDF from the mid-1970s on focused on issues such as budget, appointments, procurement, and operative performance, while leaving intact the "military mind" itself. So, the IDF could conceive a militant agenda without hindrance.

Taking these factors all together, even though the preparations for the war went on for almost a year and the public was aware of the government's intentions in part, there was no effective political opposition to the idea of launching a war, not even from the "mainstream" of the Israeli Center-Left (see Rabin, 1983, 19–31). The very nature of the lead-up conjoined with Peace Now's silence helped create a partial consent among the main political parties to the initiation of war. It was, therefore, the state's growing strength in the internal arena—the resources it allocated to beef up the army and enshrine its values— that created the conditions for the initial intervention in Lebanon and for the escalation that led, unavoidably, to war. Structurally, by becoming more potent in the military sphere through the military doctrine the state was actually compensated for its weakness in other internal spheres. As a result, the state could manage the conflict without resorting to the level of reserve-manpower extraction that otherwise would have been required, increasing state dependence on the political groups that since the 1970s had challenged its governability.

Notwithstanding the successful lead-up, owing to Sharon's maneuvers, the opening moves, whose declared goals were partially agreed upon by the main political forces, were soon expanded to include the reshaping of the political order in Lebanon with the expelling of Syrian forces and Palestinian commands from the country. Accordingly, the IDF triggered an unsuccessful clash with the Syrian forces stationed in Lebanon. Within days the IDF seized about half of Lebanon (from the border with Israel to the Beirut area). A cease-fire established under the auspices of the United States and the United Nations ended the "official" war. Nevertheless, the IDF, directed by Sharon and apparently without clear cabinet approval, provoked clashes with both Syrian and Palestinian forces to improve Israel's position toward Beirut. Eventually, although the IDF took control over part of Beirut and brought about the uprooting of the PLO commands, a "new political order" was not created in Lebanon due to the Christians' own military deficiency.

Public criticism in Israel against the war then grew louder. Nevertheless, the IDF was to remain on Lebanese soil for almost three more years as a conquering army, waiting for a political agreement with the Lebanese government to assure the security of the northern Israeli population. This was a typical "post-1967" pattern of bureaucratic behavior, namely, holding on to territory until an absolute political solution could be achieved although the Lebanese state had virtually disintegrated. Faced with aggravation of the fiscal crisis—the collapse of the big banks and the government's intervention to guarantee their shares' value was a case in point—and lacking sufficient political support, including a solid parliamentary majority, the government was reluctant to take the risks involved with a unilateral pullback from Lebanon.

During this period the IDF suffered heavy losses and a significantly increasing burden of reserve duty, insofar as the combat in Lebanon was expanded to guerilla warfare against the Lebanese Shiite groups. Shiites were initially "convenient neighbors" of Israel but their enmity had been stirred by the lengthy occupation of South Lebanon. Gradually this enmity was fanned by Iran, where a fundamentalist Shiite regime had come to power following the revolution of 1979. Thus, the government nullified the initial advantages of the war in the internal arena; witness the growing political protests against the IDF's presence on Lebanon's soil (see below). Eventually, Shiites were successful in their resistance to the Israeli occupation.

Following the elections of 1984, the Likud lost part of its power. So, the Likud and Labor formed, for the first time since the Six-Day War, a grand coalition government. It entailed the dismantling of the Alignment because Mapam objected to a coalition with the Likud. The new government was headed, on rotation basis, by Shimon Peres, a former member in Rafi's leadership and the defense minister in Rabin's cabinet (1974–77), and from 1986 by Yitzhak Shamir, ex-commander of the LHI (Fighters of Israel's Freedom), a pre-state underground organization, who succeeded Menachem Begin (see below). Yitzhak Rabin was named as defense minister. Both sides preferred an expanded coalition over a narrow one. In 1985, within a few months of its formation, the government brought about a rapid, partial withdrawal from Lebanon. It was unilateral and not conditional on the signing by the Lebanese government or by any other dominant force in Lebanon of a commitment to ensure quiet on Israel's northern border—the war's declared goal. Israel thus shifted from its "post-1967" posture.

A typical expression of an unsuccessful coping with the security dilemma manifested itself: Israel's policy of escalation, geared to recovery of deterrent capacity, actually brought about further erosion of deterrence, by stimulating the enmity of the Shiites, whose guerilla warriors exposed the army's weakness. Furthermore, deterrence also diminished because of the erosion in domestic support for the war (see below). Had the state been dominated by a "political mind-set," the logic of encouraging a Palestinian quasi-state as a replacement for fruitless guerilla warfare by Shiite forces could have been factored in. National interests could have then been defined in political rather than military terms accompanied by sharp downscaling of the competitiveness between the two political units.[1]

A similar failure repeated itself in the incomplete withdrawal from Lebanon: The army executed a pullback and concentrated forces in a narrow security zone abutting Israel's northern border. Alongside the IDF the South Lebanon Army (SLA) was also deployed in the zone. Made up of local mercenaries, that army was established, armed, trained, and funded by Israel. Its men were stationed in the forward areas of the Security Zone and bore the brunt of defending Israel's northern border against the remaining Palestinian forces and Shiite Muslim groups that soon organized against the IDF. The crisis in Lebanon showed how the state reacted to a situation in which the costs of maintaining the conflict had reached untenable levels: To offset the costs the IDF was to transfer part of its mission to an army of Arab mercenaries. The concept of "defensible borders" combined with a demilitarized buffer zone prevailed again since the SLA, sitting between the northern Israeli population and Arab forces, was to "absorb" the Lebanese-Palestinian resistance to Israeli policy.

By employing this strategy Israel failed again in establishing a formal/tacit security regime with the Shiite Muslims in South Lebanon as suggested by some military officers (Yaniv, 1994, 397–398). Rather, partial withdrawal was chosen, perpetuating friction with the Shiite population and nurturing enmity with the extremist Hizballah group spearheading the resistance. In some cases Israel had to resort to large-scale military interventions. All in all, though, the costs of the occupation were relatively low and did not arouse significant domestic political opposition. So, notwithstanding the eroded prestige of the IDF, military thought sustained its ascendancy.

The termination of the Lebanon War worked to extend the Israeli-Palestinian conflict to the occupied territories, but at the same time, it attenuated Israel's military capabilities to handle the hostilities on the latter front.

The Intifada

As agreed within the terms of the Egypt–Israel peace accord, negotiations with the Palestinians via Egypt (who represented the Palestinian side) on the constitution of Palestinian administrative autonomy in the West Bank and the Gaza Strip dragged on from 1979 until 1981 but made no headway. The sides could not agree on the meaning of "autonomy": Israel agreed to administrative autonomy without elements of sovereignty, whereas Egypt demanded territorial autonomy for the Palestinians. At the same time, Israel settled the West Bank with more than 100,000 Jews, a settlement accompanied by local frictions between Israelis and Palestinians and, most important, massive confiscation of lands. On the bottom line, Israel confiscated or brought under its military rule about 52 percent of the land in the West Bank and 30 to 40 percent of Gaza's land (Farsoun and Landis, 1990, 22).

Concurrently, Israel displayed an "iron fist" against PLO activists in the occupied territories (ibid., 19–22), accompanied by provocative activities organized by Jewish settlers and by the initiation of the Lebanon War. Rhetorically, the "iron fist" was backed by the demonization of the PLO as a terrorist organization to delegitimize internal and external pressures to hold a peace-oriented dialogue with this organization. The PLO's relatively moderate, political, rather than just military agenda, which had begun to emerge from the mid-1970s on, was rejected by Israel's government (led by both the Alignment and the Likud). Nor did Israel cooperate with American and Arab diplomatic efforts to settle the Israeli-Palestinian conflict (the 1982 Reagan Plan and Fez Plan, respectively). On top of this, on the eve of the Intifada Foreign Minister Shimon Peres concluded the clandestine London Agreement in 1987 with King Hussein of Jordan, laying the foundations for establishing a confederation between the Palestinian population in the occupied territories and the Hashemite Kingdom. (A similar formula had been rejected by the Israeli government about fifteen years before following Hussein's plan to establish a federation with the West Bank.) This agreement, however, was rejected by Prime Minister Shamir, negating any alteration of the territorial status quo. Palestinians then realized that the peace treaty with Egypt had not improved their own situation while the Lebanon War eradicated their semi-sovereign stronghold. No longer able to rely firmly on the PLO's international activity, Palestinians in the territories stepped up their resistance to the occupation, culminating in the eruption of the Intifada in December 1987 (see Tessler, 1994, 535–554, 600–612, 648–684).

The Intifada had its roots in the occupation; one of its triggers, however, was the relations between Palestinians and Jews in the Israeli labor market. Israel's economic policy since 1985 utilized unemployment to deal with the hyperinflation. This and other effects of the economic crisis had a ruinous impact on the temporary, unorganized Palestinian workforce employed in Israel, and hence on the economy in the territories, which relied heavily on those workers—in 1986 about 40 percent of the labor force of the occupied territories was employed in Israel and, unlike other groups, did not enjoy upward mobility (Saleh, 1990, 45–46; Semyonov and Lewin-Epstein, 1987, 51).

Similar to the actions taken by the Jewish workforce in the pre-state labor market when it found itself in a disadvantageous position, Palestinian workers also tried to offset their inferior economic position in the labor market through political activity at the national level. It was thus not surprising that although the uprising was driven by high school and university students, participation by youngsters who had worked in Israel was pronounced. In addition to suffering from their disadvantaged position in the labor market, they had also internalized modern values of collective action (see Hiltermann, 1990; Schiff and Yaari, 1990, 71–93; Shalev, 1990, 26). The state's goal of regularizing economic activity thus *conflicted* with its objectives in the realm of military control (Alberger, 1993).

Arguably, the Intifada not only symbolized the disintegration of the Israeli "control system" (in the terms of Kimmerling, 1989), which had included, since 1967, the population of the West Bank and the Gaza Strip. It also revealed the internal feebleness in Israel's control over its original domain. At last, central to the process sparking the uprising was Israel's overgaining from the occupied territories. Unchecked confiscation of lands and treating an exogenous labor force as a "reserve army of the unemployed" regulating the intra-Israel labor market were the main reasons for Israel's failure. Yet over-gaining was driven by the state's internal maneuvering between conflicting demands, by themselves resulting from state construction of a war-based social order. Ironically, a Jewish-Palestinian intercommunal conflict "replaced" an interethnic conflict within the Israeli Jewish community that might have been fired if the occupied territories were not exploited. As we will later see, how-ever, the very groups who had benefited from these policies, directly or indi-rectly, displayed reluctance to carry out the policies' outcomes, that is, com-bating the Intifada.

From the outset, the Intifada consisted primarily of mass demonstrations and stone throwing at the Israeli forces in the occupied territories. By and large, the Intifada did not evolve into an armed struggle against the occupation. This was due in no small measure to the influence of the PLO, based since the Lebanon War in Tunisia, which directed the Intifada. Both the timing and the intensity of the uprising took Israel by surprise. The uprising occurred during the tenure of the broad coalition government headed by Yitzhak Shamir, who had succeeded Shimon Peres—the same government that two years earlier had de-escalated the Lebanon War. Defense Minister Yitzhak Rabin set the tone for dealing with the Intifada: a military effort to suppress the riots mainly without using fire accompanied by a political effort to resolve the Israeli-Palestinian conflict. This concept was at the root of the backing that Defense Minister Rabin gave the army in the face of right-wing demands to quell the uprising with force.

External factors solidified Rabin's policy: American pressures increased and worked to delimit Israel's leverage for employing violence insofar as the United States became an hegemonic power in the region and thus no longer uti-lized aggression from Israel as a stick against the USSR (Ben-Zvi. A, 1993, 180–189). Conversely, America (especially the Bush administration) encour-aged Israel to establish channels for peace talks with the Palestinians (Arens, 1995, 112–124; Kimche, 1991, 287–309). In addition, Israel's formal/tacit security arrangements with Egypt, Jordan, and Syria had restraining effects in the Palestinian sector (Inbar and Sandler, 1995, 50–51).

Military suppression, however, proved ineffectual despite the huge loss and damage it had inflicted on Palestinian communities—about 2,000 fatalities and 18,000 injuries (Makovsky, 1996, 95). Rather, the Palestinians escalated their resistance (see Khawaja, 1993). Similar to the Lebanon War, fruitless, prolonged warfare (1987–93) was to be displaced by political negotiation whose sources will be analyzed later.

A few months after the outbreak of the Intifada, informal negotiations were held with representatives of the territories on establishing an autonomous regime in the West Bank and the Gaza Strip (Shalev, 1990, 155–158). The official Israeli approach also welcomed American mediation efforts to bring about peace negotiations. Although the PLO was now recognized as the Palestinians' representative by the United Nations and most Western countries, Israel refused to deal with an organization it branded as terrorist, a stand that had been a bedrock of both the Right and the Center-Left in Israel.

Following the elections of 1988, Yitzhak Shamir again established a Likud-led coalition with the Labor Party. In April 1990, the Labor ministers resigned from the government because the premier rejected an American initiative to hold an international conference in order to promote the peace process with neighboring Arab countries; decisive was the argument over the composition of the Palestinian delegation (Arens, 1995, 112–124; Kimche, 1991, 287–309). Nevertheless, the new government, which was led by the Likud and included parties of the extreme Right, continued the policy of its predecessor; it even moderated it by allowing schools and universities to open in the occupied territories (Arens, 1995, 291–292).

Subsequent to the Gulf War (see more below), the Likud-led government accepted the American initiative, which produced the Madrid Peace Conference in October 1991. The participants included Syria, Lebanon, Jordan, and a delegation of Palestinians from the territories that was identified with, and authorized by the PLO. Thus, the traditional stand opposing talks with the PLO began to show cracks at the Madrid Conference with the Likud-led government playing a leading role. Following the elections held in 1992, the Labor Party, headed by Yitzhak Rabin and Shimon Peres, returned to power and this time was able to rule without a coalition with the Likud. Initially, the government continued the policy of its predecessor by exploiting the peace talks with the delegation of Palestinians from the territories, talks that already moved from Madrid to Washington.

Since the Washington talks proved ineffectual as long as they were held without the attendance of the real Palestinian "master," namely, the leadership of the PLO based in Tunisia, a group within the Israeli Foreign Ministry led by Deputy Foreign Minister Yossi Beilin initiated direct, secret talks with the PLO in Oslo in 1992. These talks focused on the establishment of self-governing Palestinian rule in the West Bank and the Gaza Strip, beginning with the Gaza Strip and the Jericho area in the Jordan Valley as an interim agreement without granting formal sovereignty. With their successful conclusion, Israel recognized the PLO officially. In September 1993 on the White House lawn, Prime Minister Yitzhak Rabin and Chairman Yasir Arafat signed a Declaration of Principles on an interim settlement, which was made permanent in the Cairo Agreement of May 1994 (on the process, see Cobban, 1995, 92–104; Makovsky, 1996). A few weeks later the Palestinian National Authority was formally established in Gaza, headed by Yasir Arafat. Subsequently, in September 1995 the sides established a new agreement expanding the Palestinian Authority to the West Bank, ending the direct Israeli occupation over the majority of the

Palestinian population in its post-1967 form (Oslo II). Concurrently, advance was achieved in the talks with Syria in which Israel implicitly agreed to a complete withdrawal from the Golan Heights (Azoulay-Katz, 1996, 17–22).

As many Israelis realize, the next step will be a final agreement. It will entail the establishment of Palestinian sovereignty in the West Bank and the Gaza Strip—a sovereign state or a Palestinian-Jordanian federation; evacuation of Jewish settlements, entirely or partly; and settling the dispute concerning control over Jerusalem, which will indisputably involve a pattern of division of power among Israel, the Palestinians, and other Arab countries.

In turn, moderation on the Israeli side encouraged moderation on the Arab side. It was no more blatant than in Jordan's enthusiastic readiness to sign a peace agreement a year after the Oslo I agreement in return for negligible concessions made by Israel. Similar background triggered the establishing of low-level diplomatic relations with Morocco and Tunisia and economic relations with the Persian Gulf states. De-escalation to a large extent was a self-nurturing process, similar to the nature of escalation.

What explains the gradual shift in Israel's political and military policies toward de-escalation since the Lebanon War?

EXPLAINING DE-ESCALATION

Militarism and Materialism as Competing Values

Since similar patterns of state–group relations manifested themselves during the Lebanon War and the Intifada, both events should be analyzed within the same context. Central to the Palestinian-Israeli clashes was the exacerbation of the post-1967 asymmetry between the security burden and the return of social rewards on which state–group relations of exchange were grounded. To begin, about 650 Israelis died in the Lebanon War (about 400 during the first months and the rest during the remaining period until May 1985) and the overall economic cost was more than $2 billion (*Yediot Aharonot Supplement*, May 31, 1985, 35). Subsequently, about 100 Israelis (mostly civilians) were killed by Palestinians in the 1987–93 period (Makovsky, 1996, 95). At the economic level, the Intifada worked to erode the economic gains of the Six-Day War (see below), but its direct costs were negligible relative to past interstate wars— about $1 billion in 1988–93 (Defence Budget, 1993, 65).

Moreover, the already revealed innate contradictions within Israel's implementation of military doctrine were now aggravated. First, the character of policing missions in Lebanon and the occupied territories placed a heavy burden on infantry units. Second, because of the wars' duration and scope, it was the reserves who bore the brunt of the burden. In the case of Lebanon, this nullified the effect that had been achieved in the war's initial phase, which had been entrusted to the regular army. To put it differently, the very mechanism helping to constitute interparty agreement before the Lebanon War now worked to inflame interparty bickering. Third, as it will be recalled, offensive doctrine worked to shorten wars, unintentionally resulting in reduced domestic political costs. Boundless implementation, however, was to aggravate the extent to which the post-1967 wars were politically debated between the Left and Right (see Horowitz, 1987).

Furthermore, materialist, consumerist values became greatly salient from the 1980s, when the growth in the standard of living brought about an accumulation of enough economic resources in the middle class's hands that it could maintain independent systems of consumption vis-à-vis state-regulated ones. Flourishing of informal, even "grey" systems of education and health care, pirate cable television lines, secular bypass of religious rules, the breaking up and commercialization of the kibbutz system (the ideological vanguard of Israeli society), and more were among the new forms (see Lehman-Wilzig, 1992). Middle-class-produced "democratic capitalism," which gave birth to rituals of individualism, competition, civil rights, criticism, and so on, gradually supplanted the Mamlachtiyut-informed collectivism (Almog, 1995).

With growing materialism and the private opportunities that it entailed, the tension between materialism and militarism became more apparent. Again, it worked to increase the proportional, subjectivist value of costs and losses beyond the objective dimension at several levels. First, although the losses were quantitatively equivalent to the level of the Six-Day War, they were higher in relative terms. In the absence of a quick, celebrated victory, it was not balanced by rewards of social prestige or externally originated benefits (the Intifada even eliminated the gains of the 1967 War, as we will see).[2]

Second, unlike former wars, the state's military situation was perceived to be stable in light of the Arab countries' military deficiency. The state, then, doubly failed in functioning as a *mechanism of protection* (in the sense offered by Tilly, 1985b): It was not able to offer a convincing argument that an existential danger existed but it took unsuccessful steps to remove the amorphous danger that produced high casualties and economic burdens. In other words, consumers gradually paid a greater price for purchasing goods of lesser value (Lake, 1992). True, the formal goal was to secure the inhabitants of the north and the settlers in the occupied territories, but those who shaped the political discourse lived in the central areas of the country and did not feel threatened by the Palestinians or the Shiite militias. It was a typical failure to universalize particularist security interest. Further, even the northern population demonstrated a low level of staying power relative to past occasions when many temporarily abandoned their homes in the border and moved to the center of the country during the PLO artillery war in the north in July 1981. So the materialist syndrome afflicted those groups as well.

Third, with the materialist syndrome dominant, military service became a disruptive factor rather than a prominent avenue of social mobility. It hindered youngsters drawn from the middle class from translating their initial wealth and high-level schooling into rapid incorporation into civilian career tracks, especially as those tracks became more competitive. And the more materialist values prevailed, the less the Western middle class relied on battlefield achievements—now more pale then ever—to legitimize dominant social status.

Symptomatic were four phenomena: (1) Westerners, in greater numbers than their Oriental counterparts, advocated a cut in the security budget and criticized the inequitable distribution of the military burden among Jewish citizens (Arian, 1995, private communication). However, both groups' faith in the IDF in this regard largely declined following the Intifada (Arian, 1995a, 62–65, 70). (2) To solidify this critique, the press and groups of soldiers' parents with access to the press magnified their scrutiny of the IDF's treatment of their children. In particular, the searchlight was directed toward accidents in military operations. Although they had not highly increased, accidents became a public issue, contrary to the shroud of secrecy surrounding them in the past, indicating the growing public sensitivity to losses (see Wald, 1994, 55–57). (3) A survey done in 1995 to map preferred occupations among residents of the big cities (where the middle class dominates) revealed the prestige of the professions (*Status*, June, 1995, 8–10). Contrary to the 1960s, the golden age of the "fighter," military careers vanished from the top (see Kimmerling, 1971, on the end of the 1960s). (4) On top of this trend, the attenuated motivation of secular, Westerner youngsters to join the front-line units and do reserve duty became apparent in the mid-1990s, although felt much earlier.

As secular Westerners and mobile Orientals turned to different channels for social mobility, religious youngsters and less mobile Orientals strengthened their hold in the military. For them, military service possessed national value in its own right and as such conferred symbolic rewards. Significant was the increasing weight of the religious sector in the army following the October War through a special framework of service known as Hesder Yeshivas, in which religious youngsters could combine army service with religious studies. This trend was inspired by the same source from which Gush Emunim sprang, namely, social mobility in symbolic terms of Western, religious youngsters via military service. However, even some of the religious soldiers were drawn to secular-materialist values; hence, their motivation gradually became instrumentalist rather than ideological (Sheleg and Hadar, 1994; see, on the overall process, Beker, 1996, 60–64; Levitzky, 1996; Margalit, 1995; Zamir, 1987; and see an interview with Lieutenant Colonel Rami Dovrat, *Yediot Aharonot Supplement*, April 19, 1996, 10–16).

With the alteration of the IDF's social composition, the linkage between ideological stand and social-military status increased: In the 1981 election campaign, Westerner-dominated groups had already invoked more than ever their historical contribution to state-building and military gains to counter the Likud's Oriental-dominated constituency (see Shapiro, 1991, 169–172). Following the Lebanon War, violent clashes broke out between Center-Left Western demonstrators and Oriental right-wingers who were the main supporters of the war (Barzilai, 1992, 312). That is not *despite*, but *due* to, their heavy losses in which many of them felt pride combined with resentment toward the Left's attempts to devalue these perceived battlefield gains (see Ariely, 1983, 158). On top of that, in February 1983 a grenade thrown during a left-wing demonstration by an Oriental opponent killed one of the participants.

Religious youth, for their part, became split: Some of them, who were associated with Gush Emunim, supported the Lebanon War. But at the same time, the heavy losses among religious youngsters stimulated opposition to the enduring war by some religious leaders (see, for example, Wellman, 1985, 34–35). And when the peace process with the Palestinians took its course, it became clear that part of the soldiers belonging to the Hesder Yeshivas, under their rabbis' rules, might disobey the IDF's orders to evacuate Jewish settlements.

As for the Westerners, the more they lost their unquestioned dominance and interest in the IDF, the more they took the liberty of expressing a more autonomous, critical, stand. A cyclical process then showed itself: Middle-class groups devalued military service through their critique, leaving the stage to less-mobile Oriental and religious soldiers. In reaction to the latter's growing presence in the military, those middle-class groups further devalued military service, and so forth. So, though the presence of Orientals in the military largely grew from the 1980s on, the overall sociopolitical change devalued military service with broader implications for Orientals' achievements. With the declining of the "fighter," convertibility of a military position into a civilian one saw a momentous diminishment, with Orientals suffering most. A syndrome according to which subordinated groups were "ascending a descending escalator" was set in motion.

In sum, a gap was gradually created between material interests and the maintenance of the conflict. So, similar to the pre-1967 pattern, by realizing several groups' interests, the state in practice strengthened their position to demand more.[3] Conditions were created by which agents could dynamically reconstruct their interests in accordance with their material needs and the manner in which the state promoted this stand, that is, reconstruction toward termination of the general conflict. Precisely the very essence of militarism in Israel—its lack of cultural embeddedness—could bring about its demise. There were two concurrent processes: social agents drawn mainly from the Westerner-dominated middle class practically worked to delimit state capacity to carry out military missions by eroding the state's military capabilities. In tandem, those and other agents accepted moves of de-escalation, by themselves fueled by the former process.

The Decline of Military Capabilities

Arguably, reconstruction of interests drove the decline of military capabilities from the late 1970s on. Two factors reciprocally impacted on this process and on each other: (1) the shrinking legitimation and material capabilities enjoyed by any government to use force as a political instrument for external purposes; and (2) externally originated limits and losses.

To begin, materialism combined with growing burdens stimulated new forms of antiwar political action, initiated mainly by middle-class Westerners. This went beyond the activity by the Peace Now movement. During the Lebanon War, a political debate raged about the goals of the war while the army was still locked in combat, with a critical stand taken by most of the journalists about the deception displayed by Defense Minister Sharon (Association of Journalists, 1983, 7–18). Reservists and senior officers in uniform organized protests during their duty; "Soldiers Against Silence" carried out a permanent vigil outside Prime Minister Begin's house; soldiers' parents also demonstrated, calling themselves "Parents against Silence" (see Feldman and Rechnitz-Kizner, 1984; Zukerman-Bareli and Bensky, 1989). So again, groups invoked their military contribution to legitimize political action and by doing so their activities were more effective than those organized by purely "civilian" groups (see comparison by Wolfsfeld, 1988, 124–134).

Prominent both in the Lebanon War and in the Intifada was the Yesh Gvul ("There's a Limit") Movement advocating conscientious objection in the face of the IDF's attacks on the civilian population in Lebanon and the occupied territories (see Menuchin and Menuchin, 1985; Menuchin, 1990, respectively). By taking this stand, Yesh Gvul questioned one of the components of the state's legitimation system—the ascendancy of the army—as the dictates of one's personal conscience overrode that supremacy, Yesh Gvul maintained. The movement therefore encouraged reserve soldiers to refuse to serve in Lebanon and the occupied territories. Importantly, the group remained confined to the bounds of the "rules of discourse": It was drawn from middle-class youngsters who made their protest as reservists, rather than as conscientious citizens or in the name of moral civil values. For that reason, the group refrained from delegitimization of military service itself. It, however, remained in a minority position: The mainstream Left was choosing again to invoke military service to legitimize its political participation, thus obviously limiting its ability to downgrade military values.

Interestingly, the activity of Yesh Gvul generated less political furor than the "Letter of the High-School Seniors" had some fifteen years earlier. This is noteworthy in view of the fact that the 1980s group was a more aberrant phenomenon in terms of the norms of Israeli political culture. The difference in the public reaction is attributable to the less conservative political atmosphere of the 1980s. It was by then accepted that soldiers, both those who had served and those who had yet to serve, had the right to demand—in the name of their military participation—that they be given a say in political decisions that would shape their destiny. Moreover, the protest by the high school seniors had been an aberration in a society where the dominant groups benefited from the persistence of the conflict and objected to whatever was liable to impinge on their interests. In the 1980s, however, there were more groups who had vested interests that were incompatible with the persistence of the conflict.

Political protests marked clear boundaries of the use of violent force as a political instrument by rejecting the Lebanon War's expanded goals beyond the original version. For one thing, Peace Now and the other protest groups prompted the Center-Left, including much of the Alignment and even Likud and other coalition party figures, to oppose Sharon's maneuvers (Yishai, 1985, 379–392). At the rhetoric level, these groups for the first time took an extreme dovish position, demanding that the use of military force be curtailed, particularly as long as it did not enjoy broad consent. Some groups made a dual distinction: The expanded war was portrayed as a "war of choice," geared to achieving political objectives in the absence of an existential threat to the state's security. This, ostensibly, differentiated it from the previous wars of "no choice," although this book tells a different tale.[4] Ironically, it was the right wing that exposed the falsity of the "war of choice" argument by trying to show that it was only emulating previous governments (Yariv, 1985, 19–21).

Another distinction was made between the original, declared, and agreed upon goal of eliminating the mini-Palestinian state, and the expanded goal of establishing "a new political order" in Lebanon as a whole. IR scholars, for their part, echo this distinction, entirely or partially, explicitly or implicitly, by making a distinction between the strategic rationale of a limited war and the ideological failure of the Likud government, leading to the expanded war (see, for example, Horowitz, 1983, 1987; Lanir, 1985; Yariv, 1985). Nonetheless, "choice," as I show, is a subjective definition of security interests as much as "no choice."

True, Israeli governments had traditionally confined the wars' goals to those for which large public support could be mobilized (Horowitz, 1987), but the change was now pronounced in the boundaries of consent (or of dispute) rather than in the goals themselves. It was preceded by the dispute between Gush Emunim and Peace Now, which revealed an attempt to define the boundaries of the overall conflict far beyond the arguments taking place in 1967–73 between hawks and doves. To further illustrate, the shift in the Center-Left's behavior had already been demonstrated a year earlier, in June 1981, when the Israel air force bombed the Iraqi nuclear reactor. The center-Left had accused the government of timing the raid to win popularity in the election campaign that was then underway. In fact, timing reprisal raids to win electoral points was already a well-established pattern in Israel (Barzilai and Russett, 1990), although the practice was not placed on the public agenda until 1981.

True, the Center-Left for the first time was not part of the decision-making inner circle so it could act autonomously; however, the opposition to the Lebanon War included part of the Likud's constituency as well (Barzilai, 1992, 210), as much as leftists in Mapam did not forcefully criticize the policy of raids of the Mapai-led government in 1953–55 when the former was not part of the governing coalition. So, party affiliation is not the sole key; remember our social interests-centered explanation with its implications for political culture.

Clearly, then, the more political disputes over the use of military force intensified, the more Israel's capacity to use force declined. The state bureaucracy and the military establishment enjoyed less autonomy to operate the military because they had to carefully calculate the expected political outcomes, especially when protests were voiced by the very groups from which military personnel were drawn.

Indeed, the IDF in particular shifted its stand. Jealous of its internal integration, social status, and human and material resources, the military traditionally rebuffed attempts to tarnish its universalist status by becoming embroiled in politics. Wars, however, showed that different groups interpreted the war's results in a manner consistent with their social position and the war's effect on their status. Hence, the probability that a war would be recognized as just, or even successful, by all its participants was highly reduced. So, if in the past the IDF had gained from the state of war materially and symbolically—and thus turned to advocate a hawkish stand—now at the vortex of political storms penetrating its ranks and undermining its professional posture, the military shifted its traditional force-oriented stand. Paradoxically, the very centrality of the IDF in Israeli society by which the military had injected its mind-set into civilian statecraft now worked to restrain the military as a means of retaining its status in a politically divided society.

Effectively, political protests prompted the withdrawal from Lebanon bit by bit by voicing the losses externally inflicted on Israel: They directly induced the government to end the warfare itself in June 1982 and later contained Defense Minister Ariel Sharon's agenda of seizing West Beirut. Subsequently, the massacre of Palestinians perpetrated by Christian militia in the neighborhoods of Sabra and Shatilla in Beirut in September 1982 brought protests to new heights. In consequence, a judicial commission was appointed, eventually engendering the resignation of Sharon, who was replaced by Moshe Arens. A few months after Sharon's resignation, Premier Begin himself resigned without explanation, apparently suffering mentally from the war's outcomes, which were protested by the permanent rally in front of his house. He was replaced by Yitzhak Shamir. This reshuffling paved the way for partial withdrawal from Lebanon. Finally, the combination of economic crisis with war accounted for the Labor electoral success in 1984 in assembling a grand coalition government that conspicuously downscaled the IDF's presence in Lebanon (see Arian, 1995a, 74–76). During the entire period since the fiasco became apparent, moreover, the IDF not only cooperated with the government but also pressed strongly for withdrawal from Lebanon until the government accepted its stand (Ben Meir, 1995, 115–116).

The Intifada restimulated a fierce political controversy even more acute than that during the Lebanon War and with further limitations on state agencies' freedom of action. Right-wing groups criticized the IDF for its impotence in dealing with the Intifada and demanded that the army quell the uprising with a massive use of firepower. This critique intensified when the Intifada spread into Israeli cities, causing casualties. The Left, for its part, criticized the IDF for its use of violence against civilians, including women and children (Shalev, 1990, 141–142).

Most significant was the rise of radical right-wing forces among the now about 150,000 Jewish settlers in the West Bank. During the Intifada a growing social-cultural split emerged between the military and groups of settlers. The military leadership, drawn from secular Western communities, insisted that the IDF's mission was to contain the Intifada in order to give the political level leverage to negotiate with the Palestinians without being under violent pressures. The settlers, on their side, blamed the IDF for sympathizing with the Palestinians. They advocated total oppression of the uprising and did not hesitate to clash violently with IDF units. The extremist sector—mostly drawn from the religious settlement in Hebron and elements of Meir Kahane's racist party, Kach, which had penetrated some settlements—even formed private, illegal militias. These individuals and groups, who had initially armed themselves under the IDF's auspices for the declared purpose of self-defense, carried out operations which, at least formally, were independent of Israeli control. Some of the groups even declared the establishment of a "state of Judea" in the West Bank, expressing both their growing alienation from the formal state and the shaping of a new, distinct identity (Lustick, 1993, 409–417).

Left groups, for their part, demonstrated consistency in their political methods. However, besides the veteran Peace Now, new political movements such as "Women in Black," Ad Kahn ("No Further," organized by university professors), "The 21st Year," and organizations for human rights were also active. These groups were successful not only in restraining the IDF's activities in the territories (part of it by petitioning the High Court) but also in tightening the monitoring of the activity of the security services (Shin-Beth). Yesh Gvul saw some magnification not only by the number of those refusing to serve in the territories (which now stood at about one hundred yearly) but by the estimation that this number might grow with the intensification of the IDF's suppressive action (Lehman-Wilzig, 1992, 143).

For the first time, moreover, the underlying "rules of discourse" were cracked as new groups, energized by the persistence of the occupation, entered the political arena and invoked civil rather than military symbols to legitimize their political claims. The peace platforms of professional and women's movements thus portended an incubation of an alternative to militarism. Ironically, the rabbis' intervention in military affairs mentioned above signaled the diminishment of militarism from another angle.

The Intifada, then, aggravated the dispute involving the two schools of thought with regard to the state's substance—leftist demographic homogeneity versus rightist territorial expansion (see Kimmerling, 1993a). In light of the political deadlock, the declaration by Chief of Staff General Dan Shomron in 1988 that the Intifada could be resolved only by political, not military, means was decisive. He thus blocked political pressures to quell the uprising vigorously by marking the boundaries of the use of military force at a level that might have less affected IDF unity. After all, soldiers from both political camps took part in dealing with the Intifada (see Ben Meir, 1995, 114; Lustick, 1993, 412). As a result, the IDF was spared the disintegration that affected other armies that had engaged in highly debated police assignments, such as the French army in Algeria (see the comparison by Peri, 1990).[5]

The IDF's sensitivity was transmitted to the political level. The fact that retired General Yitzhak Rabin served as defense minister during the critical years 1987–90 was instrumental in displaying sympathy to the IDF's sensitivity. However, self-restrained use of military force also extended to the Likud-led government after the Labor ministers' withdrawal from the cabinet in 1990. The government then displayed a relatively moderate policy in its unwillingness to use massive firepower to quell the Intifada (Lustick, 1993, 412–413).

Internal pressures were backed by external ones as described above—the restraining effects of American pressures and existing regional security arrangements. In turn, military failures and the limited capacity to use force also generated constructive effects: By averting excessive bloodshed in the occupied territories, the government decreased Palestinian hostility that otherwise might have precluded political dialogue. Similarly, in an effort to arrest the spread of the Intifada into Israeli cities, the territories were closed off on a fairly frequent basis in order to prevent the entry of Palestinian workers into Israel. The closures—justified by the government in security terms—worked to inject within the public the concept of separation between the two peoples (see Makovsky, 1996, 89). A military solution then promoted a political one. Further, the external arena (the Palestinian attacks) was invoked by politicians to overcome resistance in the internal arena. And naturally, with eroded military capabilities and growing urgency to legitimize concessions, Israeli leaders voiced a more and more dovish assessment regarding Arab countries' moderation toward conciliation with Israel (see Inbar and Sandler, 1995, 54–55). Finally, due to their achievements against the IDF in Lebanon and the Intifada, Arabs were viewed by many Israelis as more equal (Almog, 1993).

Self-restraint applied to the Lebanese sector as well. Both the Likud- and Labor-led governments grasped the lesson of the Lebanon War by refraining from employing massive ground operations against the Shiite militia in South Lebanon who resisted Israel's control over the Security Zone. In this case, Israel was driven more by sensitivity to internal costs than by external pressures. To illustrate a long-term effect, the killing of nine Israeli soldiers on this front in October 1995 inflamed a political debate over the necessity of Israel's presence in South Lebanon. And the IDF contained itself to avoid damage to civilian infrastructure in general and to tourism along the northern border in particular (Friedman, 1995). Military doctrine became more affected than ever by sensitivity to human and material losses.

Finally, the Intifada's effects interlocked with the Gulf War, initiated in 1991 by an American-led international coalition (including Arab countries) against Iraq. Israel was not a formal part of the coalition but was subjected to Iraqi missile attacks aimed at Israeli cities, causing considerable property damage, although only one man was killed. However, Israel did not retaliate. American pressure (to ensure the coalition's integration) conjoined with concern for possible heavy losses prevailed against internal pressures for striking at Iraq (see Arens, 1995, 177–217). The IDF high command played a key role in restraining the cabinet (Ben Meir, 1995, xiv–xv).

Affected by the Gulf War, Israelis now became increasingly aware of the threat to their existence, namely, the potential nuclear capabilities that had been gradually acquired by Iraq, Iran, and Libya along with long-distance missiles acquired by Syria and other countries.[6] At last, helplessly "waiting" for Iraqi missiles, with many suffering from anxiety, Israelis grasped the idea that their military power was very limited (Barzilai, 1993, 139). Evidently, the power of forceful, self-confident rhetoric declined during and after the war (ibid., 139–145; Gertz, 1995, 135–173). And the Gulf War exposed Israel's ultimate dependence on a United States that both eliminated the Iraqi threat and supplied Israel with intelligence about that threat (see Handel, 1994, 576–577).

Concomitantly, from 1992 the Intifada spilled across the Green Line. Now a new Palestinian group sprang up, namely, the Hamas fundamentalist Muslim movement that drew on lower-class groups. The Rabin government failed in its attempts to suppress Hamas by deporting its activists from the occupied territories. Against the background of military deficiencies uncovered by the Gulf War and the Intifada, the traditional military doctrine based on territorial holdings proved ineffective "both against the knife and the missile," as maintained by Foreign Minister Shimon Peres (Israel Television, April 14, 1994; see also Inbar, 1996, 8–9).

Taking together the internal and external factors, IR students have rightly maintained that deterrence also diminished because of the erosion in domestic support for using force and external limitations. The state then failed in retaining a reputation for using force by which deterrence enjoys credibility (Inbar and Sandler, 1992).

Erosion of military capabilities extended to the material level as well. An analysis of the GNP indicates that from 1985 on, governments have faced growing domestic pressures to divert resources from military buildup to private consumption (a decline from 16 percent of the GDP in 1974–82 to about 11 percent in 1986; the process of decline is ongoing at the time of writing). Diversion decreased the defense budget in absolute terms, particularly from 1985, when the budget cut served the government's successful attempt to curb the 400 percent inflation (Trop, 1989; see more below).[7] Shrinking of the military industries and a sharp decline in the state's allocations for R&D were another result (Inbar, 1996, 12).

True, the Israel–Egypt peace accord removed a significant threat to Israel's security, but at the same time, the Lebanon War and the Intifada increased the costs of security. Syria's attempt from the Lebanon War to achieve strategic parity with Israel had a similar effect until 1991. Hence, not only external factors but also the growing internal tension between military needs and material well-being impacted on cutting the defense budget. Internal pressures, however, did not necessarily take the form of direct demands but were customarily indirect ones through growing social group demands to seize state resources in a consumerist society.

In a similar spirit, the IDF found itself increasingly being pushed to adjust to civilian considerations. Press and parents' scrutiny of accidents in military operations; reservists' critique of the distribution of the military burden, generating legislative attempts limiting the IDF's powers to call reservists up; homosexuals' and women's successful struggle to lift limitations on their military promotion; the press's scrutiny of issues of budgets, nominations, military performance; lifting of civilian restrictions on those who had not done military service; and moderation of military discipline were among the manifestations of this trend (see Cohen, 1995; Haberman, 1995).[8] Add to this the middle-class groups' preference for civilian channels for social mobility and shrinking budgets, and the IDF's suffering from material scarcity increased (see Inbar and Sandler, 1995, 51–55, from the IR perspective).[9]

Tension then arose between allocation of resources to deal with low-level threats such as the Intifada and other proximate threats from Syria and Lebanon and the resources geared to deal with new, long-distance threats. New opportunities that presented themselves in the global arena made it necessary for military and political elites to take a clear stand more acute: The regional system seemed to be significantly changed by the decline of the Soviet Union, formerly the Arabs' chief ally, impairing the military power of both Syria and the PLO. A sharp decrease of defense expenditures in the Arab world (Inbar and Sandler, 1992, 5), a deep crisis in the PLO, and the disintegration of the united Arab front against Israel following the Gulf War signified the diminishing threat posed by the Arab states bordering Israel. Add to this Arab countries' pragmatism, especially when they acknowledged Israel's unquestionable military supremacy (to a large extent owing to the latter's nuclear capabilities), and Israel had an opportunity to settle conflicts from an advantageous position. Nuclear proliferation, however, could have nullified these advantages. Time worked against Israel.

In sum, a mixture of crises in military doctrine with regional opportunities for de-escalation revealed themselves. Military capabilities largely declined insofar as the state's capacity to manage effectively its domestic strategies for war preparation was eroded at the level of political support. At the same time, internal and external pressures delimited Israel's capacity to exploit its capabilities. Although Israel enjoyed military supremacy, external factors devalued the original targets and Israel's means of facing new threats. So, the more the capacity to use force and deterrence shrank, the fewer options were available for statecraft other than to de-escalate or at least check the conflict. Reassessment of strategic doctrine then took place.

Reassessment of Strategic Doctrine

Louder than ever, a call for shifting from offensive to defensive military doctrine was voiced by politicians, strategic thinkers, journalists, and others advocating the IDF's adaptation to its shrinking resources and limits in using force (see, for example, Levite, 1989). A defensive posture, moreover, was largely related to another trend, namely, replacing part of the army's standard armament, particularly in the armored forces, with high-tech weapons systems to deal with distant threats and border frictions alike (see Yaniv, 1994, 388–390; Yogev, 1989).[10] Concurrently, more missions including the oppression of the Intifada were assigned to "special units," elitist and highly selective by nature (Wald, 1994, 59–63). Chief of Staff Dan Shomron stated that conception in a nutshell: Israel, he said, needed a "small, smart army." The likely result of that process could be the downsizing of the IDF through a greater use of sophisticated technology with the rise of a military-technological elite. By itself, the latter might be also used to make the army more attractive again to middle-class, well-educated youngsters.[11]

To complete the reassessment, another idea broached at the time was to shift to selective conscription, as many Western armies had already done. Selective conscription would effectively exclude, for the short term, a certain proportion of nonmobile social groups whose primary educational level was not equal to that of the well-educated middle-class groups. Social integration then would be left to the civilian educational system and the IDF would give preference to military professionalism, enabling it to build an elitist army (see Gordon, 1992). Indeed, data from 1995 reveal that the IDF practically adopted selective methods of conscription, evidenced by disqualification from military service of about a third of the Jewish population (Haberman, 1995).

Strategic reorientation conjoined with de-escalation could increase Israel's security. The establishing of a new regional order based on economic cooperation and security institutions between Israel and the relatively moderate Arab countries seemed to curb radical countries such as Iran, Iraq, and Libya, which posed a threat not only to Israel, but to moderate Muslim countries such as Egypt, Jordan, and the nascent Palestine. De-escalation could also neutralize the Arab hostility that lay behind nuclear proliferation in the Middle East; the peace-driven rise of a middle class in Arab countries, it was thought, would lessen the motivation to engage in an arms race and war (see Beilin, 1993, introduction; Peres, 1993, 1–15; 1995).

Likewise, the PLO undertook to contain the radical Hamas movement in the occupied territories, mainly the Gaza Strip, while the IDF's attempts to do so has had only limited success. Alternatively, a "cheap occupation" was at work, since the Israel–PLO agreement, at least for the short term, has not eliminated the Israeli occupation over the Palestinian population in the West Bank and Gaza Strip but has formed a new division of labor: Israel has retained its formal, sovereign rule over the territories while the control over the hostile population has been assigned to the new Palestinian Authority functioning as a "subcontractor" of Israel, as many Israelis saw it (see Makovsky, 1996, 76; Raz-Krakotzkin, 1993). No wonder that these arrangements induced the IDF command's support for the Oslo Accord (Makovsky, 1996, 102–103). No doubt, had the IDF mastered resources at the same levels of the 1970s/80s, it would have been disinclined to refresh its repertoire of doctrinary options. Scarcity inspired innovative thinking.

De-escalation interwoven with the communication of benign motives might also increase Israel's security—a successful coping with the security dilemma that cannot be done by resorting to violence. Add to this Israel's limitations in using force, and Israel directed its self-help efforts toward regional cooperation as long as it enjoyed military superiority. But if this strategy fails, de-escalation will still permit a diversion of resources previously required to manage the conflict in the proximate geographical arena to the procurement of munitions that would serve to meet long-distance threats (see Benn, 1993; Makovsky, 1996, 102–103).

Importantly, restoring Israel's deterrent capability was also invoked by proponents of de-escalation: Formal demilitarization of the borders would make manifest Israel's determination to act in case of the other side's violation, and would minimize frictions, such as the Intifada and those with the Shiite militia in South Lebanon, which exposed Israel's innate weakness (see Yaniv, 1989).

Israel was then ready to pay the price it had earlier been reluctant to pay. One component of this price was a direct dialogue with the PLO, which it previously had branded a terrorist organization, resulting in the signing of the Oslo Agreement in September 1993. Ironically, moreover, on the eve of the Lebanon War Israel rejected a similar option to establish a functional division of labor with the PLO, that is, a quasi-state in return for military calm. The other component of the political price was the acceptance of a withdrawal from the Golan Heights.

Nothing attests to Israel's realignment more than its partial reformulating security interests in political terms, that is, advancing de-escalation as a strategic goal. Formerly intent on expanding its security margins, Israel reconciled itself to the logic of taking risks in return for convertible political, partly long-term, assets. Israel, moreover, shifted from a passive posture regarding Arab hostility to an active one, seeking to shape Arab attitudes. This was seen in Israel's rescue of the PLO from disintegration (see Beilin, 1993, introduction) and, most important, in the attempt to contain radicalization and Islamization of Arab politics. Hence also Israel's moderate reaction toward the PLO/Palestinian Authority perceived violations of the Oslo Agreement, a far cry from the rigidity that characterized Israel's responses in the past. Above all, Israel switched from a "zero-sum game" that had previously inspired its methods of self-reliance to a new approach. Active assistance Israel gave to the Palestinians in establishing paramilitary power in the West Bank and Gaza Strip and the willingness to take part in modernizing the Jordanian military indicated the new approach. A new regional security institution is being formed through which Israel's security also draws from the security of its bordering states.

Arguably, despite external pressures, Israel still enjoyed considerable freedom to act externally and could have embarked on alternative paths. To evaluate the causal power of those pressures, four factors are relevant:

(1) Israel enjoyed unquestioned military superiority at the end of the Cold War. This also extended to its capacity to combat the Intifada despite the Palestinians' achievements and internal pressures.

(2) Israel was not put under the same kind of forceful pressure to withdraw from the territories as the American-Soviet pressure leading to Israel's withdrawal from the Sinai Peninsula in 1956. Nor was the American aid cut following the global change. On the contrary, Israel could have capitalized on

the internal bickering within the U.S. political system in which many politicians were annoyed at concessions toward Arab states. So, the Israeli government could retain a moderate version of status quo/de-escalation policies (beyond refraining from using fire) aimed at decreasing the conflict's costs—such as freezing the settlement project in the West Bank. That was what had been demanded by the United States, which backed Israel's reluctance to hold direct talks with the PLO, and could have satisfied certain groups within the Israeli polity. Filibustering the talks with the Palestinians was another option to escape international pressures.

(3) There was a lack of extraordinary pragmatism from the Arab side. Contrary to President Sadat's gesture (in visiting Jerusalem), Syrian and PLO leaders did not demonstrate unusual moderation before Israel demonstrated its revised posture. Yet it is clear that had Arabs displayed a rigid stand—for instance, had Syria adhered to achieving strategic parity with Israel or had the PLO been reluctant to open the secret channel for dialogue in Oslo—it might have hindered Israel's moderation. Arab countries were more passive than active.

(4) Paradoxically, the fall of the Soviet Union could have been viewed by Israel as undermining the regional order in light of the prospect that a Muslim coalition would be formed, encompassing Iran, some Arab countries, and the former Muslim Soviet Republics. Likewise, the potential that an Arab/Muslim country would acquire nuclear arms from the crumbling Soviet army was increased and the challenge to Israel's nuclear monopoly with it. Ironically, however, by establishing security regimes with the bordering countries, Israel became susceptible to pressures (mainly from Egypt) aimed at delimiting Israel's nuclear capacity by signing the Nuclear Non-Proliferation Treaty. On the contrary, in the past Israel had chosen not to follow up political opportunities for resolving the conflict, opportunities that had arisen *because* of Soviet intervention. The failure to reach an Egyptian-Israeli interim agreement in 1971/72, which was interlocked with the American-Soviet detente, is a case in point (see chapter 4).

All this attests to Israel's ability to read the same peace-prone signals as signals to maintain the status quo insofar as Arabs seemed to accept Israel's superiority (without turning to affirmative moderation), but the region still posed threats. Adjustment of military doctrine according to the internal and external pressures by both reducing the military burden through organizational changes in the military and moderating policies in the occupied territories, rather than all-inclusive de-escalation, was a real option. The international system constrained Israel but did not compel a move toward peace. Had the Arab leaders rejected the Israeli position, moreover, the risks of a renewed arms race would have seemed to be low. Indeed, this realism-informed logic was put forward by the Israeli Right (see Netanyahu, 1995, 241–361). In this spirit, Risse-Kappen (1994) argues, with respect to the Soviet Union, that Gorbachev, instead of employing reform-oriented strategies, could have embarked on the opposite road: He could have increased aggressiveness in light of the Soviet Union's decline as a means of intensifying the extractive capabilities of its state.

External, countervailing realities were then at work again—opportunities for peace and limitations with status quo opportunities and threats. Hence, the international system is not the sole determinant of Israel's ultimate preference, or at least its *timing*. In the end, moreover (if one rejects the conclusion that equal options were workable), states may remain blind to external occurrences as long as those occurrences are not compelling forces. And even if such forces become effective, states, Israel being no exception, might confront the U.S.-European bloc as did South Africa, Serbia, and Iraq—countries that overlooked global constraints. If so, we must scrutinize the manner in which internal actors filtered external opportunities and translated them into political action. Those translated signals helped fabricate strategic thinkers' mode of reading. The state's assessment is again the focal point.

True, we have factored in domestic constraints on bellicose policies but we have not completed the entire explanatory course. Domestic constraints, together with global constraints and opportunities, can elicit reassessment of bellicose policies by states but cannot alone energize a strategic shift other than by being conjoined with internal support for political concessions. Insofar as war-based relations of exchange had been molded through which social agents hardened the state's force-oriented policies in accordance with their gains, reversal moves toward de-escalation meant a structural social change rather then just a change at the level of strategic doctrine. Group protests undermining military doctrine were only part of a broader change.

We should also remember that structure in this regard means discourse. As a part of the gradual inculcation of the occupied territories as an organic ingredient of the Israeli polity, the demonization of the PLO and Yasir Arafat was deeply rooted among Israelis. Talking with the PLO was even forbidden by law. Clearly, a reconstruction of social interests could not be set in motion unless the gains entailed in the status quo lost their relevance and new actual or potential gains presented themselves to internal actors. This is the meaning of a structural change. So, who benefited from moving toward de-escalation?

MOBILIZING POLITICAL SUPPORT

Political support for the peace moves came from four, mostly new, factors: (a) the decline of benefits from the occupation; (b) the expectations of the fruits of a "peace economy"; (c) the partial dismantling of the hawkish front; and d) the support of the IDF.

(a) The decline of benefits. Beyond the general burden that had grown owing to the Lebanon War and the Intifada along the parameters outlined above, the conflict's gains diminished, impairing those groups who had previously gained from the conflict despite the general burden. Gains declined primarily because the drive of the post-1967 economic boom was now nullified.

The gigantic state-owned military industries suffered from the IDF's decreasing consumption and the worldwide crisis in the arms industry as the Cold War ended. So adverse was their situation that they have needed growing state subsidies to survive. The arms industry shrank from about 45,000 employees in the main state-owned industries during early 1980 to 28,000 workers in 1995; the process of decrease is ongoing at the time of this writing (*Ma'ariv*, May 11, 1995, 4–5). Some industries then converted a significant part of their military production to civilian goods (*Globes*, March 31, 1995, 44; *Yediot Aharonot*, March 28, 1995, 9). Military industries were no longer a significant economic lever.

Concurrently, the Intifada, by disrupting the entry of Palestinian workers into Israel, caused serious problems in various economic sectors, particularly manufacturing and industry. At the same time, Israel's economic dependence on the Palestinian workforce diminished, thanks to the arrival of nearly half a million Jewish immigrants from the former Soviet Union beginning in 1989. Lacking an organizational infrastructure, the new immigrants were dependent on the state and could therefore be exploited for blue-collar work as a partial replacement for the Palestinians. Once the Russians began to drift out of this economic segment, the government authorized the importation of 100,000 foreign workers (at the time of this writing; the informal figure is about 200,000) from Thailand, Romania, and elsewhere, a policy that was viable due to the decline of the Histadrut, presumably an opponent of moves of this kind. Thanks to this policy, the Rabin government was able to close off the territories sporadically from 1993 on and reduce the number of Palestinian workers entering Israel from 120,000 to about 25,000 to 50,000. Also the modernization of the Israeli economy beginning in the 1970s, which gave a boost to high-tech industries, weakened the position of labor-intensive business corporations. In the past those firms had benefited from the occupation and had a vested interest in its continuation (see Teitelbaum, 1984, on the post-1967 structure).

Another economic lever that declined due to the Intifada was the massive housing in the occupied territories, which could no longer be a mechanism of improvement of the standard of living. The decision made by the Rabin government in 1992 to freeze the establishment of new settlements (but not construction in existing settlements or in East Jerusalem) further accelerated this decline. Notwithstanding the freeze, the influx of immigrants from the former Soviet Union propelled massive construction within the Green Line boundaries. Indirectly and partially this was funded by American aid which, by itself, became conditional on freezing the settlement project in the occupied territories (see more below).

It is premature to assess the manner in which the decline of gains was translated into political support; however, it is safe to assume that in the absence of rigid counterinterests, the government could mobilize support more easily for the process of decolonization (in Grinberg's terms, 1994) and the military mind-set was challenged.

(b) Peace economy. The conflict's gains also declined relative to the new options entailed in a "peace economy." Peace became equated with economic growth at several levels. In 1985, the United States converted its foreign-aid loans to Israel into grants. This move, which played a key role in resolving the severe fiscal crisis (one manifestation of which was an annual inflation rate of 400 percent), became possible owing to the formation of a Labor–Likud government that de-escalated the Lebanon War. With the de-escalation in Lebanon, moreover, the government could dramatically cut the defense budget by about 8 percent; the newly released funds were diverted mainly to private consumption, over and above the growth in the GDP (Ben-Zvi. S, 1993; Trop, 1989). The linkage between military-political moderation and economic well-being for middle- and upper-class groups was augmented.

Material gains, moreover, increased since the economic measures created severe unemployment mainly in the secondary labor market, going from about 4 percent in 1984 to about 11 percent in 1992. In the Orientals' neighborhoods the rate was significantly higher. Only 1993 signified a turning point, in which the unemployment rate fell. High rates of unemployment worked to reduce costs of labor and to restrain workers (on the economic policies, see Grinberg, 1991b, 150–156; Shalev and Grinberg, 1989). Although the ethos of full employment had long been dominant in Israeli society (Shalev, 1984, 9–13), the new situation was incompatible with the more recent internalization of another ethos inspired by the prevailing materialism, that of economic efficiency (Gottlieb and Yuchtman-Yaar, 1985; Talmud, 1985), by which business corporations could improve their profitability. Evident is the absence of meaningful political opposition to the state's role in fixing the unemployment rate (Lehman-Wilzig, 1992, 77–78). However, cultural change per se did not solely account for this lack of opposition; nor did the cooperation between the main parties within the grand coalition. We ought to bring into play the state's effective reproduction of the inequitable social structure, at least in the short term, through the strategies of splitting the working class in general and the Oriental community in particular. This process was linked to peacemaking.

From the mid-1980s on (even before the economic plan took effect), many nonmobile Orientals, chiefly from poor city neighborhoods and development towns, were disappointed by the ineffectiveness displayed by the Likud-led government in the social-economic domain and became more alienated from the dominant Western culture. After all, even though the state's institutions were ruled by the Likud, the majority of whose supporters were Orientals, the interethnic gap persisted. About 10 percent of the whole Oriental community flocked from the Likud and the National Religious Party to new political frameworks.

In the elections of 1984 about 25,000 voters (1.2 percent of the total), mostly nonmobile Orientals, supported Meir Kahane's party Kach. Kach advocated expulsion of the Palestinian population, Israeli citizens and residents of the occupied territories alike, to retain Jewish homogeneity. Suffering from deep unemployment aggravated by the government's attempts to struggle with inflation after 1985, Orientals blamed their position on low-wage Palestinian workers.[12] Hence, their support for Kach grew from 1984 to 1988. Nonetheless, in 1988 the Supreme Court disqualified Kach from participating in the upcoming elections (Peled, 1990).

Concomitantly, the Intifada, by heightening the intercommunal profile of the Arab-Israeli conflict, sharpened the primordial identity of the Israeli Jewish community and thus further legitimized the presentation of traditional Oriental identity. When the Intifada expanded into Israeli cities inside the Green Line with Palestinian attacks against Israeli citizens, this traditional identity was manifested in Orientals' high presence in demonstrations held immediately after the attacks. They demanded "strong-arm" tactics against Palestinians, protested against the limitations entailed by the Israeli law on employing a tough approach, and violently attacked Palestinian workers.

Other Orientals allied with the ultra-Orthodox religious political parties, particularly the newly formed Shas (Sephardi Torah Guardians). This party was established in 1983 by pious young Orientals who were students in Ashkenazi yeshivas. The social problems they encountered when they sought acceptance in the ultra-Orthodox Ashkenazi community led them to organize politically on their own. They attracted a large following of Orientals, the majority not ultra-Orthodox, and even secular—a constituency similar to that of Kach (indeed, from 1988, a significant part of Kach's voters apparently shifted to Shas). The party did impressively well in the elections, obtaining 4 to 6 seats in the 120-member Knesset in 1984–92 and 10 seats in the elections of 1996, and becoming a part (sometimes informal) of the governing coalition (see Friedman, 1991, 175–185; Peled, 1991).

More than the Likud, Kach and Shas identified with the primordial aspects of the Israeli Jewish community. They displayed open contempt for the rule of law and for the other institutions that represented Mamlachtiyut. Through their support, the nonmobile Orientals have, in fact, registered their political protest against both Mamlachtiyut and modernity (which became strongly mixed with Westernized, globalization-oriented values from the 1990s), the two ideological constructs used to legitimate their peripheral status (see Peled, 1990). Shas, moreover, effectively worked to establish an autonomous educational-cultural system, funded by the state, to promote traditional Oriental culture, which Mamlachtiyut had supplanted. The Shas schools provided an ultra-Orthodox education and underscored the authentic elements of traditional Oriental culture, particularly the promotion of folklore.

Shas was constituted by youngsters. As social mobility in civilian tracks was blocked and as military service held no attraction for some of the Orientals in light of difficulties to attain mobility in a military losing social prestige, they were driven to attain political status divorced from the military. Shas, by establishing its own educational-cultural system, has constructed an alternative niche for accumulating symbolic and even material power. Ironically, then, conversion of power from the military to the civilian sphere had an impact even on those lacking military-accumulated resources. No wonder that the Shas groups not only developed a route distinct from military service, but also, contrary to the previous approach taken by Orientals, demanded exemption from military service for their youngsters, preferring to have them study in yeshivas. The government accepted this stand under the pressure of the powerful Orthodox political parties. Still, that arrangement increased selectivity and furthered the association of military service with the Westerners and "Westernized" Orientals. In fact, it has prevented the "others" (Palestinians and Oriental-identified alike) from taking a real part in defining the common good of the Israeli society; hence, the pervasive, legitimate acceptance of this policy. And again, the deep-seated legitimacy of the ethos of egalitarianism remained intact.

For the first time in the country's history, this Shas-based Oriental reaction marked a shift from a Likud-mobilized political action guided by ethnic motives to a construction, by political means, of a unique ethnic identity. In other words, the construction of collective belief "legitimated and sustained through cultural expression" (Enloe, 1980, 9; see also Smith, 1992, 437) became distinct from the rest of the society. The Orientals' action then effectively signaled the collapse of the successful Westerner Mamlachtiyut-based strategy to present Oriental political organizations as illegitimate because of their ethnic profile (see Herzog, 1985).

As for the state, alternately directed by two middle-class political parties, it helped fund Shas's establishment of its own system, channeling Orientals' protest into the cultural sphere, rather than the realm of social class, lest it have immediate implications for the reproduction of the social structure (see Peled, 1991). Increase of yeshiva students, moreover, created a nonproductive segment that excessively relied on state funding via Shas. Consequently, the inequitable social structure was reproduced at low cost, relative to those that might have been created had Orientals fought for altering the social structure.

So, back to my argument in chapter 5, the Shas-based activity manifested the failure of Mamlachtiyut as a strategy of de-ethnization rather than as a strategy reproducing interclass relations. So, although the shaping of ethnic identity as such signifies a failure in assimilation-oriented efforts initiated by the state, this impact might be instrumental in the state's reproduction-oriented action.

The state's policies of conflict management (partly through the IDF), which interlocked with socioeconomic regulation, thus had the unintended consequences of simultaneously augmenting Westerner-dominated middle-class superiority and splitting the Oriental collective. One part of this collective, especially the materially mobile, but also even part of the nonmobile segment, adhered to the mobility-oriented, non-ethnic track, affected by the deeply imbued belief in equal opportunities for which the military is a prominent mechanism of socialization. The nonmobile part, now after the split a relatively weak segment, turned to fortify its cultural uniqueness.

Further, the split of the whole working class was stimulated by the nonmobile Orientals' inability to cooperate with Palestinians, whose social status was identical. Because of a deep hostility between the two groups, an exclusionary strategy was adopted by many Orientals via Kach toward Palestinian laborers. Ironically, these laborers were among the factors accounting for the economic boom after the 1967 War by which the mobile Orientals benefited. Nonmobile Orientals, however, chose exclusion over cooperation with Palestinian workers to fight for a better standard of living (see Peled, 1990). In sum, a sharp class identity among poorer Orientals did not develop (see Smooha, 1993, 176–178). At this level, the Likud's ascension to power in 1977 strengthened the state's ability to remobilize the Orientals, obviating their increasing alienation under the rule of the labor parties.[13]

To the successful Shas-based strategy of splitting of the Oriental communities add the Histadrut's dramatic decline, the decline of a mechanism that voiced, albeit weakly, laborers' interests. In the late 1980s, the Histadrut's economic institutions began to collapse and gradually separated from its control, due in part to the contradiction that had emerged between their perceived social functions and the growth of the private sector under the state's auspices and the fall-off in state support.

Most striking was the enactment of the "State Health Law" in 1994, by which the state, at the end of forty years of struggle, practically separated the Histadrut and its Sick Fund. Moreover, the Histadrut became completely at the mercy of the state, as the latter assumed the collection of membership fees for the Histadrut. Recalling the argument on the decline of militarist symbols, unlike the similar struggles that took place during the 1950s and 1960s, the state-oriented groups, headed by the new general secretary Chaim Ramon (who, by leading a combined Center–Shas list, ousted Labor's control after seventy-five years of dominance) were associated with civilian professions.

Advocating dovish orientations, moreover, this group invoked socioeconomic symbols, rather than military ones, to transcend the Labor Party machine.

Consequently, the more peripheral groups were disciplined, the more business corporations could flourish and the state could gain leverage to erode welfare systems under the pressures of those corporations to lift barriers on accumulation of capital. Beyond employing unemployment, the state's autonomy was also pronounced in overt efforts, from the mid-1980s, to weaken the ruling ideology of equality in the Israeli Jewish educational system. Instead, the scales were tipped in favor of the dominant groups which could acquire education of greater value based on their differential ability (Swirski, 1990, 195–198), although the educational gaps were not widened in formal terms. Further, the policy of privatizing state- and Histadrut-owned corporations was run in the spirit that prevails in the West (see Katz, 1991) and encouraged further centralization of private capital.

At the same time, in 1995 state institutions failed to impose taxation over capital gains because of the resistance of business corporations, especially those that had sprung up under the state's auspices. Now the country's success in incorporating into global markets depended on their functioning. Concurrently, the state constantly worked to decrease the level of taxation on the upper and middle classes thanks to the cut in defense spending. For example, the government lowered its corporate income tax rate from 61 percent in 1986 to 36 percent. And the overall tax burden, which in 1986 reached the peak of 45 percent of GDP stood in 1995 at 40 percent of GDP (Israel Ministry of Finance, 1996). But at the same time, Israel's governments froze the minimum wage, abolished the subsidization of basic foodstuffs, and stiffened the criteria determining eligibility for unemployment allowances.

All of this was reflected in the income gaps between second-generation Westerners and Orientals that on average *grew* at about 10 percent between 1975 and 1992 among men and at a similar level between the preferred group (Western men) and the other Jewish groups (Western women, Oriental men, and Oriental women) (Haberfeld and Cohen, 1995). Had gaps *within* the Oriental communities been documented, it seems safe to argue that the data would show greater gaps between middle-class groups (including mobile Orientals) and nonmobile Orientals.

Equally significant, the new immigration from the former Soviet Union was absorbed mainly by market mechanisms, with the state playing a lesser role than it had in past waves of immigration (see Zarhi, 1991). The rates of unemployed and homeless people were high among those who did not enjoy social mobility. This led to calls for enacting selective immigration fitted to the country's needs and capacity to absorb newcomers.

In consequence, a new social structure arose in which the nonmobile Orientals and Israeli Palestinians were joined by nonmobile immigrants and foreign workers. Now the increase in poverty came to affect about 20 percent of the population, in particular Israeli Palestinians, Russian immigrants, and Orientals in peripheral towns. By the 1990s, then, Israel had become one of the most inegalitarian societies in the Western world.

Turning back to the discussion on the state's first years (chapter 2, table 2.1), successful reproduction laid the foundations for the state's shift from the trajectory of state-directed absorption to that of a market-oriented, capitalist-style absorption with restraining effects on the potential for war.

Sturdy bonds among effective reproduction, empowerment of business corporations, and the decline of welfare systems impacted peacemaking, as figure 6.1 shows. To begin, the newly tailored peace-consumerism package could not take root unless war lost a great deal of its instrumentality in retaining the social order. Symptomatic was the phenomenon that, unlike in former instances, state agencies were no longer inclined to invoke external threats as a means of restraining social pressures. Strict capitalist values, rather than the old patterns of Mamlachtiyut, legitimized inequality in the Israeli society of the 1980s and 1990s. This also had implications for the solidification of a peace-oriented political discourse.

The lessening linkage between interethnic reproduction and the state of war was no more blatant than in the IDF's withdrawal from its social integration missions evidenced by disqualification from military service of about a third of the Jewish population, apparently nonmobile Orientals, ultra-Orthodox and

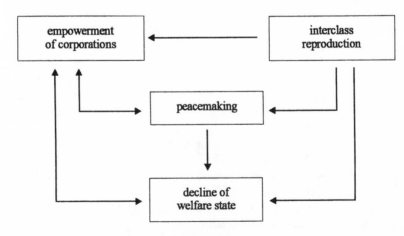

Figure 6.1
Peacemaking and Welfare Systems

some upper-middle-class youngsters (Haberman, 1995). As a senior officer implied, even in the mid-1990s the IDF reflected the inequalities in Israeli society as seen by the limited number of nonmobile groups staffing elite units (see an interview with Lieutenant Colonel Rami Dovrat, *Yediot Aharonot Supplement*, April 19, 1996, 15–16). Similar to former instances, moreover, reshaping of criteria for promotion and devaluation of Orientals' present accomplishments in the military, now in a consumerist, de-escalation-prone society, went together. But unlike in former instances, the diminishment of inclusiveness suggests that the intrinsic tension between professionalism and social tasks began to be questioned, if not decided. To a large extent, this transformation attests to the IDF's prioritizing professional considerations. Its reproduction-oriented policies were, as this book has repeatedly argued, an unintended consequence of its professional posture. Reproduction-oriented roles now waned.

At the same time, the very transformation to selective conscription shows the extent to which the mission of social integration became marginal at the political level. We, moreover, remember that mass conscription depended on an effective welfare system by which obstacles to uninterrupted participation of peripheral groups in the military are lifted and the educational system qualifies them to be soldiers (for comparison, see Porter, 1994, 195–241; Shaw, 1988; Skocpol, 1992, on the warfare-welfare state). So, the more the IDF adopted selective methods, the greater the state's leverage to erode welfare systems without taking short-term risks in the domain of legitimation (albeit with neglected long-term risks; see below).[14]

Reciprocal relations between the empowerment of business corporations and peacemaking took their course as figure 6.1 shows: Directly, the decline of welfare gave rise to a sector supporting peacemaking for strict business calculations (see more below); indirectly, capital forces' support for the peace moves was fueled by the de-escalation-stimulated decline of welfare systems, increasing their satisfaction as the ability to accumulate capital became smoother than ever. Invoking the innate rationale of the global system (such as marketability, competitiveness, etc.), firms also acquired further capacity to eliminate internal obstacles to exploitation of the labor force within a "flexible" labor market (of which the importation of foreign workers was a part). Simply put, globalization benefits mainly the dominant groups (for a comparative analysis, see Gill, 1995; Tilly, 1995d). The eradication of welfare systems then became an integral ingredient of the peace economy.

Material gains equaled de-escalation once again. This happened when Washington approved loan guarantees worth $10 billion to help Israel absorb the influx of immigrants from the former Soviet Union. The guarantees were given to the Rabin government in 1992 only after it had agreed, in line with its political approach, to freeze the establishment of new settlements in the occupied territories—a condition that had been rejected by the right-wing Likud government under Yitzhak Shamir a year before. Naturally, the increase in aid, conditional on the peace process, augmented support for the government's new approach among the many groups in the upper and middle class that benefited from the American largesse.

Of great importance was the moderation of the main "clients" of this aid, the new immigrants, 58 percent of whom in the elections of 1992 had favored the center-left parties while only 34 percent advocated (a few months earlier) return of territories (Fein, 1995, 168–173). Again, a material stand overshadowed ideological preferences and tipped the scale in favor of electoral change—the return to power of the Labor Party led by Yitzhak Rabin and Shimon Peres (Arian and Shamir, 1995, 29–30), who speeded up the peace moves.

It is thus worth emphasizing that Israel's growing dependence on the American funds has not meant, by itself, erosion in its autonomy relative to external forces (as claimed by Barnett, 1992, 228–243), but rather in its autonomy vis-à-vis internal dominant groups as the social order relied on the role played by the funds in the permanent rising of the standard of living. American aid, *mediated* by social forces, worked to moderate the Israeli approach.

Expected material benefits fueled peace-oriented support at other levels as well in addition to the de-escalation-incited tax cut mentioned above. As the dialogue with the Palestinians made progress, it gave a boost to new economic forces, mainly business corporations, private and state-owned alike. In particular they looked to economic cooperation with the European Union and the United States unrestricted by the Arab boycott, which gradually vanished as the peace process advanced. In like manner, other businessmen were motivated by the enormous potential for Israeli economic relations with the Arab world, particularly the Gulf states. Moving labor-intensive production branches to Arab countries, where labor costs are significantly lower than in Israel, was another option considered by manufacturers (see, for example, Friedlin, 1996, on the textile industry).

Even the boost given to the Israeli stock market by the PLO–Israel agreement created a clear linkage between business interests (and many ordinary citizens who were indirectly involved with this market by their savings) and peace. Immense entrance of American, European, and Asian companies into the Israeli market to invest capital, purchase companies, and market goods signified another form of linkage between peace and economic boom with further augmentation of forces supporting peace. No wonder that members of the Israeli business-managerial elite supported the peace process publicly (see Ramirez, 1995; Rosenberg, 1995; Swirski, 1993).

Domestic forces thus played a key role in translating into peace moves the signals of the changing international system following the end of the Cold War. Interests then realized ideology and vice versa. New ideology was apparent not only in the new images of Arabs, but new global-universalist cultural frames of mind emerged as well among middle-class groups, displacing some of the post-1967 force-oriented symbols (Almog, 1993; Hareven, 1993; Gertz, 1995, 135–173). This development is worth emphasizing, as many people, primarily intellectuals, who had taken part in both constructing and injecting the post-1967 military-originated frames of thought, now became swept up in the new trends.

Global trends possibly nurtured the new Israeli outlook on the Arab world and shaped political stands, as neoliberal and constructivist scholars have theoretically claimed (see, for example, Deudney and Ikenberry, 1991; Lebow, 1994; Rhodes, 1995; Risse-Kappen, 1994; Wendt, 1992). But it seems safe to claim that global ideas would have signified no more than futile thoughts, as had many "imported" ideas during former periods, in the absence of several conditions—a fit between ideas and interests, real obstacles erected to maintaining the state of war, and conditions that generated the dominant group's exposure to global trends, that is, the state-led rise in the standard of living. Simply put, the social structure accounts for the manner in which different societies are affected by exogenous trends. Equally significant, the value of the assets over which Israelis and Arabs disputed—the territories—was minimized in Israeli eyes insofar as gains from such assets declined. Hence, the openness to new ideas that worked to universalize, and thus to legitimize, the actualization of new material interests.[15]

Taking together the cumulative impact of the decline of old gains with the rise of new ones, growing moderation among Israeli Jews, Westerners and Orientals alike, became apparent following the Intifada (Arian, 1995a, 115).[16] As one right-wing speaker claimed, the bourgeois Left successfully made its materialist formula hegemonic (Unger, 1993).

Israeli Palestinians also took their part as the Labor-led government was supported, for the first time, by the Israeli Palestinian parties. Within a two-bloc system, the Palestinians' electoral weight increased to the degree that even the Likud attempted to mobilize their support (Arens, 1995, 20). And, ironically, some Israeli Palestinians' refrain from wholeheartedly casting their ballots for Prime Minister Shimon Peres in the elections of 1996 (registering their protest against the government's hard-line policies in Lebanon and toward the Palestinian Authority, see more below) paved the way for the victory of the Likud leader, Benjamin Netanyahu. Israeli Palestinians then paradoxically gained from the conflict-originated bickering that split the Israeli polity. Likewise, inspired by the effort to curtail the penetration of the Intifada into the Green Line alongside other considerations, differentiation was made between the Palestinians who were Israeli citizens and those residing in the occupied territories. This was done by cementing the civil status of the former in contrast to the deprivation of civil rights suffered by the latter (Peled, 1992, 439). In addition to the Palestinians' success in improving their lot in the labor market by, paradoxically, taking advantage of their economic isolation (Lewin-Epstein and Semyonov, 1994) and other achievements in education (see chapter 4), new, independent, political forms have arisen, such as the Arab Democratic Party and the Islamic Movement. Some of them sought more than ever to increase the Israeli Palestinians' integration into the core of Israeli society (see Al-Haj, 1993).

Needless to say, Israeli Palestinians also had an interest in the termination of the conflict by which a major barrier to their integration would be removed (see Rekhess, 1995). Further, the more this community was viewed as loyal to the Jewish state, the less the state of conflict was invoked to legitimize discrimination against Israeli Palestinians.[17] By taking part in supporting peacemaking, and thus helping the government overcome its narrow parliamentary base, Israeli Palestinians became more legitimate political participants, albeit still not in a complete fashion.

(c) The partial dismantling of the hawkish front. The change of government in 1992 was accompanied by the creation of a unique political alliance between the nonmobile Orientals and the Westerner-dominated middle class embodied in the coalition government formed among Labor, the left-wing bloc, and the ultra-Orthodox Shas Party and, in part, the Israeli Palestinian parties. Shas's critical support for the 1993 agreement with the PLO (Oslo I, although it moderately opposed Oslo II) began to splinter the Orientals' hawkish image. The modification of the hawkish stance is attributable not only to the moderate version of the traditional Sephardic attitude to the idea of "Whole Land of Israel" but also to the fact that Shas did not represent the segment of the Orientals that enjoyed social mobility via military service. Consequently, part of this group was more prone than other Orientals to support a policy that would alter the force-oriented thrust of Israeli society—even though they themselves believed in force and had, in part, tended to support Rabbi Kahane's party. In practice, this group distinguished between the primordial source of its hostility toward the Arabs and the instrumental source of its pragmatic approach toward the peace process, whether for short-term political reasons or to build a bridge to the Westerners.

It seems safe to assume that had the state strategies of splitting not taken their course, the Likud could have retained its hold among Oriental constituencies and thus avoided a crack in the hawkish front. Back to figure 6.1, strategies of interethnic reproduction impacted on peacemaking from this particular direction as well.

Cracks were also apparent in the settlers' organizing in the West Bank. To recall, Gush Emunim gradually became a bureaucracy managing part of the colonial project in the West Bank and as such, was dependent on the state's favors (see Goldberg, 1993; Moskovitch, 1992, 91–92). The movement underwent a process of gradual moderation and eventually had no ideological alternative to offer. By the 1990s Gush Emunim lost its political potency as a movement; an internal split among the settlers resulted in loss of parliamentary representation by the settlers' party, Tehiya (Shamir and Arian, 1995, 6). No wonder that the Oslo Agreement took the settlers by surprise, despite steps indicating the Rabin government's depth of political flexibility. In the absence of effective organizing by this sector, the government could steer its own policies without interference. Effective resistance was to emerge only at a later stage, with opposition to Oslo II.

With the linkage between social stand and the peace process, moreover, no wonder that the right wing has failed to enlist the support of its own constituency to protest activities against the new moves. And activities organized by Jewish settlers in the occupied territories have not attracted those who resided within the Green Line with the exception of religious extremists. *Passive*, not only, active support energized peacemaking. So, many groups that had previously had an interest in the conflict's perpetuation now reversed their position toward de-escalation or at least passively accepted the peace moves. All in all, the political shift embraced the majority of the middle class, regardless of its party affiliation, as public opinion surveys show (Arian, 1995b, 1996) and as the gradual moderation of the Likud Party confirms. The war-based social structure was being dismantled. This accounted for the Labor-led government's successful mobilization of political support despite its narrow parliamentary base.

Still, hesitating to clash with Jewish settlers—a clash that might extend to a bitter political struggle over the very underpinnings of the Israeli polity—Israel's government put off the determination of these settlements' fate until the final agreement and accepted the status quo. Its commitment to the settlers' security, moreover, greatly affected the IDF's redeployment in the territories. The PLO's cooperation was helpful to Israel's maneuvering.

With widespread active and passive support for the peace policies, only the margins of the right wing challenged the government, mostly drawn from the religious settlement in Hebron and the Kahane–Kach movement. Settlers remained the only beneficiaries of the occupation. Then, the more the fate of the Golan Heights and the West Bank was put in question, the more political bickering intensified. In case of total withdrawal from the West Bank, those groups might clash violently with IDF troops. Indeed, two dramatic, unprecedented events attest to this potential.

The first event was the massacre of Muslim worshipers perpetrated by a lone Jewish settler-gunman at a mosque in Hebron in February 1994. Although the Kach Movement was outlawed following the event, its zealots remained committed to their attempts to erect local, violent resistance both against the

IDF—now viewed as an enemy—and the Palestinians. More than ever, young-sters who grew up in these settlements became a target of political, even para-military organizing (Kimmerling, 1995). This has borne the potential for inten-sifying Jewish-Palestinian clashes ensuing from the IDF's partial withdrawal from the West Bank. The second event was the assassination of Prime Minister Yitzhak Rabin in November 1995 by an Oriental religious gunman after Rabin had ended his speech at a peace rally in Tel Aviv. Foreign Minister Shimon Peres succeeded Rabin but lost the 1996 elections for the Likud leader, Benjamin Netanyahu. Still at the time of this writing, it is premature to estimate all the implications of this event both on the direction of peacemaking and on the reshaping of political culture in Israel.

(d) The IDF's support. The military supported, even prompted, the moves within the state bureaucracy. In 1991, Military Intelligence submitted to the government an opinion by General Uri Sagie stating that Syria was bent on reaching a political settlement with Israel because it realized that strategic equality with Israel was no longer a viable option. That assessment helped induce the Likud government to participate in the Madrid Conference over its traditional reluctance.[18] Subsequently, the army's support was demonstrated in its cooperation with the political level in working out the agreements with the PLO, in its backing of deep pullback in the Golan Heights, and in the public support given by the generals to the government's move.

All of this was a departure from the traditional, functional division of labor between military and civilian institutions. Still, the agreements with the PLO were formulated in military terms under the auspices of high-ranking generals who took an active part in conducting the diplomatic talks following an intermezzo of the Foreign Ministry's secret talks in Oslo. So, the IDF's position was still cast within the underlying relations of exchange between the IDF and the politicians by which the military exchanged political subordination for partnership in steering foreign policies. With the IDF's affirmative sup-port, the government could overcome domestic resistance that otherwise would have presented more obstacles.

Interestingly, the IDF, by supporting peace moves, helped erode its own long-term social status. But only a military whose officer corps' civilian pro-motion relies to a large extent on the military's present social status might smoothly adjust its professional considerations to sociopolitical, dynamic change. Demilitarization now showed more signs.

Taken together, internal support joined with internal hindrances to belli-cose moves and tipped the scale for reading the new external reality as oppor-tunities for de-escalation rather just new risks or opportunities to retain the status quo. Strategic reassessment could not be realized otherwise. At last, those occurrences depicted as strategic opportunities for decision-makers were perceived as material opportunities for social groups. Mutual fit accounted for the moves and the success in enlisting support for them. The Likud government led by Yitzhak Shamir was indeed aware of the multitude of limitations and opportunities, as shown by its unexpected, relatively moderate policies. Nevertheless, this government failed to exploit the Madrid talks. And its insistence on continuing to establish new settlements in the West Bank in defiance of American pressures, combined with the intensification of Palestinian attacks within the Green Line boundaries, affected electoral outcomes in 1992 stimulated by an increasingly moderate electorate (see Makovsky, 1996, 84–87). The political comeback of the Labor Party headed by Yitzhak Rabin and Shimon Peres in 1992 was the result.

Rabin and Peres read the new reality more forcefully than had their predecessors (see ibid., 111–113). By nature, they were more sensitive to pressures from business corporations, middle-class groups and the IDF (with its constitutive social groups), the traditional pillars of the Labor Movement. So, the Labor leaders did not change the direction that the Likud-led government had actually accepted beginning with the peace accord with Egypt in 1979, but intensified efforts toward de-escalation. Hence, the openness to new initiatives central to which was that of Deputy Foreign Minister Yossi Beilin, produced the Oslo talks in 1992. Exogenous constraints rather than voluntary acts were at work. (Again, my analysis centers on the context of decision-making, the previously created processes setting the political boundaries within which decision-making was structured [see also my remarks in chapter 3 and chapter 4, note 2]).

AFTER OSLO

The transition from de-escalation to all-inclusive peace is fragile not only because of external obstacles. Progress also depends on the congruence between the peace process and the interests of major Israeli groups. Disappointment in the process's effects on the improvement of the standard of living in Israel might erect obstacles to the process and even reverse it, notwithstanding the domestic support that has been rigid enough to set the shift so far.

Crucial here are the sharp distinctions that have emerged in the process of peace-making between those benefiting from peace—the Westerner-dominated middle-class—and those frozen in a backward position—nonmobile Orientals conjoined by some of the Russian immigrants and Israeli Palestinians. Middle-class Jews gained from unprecedented peace-incited economic growth which boosted consumerism, raised incomes, and decreased the overall tax burden (due to the cut in defense spending). To recall, at the same time, the governments eradicated the welfare systems. Peace-making also contributed to greater income inequalities by intensifying competition among Jewish and immigrant foreign workers in low-paid labor market segments, while the freeze of settlements in the occupied territories greatly increased the cost of housing, making it less affordable for low-wage groups. Paradoxically, the Labor-led government, which took power in 1992 owing to a slim, even coincidental, margin of support among Russian immigrants, worked more than any previous government to mold a regional coalition open to peace but made no serious attempt to do so at home.

By making the peace process a source of loss for low-status groups in Israel, the Labor-led government further alienated those groups at the electoral level, pushing them toward Likud as the latter's victory in the elections of 1996 confirms. It is no wonder, then, that those groups approved of attempts made by right-wing and religious movements to inculcate both existential anxieties about Hamas and Hezbolla terror attacks, which escalated after Oslo II (see Arian, 1996, 6), and cultural fears about peace-inspired "westernization" of Israeli society.

Crucial events—the closure Israel imposed on the Palestinian Authority-ruled territories in the Spring of 1996 following the Hamas' attacks in Israeli cities, the tension emerging on the Israel-Syria border in the Summer of 1996 following the Likud-led government's rejection of its predecessor's commitments to Syria and, most importantly, the violent clashes that erupted between the IDF and the Palestinian militia of September 1996 following the Netanyahu government's slowing down of the implementation of the Oslo agreements—all demonstrate the extent to which reescalation is still a viable path which is supported, even electorally fueled, by those who lose from peace.

In the long term, moreover, socio-economic polices might lay the foundations for the creation of a hawkish front, composed of socially nonmobile groups, settlers questioning the legality of the state's action (see Lustick, 1993, 386–395), and religious groups, the major losers from peace, that will halt the peace process. After all, peacemaking not only facilitates erosion of the welfare state but, at the same time, it might also eliminate barriers to political action by peripheral groups (all significantly increased their political representation in the Knesset in the elections of 1996). The less the social value of military service, the less the efficacy of welfare systems, the less the integrative effects of the external conflict, and the more that westernization dominates Israel culture, the more these groups might be motivated to fight for social mobility, register their protests, or embark on the ethnic identity-oriented avenue.[19] They might even create frameworks for cooperation in the absence of conflict-originated political barriers. A fight of this kind might call into question the future viability of reproduction of interclass relations.

Yet it is safe to predict, for the short term, that in the absence of a significant change in the regional system, and in the absence of internal change taking the form of a sharp decline in the domestic gains effectively produced and expected to be produced shortly from peace, any government's attempt to reverse the process (implicitly or explicitly) will face internal resentment. That will be so particularly if the revised policy entails new costs, such as a reemergence of violent clashes between Palestinians and Israeli troops triggered by Jewish settlers' provocations or an intolerable tension between Israel and the Western bloc with the economic implications that it entails. Consumerism-incited de-escalation might impede reversal. Groups' resistance to bellicose moves similar to the Lebanon War and the Intifada might reveal themselves again. State-directed aggrandizement of the middle class and powerful corporations thus means not only diminishing state autonomy in the socioeconomic domain (Shalev, 1992, 309) but also in the military domain.

Thus, future governments, such as the Likud-led government headed by Benjamin Netanyahu that took power again in the elections of 1996, might change the focus of the process or attempt to slow down its course. But it is less likely that could insistently reverse it without a considerable reason, as the Netanyahu government's acknowledgment, albeit reluctantly, of the Oslo agreements manifests.

Critical, however, is the reengineering of the IDF. Since the Israeli military tends to adopt selective policies of recruitment and turns the officer corps from "call" to occupation, it is likely that unlike the "war army" that was largely drawn from elite groups, given the growing reservations displayed by middle-class youngsters toward military service, the "peace army" possibly would be inclined to accept growing recruitment of peripheral groups. Religious youngsters, nonmobile Orientals and nonmobile immigrants (ex-Soviet and Ethiopians), and even, for the long term, Israeli Palestinians and foreign workers in the process of becoming citizens, might be the new constituent groups. These groups' motivation to carry out bellicose missions would derive from the social status they could acquire through military service relative to civilian tracks and their satisfaction with their position in the "peace society." Remilitarization of part of the IDF is a likely outcome.

For an army engaged in intensive, daily encounters with Arab armed forces, mostly Palestinian and Shiite, militarization might take the army back to periods when it incubated hard-line policies. In this case, the state might regain part of its autonomy to employ military policies by lessening its dependence upon mass conscription drawn from middle-class groups. A "third wave," professional military preparing to meet distant threats (and maybe establish cooperation with other regional armies or a military pact with America) would be supplemented by forces dealing with current security (see notes 10–11).[20]

The key to legitimizing the peace process lies in the adoption of more equitable social policies. Otherwise, the durable equation of potential domestic social unrest with militant policies externally might reverse the already fragile peace-making. A melange of a remilitarized military and a bloc of peace-losers, together with external events and difficulties in settling disputable problems between Israel and its surrounding states, might reinflame the conflict and even expand it into an Islamic-Jewish conflict. Israel's ability to resolve this problem will, therefore, constitute the major future test of the Israeli society.

CONCLUSIONS

The lead-up to de-escalation of the Arab-Israeli conflict, beginning with the 1979 Israel–Egypt peace accord, was grounded on two major pillars (see figure 6.2, which summarizes the arguments presented in chaptesr 5–6).

First, the external pillar was the waning of the Soviet Union as a regional power (beginning in 1973) with the dual implications that it effected: (1) the limitations the process set on the freedom for military action enjoyed by Israel (via the American shift from status quo to peace policies, restraining both quarrelling sides); and (2) peace opportunities embodied by the gradual moderation of Arab states (further vitiating Israel's military thrust). The second pillar, an internal one, was the growing materialism and consumerism in Israeli society owing to the Six-Day War's benefits (including American largesse) and the state's effective construction of an inequitable social structure. Together with the empowerment of the Western bloc ensuing in the decline of the Soviet Union, this process amplified trends toward globalization. Through this general process, middle-class groups were less prepared to combat bordering countries or sacrifice their property for war, and more vulnerable to losses inflicted by those countries. Hence, they were more inclined to carefully listen to global processes and Arab peace signals. Cycles of protest, empowerment of the dovish front, and more monitoring of the military were the results. At the same time, the very overgaining from the 1967 War's fruits caused military failures directly inasmuch as gaining triggered the eruption of the Intifada.

So, with shrinking internal legitimation and resources and diminishing external freedom of operation, Israel's military capabilities gradually declined as a series of military failures demonstrates. Military decline was aggravated by the intensification of support for peace owing to military failures changing Arabs' images in Israeli eyes, and effects of changes in the Arab world. At bottom, Israel was motivated to embark on the road toward de-escalation. Following the peace accord with Egypt, however, internal pressures to reverse/nullify some of the accord's impacts led to a temporary re-escalation in the Lebanon War and the policies toward the Palestinians in the occupied ter-

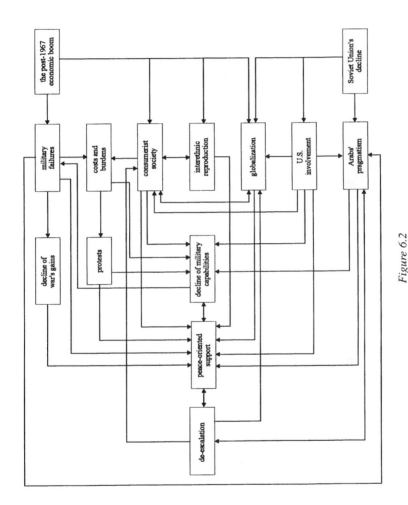

Figure 6.2
The Variables of Peacemaking

ritories. Following these military adventures, not only growing costs manifested themselves but also a gradual decline of the post-1967 gains.

As these occurrences added to the former domestic processes, accompanied by new opportunities that the peace economy offered, the leading groups regarded the end of the Cold War as an opportunity for de-escalation. Reversal of Israel's military moves toward the resumption of de-escalation then showed itself, accelerated by the Labor's return to power in 1992. As figure 6.2 summarizes the overall analysis, cyclical motions prevailed in the relations among the causal factors. The self-fulfilling nature of de-escalation, its internal effects on the middle class (a rise in the standard of living, and hence of consumerism), and the reinforcement of globalization made the process hardly reversible.

It thus also seems safe to assume that had Israel been faced with similar internal pressures to de-escalate in past periods, it would have been inclined to carefully read peace signals, albeit minor ones, being transmitted from Arab states and then would have followed up on peace initiatives.

Paradoxically, the more the state strategies of war preparation rely on a pattern of exchange within the framework of materialist militarism, the more the opportunity for "exit" (as defined in chapter 1) is available to agents. By exit, agents can either raise the expected return for their "non-exit" or impair social arrangements by clinging to exit. And the more the elements of consent were symbolized by the architects of the military doctrine (see Horowitz, 1987), the more participating agents were empowered to crack this doctrine. And when the war-based creation of new resources (material and symbolical alike) was not viable anymore, the state's reconstruction of social interests toward retaining the state of war was scarcely workable. On the contrary, groups reconstructed state security interests. So, the same concatenation of interests that had hardened Israel's posture in the aftermath of the Six-Day War was now reconstructed in part and identified with the goal of de-escalating the war. Structural relations of exchange revealed themselves as a reality of contractual relations rather than as an abstract notion, by which the state either accumulates autonomous power or undergoes crisis.

Students of Israeli society and politics, notably those belonging to the critical wing, have discerned a hardening in the functioning of the intrastate mechanisms that nourished the conflict, especially after the 1967 War. Those mechanisms ranged from the occupation's impacts on regulation of the labor market and the social order with it (Grinberg, 1991b, 1993a, 1993b; Peled, 1990; Shalev, 1992), to the occupation's symbolic impacts on the forces attracted to tradition in Israel (Kimmerling, 1989, 1993a; Lustick, 1993, 417–436). Central to this view, implicitly or explicitly, are the multiple symbolic and material gains of several leading groups. Slashing those gains by reverting to the pre-1967 reality would thus entail internal crisis. It is premature to completely assess this outlook. Suffice it to say that the dialectical dimension of Israel's hold in the occupied territories has been overlooked by many scholars. Innate crisis, not necessarily linear gains and losses, was at stake, as this chapter illustrates. Furthermore, those gains and losses had implications for military capabilities on which the sustenance of symbolic and material gains was conditioned. By delinking war's consequences from military capabilities and military doctrine, scholars have neglected essential driving forces that account for peace and war.

CHAPTER 7

Conclusions: Trial and Error

Highlighting processes of "natural selection," Milton Friedman uses the example of a billiard player: "If [the player] is asked how he decides where to hit the ball, [he] may say that he 'just figures it out'" (Friedman, 1953, 22). But actually, Friedman claims, players, like businessmen, are guided by "natural selection" based on habitual reaction, random chance, or whatnot rather than strict rationality. Through this type of selection, players and businessmen (and, we might add, politicians and generals) strive to achieve maximization of gains ("returns" in Friedman's theory) up to a relatively satisfying point. Failure leads not only to losses but may also drive the player out of the game (ibid.).

A similar, albeit far more complicated pattern of trial and error was evident in the manner by which the Israeli state selected its foreign, military, and social policies. Selection passed through experiments—purposive action whose results fell sometimes far from the underlying intentions—up to a relatively satisfying point. Why did errors occur and how were they corrected?

As I have already noted (see chapter 1), the observable dimension of structural relations, that is, the declarative, purpose-oriented dimension of agents' action, is naturally erroneous. Agents underestimate, even overlook, structural limitations imposed on them and on other agents and the extent to which structural relations permit the participating agents to accumulate power and bring about structural change. Errors mean that agents unintentionally provoke other agents' resistance, leaving the former with no space except for reversal moves.

Informed by the consequences of trial and error, both sides possess the capacity to recalculate their expected/actually experienced outcomes relative to their past conditions, present well-being, and future expectations. "Natural selection," then, governs agents' activity up to the point that satisfies most of them, be it through their active selection or passive response to the moves of other agents, including the state (through its methods of reconstruction). Unlike

Friedman's anecdote, the balls do not just passively react to the cue.

The manner in which errors are corrected, however, also engineers the next trial-and-error course as long as corrections (re)produce/transform structures having the underlying tension among agents' interests and the invisibility of structures and their elicited interests (see also Tilly, 1995a). So it happens in our story: The path of state-directed absorption of Oriental immigration, by which an inequitable social structure was molded, was prioritized over other avenues. But this happened only after the main alternative, an egalitarian model, was realized and practically "corrected" by means of the middle class's resistance to the austerity measures. Crucial, then, was state agencies' misreading of the materialist interests underpinning their previously constructed structural relations with the Westerner groups and the power stored by the latter. Creation of an inequitable ethno-class structure corrected former errors but also made Israel's foreign-military policies captive to its commitments to promote the well-being of the Westerner-dominated middle class. Again, miscalculation of social groups' interests and power generated errors the state made by selecting methods to combat infiltrations during the 1950s that demanded relatively high sacrifice for relatively small returns. Equating sacrifice with gains, state agencies escalated the border war, shifted from a defensive-diplomatic avenue to a bellicose one and, thus, mobilized domestic support. The results of that bellicosity-based error correction—empowerment of the military establishment and middle-class groups—drove the state toward further escalation and later entrenchment of the 1967 territorial gains. So, both groups worked to correct through trying and erring in relatively moderate stands regarding the fate of the occupied territories. Only entrenched occupation fit the groups' gradually constructed expectations. Again, state agencies miscalculated domestic pressures.

Nevertheless, precisely because of middle-class groups' acquiring further power due to the occupation, they could not tolerate the errors innate in the state's socially incited overproduction of gains. Multiple forms of internal burdens and losses during the 1970s and 1980s were the result of overproduction. As for the state, its agencies worked on the assumption that middle-class youngsters were motivated to seek prestige by means of battlefield achievements (the intentional tier of interest). State agencies, however, ignored the materialist interests underlying those motivations (the structural tier), termed in this book "materialist militarism." Hence, agents' capacities to embark on alternative tracks other than military service, which also added to their growing reservation toward military service, was overlooked. This error accounted for the state's mistaken moves in the regional arena after the October War.

Agents' interference with the running of the originally chosen force-oriented policies until de-escalation prevailed was the epitome of correction of policy. By itself, as chapter 6 implies, de-escalation was a course of trial rather than a terminal station as long as its implementation affected social agents who might push for correcting newly created or newly revealed errors by operating their yet invisible power.

Social interests matter only by virtue of their structural context. Limitations set on agents' action, contradictory interests, the tension between rhetoric and practice, and dynamic changes accounting for processes of construction/reconstruction, are all insights exclusively attained through the lens of this context. Understanding of political processes thus entails an exposure of alternative trajectories of action that presented themselves, implicitly or explicitly, to the agents involved. What did not occur is no less significant in tracing processes than what happened. Reading a "history of alternatives" (in Pappe's terms, 1993, 108) follows from this perception. Otherwise, we cannot understand the real strength of the chosen route, the structures that agents construct through their choices and actions, and then the manner in which agents calculate newly apparent alternative options of adherence or exit.

Trial-and-error strategies impacted not only on the manner by which Israel conducted its foreign and social policies, but also on the relations of power in the entire region. Drawing on the three-domain framework of state action (chapter 1, figure 1.2), the case of Israel suggests an extended comprehension of the functioning of the modern state as a nexus between two arenas of action. The dialogue between IR and statist theories illuminates the extent to which domestic war-based structures molded and were molded by interest-driven agents facilitating, propelling, hardening, and precluding certain external state actions. By doing so, domestic forces decreased the repertoire of options presented in the international system from which states could select their foreign-military policies. This study has therefore further linked the transition from state features to its actual performance in the external arena via the selection of foreign-military policies (see chapter 1, figure 1.1). This being the case, the various schools of thought might improve their explanatory power.

As I admitted in the introduction to this book, Israel's path from war to de-escalation presents an elegant picture regarding the impact of the international system on Israel's moves. Hence, the natural temptation is to see in this system an explanation for Israel's policies. Nevertheless, Israel did what it did not merely because of global forces but because external forces worked in coordination with internal forces. To a large extent, they reciprocally enhanced each other (as figure 6.2 shows). Consequently, reciprocal effects of internal and external state action have contributed to the molding of both the regional system and Israeli society. Figure 7.1 summarizes the process.

Flexible geopolitics permitted, but did not compel, bellicose moves by Israel in the early 1950s. Nonetheless, it was mainly the internal set of interests that simultaneously facilitated and drove Israel to take advantage of external conditions. Other options the international system offered were gradually ruled out. In turn, by capitalizing on a moderately threatening regional system, Israel

EXTERNAL   INTERNAL

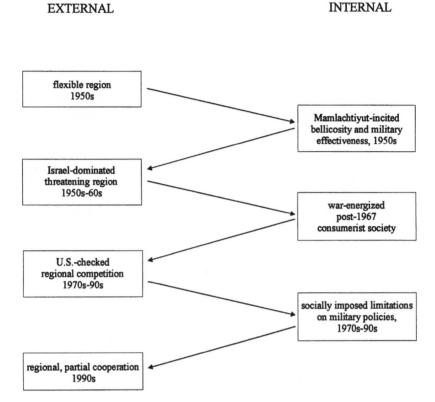

Figure 7.1
The Reciprocal Effects of Internal and External State Action—An Overview

could stabilize social order internally. Translating social order into military capabilities, bellicosity in the 1950s played a key role in shaping a threatening regional environment by serving the Soviet Union's endeavors to penetrate the region through its alliances with Egypt and Syria. Concurrently, Israel's impressive translation of internal extraction of resources into military power and battlefield gains attracted France and later the United States to ally with Israel beginning in the 1950s. Incorporation of the Middle East into the Cold War was the result.

Converting its regional domination into middle-class improvements following the 1967 War, Israel was inclined to exploit the war's gains to the utmost. The entrenched conflict had contradictory implications. First, it inflicted losses on the Soviet Union's Arab allies, by which Israel practically served the U.S. attempts to drive the USSR out of the latter's regional strongholds. At the same time, enduring conflict cracked Israel's military capabilities because of the disharmony between a growing military burden and the rise of a consumerist society in Israel. Increasing dependence on the United States was the consequence, generating regional competition held in check by the United States through the Israel–Egypt peace accord and other restraining effects. This happened long before the "formal" collapse of the Soviet Union.

Still, even the relatively low costs this competition demanded from Israel worked to amplify socially imposed limitations. Social change decreased motivation for the kind of sacrifice that conflict with the Western bloc (mainly the United States after becoming the major power in the region) over the fate of the Arab-Israeli conflict would have meant. Democracy (within the Jewish sector) enabled the main social groups to voice their grievances. A sharp tension between Israel and the dominant states was then averted and punitive moves (like the international sanctions against South Africa, Iraq, and Serbia) with it. Likewise, a Western-style society made the main groups more sensitive to the trends that prevailed, at least temporarily, in the post–Cold War, America-dominated world system, notably demilitarization and globalization. Ultimately, Israel was inclined to take part in designing the "New Middle East."

Reciprocal impacts of this kind might encourage constructivists to explicate their process of "state socialization" through the terrains of domestic, interest-driven filters and their impact on the creation of intersubjective meanings generated by structural distribution of power *inwardly*, not only at the interstate level. In a similar fashion, the case of Israel suggests that the state is not simply bound by the limitations set by the two arenas of its functioning (see Barnett, 1992; Mastanduno et al., 1989; Putnam, 1988; Starr, 1994). Rather, it may use each arena to overcome problems it faces in the other arena.

In line (partially) with constructivist arguments, global systems and external occurrences may be studied not only through their "objective properties" but also through their subjective dimension. This refers to the manner in which internal agents receive and evaluate external signals and filter them into demands, cooperation, sacrifice, protest, and so on, according to their position relative to expected outcomes of those occurrences. In fact, the state "learns" and "understands" occurrences taking place in the external arena owing to the information transmitted by domestic agents. Military capabilities, moreover, can be analyzed by factoring in the societal support for employing violent force with the material resources for military buildup that it entails. This process results in narrowing the scope of options offered by the global arena. External occurrences also contextualize internal agents' activity and thus form their relative power to leave their imprint on statecraft. "State assessment," in neorealist terms, may also gain more analytical tools to understand how international distribution of power, in conjunction with internal, societal distribution, largely impacts on the state's selection of its avenues in the global system, and vice versa. A bridge between globally constructed structural variables and a theory of foreign policy is thus in reach. Distribution of power, thereby, might be switched from an independent variable to a dependent one, namely, the outcome of the interplay among international factors, states and, domestic agents, which cumulatively transform world orders (see Cox, 1981, 139–141).

Making distribution of power a dependent variable is the old business of statist theories. But by studying the creation of power through the lens of domestic interests, statist theories may not only explain how states, constrained by their domestic social order, utilize global anarchy for internal empowerment by means of crafting capacity for managing war. They may also transform war's effects into causal mechanisms fueling external moves via those agents benefiting or losing from internal effects of external action. Social order, then, is not only a determinant of war and war preparation, but also an effect and a driving force. War-making and peacemaking, moreover, are processes that simultaneously are constructed by social structures and construct social structures, rather then being just political processes. As such, building on scientific realism permits exemplification of both hardening mechanisms impacting on foreign policies and the inherent potential for crisis within structural arrangements that might lead to decline of military capabilities.

Indeed, elaborating distribution of power and intersubjective meanings through the contour of the state's internal features lays the foundations for better understanding the regional order in the Middle East (and elsewhere), although this study addresses the behavior of the Israeli side alone. Still, the behavior of the Arab side suggests that it also had an interest in perpetuating the conflict and later in reversing its thrust. Clearly, only a conjunction of interests could mutually nurture the conflict by furnishing the states involved with sufficient capabilities and mutually constructing intersubjective meanings and shared images (from moderate to harsh competition and from competition to middling cooperation). However, Arab motives were not factored in by a method that could evaluate the proportional effect of the Arab factor in relation to the Israeli ones. An interwoven analysis of each side's motives and their contributions to the dynamic evolution of the conflict might shape a systemic explanation. If so, not only a deeper historical understanding of the conflict's evolution can be achieved, but also a broader theoretical comprehension of the relations among the global system, the state, and social structures than this study presents.

Notes

CHAPTER 1

1. As Levy (1989, 226) explains: "Because actions a state takes to increase its security often decrease the security of other states, which feel then compelled to take countermeasures to increase their own security, which in turn are threatening to others, and so forth, actions taken to increase security often generate an action-reaction spiral. This spiral . . . may actually decrease the security of all by increasing tensions and hence the probability of war."

2. On the American experience, see also Wolfe, 1977, 186–199; Hooks and McLauchlan, 1992; on postrevolutionary Iran, Skocpol, 1988; and on the general level, Feagin and Riddell, 1990; Jaggers, 1992.

3. Similarly, other IR scholars focus on the manner in which democracy restrains war-prone orientations (Lake, 1992; Russett, 1990; Russett and Maoz, 1990; Weede, 1992) or how culture shapes military doctrine (Kier, 1995; Silver, 1994). For neorealists, on the contrary, domestic regime and culture play no significant part in international politics.

4. Even in revisionist versions of neorealism in which internal structures matter, the state's stand vis-à-vis the vertical social structure is not conceptualized at all (Mastanduno et al., 1989; Ruggie, 1983).

5. See also the critique of Wallerstein's world system theory (1974) by Dale, 1984; Skocpol, 1977; Wendt, 1987, 344–349. A common focus of these criticisms is Wallerstein's neglect of the role of individual states in structuring the world system by virtue of the formers' internal structure and capacities.

6. Successful inculcation of an external threat is instrumental in legitimizing militarism. Still, even proponents of militarism (see, for example, Berghahn, 1982;

Mann, 1987; Geyer, 1989; Vagts, 1959) tend to downplay the fact that, after all, an external threat, real or imaginary, is at stake, not only a cultural pattern (see Oakes, 1994, on the American home front during the 1950s for illustration of a threat injection). Missing, however, is systematic theorizing about the role played by domestic groups in driving/facilitating bellicosity relative to external occurrences and their reciprocal effects. Mann (1993, 740–799), who has put forward a sociological, alternative explanation to those furnished by realists, tracing the breakout of World War I, replicated the same lacuna. However, Mann's narration of the unique interests of military establishment and "militarized" social groups is very helpful in designing the track taken by this study.

7. Interests refer to any form of agentic action, be it interest group, ethnic group, and so on.

8. Accumulation of power is then viable when, from agents' point of view, those conditions on which their adherence to the structure had been grounded change, a kind of asymmetric exchange. Potential, invisible power then becomes apparent when agents break the "rules of the game," even employing or threatening to employ the option of exit. For those agents' counterparts, an error becomes apparent that has implications for the stability of social relations.

9. For example, American corporations, whose assets in Third World countries had been nationalized, usually appealed to their own government to take diplomatic, economic, even military measures to save American investments. Equation of corporations' interests with security of supply of raw materials was highly invoked (Krasner, 1978).

10. For example, American corporations identified global opportunities in trade and finance that would entail America's abandonment of its isolationist approach after World War I. Domestic debate between "isolationist" and "internationalist" clusters of interests accounts for the zigzagging of American foreign policy (see Frieden, 1988). In a similar fashion, the financially driven, rigid approach toward Japan demonstrated by a coalition of business corporations led by J. P. Morgan played a large role in stimulating the Pacific War (Nolt, 1994). So, too, commercial interests played a decisive role in stimulating the rivalry between Germany and Britain from the end of the nineteenth century, culminating in World War I. Rock has suggested that these interests nourished both the naval rivalry between the countries and hostile opinions and fears among the two sides' leaderships, bringing about the violent clash (Rock, 1989, 76–82).

11. Marxist and neo-Marxist theoreticians have established the linkage between state competitiveness and internal capital accumulation due to the mitigation of interclass tensions (Lenin, 1968), arms production (Block, 1980; Kaldor, 1984; Luxemburg, 1951; Mackenzie, 1983), and protection of external assets (Baran and Sweezy, 1966; see also the debate in Szymanski, 1977, on this linkage). My argument, however, shuns the economic reductionism of the Marxist/neo-Marxist approach, and the reduction of external state action to the internal arena. Rather, the role, whether autonomous or not, played by the international system in shaping a state's action is projected in conjunction with

internal mechanisms, in part analyzed in line with neo-Marxist approaches. Moreover, as I have argued, social agents might gain from the state of war not only directly, as proponents of neo-Marxism argue, but also indirectly insofar as war cements a state's internal control by which it gains more leverage to benefit agents and to regulate interclass/interethnic tensions.

12. Historically, the scope of citizenship in Europe increased from the end of the eighteenth century on in return for the imposition of direct statist rule with the constitution of mass armies based on conscription of the domestic population rather than mercenaries (Thomson, 1994). Social groups then capitalized on their participation in war and in preparations for war to claim and attain political and material resources or rights from the state. As for the state, it was willing to accede as a means of mobilizing for war. Consequently, wars accelerated the allocation of civil, political, and social rights to those who had borne the burden of war (Andreski, 1971; Feld, 1975; Janowitz, 1976; Marwick, 1988; Shaw, 1988; Tilly, 1994, 1995b; Titmus, 1976, 75–87).

13. Furthermore, even the evaluation of external assets is recontextualized according to changes in the state's capacity to compete with other states as long as the expectations of state agencies and particularist groups are derived from that capacity (a movement from mobilization to evaluation). Likewise, the option to reward social and political groups through foreign-military policies might drive state agencies to act externally (see Gurr, 1988; Mastanduno et al., 1989, 466–467), for example, using external force to increase electoral support (Morgan and Bickers, 1992). This acquires value only through previously constructed force-oriented discourse.

14. Peace movements attributing Israel's occupation in the West Bank to settlers' interests may serve as an example of deuniversalization. Likewise, the options to achieve peace with Syria devalued the Golan Heights as a strategic asset.

15. It has become more and more established among scholars of public opinion that political attitudes are structured along socioeconomic variables (see, for example, Arian, 1995a, 114–119; Maggiotto and Wittkopf, 1981).

16. For example, see the conflict of interests sparked between small businesses and big corporations with respect to President Truman's military agenda in the early 1950s (Lo, 1982).

17. The relations between state action and social structure are not functional, causal relations in the sense that a phenomenon is explained in terms of its consequences (see Stinchcombe, 1968, 85–91).

18. My arguments are largely informed by critical historians who have greatly contributed by exposing Israel's force-oriented preference along critical, historical milestones. Nonetheless, similar to IR scholars, the basic weakness of their perception lies, arguably, in the absence of an attempt to provide a comprehensive explanation of why Israel, during its early years, preferred a force-oriented approach over extracting the potential for peace (see mainly Morris, 1988, 1993; Pappe, 1992).

19. Contingent realism suggests that self-help principles induce states to act as security-seekers rather than to seek to maximize relative power over their adversaries, as proponents of standard neorealism maintain. Accordingly, states draw their policies from considerations of how much and what type of military capabilities they can produce with their power relative to the international environment. So, "when the risks of competition exceed the risks of cooperation, states should direct their self-help efforts toward achieving cooperation" (Glaser, 1994/95, 60). Cooperation might be feasible, even indispensable, under two main conditions: (1) when a state is more afraid of the costs of an arms race or of being made vulnerable by its consequences than of the risks of being cheated by the other side; and (2) when by accepting arms control or employing unilateral defensive policies a state might decrease both its own and its adversary's uncertainty about the other's motives. Arms control and defensive policies are then the main features of cooperation. Thus, an increase in the adversary's security reduces the probability of conflict, averting the spiraling process innate in coping with the *security dilemma*.

20. See also my critique of Barnett, 1992, who confines himself to Israel's material strategies of war preparation and overlooks the question of legitimation.

21. It is worth emphasizing that *unintended consequences* are not necessarily undesirable, nor are they a perverse outcome (in Hirschman's terms, 1991, 11–42); they can sometimes even be an indirect realization of agents' interests.

CHAPTER 2

1. I distinguish "Orientals" from the "Sephardim," a religious category; not all Sephardim are Orientals. The term "Orientals" does not blur the distinct ethnic identity of these communities, though they constructed their distinctiveness only at the end of the 1970s with the failure of the attempts toward coerced assimilation. Likewise, the category of "Israeli Palestinians" does not blur the ethnic-national identity of Palestinians while the dominant Jewish groups endeavored to construct alternative identities, evidenced by the diversity of epithets ("the minorities," "Israeli Arabs," etc.) (see Rabinowitz, 1993). Unlike "Ashkenazi," "Western" is a nonreligious category epitomizing the cultural identity and common social position of those who immigrated from Europe or America, including non-Oriental Sephardim. Still, because Russian and Polish Jews, i.e., Ashkenazis, are the dominant communities among the Westerners, "Ashkenazi" is the term popular with many Westerners and Orientals.

2. Composed of members sharing common status in the labor market and similar cultural identities that both gradually elicited similar interests and patterns of political action, each ethnic group is termed a class with respect to the 1950s/60s.

3. My analysis, drawn from the scholarly critique of Israeli society, rejects the "mainstream" study of the construction of Israel's social structure which is mainly informed by the school of modernization associated with Eisenstadt (1967, 1985). Unlike this school, the critical analysis suggests that an inequitable social structure

within the Jewish community has been rigidified by economic, political, and symbolic arrangements structured by the Westerners who had taken advantage of their control over the dominant institutions (such arrangements are described more fully in the rest of this chapter). The extent to which the state functioned as a universalist entity on behalf of the whole Jewish community is thus questioned by several versions of the critical scholarship. Seen within this context, interethnic gaps perceived as class-based, long-lived, and fixed rather than as a temporary phenomenon contradicted the declared government policies (see Smooha, 1984a, for alternative explanations for the interethnic gaps). Moreover, mainstream scholars have not addressed the linkage between the social position of Orientals and Israeli Palestinians. Eisenstadt (ibid.) even conceptually dislocates Israeli Palestinians from Israeli society.

4. Methodologically, party emissaries in state institutions (the prime minister and other ministers, in particular) might embody the state and the party simultaneously. The line between the spheres is the person's functional role and orientation rather than his or her formal position. In similar fashion, the state is presented at once as a web of structural arrangements, a bureaucracy, and a collection of individual actors. Those are the forms through which the state practically reveals itself. Though the state is structurally limited by dominant groups' preferences, the state simultaneously bargains through multiple agencies with multiple actors over available resources. Outcomes of this bargaining are only strategically determined by the underlying constraints; a large space is open to decisions standing at odds with dominant groups' preferences. This is the meaning of a state's "relative autonomy" (see Mann, 1993, 81–88; see more in note 12). At another level, state–party conflicts might run their course through party channels and take the form of bickering among party groups; each represents its own rationale according to its power position vis-à-vis the state. Conflicts result in a decision pertinent to the party's stand toward state empowerment.

5. See, for example, the comparative analysis by Skocpol (1988) on the Iranian military following the Muslim revolution, which was inundated with new recruits at the prompting of the Muslim elites, as a means of weakening the hold of the secular elites in the military.

6. A similar argument is made by Swirski (1988, 54–68) in connection with IQ testing in Israel. The tests, he maintains, which were cloaked in a scientific aura, had the effect of perpetuating the arrested state of the Orientals in the educational system. Because the tests were keyed to a "Western" system of selection that was utterly foreign to the Orientals, they ended up rationalizing the Orientals' backwardness.

7. Althusser (1976) has noted, in this connection, that the state's ideological mechanisms reproduce the relations of production by means of an ideology that constitutes individuals as subjects but also makes them feel like autonomous actors. Ideology, Althusser argues, is reflected in practices that distort the meaning of the relations of production.

, 8. At another level, with instrumentalist symbols in the center, Mamlachtiyut left its imprint as a political discourse emphasizing the supremacy of technocratic values over traditional ideological principles. Drawing on Western Europe's similar experience in the aftermath of World War II, the state impacted on the transformation of the nature of political discourse by increasing internal power and penetrating social-civilian sectors that had previously enjoyed partial autonomy. State encroachment released the individual from dependence on the social-political networks that had dictated the ideological thrust of the dialogue, and class conflicts gave way to the creation of pragmatically oriented channels of dialogue, strengthening the bureaucratic class with its associated values (see Barnes, 1966; Kirchheimer, 1968). Further, the more the state penetrated new social spheres, the more the political discourse addressed operative aspects related to the agenda of the state organizations and the resources allocated by them (see Skocpol, 1985, 21–25; Tarrow, 1994, 62–78). Far from a vision of building a new society, this political discourse focuses on short-term goals for which broad political consent can be mustered. The result was a gradual neutralization of the longstanding debate between right and left wings, thus blunting a mechanism that could have engendered social awareness among peripheral groups. Such a process inherently reinforces the legitimation of the existing social order (see, for comparison, Held, 1989, 99–137, on the working class in Britain).

9. It is worth emphasizing that my argument compares the Western male to the Oriental male. But the army's universalism has also affected its recruitment policy toward women. The IDF enacted at its foundation compulsory conscription for women. Formally, all women aged eighteen to twenty have had to serve for twenty-four months. The conscription of women has been based, in large measure, on the ethos of sexual equality, a prominent element in the Zionist pioneering ethos. But if the ethos has been egalitarian, the practice has been different: The army has recruited only some Jewish women, exempting those who are religious, married, or poorly educated, especially Oriental women. Consequently, only about 60 percent of Israeli women actually serve. Furthermore, even though women serve in mixed units with men, they are limited to auxiliary professions and are barred from combat positions (Goldman and Wiegand, 1984; Yuval-Davis, 1985). Consequently, the IDF, like many other militaries, has symbolically associated the "fighter" with men, and thereby played a significant role in injecting masculine stereotypes into the public discourse (at the comparative level, see Enloe, 1988). Women—Westerners and Orientals alike—therefore have had a limited capacity to convert power from the military to the civilian sphere, and men's social power is buttressed instead.

10. It can be argued that the rationalism embodied in the Mamlachtiyut was, in large measure, a substitute for the practices of the free market, which Habermas (1971, 81–122) posits as the source of the legitimation of the modern capitalist order. In other words, whereas in the West the practices of the free market supported the granting of differential rewards and helped bring into being structures that both rely on and support this mode of allocation, in Israel it was Mamlachtiyut that fulfilled this role.

11. The dominant school, a part of the "mainstream" mentioned in note 3, has failed to analyze the institutional barriers to the promotion of Orientals within the military, nor has it addressed the mobility of Orientals *relative* to Westerners. Both this school and Smooha's criticism (1984b) of the IDF as reflecting the ethnic division in society also

neglect to explore (1) the resources of social power accumulated by each ethnic group during, and due to, military service, (2) how those resources are converted into social power *outside* the military, and (3) how this conversion affects interethnic relations (see Azarya, 1983; Azarya and Kimmerling, 1980; Horowitz and Kimmerling, 1974; Horowitz and Lissak, 1989; Lissak, 1984a; Rapoport, 1962). This analytic tendency also reflects the limitations of the modernization approach taken by some scholars (see, for example, Bienen, 1983; Dietz et al., 1991; Fidel, 1975; Harries-Jenkins, 1982; Huntington, 1968; Janowitz, 1964; Pye, 1962; Stepan, 1978; Williams, 1994, 69–71).

12. The concept of "state autonomy" generally refers to the modern state's ability to act without its policy reflecting the preferences of dominant groups (for examples of state-centered approaches, see Ellis, 1992; Nordlinger, 1981; Poggi, 1978; Skocpol, 1985). The manner in which I use this term refers not only to the outcome itself, the focus of the state-centered approach, but also to the relations of exchange by which this autonomy came about. Autonomy, I claim, extended to the main groups' stand vis-à-vis the state within a framework of interests-based exchange rather than just state capacity. For that reason, Poulantzas's (1978) classic designation is more suitable to my conceptualization (see also Giddens, 1985, 201–209; Tilly, 1992, on the state-civilian sectors' relations of exchange generating the formation of the European democratic state). Furthermore, my analysis draws a distinction between two forms of state autonomy: (1) state autonomy to act *in defiance* of dominant groups' preferences but within the limits of previously established relations of social power and (2) state autonomy achieved by *reconstructing* dominant groups' interests, blurring their initial preferences and thus changing those relations of social power (see the next chapters).

13. Mamlachtiyut was a political discourse in the sense that it embodied a mutually constitutive combination of rhetoric with practice, defining reality and implanting it in an apparently self-evident way (at the theoretical level, see Dreyfus and Rabinow, 1982; Foucault, 1982; Hoy, 1986; Taylor, 1984).

CHAPTER 3

1. This was a part of what Blain (1994, 828) defines as a "politics is war" strategy of gaining support for mobilization by invoking military rhetoric expressed in "discursive features associated with systems of differentiation, objectives and aims, tactics, institutionalization, and rationalization."

2. A comparative study of state-building experienced concurrently by Japan and Germany in the late nineteenth century reveals a similar pattern in each state's attitude toward the constituting social-political force—the Samurai in Japan and the Junkers in Germany (see Berghahn, 1982).

3. The fragmented boundaries are extremely reflected in the cultural domain. Examples include the military broadcasting station (*Gallei Zahal*), which disperses civilian contents; the mixed civilian-military character of the military education's content (Bowden, 1976); and the operation of the *Gadna*, a mechanism employed in high schools to prepare youth for military service (Eaton, 1969).

4. The IDF fulfilled its disciplinary missions by means of techniques that are in part common to all modern armies and in part unique. One unique element was the apparently informal nature of military discipline, which mitigated the repressive character of military service and bolstered the individual's consciousness that he or she was part of a voluntary social activity, even if it involved administrative coercion and a hierarchical organization. In addition, the IDF's distinctive conscription model placed the Jewish youngsters under military control for a prolonged period, with debilitating effects on the energy available to them for civilian political activity (Levy, 1993, 134–140). The result was that the military functioned as a mechanism that weakened the political potential of the young generation, a function that fit the state's internal expansion, as I mentioned above. The military organizations had begun to play this role in the pre-state era (Ben-Eliezer, 1993; Shapiro, 1984a, 122–124), but the IDF refined it and performed it more effectively after the state's establishment.

Viewed from a broader perspective, Foucault (1977, 139–170) has grouped the modern military among factories, hospitals, and schools as mechanisms of internalizing habits of discipline and obedience among the individuals subjected to their rule. As such, they played a significant role during the transition from the traditional to a modern social order. The military employed several unique methods (learning, use of space, repetition, coordination, measurement, etc.) of internalizing discipline by making the individual the subject of his own training; that is, the discipline worked from *within* not from *outside*. Hence, discipline became objective, and as such, it kept dependence on external means of coercion to a minimum, which also reduced the subject's capacity to resist the operation of power. In this way, the operation of power became a mechanism that shaped order, and not only maintained it. The military thus supported the assimilation of individuals into the framework of the modern order instead of retaining its former role of merely confronting an external order (ibid., 139–170; for further elaboration, see Dandeker, 1990; Giddens, 1982, 222–223; Mitchell, 1991a, 93–94; 1991b, 34–42).

5. At the comparative level, in the United States the internal power of the state increased following the country's entry into World War II. The growth of security needs was nurtured by the constant development of military technology, so that it became imperative for the state to intensively extract civil resources and to direct private industry, a domain that had previously been largely autonomous from state intervention (Hooks, 1990, 1993, 1994; Hooks and McLauchlan, 1992). In another sphere, Tilly (1992, 107–121) shows how, for example, the bellicose orientation of postrevolutionary France augmented the state's ability to extract resources such as manpower and money, and thereby diminished the power of the prerevolutionary elites and established a direct dialogue with the citizenry.

6. See, for comparison, the case of European militarism in the 1914–45 period. The state in some countries achieved total domination over political space when militarism marked the collapse of boundaries between politics and the military within the state and between state and society, as the latter was mobilized by the state for the war effort (see Geyer, 1989, 71–81).

7. At the comparative level this argument is reinforced by Shafir (1989, 12–14), who adduces historical evidence (Kenya, Rhodesia, Canada, and others) for a connection

between establishing settlements in frontiers not demarcated by a border, and the shaping of political institutions that realize the "demographic interest" of the new settlers, namely, to accumulate land and control its allocation. This mechanism brought about the emergence of a centralistic, interventionist state. Shafir's conceptual system differs from the one that informs the present work. Nevertheless, the mechanism of settlement in an "open frontier" can be linked to the development of a centralistic state in which the protection of the settlers helps nurture the centralism (see also Kimmerling, 1983).

8. Viewed from a broader perspective, a shift from political control by those political networks from which the military command drew to state control might engender problems of this kind up to the point of reinstitutionalization. See, for example, Mann's (1993, 436–440) argument about similar effects of the shift undergone by European armies following the nineteenth century's revolutionary wars marking autonomization of militaries vis-à-vis the old regimes' networks.

9. Therein lies the modern military's distinctiveness as compared with its traditional forebear, which had been both virtually autonomous and closely affiliated with, and funded by, particularist power centers. Yet even in the transition to the modern model, conditions to restrain militaries were not created in the absence of militaries' dependence on civil bureaucracies, be it because the military buildup was funded by an external power (as in many Third World countries) or because the mode of organization of the major social classes in society impeded the state's extraction (as in some Latin American countries). Nor did group pressures to attain access to political control in return for military participation emerge (see Giddens, 1985, 249–254; Tilly, 1992, 192–225).

10. This explanation, drawn from the school of "state formation" for the nature of the supervision exercised by the political authorities over the army, differs from that proposed by the dominant approach in the study of the Israeli army (see Halpern, 1962; Horowitz, 1977, 1982; Lissak, 1984b; Peri, 1983; Perlmutter, 1969; Schiff, 1992, 1995).
I formulate the relations between militaries and civilian agencies in terms of *structural relations of exchange*, whereby the military accepts the politicians' supervision for political, symbolic, and material resources, by themselves drawn upon the extent to which the sociopolitical sphere is militarized. Instead of conceptualizing the relations as civilian power exercised *over* the military, as has traditionally been done, exchange suggests that each side, simultaneously, gains and foregoes assets, material and symbolic alike, through the creation of institutional arrangements. Consequently, the military's stand in accepting/rejecting political supervision is further understood as long as its structural limitations to act otherwise and the losses that it entails are put at stake. At the bottom line, each side's satisfaction with the overall consequences, intended and unintended alike, fuels its motivation to cling to the created structural relations. Further, the offered perspective addresses the dynamics of the evolution of the institutional arrangements according to changes in each side's power, hence the extent to which the military depended on civilian agencies. However, Israeli accounts of the different structures of control have not asked what explains the military's acceptance of its subordination to the political level relative to alternative options. Simply put, any analysis of power relations should start from this point.

By showing that militarization-produced gains for the military accounted for cementing political control, the offered perspective links the ostensibly contradictory trends of increasing political (formal) control and the militarization of the modern state (see Tilly, 1995c). "Mainstreamer" in military sociology, including the Israeli wing, has failed to address this connection (examples of the mainstream approach are Edmonds, 1988; Feld, 1968; Finer, 1976; Huntington, 1964; Janowitz, 1968, 1971; Larson, 1974; Luckham, 1971; Sarkesian, 1984; Segal et al., 1974; Stepan, 1978; 1988; Van-Doorn, 1976; see also Shaw's criticism of military sociology: 1991, 73–76). Even for proponents of militarism, the rise of militarism is perceived as a process by which the military ascended over civilian institutions (see, for example, Albrecht, 1980; Vagts, 1959) or, at least, civil forces were guiding militarization without changing the form of political control (see, for example, Aron, 1979; Geyer, 1989; Mills, 1956; Regehr, 1980). Israeli proponents of militarism, although they describe the dynamic evolution of Israeli militarism, refrain from analyzing its effects on political control over the IDF (see Ben-Eliezer, 1995; Carmi and Rosenfeld, 1988; Kimmerling, 1993b).

Boldly put, contrary to what has been surmised by most students of military–civilian relations in Israel, state agencies molded arrangements of control over the IDF not *despite* but *due* to the militarization of society and politics. At the broader theoretical level, contrary to the existing scholarship on militarization, as long as militarization increases the state's capacity to extract internal resources concurrently with the military's gains, militarization works to *restrain* the autonomous power held by the military, rather than *bolstering* this power.

Finally, militarization also set the cultural-political boundaries within which political-civilian institutions control the military. So, formal arrangements do not appear in my account as a sufficient condition for effective control. Rather, the searchlight is put on the cultural-political boundaries within which those relations of control are structured, and hence, the level in which the military mind-set is privileged over civilian-dominated statecraft regardless of, even stimulating, that control. After all, even in countries categorized as "garrison states" (see Lasswell, 1941) militaries are somewhat controlled (Aron, 1979), but control is confined to a previously constructed cultural-political structure bounding decision-making to a narrow range of alternative options. The mentioned Israeli mainstream military sociologists have repeated this neglect as well.

CHAPTER 4

1. Yaniv and Maoz (1984) quantitatively analyze Israel–Syria military clashes during the years 1948–82 and find that since Israel acted in a deterrence-seeking fashion, it clung to escalation while Syria confined its reaction to the event itself.

2. Theoretically, given that the military doctrine, military buildup, and the lead-up are key factors in the outbreak of the war, a purely crisis-centered perspective is implausible (see Holsti, 1989, for the IR school of crisis management). Leaders' perceptions— through which they read the situation as a threat to Israel's existence, especially under conditions of stress and lack of information (Brecher, 1980, 37–41, 94–103)—are of less importance than other variables: (1) the conditions that generated the crisis in question

and (2) the previously created conditions, external and internal, narrowing the leaders' scope of consideration, such as the widely installed ascendancy of military mind-set with the resources that it entailed (see my critique on Brecher in chapter 3).

3. To illustrate long-term effects on higher education, while in 1961 only 3 percent of foreign-born Orientals and 4.5 percent of Israeli-born Orientals had 13+ years of schooling, in 1982 the rates were 10 percent and 11.5 percent, respectively. But for Westerners, in 1961 about 13 percent of foreign-born Westerners and 20 percent of Israeli-born Westerners acquired higher education, while in 1982, the numbers were 29 percent and 43 percent, respectively (Ben-Porath, 1986a, 158–159). Gaps among the Israeli-born in each ethnic group, then, saw no more than a slight decline during twenty years.

4. Grinberg argues that state's autonomy was impaired as a result of the creation of a coalition between the military establishment and the Histadrut, the main beneficiaries from the occupation. Hence, the state was inclined to maintain the occupation and further leaned to display responsiveness toward the Histadrut's claims. This argument is valid if the conception of the state's autonomy is reduced to state–Histadrut relations at the level of everyday give and take while neglecting the creation of a structural dependence of the Histadrut on the state. Grinberg, moreover, conceptually fails to explain how it is possible that the state was weakened while the military was strengthened. He also fails to address the wide range of gains that helped materialize the state's capacity to maintain its reproduction-oriented action in the interethnic domain. Finally, Grinberg neglects the levels at which the Histadrut's capacity to mobilize the political support of Orientals and Israeli Palestinians actually declined due to the entrenchment of the Arab-Israeli conflict and despite its ostensible empowerment, as chapters 5–6 show.

5. In this connection Marcuse (1964, 33–34) argues, at the theoretical level, that military production brought about a convergence of interests between the business corporations and the trade unions as it became a mechanism of creating/keeping jobs. This capitalist mechanism of "uniting contradictions" precludes a possibility of social change.

6. In addition, Israel provided other benefits, such as operating ports to replace the paralyzed Suez Canal; petroleum production in Sinai; tax collection in the territories (nullified by costs of military administration); tourism; increased financial support from the Jewish diaspora, and so on (Kanovsky, 1970, 54–67).

7. Marx, in his essay "The Eighteenth Brumaire of Louis Bonaparte" (1963, 130), showed that the peasants' service in the army of Napoleon III bestowed on them the prestige that was a basic element of their loyalty to a social order that in fact vitiated the social interests of their class. Moreover, Mann (1987) notes that the introduction of mass conscription in the European armies at the end of the nineteenth century conferred the status of membership in the political community on the middle class. Consequently, they supported belligerent actions that nonetheless conflicted with their own social interests (see also Best, 1989, 24–25, on workers' movements' support and the discussion by Tocqueville, 1967, 59–64, on the American army).

8. Viewed from a broader perspective, the high price of protection the state "sells" to its citizens is instrumental for channeling peripheral groups' protests from the social domain to the military-political one (see the variety of illustrations in Moskos, 1970, 108–111; 1984, 142–143; Pedersen, 1990; Young, 1984).

9. It is worth emphasizing that these figures are approximations insofar as the overall analysis is grounded on assumptions rather than solid facts. Since the idea of the military as an interethnic "melting pot" is one of the "sacred cows" of Israeli society, formal data about the actual mobility of Orientals in the IDF are not available—unlike, for instance, the U.S. military with regard to the promotion of African Americans.

10. Exploration of highly developed economies has recently refuted Andreski's classic project (1971) in which he claimed that high military participation ratios increase income inequalities. The more society is economically developed, the less skills learned in the military are transferrable to the civilian labor market (Weede, 1993). Data about the social mobility of African American veterans in American society confirm this argument (Segal and Verdugo, 1994, 628; Teachman et al., 1993, 304–305).

11. Transferability of skills is not simply a mechanical construct of the labor market. It is built on social networks that rank the value of jobs and the categorically framed groups' qualifications to perform those jobs, relative to the comparable ranking of jobs and groups in the military. From this is derived the social acknowledgement of qualification of veterans to convert their military positions into civilian positions. So, status attained by a subordinated group in the military socially matters only by virtue of the degree to which its performance is symmetrically and highly appreciated by the other social networks in society. Group accomplishments then become the main "currencies" for relations of exchange between groups. This allows for the subordinated groups' expropriation of symbols previously and exclusively utilized by dominant groups to legitimize their superior position. Subordinated groups can then invoke their military gains to demand quid pro quos in civilian terms. Networks built on those symbols (such as the military-industrial complex) might then be expanded to include the subordinated group's members, now acknowledged by members of dominant social networks as qualified to convert military to civilian jobs. As for the subordinated group, the more those conditions show themselves, the more this group will be motivated to opt for the military-based avenue of social integration. Class/ethnic identity-waxing is thus less likely to appear.

12. Three writers were part of the decision-making circle: Mordechai Gazit served as the senior political adviser to Prime Minister Golda Meir; Yitzhak Rabin was ambassador to the United States at the time; and Gad Yaacobi served as a cabinet minister during 1974–77. A similar opinion has also been stated by General Mordechai Hod, then the commander of the air force (*Ha'aretz* Supplement, April 12, 1996, 20). But see also the version of Aaron Yariv (1985, 24), the head of Military Intelligence during that period, claiming that Israel really made a serious attempt to obtain an agreement.

13. Some scholars argue that the political system suffered from "paralysis" in the light of the bickering between doves and hawks (for example, Beilin, 1985; Lustick,

1993, 362–366; Shapiro, 1991, 151–159). However, as the occupation's beneficiaries, doves and hawks alike took part in solidifying the status quo as long as their debates were confined to the military school rather than embodying two distinct, incompatible alternatives.

CHAPTER 5

1. By comparison, Mann (1985) identified within the state-building process the state's tendency to strengthen civilian power centers as part of its very penetration of the society. At a later stage, however, these centers accumulate power with which they try to remove the state from its penetrative positions. In Mann's terms, they impair the state's "infrastructural power" (for a similar analysis of dialectical relations between the state and civilian power centers, see Badie and Birnbaum, 1983, 55–59; Migdal, 1988).

2. Political opportunity structure is "consistent . . . dimensions of the political environment that provide incentive for people to undertake collective action by affecting their expectations for success or failure" (Tarrow, 1994, 85). Increasing access to political participation, unstable alignments, divided elites, and a state's weakness to meet some groups' expectations are among the dimensions of political opportunity structure (ibid., 85–90).

3. The fact that the Orientals consider army service to be a social asset was shown also in anthropological observations of such a group during their military service. The study found that in card games played by reserve soldiers in mixed Oriental-Western units, the Orientals created a social insularity geared to show their superiority over the Westerners (Feige and Ben-Ari, 1991).

4. See, by comparison, Geyer (1989, 93–94) on the emergence of peripheral groups' protest in the defeated countries in the aftermath of World War I. Furthermore, Smith (1981) identified, in the theoretical context, the likelihood that a lengthy war will bolster ethnic identities. A short war, in contrast, helps cement social cohesiveness and blurs communal distinctions. That hypothesis fits in with my argument on the connection between shortening the duration of wars and reducing the costs of maintaining the conflict. Those costs increased, I maintain, in the case of a protracted war such as the War of Attrition, in which the primary burden fell on the regular army, where the Orientals were overrepresented relative to their numbers in the population.

5. Under the state's auspices, Hevrat Ha'Ovdim, the Histadrut's holding company, abandoned its social-welfare approach and became a business corporation in every respect, competing with other corporations in a capitalist business environment. This process further sharpened the alienation between the Histadrut and the workers, particularly the many Orientals, and nowhere more so than in the development towns where Orientals were employed by Hevrat Ha'Ovdim's industries, including those of the Kibbutz Movement. The Histadrut's "schizophrenia" became pronounced, as it was perceived to function as both a trade union and a business (Grinberg, 1991b, 64–83).

6. A state-produced loss of political support within three constituencies engendered the waning of the Alignment: upper middle class, Orientals, and Israeli Palestinians. Middle-class voters turned to support the DMC. It was founded in 1976 by retired General Yigael Yadin, who had served as the IDF's second chief of staff. The DMC's founders included, similar to Rafi, personalities who were identified with the technocracy of the Labor Party and the Histadrut, some of them retired generals. Symptomatic was the DMC's advocacy of reasserting the state's internal control, in such demands as their call for a revision of the electoral system in order to give the government far greater powers (Urieli and Barzilay, 1982). With the post-1967 rise of standard of living and the state's gradual universalization and its neutralization of the party-based power centers, voters dependent on the Histadrut and state agencies declined. Part of them could therefore take on their mother party, the Alignment. The DMC's success in 1977 (it obtained 15 seats in the 120-member Knesset) came at the expense of the Alignment.

Furthermore, similar to the Orientals' realignment as noted above, Israeli Palestinians turned to a more national stand, giving growing support to the Communist Party and other autonomous organizing. Not only "the Day of the Land" (see chapter 4) accounts for this switch, but also the growth of material and political expectations among the Palestinians—who also improved their lot following the Six-Day War. Those expectations were at odds with the state's security-oriented policies and the decline of the Histadrut, which could not restrain or mobilize Israeli Palestinians at the level it had before.

So, to a large extent, this political change reflected a socially originated shift in the political division of labor between the state and the parties. This goes beyond the explanations furnished by Israeli scholars, whether, for example, centered on the electorate (Shamir and Arian, 1982), on political entrepreneurs (Goldberg, 1986; Shapiro, 1991), or on the cultural-symbolic effects of enduring occupation on domestic realignment (Kimmerling, 1983; Shapiro, 1996, 113–114).

7. At the theoretical level, whereas overt policies and ascriptive criteria based on ethnic categorization deprive subordinated groups of the capacity to resist repression, they also create for the long term a subordinated racial identity that acts as a potential basis for resistance (Marx, 1996, 200). In the case of Israel, however, it was the ostensible universalism that worked for a long time to stifle Oriental organizing. On the other hand, tension between reality and the expectations produced by universalism created a base for political mobilization in which the same "melting-pot" symbols previously invoked to obstruct ethnic organization were now used to demand substantiation of unity. But it was the centrality of war that contextualized collective action, creating the suitable opportunity structure.

8. It is for this reason that Barnet (1972, 13–15) argues, in the context of the Vietnam War, that the preponderance of technology and logistics in modern warfare dulls the conscience of soldiers and disinclines them to engage in political activity after the war.

9. The Gush Emunim–IDF clash was a limited one. Even when the Jewish settlement of Yamit, in northern Sinai, was evacuated in 1982, marking the final phase of Israel's withdrawal from the Sinai, the settlers—specifically, those who were led by

Gush Emunim—showed restraint in resisting the army's operation. They portrayed the IDF as the victim of the political settlement, not as one of its architects (Aran, 1985).

10. No wonder that the 1980s saw a steep rise in the importance of another state agency—the courts. It found expression in a dramatic increase in the number of groups and individuals that turned to the Supreme Court, in its capacity as the High Court of Justice, to arbitrate between them and the state's executive agencies. Gradually the Supreme Court began to intervene more extensively in areas it had previously avoided, notably the appointment and election of public officials, the government's resource allocation policies, and even the army's activity in the territories (Mautner, 1993, 101–108). This had the effect of reducing the government's operative autonomy, but at the same time, the government could draw on the assistance of another state agency—the courts—to implement its policy in the face of conflicting pressures. Moreover, the Supreme Court was generally perceived to be above politics—in the narrow sense in which the term "politics" was understood by most of the groups in Israel—even if its decisions generally upheld the value system of the dominant groups (ibid., 128–130; on the public's high confidence in courts, see Barzilai et al., 1994, 54–55).

11. Some scholars (especially Horowitz and Lissak, 1989; Shapiro, 1991) deemed the waning of Westerners' exclusiveness in the political domain, accompanied by the Alignment's decline, as a political crisis. Their work reflects two conceptual failures. First, they conceptualize the Orientals' entrance into the political arena exclusively through the Western elites' eyes. Second, they have not conceptualized variants in state autonomy: its reliance on the Histadrut and Mapai in the 1950s was now converted into imprisonment by big corporations and other forces that gained from the conflict. Reconstruction of power relations, rather than a state crisis, was manifest.

CHAPTER 6

1. This option is overlooked by Israeli IR scholars inspired by neorealist concepts (see, for example, Horowitz, 1983, 1987; Lanir, 1985; Yariv, 1985).

2. For the first time in the country's history, Israel Television documented the funerals of the slain, amplifying the sense of loss. By comparison, in the 1948 War, when the state fought for its perceived sheer survival, about 6,000 youngsters were killed (a tenth of the entire young generation, fifty times more than in the Lebanon War in proportional terms). The press, however, did not report the losses (Gertz, 1995, 66).

3. The case of Israel is similar to other instances in which a cyclical motion took place: internal-state expansion-> growth in living standard-> stimulation of social demands-> state expansion, and so forth. At the extreme, a "legitimation crisis" may be set in motion (for different versions, see Gold et al., 1975, 37–41; Habermas, 1975, 1987; Herring, 1987; O'Connor, 1973; Offe, 1975; Wolfe, 1973, 1977; see also the conservative version taken by Brittan, 1975; Crozier et al., 1975; for comparison between approaches, see Held, 1989).

4. More than once Israel defined, implicitly or explicitly, an expanded war goal oriented to altering the political reality. To recall: The cooperation with France and Britain in the Suez War; General Rabin's declaration that Israel's moves of escalation in 1967 aimed at toppling the Ba'ath regime in Syria (Haber, 1987, 146); and the same Rabin's (now ambassador to Washington) suggestion to employ strategic blows in Egypt during the War of Attrition as a means of overthrowing the Nasserist regime (Bar-Or, 1994, 39–40). Even the Alignment-led government's first intervention in the civil war in Lebanon aimed at sustaining the Christians' dominance.

5. Other mechanisms as well were instrumental to escape a short-term army disintegration. The interethnic conflict has not been aggravated following the Intifada due to the modus vivendi created between Likud and Labor and the channeling of Orientals' frustration into the cultural sphere via the Shas Party (see below). Significant was the role played by the political discourse. Inspired by the cooperation between Right and Center-Left, the political discourse as it was reflected in the media constructed the Intifada as a violation of order while minimizing the IDF's role as an oppressive force (Levy, 1992). The military's policy of assigning a great deal of the policing missions—those liable to stimulate political awareness among the soldiers—to regular forces, particularly "special units," was also instrumental to the IDF's integration. The professional aspect aside, the army could reduce the political costs of suppressing the mass uprising. Troops of this kind had limited political awareness, not only because of their young age but also because they were prone to develop professional pride by the very fact of being called "special forces." Finally and most important, a tacit coalition of forces, that is, the groups that comprised the Westerner-dominated middle class from both the political Right and Left, still had a vested interest in preserving the IDF's status by distancing it from political disputes. Hence, the right wing's relatively moderate stand restrained it from pushing the military to up the ante of violence as a means of oppressing the uprising even when the Likud-led coalition succeeded the grand coalition in 1990. As for the mainstream Left, it distinguished between opposition to the occupation and the army's instrumental functioning, which was said to transcend political disputes (see, for example, Ben-Ari, 1990, on the mechanisms of differentiation that reservists developed between their civilian and military experiences).

6. Again, the spread of nuclear weapons was a typical product of the manner in which Israel coped with the security dilemma inasmuch as to a large extent states in the region reacted to Israel's nuclear project.

7. Considering that the price of weapons systems became higher in absolute terms as long as they became based on technology instead of labor-intensive systems, and shrinking budgets had acute meaning from the IDF's point of view.

8. Again, militarization, which accounted for the growing burden, also propelled political participation by which the military became further monitored. Clearly, until the post-1967 milestone the Jewish citizenry did not play an active role in monitoring military activities but passively tolerated military policies.

9. Weakening links between military service and substantive citizenship (Shaw, 1991, 174–180; Silver, 1994) and militaries' transition from "institution" to "occupation" (Moskos, 1986) typify the global diminishment of militaries as prestigious institutions (see also Harries-Jenkins, 1976; Van-Doorn, 1975).

10. The gradual revision of the military doctrine was apparent in the 1993 Operation Accountability and the 1996 Grapes of Wrath, mounted against Hezbollah militia, when friction between that fundamentalist Lebanese-Shiite movement and the IDF and the South Lebanon Army increased in southern Lebanon. In these operations the conception formulated by the chief of staff in the early 1990s, General Ehud Barak, was implemented. This called for "transferring fire to the enemy's territory"—supplanting the traditional doctrine of "transferring the war to the enemy's territory." The new approach involved the use of state-of-the-art technology, particularly in air power and artillery, to attack targets without endangering Israeli ground forces. Israel in fact achieved its short-term military objectives. The short operations, which caused hundreds of Lebanese civilian casualties and inflicted tremendous damage, did not arouse significant domestic political opposition inasmuch as Israel used weapons systems that heightened the level of alienation between fighter and victim. Israel again grasped the lessons of the Lebanon War.

11. Those weapons systems might be strategic systems and weapons based on technology, knowledge, and information instead of labor-intensive systems—in short, a "third wave" of military technology, as it is termed by Toffler and Toffler (1993) inspired by the Gulf War (and which found its partial expression in Operation Accountability and Grapes of Wrath).

12. For illustration, unemployment in 1986 stood at 11 percent in development towns compared to 6.5 percent at the national level (Peled, 1991, 9).

13. Part of that remobilization manifested as dramatic increases in the political representation of Orientals by the biggest parties. Ironically, however, while Orientals account for about 40 percent of the big parties' lists for the 1996 elections, political representation and inequality marched together (*Ha'aretz*, March 29, 1996, b2).

14. The case of Britain exemplifies this argument. The state, during the aftermath of the Second World War, developed a centralist form of social-economy coordination from the centralist form of war management. The shift from conventional-based to nuclear-based strategic doctrine, running from the late 1950s, contributed to the decline of the centralist welfare state, because the decline of military participation was a necessary, if not a sufficient, condition for the break-up of the political-social consensus (Shaw, 1987; 1988, 104–107).

15. As some scholars maintain, democracy might restrain war-prone orientations against other democracies (Lake, 1992; Russett, 1990; Russett and Maoz, 1990; Weede, 1992). However, democratization, as the case in point suggests, sprang from the societal ascendancy of materialism by which new groups endeavored to take part in formulating the military doctrine through which they restrained the use of force.

16. For example, consider an extremist hawkish stand as 5 and extremist dovish stand as 1: the mean scores obtaining from public opinion surveys were 3.1 in 1987 (before the Intifada had broken out) and 2.4 in 1993 (Arian, 1995a, 114–115).

17. It is possible that the peace process (or its pause) would propel political autonomization of Israeli Palestinians, leading to the rising of a radical stand toward the state, or demands geared to political autonomy within the Israeli state, and even to greater linkage with whatever Palestinian entity the future holds.

18. This suggests that the IDF's shift took place in part under the Likud government when Moshe Arens served as a "civilian" defense minister. Thus, the IDF's reorientation cannot be exclusively attributable to the military authority of Prime Minister and Defense Minister Rabin who conducted the peace moves in 1992–95.

19. A clear expression of this trend was the Ethiopian Jews' violent protest in January 1996. Ethiopians were absorbed beginning in 1985 and relegated to backward positions in the labor market. The direct trigger, however, was the disclosure that medical authorities "dumped" blood donated by this ethnic group because of a proportionally high rate of HIV and other diseases among Ethiopian immigrants. But the protests highlighted a deep frustration with the terms of absorption, which were likened to those of Orientals during the 1950s. Under conditions of market-oriented absorption, it took very few years for an ethnic group that accounts for only about one percent of the total population to put forward its demands loudly in a demonstration that included a great number of the adult members of this group. Under conditions of state-led absorption, Orientals, who accounted for more than 30 percent of the total population during the early 1950s, reacted far more obediently.

20. De-escalation, entwined with the long-distance nuclear threat, could keep the Arab-Israeli conflict viable, with the state retaining part of the war-produced gains germane to its third domain by maintaining war preparation geared toward an "abstract belligerence," to use Wolfe's term (1984, 245). That would combine force-oriented rhetoric with minor demands for sacrifice (see also empirical support in Russett, 1989, 176–179).

Bibliography

Abramov, Zalman S. 1995. *A Party that Failed—Its Idea Prevailed.* Tel Aviv: Dvir (Hebrew).

Alberger, Zvi. 1993. "From Economic Regression to the 'Intifada': A Critical Examination of the Crisis of the Israeli State in the 1980s." Unpublished manuscript, Department of Political Science, Tel Aviv University (Hebrew).

Albrecht, Ulrich. 1980. "Militarism and Underdevelopment." In *Problems of Contemporary Militarism*, eds. Asbjorn Eide and Mark Thee. New York: St. Martin's Press.

Alexander, David. 1985. *Satiric Theater in Israel.* Tel Aviv: Sifriat Hapoalim (Hebrew).

Alford, Robert, and Roger Friedland. 1985. *Powers of Theory: Capitalism, the State and Democracy.* Cambridge: Cambridge University Press.

Al-Haj, Majid. 1993. "The Changing Strategies of Mobilization among the Arabs in Israel: Parliamentary Politics, Local Politics, and National Organizations." In *Local Communities and the Israeli Polity: Conflict of Values and Interests*, ed. Efraim Ben-Zadok. Albany: SUNY Press.

Allison, Graham T. 1969. "Conceptual Models and the Cuban Missile Crisis," *American Political Science Review* 63: 689–718.

Allon, Yigal. 1989. *The Efforts to Reach Peace.* Tel Aviv: Hakibbutz Hameuchad Publishing House (Hebrew).

Almog, Oz. 1993. "The Death of the Bad Arab," *Politica* 51: 20–25 (Hebrew).

———. 1995. "The Secular Rabbis," *Ha'aretz*, December 29: 19 (Hebrew).

Althusser, Louis. 1976. "Ideology and Ideological State Apparatuses." In *Essays on Ideology.* London: Verso.

Amir, Shmuel. 1986. "Educational Structure and Wage Differentials of the Labor Force in the 1970s." In *The Israeli Economy: Maturing through Crises*, ed. Yoram Ben-Porath. Cambridge, Mass.: Harvard University Press.

Amir, Yehuda. 1967. "Adjustment and Promotion of Soldiers from Communal Settlements," *Megamot* 15: 250–258 (Hebrew).

——— , et al. 1975. "Effects of Interethnic Contact on Friendship Choices in the Military," *Megamot* 21: 287–294 (Hebrew).

Amitay, Yossi. 1986. *The United Workers' Party (Mapam) 1948–1954: Attitudes on Palestinian-Arab Issues*. Tel Aviv: Gome (Hebrew).

Amitzur, Ilan. 1995. *Embargo, Power, and Military Decision in the 1948 Palestine War*. Tel Aviv: Ma'arachot (Hebrew).

Andreski, Stanislav. 1971. *Military Organization and Society*. Berkeley: University of California Press.

Andrews, Bruce. 1975. "Social Rules and the State as a Social Actor," *World Politics* 27: 521–540.

——— . 1984. "The Domestic Content of Behavioral Desire," *International Organization* 38: 321–327.

Aran, Gideon. 1985. *The Land of Israel—Between Religion and Politics*. Jerusalem: Jerusalem Institute for Israel Studies (Hebrew).

Arens, Moshe. 1995. *Broken Covenant: American Foreign Policy and the Crisis Between the U.S. and Israel*. New York: Simon and Schuster.

Arian, Asher. 1975. "Were the 1973 Elections in Israel Critical?" *Comparative Politics* 8: 152–165.

——— . 1977. "The Passing of Dominance," *Jerusalem Quarterly* 5: 20–32.

——— . 1995a. *Security Threatened: Surveying Israeli Opinion on Peace and War*. New York: Cambridge University Press.

——— . 1995b. *The Peace Process and Terror: Conflicting Trends in Israeli Public Opinion in 1995*. Tel Aviv: Tel Aviv University, Jaffee Center for Strategic Studies.

——— . 1996. *Israeli Security Opinion, February 1996*. Tel Aviv: Tel Aviv University, Jaffee Center for Strategic Studies.

——— , and Michal Shamir. 1983. "The Primarily Political Functions of the Left-Right Continuum," *Comparative Politics* 15: 139–158.

——— , and Michal Shamir. 1995. "Two Reversals: Why 1992 Was Not 1977." In *The Elections in Israel 1992*, eds. Asher Arian and Michal Shamir. Albany: SUNY Press.

Ariely, Yehoshua. 1983. "The Israeli Democracy under the Test of the Lebanon War." In *Lebanon: The Other War*, ed. Rubik Rosenthal. Tel Aviv: Sifriat Hapoalim (Hebrew).

Aron, Raymond. 1979. "Remarks on Lasswell's 'The Garrison State,'" *Armed Forces and Society* 5: 347–357.

Aronoff, Myron J. 1993. "The Origins of Israeli Political Culture." In *Israeli Democracy under Stress*, eds. Larry Diamond and Ehud Sprinzak. Boulder, Colo.: Lynne Rienner Publishers.

Aronson, Shlomo. 1974. "A Framework for Analysis of the Linkage Between Foreign and Defense Policy and the Internal Political Structure in Israel, 1948–1971," *Medina, Mimshal Viyahasim Benleumiyyim* 5: 109–118 (Hebrew).

———. 1992. *The Politics and Strategy of Nuclear Weapons in the Middle East: Opacity, Theory, and Reality, 1960–1991, An Israeli Perspective*. Albany: SUNY Press.

———, and Dan Horowitz. 1971. "The Strategy of Controlled Retaliation—The Israeli Case," *Medina, Mimshal, Viyahsim Benleumiyim* 1: 77–99 (Hebrew).

Ashley, Richard. 1984. "The Poverty of Neo-Realism," *International Organization* 38: 225–286.

Association of Journalists. 1983. "War Without Consensus." In *The Yearbook of the Association of Journalists*. Tel Aviv: Association of Journalists (Hebrew).

Avnery, Uri. 1968. *Israel Without Zionists*. London: Macmillan Press (Hebrew Version: Avnery, Uri. 1969. *The Seventh Day War*. Tel Aviv: Daf Hadash).

Azarya, Victor. 1983. "The Israeli Armed Forces." In *Civic Education in the Military*, eds. Morris Janowitz and Stephen Westbrook. Beverly Hills, Calif.: Sage Publications.

———, and Baruch Kimmerling. 1980. "New Immigrants in the Israeli Armed Forces," *Armed Forces and Society* 6: 455–482.

Azoulay-Katz, Orly. 1996. *Sysiphos' Catch*. Tel Aviv: Miskal (Hebrew).

Badi, Joseph. 1963. *The Government of the State of Israel*. New York: Twayne.

Badie, Bertrand, and Pierre Birnbaum. 1983. *The Sociology of the State*. Chicago: University of Chicago Press.

Baran, Paul, and Paul Sweezy. 1966. *Monopoly Capital: An Essay on the American Economic and Social Order*. New York: Monthly Review Press.

Bar-Haim, Aviad. 1987. "Patterns of Ethnic Integration among the Israeli Military Elite," *Megamot* 30: 276–287 (Hebrew).

Barnes, Samuel. 1966. "Ideology and the Organization of Conflict: On the Relationship Between Political Thought and Behavior," _Journal of Politics_ 28: 513–530.

Barnet, Richard J. 1972. _Roots of War._ New York: Atheneum.

Barnett, Michael N. 1990. "High Politics Is Low Politics: The Domestic and Systemic Sources of Israeli Security Policy, 1967–1977," _World Politics_ 42: 529–562.

———. 1992. _Confronting the Costs of War: Military Power, State, and Society in Egypt and Israel._ Princeton, N.J.: Princeton University Press.

Bar-On, Avner. 1981. _The Stories That Have Never Been Told._ Tel Aviv: Edanim Publishers (Hebrew).

Bar-On, Mordechai. 1985. _Peace Now: The Portrait of a Movement._ Tel Aviv: Hakibbutz Hameuchad Publishing House (Hebrew).

———. 1992. _The Gates of Gaza: Israel's Defence and Foreign Policy, 1955–1957._ Tel Aviv: Am Oved Publishers (Hebrew).

Bar-Or, Amir. 1989. "Preemptive Counterattack and Its Development in Yigal Allon's Security Thinking," _Medina, Mimshal Viyahsim Benleumiyim_ 30: 61–79 (Hebrew).

———. 1994. "The Government of Israel's Decision to Employ Deep-Penetration Bombing in Egypt," _Ma'arachot_ 334: 32–41 (Hebrew).

Bar-Siman-Tov, Yaacov. 1988. "The Bar-Lev Line Revisited," _Journal of Strategic Studies_ 11: 149–176.

———. 1995. "Security Regimes: Mediating Between War and Peace in the Arab Israeli Conflict." In _Regional Security Regimes: Israel and Its Neighbors_, ed. Efraim Inbar. Albany: SUNY Press.

Bartov, Hanoch. 1978. _Dado: A Biography._ Tel Aviv: Sifriat Ma'ariv Library (Hebrew).

Barzilai, Gad. 1992. _A Democracy in Wartime: Conflict and Consensus in Israel._ Tel Aviv: Sifriat Hapoalim (Hebrew).

———. 1993. "Society and Politics in War: The Israeli Case." In _The Gulf Crisis and Its Global Aftermath_, eds. Gad Barzilai et al. London: Routledge.

———, and Bruce Russett. 1990. "The Political Economy of Israeli Military Action." In _The Elections in Israel 1988_, eds. Asher Arian and Michal Shamir. Boulder, Colo.: Westview Press.

———. et al. 1994. _The Israeli Supreme Court and the Israeli Public._ Tel Aviv: Papyrus (Hebrew).

Bar-Zohar, Michael. 1975. _Ben-Gurion._ Jerusalem: Keter Publishing House (Hebrew).

Be'er, Israel. 1966. _Israel's Security._ Tel Aviv: Hamikam (Hebrew).

Beilin, Yossi. 1984. *Sons under Their Fathers' Shadow*. Tel Aviv: Revivim (Hebrew).

————. 1985. *The Price of Unity*. Tel Aviv: Revivim (Hebrew).

————. 1987. *The Roots of Israeli Industry*. Jerusalem: Keter Publishing House (Hebrew).

————. 1993. *Israel—40 Plus : A Political Profile of Israel Society in the 1990s*. Tel Aviv: Yediot Aharonot Books (Hebrew).

Beker, Avichai. 1996. "A Yarmulke March," *Ma'ariv Supplement*, March 8: 60–64 (Hebrew).

Ben-Ari, Eyal. 1990. "Soldiers with Masks: The IDF and the Intifada." In *The Seventh War: The Effects of the Intifada on the Israeli Society*, ed. Reuven Gal. Tel Aviv: Hakibbutz Hameuchad Publishing House (Hebrew).

Ben-Dor, Gabriel. 1973. "The Military in the Politics of Integration and Innovation: The Case of the Druze Minority in Israel," *Asian and African Studies* 9: 339–369.

————. 1977. "Politics and Military in Israel of the 1970s." In *The Political System in Israel*, eds. Moshe Lissak and Emanuel Guttman. Tel Aviv: Am Oved Publishers (Hebrew).

Ben-Eliezer, Uri. 1984. "Israel's Native-Born Generation: Social Superiority Conditioned by Political Inferiority," *Medina, Mimshal Viyahsim Benleumiyim* 23: 29–49 (Hebrew).

————. 1993. "The Meaning of Political Participation in a Nonliberal Democracy: The Israeli Experience," *Comparative Politics* 25: 397–412.

————. 1994. "The Nation-in-Arms and War: Israel During Its First Years," *Zmanim* 49: 51–65 (Hebrew).

————. 1995. *The Emergence of Israeli Militarism 1936–1956*. Tel Aviv: Dvir (Hebrew).

Ben-Gurion, David. 1971. *Uniqueness and Destiny*. Tel Aviv: Ma'arachot (Hebrew).

————. 1981. " The Military and the State," *Ma'arachot* 279–280: 2–11 (Hebrew).

Benjamini, Haim. 1984. "The Six-Day War, Israel 1967: Decisions, Coalitions, Consequences, A Sociological View." In *Israeli Society and Its Defense Establishment*, ed. Moshe Lissak. London: Frank Cass.

Ben Meir, Yehuda. 1995. *Civil-Military Relations in Israel*. New York: Columbia University Press.

Benn, Aluf. 1988. "A Wall to His People." In *Heroes of Israel*, ed. Michael Bar-Zohar. Tel Aviv: Ministry of Defense (Hebrew).

————. 1993. "When Comprehensive Peace Comes," *Ha'aretz*, September 29: 16 (Hebrew).

Ben-Porath, Yoram. 1986a. "Diversity in Population and in the Labor Force." In *The Israeli Economy: Maturing through Crises*, ed. Yoram Ben-Porath. Cambridge, Mass.: Harvard University Press.

―――. 1986b. "Introduction." In *The Israeli Economy: Maturing through Crises*, ed. Yoram Ben-Porath. Cambridge, Mass.: Harvard University Press.

―――. 1986c. " The Entwined Growth of Population and Product, 1922–1982." In *The Israeli Economy: Maturing through Crises*, ed. Yoram Ben-Porath. Cambridge, Mass.: Harvard University Press.

Ben-Rafael, Eliezer. 1982. *The Emergence of Ethnicity: Cultural Groups and Social Conflict in Israel*. Westport, Conn.: Greenwood Press.

Ben-Zadok, Efraim. 1993. "Oriental Jews in the Development Towns: Ethnicity, Economic Development, Budgets, and Politics." In *Local Communities and the Israeli Polity: Conflict of Values and Interests*, ed. Efraim Ben-Zadok. Albany: SUNY Press.

Benziman, Uzi. 1985. *Sharon—An Israeli Caesar*. New York: Adama Books.

―――, and Atallah Mansour. 1992. *Subtenants*. Jerusalem: Keter Publishing House (Hebrew).

Ben-Zvi, Abraham. 1993. "A Changing American-Israel Relationship." In *The Gulf Crisis and Its Global Aftermath*, eds. Gad Barzilai et al. London: Routledge.

Ben-Zvi, Shmuel. 1993. *Security Expanses and the National Economy*. Tel Aviv: Tel Aviv University, Pinhas Sapir Center for Development (Hebrew).

Berger, Herzl. 1955. "The Balancing Account of the 1955 Knesset Elections," *Molad* 84: 259–261 (Hebrew).

Berghahn, Volker Rolf. 1982. *Militarism: The History of an International Debate, 1861–1979*. New York: St. Martin's Press.

Berglas, Eitan. 1984. "The Defense Burden upon the Israeli Economy." In *The Price of Power*, eds. Zvi Offer and Avi Kober. Tel Aviv: Ministry of Defense (Hebrew).

―――. 1986. "Defense and the Economy." In *The Israeli Economy: Maturing through Crises*, ed. Yoram Ben-Porath. Cambridge, Mass.: Harvard University Press.

Bernstein, Deborah, and Shlomo Swirski. 1982. "The Rapid Economic Development of Israel and the Emergence of the Ethnic Division of Labor," *British Journal of Sociology* 33: 64–85.

Best, Jeffrey. 1989. " The Militarization of European Society, 1870–1914." In *The Militarization of the Western World*, ed. John R. Gillis. New Brunswick, N.J.: Rutgers University Press.

Bienen, Henry. 1983. "Armed Forces and National Modernization: Continuing the Debate," *Comparative Politics* 16: 1–16.

Bishara, Azmi. 1993. "On the Question of the Palestinian Minority in Israel," *Theory and Criticism* 3: 7–20 (Hebrew).

Blain, Michael. 1994. "Power, War, and Melodrama in the Discourse of Political Movements," *Theory and Society* 23: 805–837.

Block, Fred. 1980. "Economic Instability and Military Strength: The Paradoxes of the 1950 Rearmament Decision," *Politics and Society* 10: 35–58.

Bourdieu, Pierre, and Loic J. D. Wacquant. 1992. *An Invitation to Reflexive Sociology*. Chicago: University of Chicago Press.

Bowden, Tom. 1976. *Army in the Service of the State*. Tel Aviv: Tel Aviv University.

Brecher, Michael. 1980. *Decisions in Crisis: Israel, 1967 and 1973*. Berkeley: University of California Press.

———. 1974. *Decisions in Israel's Foreign Policy*. London: Oxford University Press.

Brittan, Samuel. 1975. "The Economic Contradictions in Democracy," *British Journal of Political Science* 5: 129–159.

Carmi, Shulamit, and Henry Rosenfeld. 1993. "The Emergence of a Militaristic Nationalism in Israel." In *Israeli Society: Critical Perspectives*, ed. Uri Ram. Tel Aviv: Breirot (Hebrew).

Cobban, Helena. 1995. "Israel and the Palestinians: From Madrid to Oslo and Beyond." In *Israel under Rabin*, ed. Robert O. Friedman. Boulder, Colo.: Westview Press.

Cohen, Avner. 1996. "Cairo, Dimona, and the June 1967 War," *Middle East Journal* 50:190–210.

Cohen, Eric. 1989. "Citizenship, Nationality and Religion in Israel and Thailand." In *The Israeli State and Society: Boundaries and Frontiers*, ed. Baruch Kimmerling. Albany: SUNY Press.

Cohen, Mitchell. 1987. *Zion and State: Nation, Class and the Shaping of Modern Israel*. New York: Basil Blackwell.

Cohen, Stuart A. 1995. "The Israeli Defense Forces (IDF) from a 'People Army' to a 'Professional Military'—Causes and Implications," *Armed Forces and Society* 21: 237–254.

Cohen, Yinon. 1988. "War and Social Integration: The Effects of the Israeli-Arab Conflict on Jewish Emigration," *American Sociological Review* 53: 908–918.

Connolly, William E. 1993. *The Terms of Political Discourse*. Oxford: Basil Blackwell.

Cox, Robert W. 1981. "Social Forces, States and World Orders: Beyond International Relations Theory," *Millennium* 10: 126–155.

Creveld, Martin van. 1993. *Nuclear Proliferation and the Future of Conflict*. New York: Free Press.

Crozier, Michel, et al. 1975. *The Crisis of Democracy*. New York: New York University Press.

Dale, Roger. 1984. "Nation State and the International System: The World-System Perspective." In *The Idea of the Modern State*, eds. George McLennan et al. Milton Keynes: The Open University Press.

Dandeker, Christopher. 1990. *Surveillance, Power and Modernity: Bureaucracy and Discipline From 1700 to the Present Day*. New York: St. Martin Press.

Dayan, Moshe. 1976. *The Story of My Life*. Jerusalem: Edanim Publishers (Hebrew).

———. 1981. *Shall the Sword Devour Forever? Breakthrough—A Personal Account of the Egypt-Israel Peace Negotiations*. Tel Aviv: Edanim Publishers (Hebrew).

Deudney, Daniel, and G. John Ikenberry. 1991. "Soviet Reform and the End of the Cold War," *Review of International Studies* 17: 225–250.

Deutsch, Karl W. 1985. "Introduction." In *Studies of Israeli Society*, vol. 3: *Politics and Society in Israel*, ed. Ernest Krausz. New Brunswick, N.J.: Transaction Books.

Dietz, Henry et al. (eds.). 1991. *Ethnicity, Integration, and the Military*. Boulder, Colo.: Westview Press.

Ditomaso, Nancy. 1978. "The Organization of Authority in the Capitalist State," *Journal of Political and Military Sociology* 6: 189–204.

Domhoff, William. 1986. "State Authority and the Privileged Position of Business: An Empirical Attack on a Theoretical Fantasy," *Journal of Political and Military Sociology* 14: 149–162.

Dowty, Alan. 1975. "Israel's Nuclear Policy," *Medina, Mimshal Viyahsim Benleumiyim* 7: 5–27 (Hebrew).

Dreyfus, Hubert, and Paul Rabinow. 1982. *Michel Foucault: Beyond Structuralism and Hermeneutics*. Chicaco: University of Chicago Press.

Easton, David. 1965. *A System Analysis of Political Life*. New York: Prentice Hall.

Eaton, Joseph. 1969. "Gadna: The Israeli Youth Corps," *The Middle East Journal* 23: 471–483.

Edelist, Ran, and Ron Maiberg. 1986. *Hotel Palestine*. Tel Aviv: Modan (Hebrew).

Edmonds, Martin. 1988. *Armed Services and Society*. Boulder, Colo.: Westview Press.

Ehrlich, Avishai. 1987. "Israel: Conflict, War and Social Change." In *The Sociology of War and Peace*, eds. Colin Creighton and Martin Shaw. London: Macmillan Press.

Eisenstadt, Shmuel Noah. 1948. *Introduction to the Research of the Sociological Structure of Oriental Jews*. Jerusalem: The Szold Institute (Hebrew).

————. 1958. "The New Youth Revolt," *Megamot* 9: 95–102 (Hebrew).

————. 1967. *Israeli Society*. London: Wiedenfeld and Nicolson.

————. 1985. *The Transformation of Israeli Society: An Essay in Interpretation*. Boulder, Colo.: Westview Press.

Eitan, Rafael. 1985. *Raful: The Story of a Soldier*. Tel Aviv: Sifriat Ma'ariv Library (Hebrew).

Elam, Yigal. 1990. *The Executors*. Jerusalem: Keter Publishing House (Hebrew).

Ellis, Richard J. 1992. "Pluralist Political Science and the State: Distinguishing Between Autonomy and Coherence," *Polity* 24: 569–589.

Enloe, Cynthia. 1980. *Ethnic Soldiers: State Security in Divided Societies*. Athens: The University of Georgia Press.

————. 1988. *Does Khaki Become You? The Militarization of Women's Lives*. London: Pandora Press.

Eshed, Haggai. 1979. *Who Gave the Order?—The Lavon Affair*. Jerusalem: Edanim Publishers (Hebrew).

Etzioni, Amitai. 1954. "On Qibya," *Beterem* 2: 9–10 (Hebrew).

Etzioni-Halevi, Eva. 1975. "Protest Politics in the Israeli Democracy," *Political Science Quarterly* 90: 497–520.

Evron, Boaz. 1988. *A National Reckoning*. Tel Aviv: Dvir (Hebrew).

Evron, Yair. 1987. *Israel's Nuclear Dilemma*. Tel Aviv: Hakibbutz Hameuchad Publishing House (Hebrew).

————. 1989. "Israel's Foreign Policy and Defense Policy: Structural and Personal Aspects, 1949–1956," *Hatziyonut* 14: 219–230 (Hebrew).

Farjoun, Emanuel. 1983. "Class Divisions in Israeli Society," *Khamsin* 10: 162–167.

Farsoun, Samih K., and Jean M. Landis. 1990. "The Sociology of an Uprising: The Roots of the Intifada." In *Intifada: Palestine at the Crossroads*, eds. Jamal R. Nassar and Roger Heacock. New York: Praeger Publishers.

Feagin, Joe, and Kelly Riddell. 1990. "The State, Capitalism and World War II—the U.S. Case," *Armed Forces and Society* 17: 53–79.

Feige, Michael, and Eyal Ben-Ari. 1991. "Card Games in an Israeli Army Unit: An Interpretive Case Study," *Armed Forces and Society* 17: 429–448.

Fein, Aharon. 1995. "Voting Trends of Recent Immigrants from the Former Soviet Union." In *The Elections in Israel 1992*, eds. Asher Arian and Michal Shamir. Albany: SUNY Press.

Feld, Maury D. 1968. "Professionalism, Nationalism and the Alienation of the Military." In *Armed Forces and Society*, ed. Jacques Van-Doorn. The Hague: Mouton.

———. 1975. "Military Professionalism and the Mass Army," *Armed Forces and Society* 1: 191–214.

———. 1977. *The Structure of Violence—Armed Forces as Social Systems*. Beverly Hills, Calif.: Sage Publications.

Feldman, Shai, and Ada Rechnitz-Kizner. 1984. *Deception Consensus and War: Israel in Lebanon*. Tel Aviv: Tel Aviv University, Jaffee Center for Strategic Studies.

Fidel, Kenneth. 1975. "Militarism and Development: An Introduction." In *Militarism in Developing Countries*, ed. Kenneth Fidel. New Brunswick, N.J.: Transaction Books.

Finer, Samuel. 1975. "State and Nation-Building in Europe: The Role of the Military." In *The Formation of National States in Western Europe*, ed. Charles Tilly. Princeton, N.J.: Princeton University Press.

———. 1976. *The Man on Horseback: The Role of the Military in Politics*. Harmondsworth, Middlesex: Penguin Books.

Fischer, Shlomo. 1991. "Two Patterns of Modernization: On the Ethnic Problem in Israel," *Theory and Criticism* 1: 1–22 (Hebrew).

Fishelson, Gideon, et al. 1980. "Ethnic Origin and Income Differentials among Israeli Males, 1969–1976." In *Israel—A Developing Society*, ed. Asher Arian. Tel Aviv: Tel Aviv University.

Flapan, Simha. 1987. *The Birth of Israel: Myths and Realities*. London: Croom Helm.

Foucault, Michel. 1977. *Discipline and Punish: The Birth of the Prison*. New York: Pantheon Books.

———. 1982. "Afterword: The Subject and Power." In *Michel Foucault: Beyond Structuralism and Hermeneutics*, eds. Hubert Dreyfus and Paul Rabinow. Chicago: University of Chicago Press.

Frieden, Jeff. 1988. "Sectoral Conflict and U.S. Foreign Economic Policy, 1914–1940," *International Organization* 42: 59–83.

Friedlin, Jennifer. 1996. "The Textile Industry: From Lodz to Amman," *The Jerusalem Post*, March 8 (http://www.jpost.co.il/companies.html).

Friedman, Menachem. 1991. *The Haredi (Ultra-Orthodox) Society—Sources, Trends and Processes*. Jerusalem: The Jerusalem Institute for Israeli Studies (Hebrew).

Friedman, Milton. 1953. *Essays in Positive Economics*. Chicago: University of Chicago Press.

Friedman, Thomas. 1995. "I Dial Therefore I Exist," *New York Times*, October 29: 15E.

Gaddis, John Lewis. 1992/93. "International Relations Theory and the End of the Cold War," *International Security* 17: 5–58.

Gal, Reuven. 1986. *The Portrait of the Israeli Soldier*. Westport, Conn.: Greenwood Press.

Galnoor, Itzhak. 1982. *Steering the Polity: Communication and Politics in Israel*. Beverly Hills, Calif.: Sage Publications.

Gazit, Mordechai. 1984. *The Peace Process*. Tel Aviv: Yad Tabenkin (Hebrew).

Gazit, Shlomo. 1985. *The Stick and the Carrot: The Israeli Administration in Judea and Samaria*. Tel Aviv: Zmora-Bitan Publishers (Hebrew).

Geist, Benjamin. 1975. "The Six-Day War: Decision-Making in Crisis," *Medina, Mimshal Viyahsim Benleumiyim* 8: 75–67 (Hebrew).

Gelber, Yoav. 1986. *The Dissolution of the Palmach*. Tel Aviv: Schocken Publishing House (Hebrew).

———. 1989. "Ben-Gurion and the Establishment of the I.D.F.," *The Jerusalem Quarterly* 50: 56–80.

Gertz, Nurith. 1983. "Few Against Many: The Rhetoric and Structure of Begin's Electoral Speeches," *Siman Kria* 16–17: 106–126 (Hebrew).

———. 1983. *Generation Shift in Literary History: Hebrew Narrative Fiction in the Sixties*. Tel Aviv: The Porter Institute for Poetics and Semeiotics, Tel Aviv University (Hebrew).

———. 1985/86. "Within the Eternal Present, Without Hopes, Without Memories," *IGRA* 2: 263–298 (Hebrew).

———. 1988. "The Reflection of Social Myths in Literary and Political Texts During the Yishuv and State Period." In *Perspectives on Culture and Society in Israel*. Tel Aviv: The Open University (Hebrew).

———. 1995. *Captive of a Dream: National Myths in Israeli Culture*. Tel Aviv: Am Oved Publishers (Hebrew).

Geyer, Michael. 1989. "The Militarization of Europe, 1914–1945." In *The Militarization of the Western World*, ed. John R. Gillis. New Brunswick, N.J.: Rutgers University Press.

Giddens, Anthony. 1982. *Profiles and Critiques in Social Theory*. Berkeley: University of California Press.

———. 1984. *The Constitution of Society: Outline of the Theory of Structuration*. Cambridge: Polity Press.

————. 1985. *The Nation State and Violence*. Cambridge: Polity Press.

Gill, Stephen. 1995. "The Global Panopticon? The Neo-Liberal State, Economic Life and Democratic Surveillance," *Alternatives* 20: 1–49.

Gilpin, Robert G. 1984. "The Richness of the Tradition of Political Realism," *International Organization* 38: 287–304.

Glaser, Charles L. 1994/95. "Realists as Optimists: Cooperation as Self-Help," *International Security* 19: 50–90.

Golan, Mati. 1976. *The Secret Talks of Henry Kissinger*. Tel Aviv: Schocken Publishing House (Hebrew).

————. 1982. *Peres*. Tel Aviv: Schocken Publishing House (Hebrew).

Gold, David A., et al. 1975. "Recent Developments in Marxist Theories of the Capitalist State" (Part II), *Monthly Review* 6: 36–51.

Goldberg, Giora. 1986. "The Struggle for Legitimacy—Herut's Road from Opposition to Power." In *Conflict and Consensus in Jewish Political Life*, eds. Stuart A. Cohen and Eliezer Don-Yehiya. Ramat-Gan: Bar-Ilan University Press.

————. 1991. "Ben-Gurion and the People's Front," *Medina, Mimshal Viyahsim Benleumiyim* 35: 51–66 (Hebrew).

————. 1992. *Political Parties in Israel—From Mass Parties to Electoral Parties*. Tel Aviv: Ramot Publishing (Hebrew).

————. 1993. "Gush Emunim New Settlements in the West Bank: From Social Movement to Regional Interest Group." In *Local Communities and the Israeli Polity: Conflict of Values and Interests*, ed. Efraim Ben-Zadok. Albany: SUNY Press.

Goldman, Nancy L., and Karl L. Wiegand. 1984. "The Israeli Women in Combat." In *The Military, Militarism, and the Polity: Essays in Honor of Morris Janowitz*, ed. Michael Louis Martin and Ellen Stern-McCrate. New York: The Free Press.

Goodwin, Jeff, and Theda Skocpol. 1989. "Explaining Revolutions in the Contemporary Third World," *Politics and Society* 17: 489–509.

Gordon, Shmuel. 1992. "In Favor of Selective Service," *Ma'arachot* 328: 32–36 (Hebrew).

Goren, Dina. 1975. *Secrecy, Security and the Press Freedom*. Jerusalem: Magnes Press (Hebrew).

————. 1977. *Report and Criticism*. Jerusalem: Institute for Communication, Hebrew University (Hebrew).

Gottlieb, Avi, and Ephraim Yuchtman-Yaar. 1985. "Materialism, Postmaterialism, and Public Views on Socioeconomic Policy: The Case of Israel." In *Studies of Israeli Society*, vol. 3: *Politics and Society in Israel*, ed. Ernest Krausz. New Brunswick, N.J.: Transaction Books.

Greenberg, Yitzhak. 1993. "The Defense Ministry and the General Staff: The Debate over Control of the Defense Budget, 1949–1967," *Medina, Mimshal Viyahsim Benleumiyim*, 38: 49–76 (Hebrew).

Grinberg, Lev Luis. 1991a. *The Israeli Labor Movement in Crisis, 1955–1970*. Doctoral dissertation, Department of Sociology, Tel Aviv University (Hebrew).

––––––. 1991b. *Split Corporatism in Israel*. Albany: SUNY Press.

––––––. 1993a. *The Histadrut above All*. Jerusalem: Nevo Publishing House (Hebrew).

––––––. 1993b. "The Crisis of Statehood in a Weak State and Strong Political Institutions in Israel," *Journal of Theoretical Politics* 5: 89–107.

––––––. 1994. "A Theoretical Framework for the Analysis of the Israeli Palestinian Peace Process," *International Review of Sociology* 1: 68–89.

Gurr, Ted Robert. 1988. "War, Revolution and the Growth of the Coercive State," *Comparative Political Studies* 21: 45–65.

Haber, Eytan. 1987. *War Will Break Out Today*. Tel Aviv: Edanim Publishers (Hebrew).

Haberfeld, Yitchak, and Yinon Cohen. 1995. *Schooling and Income Gaps Between Western and Eastern Jews in Israel, 1975–1992*. Tel Aviv: Tel Aviv University, Golda Meir Institute for Social and Labour Research.

Haberman, Clyde. 1995. "Israel's Army, Once Sacrosanct, Is Now Becoming Deglamourized," *New York Times*, May 31: 10a.

Habermas, Jurgen. 1971. *Toward a Rational Society: Student Protest, Science and Politics*. London: Heinemann.

––––––. 1975. *Legitimation Crisis*. Boston: Beacon Press.

––––––. 1987. "What Does a Legitimation Crisis Mean Today? Legitimation Problems in Late Capitalism." In *Legitimation and the State*, ed. William Connolly. Oxford: Basil Blackwell.

Hacohen, Devora. 1994. *From Fantasy to Reality: Ben-Gurion's Plan For Mass Immigration, 1942–1945*. Tel Aviv: Ma'arachot (Hebrew).

Halpern, Ben. 1962. "The Role of the Military in Israel." In *The Role of the Military in Underdeveloped Countries*, ed. John Johnson. Princeton, N.J.: Princeton University Press.

Handel, Michael. 1973. *Israel's Political-Military Doctrine*. Cambridge, Mass.: Harvard University, Center for International Affairs.

————. 1994. "The Evolution of Israeli Strategy: The Psychology of Insecurity and the Quest for Absolute Security." In *The Making of Strategy: Rulers, States, and War*, eds. Williamson Murray et al. New York: Cambridge University Press.

Hareven, Shulamit. 1993. "The New Dictionary," *Politica* 51: 28–31 (Hebrew).

Harries-Jenkins, Gwyn. 1973. "The Victorian Military and the Political Order," *Journal of Political and Military Sociology* 1: 279–289.

————. 1976. "Legitimacy and the Problem of Order." In *The Military and the Problem of Legitimacy*, eds. Gwyn Harries-Jenkins and Jacques Van-Doorn. London: Sage Publications.

————. 1982. "The Sociology of Military Institution Today." In *Sociology, the State of the Art*, eds. Thomas Burton Bottomore et al. London: Sage Publications.

Hechter, Michael. 1992. "Rational Choice Theory and Historical Sociology," *International Social Science Journal* 133: 367–373.

Held, David. 1989. *Political Theory and the Modern State*. Cambridge: Polity Press.

————. 1991. "Democracy, the Nation-State and the Global System." In *Political Theory Today*, ed. David Held. Stanford: Stanford University Press.

Hermann, Tamar. 1989. *From "Brit Shalom" to "Peace Now": The Pragmatic Pacifism of the Peace Camp in Israel*. Doctoral dissertation, Department of Political Science, Tel Aviv University (Hebrew).

Herring, Cedric. 1987. "Alienated Politics and State Legitimacy: An Assessment of Three Neo-Marxian Theories," *Journal of Political and Military Sociology* 15: 17–31.

Herzog, Hanna. 1985. "Social Construction of Reality in Ethnic Terms: The Case of Political Ethnicity in Israel," *International Review of Modern Sociology* 15: 45–61.

Hiltermann, Joost R. 1990. "Work and Action: The Role of the Working Class in the Uprising." In *Intifada: Palestine at the Crossroads*, eds. Jamal R. Nassar and Roger Heacock. New York: Praeger Publishers.

Hintze, Otto. 1975. *The Historical Essays of Otto Hintze*, ed. Felix Gilbert. New York: Oxford University Press.

Hirschman, Albert O. 1970. *Exit, Voice, and Loyalty: Responses to Decline in Firms, Organizations, and States*. Cambridge, Mass.: Harvard University Press.

————. 1991. *The Rhetoric of Reaction: Perversity, Futility, Jeopardy*. Cambridge, Mass.: The Belknap Press of Harvard University Press.

Holsti, Ole R. 1989. "Crisis Decision Making." In *Behavior, Society, and Nuclear War*, eds. Philip E. Tetlock et al. New York: Oxford University Press.

Hooks, Gregory. 1990. "The Rise of the Pentagon and U.S. State Building: The Defence Program as Industrial Policy," *American Journal of Sociology* 96: 358–404.

————. 1993. "The Weakness of Strong Theories: The U.S. State's Dominance of the World War II Investment Process," *American Sociological Review* 58: 37–53.

————. 1994. "Regional Processes in the Hegemonic Nation: Political, Economy, and Military Influences on the Use of Geographic Space," *American Sociological Review* 59: 746–772.

————, and Gregory McLauchlan. 1992. "The Institutional Foundation of Warmaking: Three Eras of U.S. Warmaking, 1939–1989," *Theory and Society* 21: 757–788.

Horowitz, Dan. 1960. "Between Pioneer Society and Like All Other Nations," *Molad* 113–114: 571–580 (Hebrew).

————. 1973. *Israel's Conception of National Security: The Constant and the Changing in Israeli Defence Doctrine.* Jerusalem: Hebrew University (Hebrew).

————. 1977. "Is Israel a Garrison State?" *The Jerusalem Quarterly* 4: 58–75.

————. 1979. "The Control of Limited Military Operations: The Israeli Experience." In *International Violence: Terrorism, Surprise and Control*, ed. Yair Evron. Jerusalem: The Leonard David Institute for International Relations.

————. 1982. "The Israel Defence Forces: A Civilianized Military in a Partially Militarized Society." In *Soldiers, Peasants and Bureaucrats*, eds. Roman Kolkowicz and Andrze Korbousky. London: George Allen and Unwin.

————. 1983. "The War in Which National Consensus Broke." In *The Lebanon War— Between Protest and Compliance*, ed. Giora Rosen. Tel Aviv: Hakibbutz Hameuchad Publishing House (Hebrew).

————. 1985. "The Constant and the Changing in Israeli Strategic Thinking." In *War by Choice*, ed. Josef Alpher. Tel Aviv: Hakibbutz Hameuchad Publishing House (Hebrew).

————. 1987. "Strategic Limitations of 'a Nation in Arms,'" *Armed Forces and Society* 13: 277–294.

————, and Baruch Kimmerling. 1974. "Some Social Implications of Military Service and the Reserve System in Israel," *Archives Europeennes de Sociologie* 15: 262–276.

————, and Moshe Lissak. 1978. *Origins of the Israeli Polity: Palestine under the Mandate.* Chicago: University of Chicago Press.

————, and Moshe Lissak. 1989. *Trouble in Utopia: The Overburdened Polity of Israel.* Albany: SUNY Press.

Hoy, David Couzens. 1986. "Power, Repression, Progress: Foucault, Lukes and Frankfurt School." In *Foucault: A Critical Reader*, ed. David Couzens Hoy. New York: Basil Blackwell.

Huntington, Samuel Phillips. 1964. *The Soldier and the State: The Theory and Politics of Civil-Military Relations*. New York: Vintage Books.

————. 1968. *Political Order in Changing Societies*. New Haven, Conn.: Yale University Press.

Hurewitz, J. C. 1969. *Middle East Politics—The Military Dimension*. London: Pall Mall Press.

Idan, Asher. 1983. "On War and Equality," *Apirion* 1: 41 (Hebrew).

Inbar, Efraim. 1996. "Contours of Israeli New Strategic Thinking," *Israel Studies Bulletin* 11: 7–13.

————, and Shmuel Sandler. 1992. "The Diminishing Israeli Deterrent," *Israel Studies Bulletin* 7: 4–7.

————, and Shmuel Sandler. 1995. "The Changing Israeli Equation," *Review of International Studies* 21: 41–59.

Isaac, Jeffrey C. 1987a. *Power and Marxist Theory—A Realist View*. Ithaca: Cornell University Press.

————. 1987b. "Beyond the Three Faces of Power: A Realistic Critique," *Polity* 20: 4–37.

————. 1987c. "After Empiricism: The Realist Alternative." In *Idioms of Inquiry: Critique and Renewal in Political Theory*, ed. Terence Ball. Albany: SUNY Press.

Israel Ministry of Finance, International Division. 1996. *Structural Reform* (http://www.macom.co.il/Government/MOF.html).

Jaggers, Keith. 1992. "War and the Three Faces of Power: War Making and State Making in Europe and the Americas," *Comparative Political Studies* 25: 26–92.

Janowitz, Morris. 1968. "Armed Forces and Society: A World Perspective." In *Armed Forces and Society*, ed. Jacques Van-Doorn. The Hague: Mouton.

————. 1971. *The Professional Soldier: A Social and Political Portrait*. New York: The Free Press.

————. 1976. "Military Institutions and Citizenship in Western Societies," *Armed Forces and Society* 2: 185–226.

Kahana, Reuven, and Shlomit Cnaan. 1973. *The Press Behavior under Security Stress and Its Impact on Public Support for the Government*. Jerusalem: Eshkol Institute (Hebrew).

Kalderon, Nissim. 1984. *The Second Year of the War*. Tel Aviv: Siman Kria Books (Hebrew).

Kaldor, Mary. 1984. "Warfare and Capitalism." In *Exterminism and Cold War*, ed. Edward Palmer Thompson. London: Verso.

Kanovsky, Eliyahu. 1970. *The Economic Impact of the Six-Day War, Israel, the Occupied Territories, Egypt, Jordan*. New York: Praeger Publishers.

Karpel, Dalia. 1993. "I Am an 'Alien Corn,'" *Ha'aretz Supplement*, January 15: 39–40 (Hebrew).

Katz, Yitzhak. 1991. "The Privatization in Israel—1962–1987," *Medina, Mimshal Viyahsim Benleumiyim* 35: 133–145 (Hebrew).

Keohane, Robert O. 1986. "Neorealism and the Study of World Politics." In *Neorealism and Its Critics*, ed. Robert O. Keohane. New York: Columbia University Press.

Keren, Michael. 1983. *Ben-Gurion and the Intellectuals: Power, Knowledge and Charisma*. Decatur: Northern Illinois University Press.

————. 1986. *The Open Society and the Challenge of War: Israel 1963–1967*. Tel Aviv University, Pinhas Sapir Center for Development.

————. 1988. "The Hebrew Intellectual and the Shock of State's Emergence." In *Perspectives on Culture and Society in Israel*. Tel Aviv: The Open University (Hebrew).

————. 1989a. *The Pen and the Sword: Israeli Intellectuals and the Making of the Nation State*. Boulder, Colo.: Westview Press.

————. 1989b. "The Intelligentsia in Israel and the Political Establishment," *Hatziyonut* 14: 241–251 (Hebrew).

————, and Giora Goldberg. 1980. "Technological Development and Ideological Change." In *Israel—A Developing Society*, ed. Asher Arian. Tel Aviv: Tel Aviv University.

Kese, Zvi. 1986. "Teachers and Students," *Politica* 10–11: 36–41 (Hebrew).

Khalidi, Rashid. 1986. *Under Siege: P.L.O. Decisionmaking During the 1982 War*. New York: Columbia University Press.

Khawaja, Marwan. 1993. "Repression and Popular Collective Action: Evidence from the West Bank," *Sociological Forum* 8: 47–71.

Kibbutz Movement. 1967. *Fighter's Talk*. Tel Aviv: Kibbutz Movement (Hebrew).

Kier, Elizabeth. 1995. "Culture and Military Doctrine: France Between the Wars," *International Security* 19: 65–93.

Kiess, Naomi. 1978. "Policy and Public Opinion." In *Diplomacy and Confrontation: Selected Issues in Israel's Foreign Policy, 1948–1978*, ed. Benjamin Neuberger. Tel Aviv: The Open University (Hebrew).

Kimche, David. 1991. *The Last Option: After Nasser, Arafat and and Sadam Hussein, The Quest for Peace in the Middle East.* London: Widenfeld and Nicolson.

Kimmerling, Baruch. 1971. "The Status Perception of Security Roles in Israel," *Medina, Mimshal Viyahsim Benleumiyim* 2: 141–149 (Hebrew).

———. 1976. "The Management of the Jewish-Arab Conflict and Nation-Building Processes During the Mandate," *Medina, Mimshal Viyahsim Benleumiyim* 9: 35–66 (Hebrew).

———. 1979. "Determination of the Boundaries and Framework of Conscription: Two Dimensions of Civil-Military Relations in Israel," *Studies in Comparative International Development* 14: 22–41.

———. 1983. *Zionism and Territory: The Socio-Territorial Dimensions of Zionist Politics.* Berkeley: University of California, Institute for International Studies.

———. 1985a. *The Interrupted System: Israeli Civilians in War and Routine Times.* New Brunswick, N.J.: Transaction Books.

———. 1985b. "The Reopening of the Frontiers, 1967–1982." In *Studies of Israeli Society*, vol. 3: *Politics and Society in Israel*, ed. Ernest Krausz. New Brunswick, N.J.: Transaction Books.

———. 1985c. "Between the Primordial and the Civil Definition of the Collective Identity: Erertz Israel or the State of Israel?" In *Comparative Social Dynamics: Essays in Honor of S. Eisenstadt*, eds. Eric Cohen et al. Boulder, Colo.: Westview Press.

———. 1989. "Boundaries and Frontiers of the Israeli Control System: Analytical Conclusions." In *The Israeli State and Society: Boundaries and Frontiers*, ed. Baruch Kimmerling. Albany: SUNY Press.

———. 1992. "Sociology, Ideology and Nation Building: The Palestinians in Israeli Society," *American Sociological Review* 53: 446–460.

———. 1993a. "State Building, State Autonomy and the Identity of Society: The Case of Israel," *Journal of Historical Sociology* 6: 396–429.

———. 1993b. "Militarism in Israeli Society," *Theory and Criticism* 4: 123–140 (Hebrew).

———. 1995. "Children in an Ideological Bubble," *Ha'aretz*, May 19: 17 (Hebrew).

Kirchheimer, Otto. 1968. "The Transformation of the European Party Systems." In *Comparative Politics: Notes and Readings*, eds. Roy C. Macridis and Bernard Brown. Homewood, Ill.: Dorsey Press.

Kleiman, Aharon. 1986. "Israel's Arms Sales: Present and Future." In *Strategic Yearbook*. Tel Aviv: Tel Aviv University, Jaffee Center for Strategic Studies (Hebrew).

———. 1995. "The Israel-Jordan Tacit Security Regime." In *Regional Security Regimes: Israel and Its Neighbors*, ed. Efraim Inbar. Albany: SUNY Press.

Kocs, Stephen A. 1995. "Territorial Disputes and Interstate War, 1945–1987," *Journal of Politics* 57: 159–175.

Krasner, Stephen D. 1978. *Defending the National Interest: Raw Material Investments and U.S. Foreign Policy*. Princeton, N.J.: Princeton University Press.

———. 1984. "Approaches to the State: Alternative Conceptions and Historical Dynamics," *Comparative Politics* 16: 223–246.

Kraus, Vered, and Robert W. Hodge. 1990. *Promises in the Promise Land: Mobility and Inequality in Israel*. Westport, Conn.: Greenwood Press.

Kreitler, Hans, and Shulamit Kreitler. 1964. "The Attitude of Israeli Youth Towards Social Ideals," *Megamot* 13: 174–183 (Hebrew).

Lake, David A. 1992. "Powerful Pacifists: Democratic States and War," *American Political Science Review* 86: 24–37.

Lang, Kurt. 1972. *Military Institutions and the Sociology of War*. Beverley Hills, Calif.: Sage Publications.

Lanir, Zvi. 1983. *Fundamental Surprise—the National Intelligence Crisis*. Tel Aviv: Tel Aviv University, Jaffee Center for Strategic Studies (Hebrew).

———. 1985. "The Political Goals and Military Targets in Israeli Wars." In *War by Choice*, ed. Josef Alpher. Tel Aviv: Hakibbutz Hameuchad Publishing House (Hebrew).

Laor, Yitzhak. 1993. "The Atrocious Reflection of Arabs in the Israeli Press," *Hadashot*, August 27: 10–11 (Hebrew).

Larson, Arthur. 1974. "Military Professionalism and Civil Control: A Comparative Analysis of Two Interpretations," *Journal of Political and Military Sociology* 2: 57–72.

Lasswell, Harold D. 1941. "The Garrison State," *American Journal of Sociology* 46: 455–468.

Lebow, Richard Ned. 1994. "The Long Peace, the End of the Cold War, and the Failure of Realism," *International Organization* 48: 249–277.

Lehman-Wilzig, Sam N. 1990. *Stiff-Necked People, Bottle-Necked System: The Evolution and Roots of Israeli Public Protest, 1949–1986*. Bloomington and Indianapolis: Indiana University Press.

———. 1992. *Wildfire: Grassroots Revolts in Israel in the Post-Socialist Era.* Albany: SUNY Press.

Lenin, Vladimir Ilich. 1968. *Imperialism: The Highest Stage of Capitalism.* Moscow: Progress Press.

Levite, Ariel. 1988. *Offense and Defense in Israeli Military Doctrine.* Tel Aviv: Hakibbutz Hameuchad Publishing House (Hebrew).

———. 1989. "The Best Defense Is Not Necessarily Offense," *Politica*: 26: 44–47 (Hebrew).

Levitzky, Naomy. 1996. "The IDF Closed Its Eyes," *Yediot Aharonot Yom Kippur Supplement*, September 22: 19–21 (Hebrew).

Levy, Daniel. 1992. "The Ideological Role of TV News: The Coverage of Intifada in Israel Television," *Patuach* 1: 9–30 (Hebrew).

Levy, Jack S. 1986. "Organizational Routines and the Causes of War," *International Studies Quarterly* 30: 193–222.

———. 1989. "The Causes of War: A Review of Theories and Evidence." In *Behavior, Society, and Nuclear War*, eds. Philip E. Tetlock et al. New York: Oxford University Press.

Levy, Yagil. 1993. *The Role of the Military Sphere in the Construction of Social-Political Order in Israel.* Doctoral dissertation, Department of Political Science, Tel Aviv University (Hebrew).

———. 1995. "Controlling the Invisible: The Deficient Political Control of the Modern Military." New School for Social Research, Center for Studies of Social Change (Working Paper No. 208).

———, and Yoav Peled. 1994. "The Utopian Crisis of the Israeli State." In *Critical Essays on Israeli Social Issues and Scholarship—Books on Israel*, vol. 3, eds. Russell A. Stone and Walter P. Zenner. Albany: SUNY Press.

Lewin-Epstein, Noah, and Moshe Semyonov. 1994. "Sheltered Labor Markets, Public Sector Employment, and Socioeconomic Returns to Education of Arabs in Israel," *American Journal of Sociology* 100: 622–651.

Liebman, Charles. 1989. "Conceptions of 'State of Israel' in Israeli Society," *Medina, Mimshal Viyahsim Benleumiyim* 30: 51–60 (Hebrew).

———, and Eliezer Don-Yehiya. 1983. *Civil Religion in Israel: Traditional Judaism and Political Culture in the Jewish State.* Berkeley: University of California Press.

Lissak, Moshe. 1953. "The Youth and the Social Changes in the State of Israel," *Beterem* 4: 23–26 (Hebrew).

————. 1984a. "A Response: Theses for Discussion or Preliminary Attitudes," *Medina, Mimshal Viyahsim Benleumiyim* 22: 33–38 (Hebrew).

————. 1984b. "Paradoxes of Israeli Civil-Military Relations: An Introduction." In *Israel and Its Defence Establishment*, ed. Moshe Lissak. London: Frank Cass.

Lo, Clarence Y. H. 1982. "Theories of the State and Business Opposition to Increased Military Spending," *Social Problems* 29: 424–438.

Love, Kenneth. 1969. *Suez: The Twice Fought War*. New York: McGraw-Hill.

Luckham, A. R. 1971. "A Comparative Typology of Civil-Military Relations," *Government and Opposition* 6: 9–35.

Lustick, Ian Steven. 1980. *Arabs in the Jewish State: Israel's Control of a National Minority*. Austin: University of Texas Press.

————. 1988. *For the Land and the Lord: Jewish Fundamentalism in Israel*. New York: Council on Foreign Relations.

————. 1993. *Unsettled States, Disputed Lands: Britain and Ireland, France and Algeria, Israel and the West Bank-Gaza*. Ithaca: Cornell University Press

Luxemburg, Rosa. 1951. *The Accumulation of Capital*. London: Routledge and Kegan Paul.

MacKenzie, Donald. 1983. "Militarism and Social Theory," *Capital and Class* 19: 33–73.

Maggiotto, Michael A., and Eugene R. Wittkopf. 1981. "American Public Attitudes Toward Foreign Policy," *International Studies Quarterly* 25: 601–631.

Makovsky, David. 1996. *Making Peace with the PLO: The Rabin Government's Road to the Oslo Accord*. Boulder, Colo.: Westview Press.

Mann, Michael. 1984. "Capitalism and Militarism." In *War, State and Society*, ed. Martin Shaw. London: Macmillan Press.

————. 1985. "The Autonomous Power of the State," *Archives Europeennes de Sociologie* 24: 185–213.

————. 1987. "The Roots and Contradictions of Modern Militarism." *New Left Review* 162: 35–50.

————. 1988. *States, War and Capitalism: Studies in Political Sociology*. London: Basil Blackwell.

————. 1993. *The Sources of Social Power*, vol. 2: *The Rise of Classes and Nation-States, 1760–1914*. New York: Cambridge University Press.

Marcuse, Herbert. 1964. *One-Dimensional Man: Studies in the Ideology of Advanced Industrial Society*. Boston: Beacon Press.

Margalit, Dan. 1995. "Back to 'The Best for Aircraft,'" *Ha'aretz*, April 6: 14 (Hebrew).

Marwick, Arthur. 1988. *War and Social Change*. New York: St. Martin's Press.

Marx, Anthony W. 1996. "Race-Making and the Nation-State," *World Politics* 49: 180–208.

Marx, Karl. 1963. *The Eighteenth Brumaire of Louis Bonaparte*. New York: International Publishers.

Mastanduno, Michael, et al. 1989. "Toward a Realist Theory of State Action," *International Studies Quarterly* 33: 457–474.

Mautner, Menachem. 1993. *The Decline of Formalism and the Rise of Values in Israeli Law*. Tel Aviv: Ma'agalay Da'at Publishing House (Hebrew).

Mearsheimer, John J. 1990. "Back to the Future: Instability in Europe after the Cold War," *International Security* 15: 5–56.

———. 1994/95. "The False Promise of International Institutions," *International Security* 19: 5–49.

Medding, Peter Y. 1972. *Mapai in Israel—Political Organization and Government in a New Society*. Cambridge: Cambridge University Press.

———. 1990. *The Founding of Israeli Democracy, 1948–1967*. New York: Oxford University Press.

Menuchin, Ishai. 1990. *On Democracy and Obedience*. Jerusalem: The "Yesh Gvul" Movement and Siman Kria Books (Hebrew).

———, and Dina Menuchin. 1985. *The Limits of Obedience*. Tel Aviv: The "Yesh Gvul" Movement and Siman Kria Books (Hebrew).

Michael, Sami. 1984. *These Are the Tribes of Israel*. Tel Aviv: Sifriat Hapoalim (Hebrew).

Migdal, Joel S. 1988. *Strong Societies and Weak States: State-Society Relations and State Capabilities in the Third World*. Princeton, N.J.: Princeton University Press.

———. 1989. "The Crystallization of the State and the Struggles over Rulemaking: Israel in a Comparative Perspective." In *The Israeli State and Society*, ed. Baruch Kimmerling. Albany: SUNY Press.

Miliband, Ralph. 1969. *The State in Capitalist Society*. New York: Basic Books.

Mills, C. Wright. 1956. *The Power Elite*. London: Oxford University Press.

Milstein, Uri. 1974. *By Blood and Fire, Judea*. Tel Aviv: Lewin-Epstein-Modan Publishers (Hebrew).

Mintz, Alex. 1985. "Military-Industrial Linkages in Israel," *Armed Forces and Society* 12: 9–24.

————. 1987. "Arms Production in Israel," *The Jerusalem Quarterly* 42: 89–99.

Miron, Dan. 1985/86. "From Creators and Builders to Homeless," *IGRA* 2: 71–135 (Hebrew).

————. 1987. "An Israeli Document: On the Platform of the Movement for Integrity of the Land of Israel," *Politica* 13: 31–45 (Hebrew).

Mishal, Nissim. 1978. *The Broadcasting Authority: Political Dynamics*. Unpublished M.A. thesis, Department of Political Science, Bar-Ilan University (Hebrew).

Mitchell, Timothy. 1991a. "The Limits of the State: Beyond Statist Approaches and Their Critics," *American Political Science Review* 85: 77–96.

————. 1991b. *Colonising Egypt*. Berkeley: University of California Press.

Mor, Ben D. 1991. "Nasser's Decision Making in the 1967 Middle East Crisis: A Rational-Choice Explanation," *Journal of Peace Research* 28: 359–375.

Morgan, Clifton T., and Kenneth N. Bickers. 1992. "Domestic Discontent and the External Use of Force," *Journal of Conflict Resolution* 36: 25–52.

Morris, Benny. 1988. *The Birth of the Palestinian Refugee Problem, 1947–1949*. Cambridge: Cambridge University Press.

————. 1993. *Israel's Border Wars 1949–1956: Arab Infiltration, Israeli Retaliation, and the Countdown to the Suez War.* Oxford: Clarendon Press.

Moskos, Charles C. 1970. *The American Enlisted Man: The Rank and File in Today's Military*. New York: Russell Sage Foundation.

————. 1984. "The Citizen-Soldier and the All-Volunteer Force." In *The Military, Militarism, and the Polity: Essays in Honor of Morris Janowitz*, eds. Michael Louis Martin and Ellen Stern-McCrate. New York: Free Press.

————. 1986. "Institutional/Occupational Trends in Armed Forces: An Update," *Armed Forces and Society* 12: 377–382.

Moskovitch, Avital. 1992. *Generational Analysis of "Gush-Emunim."* Unpublished M.A. thesis, Department of Political Science, Tel Aviv University (Hebrew).

Nagel, Joane. 1995. "Resource Competition Theory," *American Behavioral Scientist* 38: 442–458.

Nahon, Yaacov. 1987. *Patterns of Educational Expansion and the Structure of Occupational Opportunities*. Jerusalem: Jerusalem Institute for Israel Studies (Hebrew).

————. 1993a. "Educational Expansion and the Structure of Occupational Opportunities." In *Ethnic Communities in Israel: Socio-Economic Status*, ed. Shmuel Nohah Eisenstadt. Jerusalem: Jerusalem Institute for Israel Studies (Hebrew).

———— . 1993b. "Occupational Status." In *Ethnic Communities in Israel: Socio-Economic Status*, ed. Shmuel Nohah Eisenstadt. Jerusalem: Jerusalem Institute for Israel Studies (Hebrew).

Naor, Aryeh. 1986. *Cabinet at War: The Functioning of the Israeli Cabinet During the Lebanon War, 1982*. Tel Aviv: Lahav (Hebrew).

Naor, Mordechai. 1988. *Laskov*. Jerusalem: Ministry of Defense and Keter Publishing House (Hebrew).

Narkiss, Uzi. 1991. *Soldier of Jerusalem*. Tel Aviv: Ministry of Defense (Hebrew).

Neeman, Yuval. 1985. "The Formation of the National Security System in a Crystallized Nation." In *Israel Security and Economy in the 1980's*, ed. Zvi Lanir. Tel Aviv: Ministry of Defense (Hebrew).

Negbi, Moshe. 1985. *Paper Tiger: The Struggle for a Press Freedom in Israel*. Tel Aviv: Sifriat Hapoalim (Hebrew).

———— . 1990. "The Occupation, Intifada and the Israeli Democracy." In *On Democracy and Obedience*, ed. Ishai Menuchin. Jerusalem: The "Yesh Gvul" Movement and Siman Kria Books (Hebrew).

Netanyahu, Benjamin. 1995. *A Place Among the Nations*. Tel Aviv: Edanim Publishers (Hebrew).

Nolt, James H. 1994. *Business Conflict and the Origins of the Pacific War*. Doctoral dissertation, University of Chicago.

Nordlinger, Eric A. 1981. *On the Autonomy of the Democratic State*. Cambridge, Mass.: Harvard University Press.

Oakes, Guy. 1994. *The Imaginary War: Civil Defence and American Cold War Culture*. New York: Oxford University Press.

O'Connor, James. 1973. *The Fiscal Crisis of the State*. New York: St. Martin's Press.

Ofer, Gur. 1986. "Public Spending on Civilian Services." In *The Israeli Economy: Maturing through Crises*, ed. Yoram Ben-Porath. Cambridge, Mass.: Harvard University Press.

Offe, Claus. 1975. "The Theory of Capitalist State and the Problem of Policy Formation." In *Stress and Contradiction in Modern Capitalism: Public Policy and the Theory of the State*, eds. Leon Lindberg et al. Lexington, Mass.: D. C. Heath.

Oren, Amir. 1983. "The Road to Beirut." In *The Lebanon War—Between Protest and Compliance*, ed. Giora Rosen. Tel Aviv: Hakibbutz Hameuchad Publishing House (Hebrew).

Organski, A. F. K., and Jack Kugler. 1980. *The War Ledger*. Chicago: University of Chicago Press.

Outhwaite, William. 1987. *New Philosophies of Social Science*. London: Macmillan Education.

Oz, Amos. 1983. *In the Land of Israel*. New York: Harcourt Brace Jovanovich Publishers.

Pail, Meir. 1979. *The Emergence of Zahal (I.D.F.)*. Tel Aviv: Zmora Bitan Modan Publishers (Hebrew).

Pappe, Ilan. 1992. *The Making of the Arab-Israeli Conflict, 1947–1951*. London: I. B. Tauris Publishers.

————. 1993. "New History of the 1948 War," *Theory and Criticism* 3: 99–114 (Hebrew).

Pedersen, Susan. 1990. "Gender, Welfare, and Citizenship in Britain During the Great War," *American Historical Review* 95: 983–1006.

Pedhatzur, Reuven. 1996. *The Triumph of Embarrassment: Israel and the Territories After the Six-Day War*. Tel Aviv: Bitan (Hebrew).

Peled, Yoav. 1990. "Ethnic Exclusionism in the Periphery: The Case of Oriental Jews in Israel's Development Towns," *Ethnic and Racial Studies* 13: 345–367.

————. 1991. "Explaining Religious Voting among Oriental Jews in Israel: A Cultural Division of Labour Approach." Unpublished manuscript.

————. 1992. "Ethnic Democracy and the Legal Construction of Citizenship: Arab Citizens of the Jewish State," *American Political Science Review* 86: 432–443.

Peres, Shimon. 1993. *The New Middle East*. New York: Henry Holt.

————. 1995. "The Privatization of Peace," *Middle East Business Today—A Special Supplement from the Jerusalem Post*: 16–18.

Peri, Yoram. 1983. *Between Battles and Ballots—Israeli Military in Politics*. London: Cambridge University Press.

————. 1990. "The Impact of the Intifada on the I.D.F." In *The Seventh War: The Effects of the Intifada on Israeli Society,* ed. Reuven Gal. Tel Aviv: Hakibbutz Hameuchad Publishing House (Hebrew).

————, and Moshe Lissak. 1976. "Retired Officers in Israel and the Emergence of a New Elite." In *The Military and the Problem of Legitimacy*, eds. Gwyn Harries-Jenkins and Jacques Van Doorn. London: Sage Publications.

————, and Amnon Neubach. 1984. *The Military-Industrial Complex in Israel: A Pilot Study*. Tel Aviv: International Center for Peace in the Middle East (Hebrew).

Perlmutter, Amos. 1969. *Military and Politics in Israel: Nation-Building and Role Expansion*. London: Frank Cass.

Pitovsky, Itamar. 1990. "Shooting and Crying." In *On Democracy and Obedience*, ed. Ishai Menuchin. Jerusalem: The "Yesh Gvul" Movement and Siman Kria Books (Hebrew).

Poggi, Gianfranco. 1978. *The Development of the Modern State: A Sociological Introduction.* Stanford: Stanford University Press.

Polanyi, Karl. 1944. *The Great Transformation.* New York: Farrar and Rinehart.

Popper, Micha, and Avihu Ronen. 1989. *On Leadership.* Tel Aviv: Ministry of Defense (Hebrew).

Porter, Bruce D. 1994. *War and the Rise of the State: The Military Foundations of Modern Politics.* New York: Free Press.

Posen, Barry R. 1988. *The Sources of Military Doctrine: France, Britain, and Germany Between the World Wars.* Ithaca: Cornell University Press.

Poulantzas, Nicos. 1978. *Political Power and Social Classes.* London: Verso.

Preuss, Teddy. 1984. *Begin—His Regime.* Tel Aviv: Keter Publishing House (Hebrew).

Putnam, Robert D. 1988. "Diplomacy and Domestic Politics: The Logic of Two-Level Games," *International Organization* 42: 427–460.

Pye, Lucian. 1962. "Armies and the Problem of Political Modernization." In *The Role of the Army in Underdevelopment Countries*, ed. John Johnson. Princeton, N.J.: Princeton University Press.

Raanan, Uri. 1955. "A Study of the 1955 Knesset Election Results," *Molad* 84: 262–267 (Hebrew).

Rabin, Yitzhak. 1979. *Service Book.* Tel Aviv: Sifriat Ma'ariv Library (Hebrew).

———. 1983. *The War in Lebanon.* Tel Aviv: Am Oved-Tarbut Vechinuch (Hebrew).

Rabinovich, Itamar. 1991. *The Road Not Taken: Early Arab-Israeli Negotiations.* Jerusalem: Maxwell-Macmmillan-Keter Publishing (Hebrew).

Rabinowitz, Dani. 1993. "Oriental Nostalgia: The Transformation of the Palestinians into 'Israeli Arabs,'" *Theory and Society* 4: 141–151.

Radom, Matthew. 1968. "Military Officers and Business Leaders—An Israeli Study in Contrasts," *Columbia Journal of World Business* 3: 27–34.

Rafael, Gideon. 1981. *Destination Peace: Three Decades of Israeli Foreign Policy.* Jerusalem: Edanim Publishers (Hebrew).

Ramirez, Anthony. 1995. "After Assassination, Israel Is a Fragile Market," *New York Times*, October 12: 3F.

Rapoport, David. 1962. "A Comparative Theory of Military and Political Types." In *Changing Patterns of Military Politics*, ed. Samuel P. Huntington. New York: Free Press.

Raz-Krakotzkin. 1993. "It Is the Same Old Rabin," *Politica* 51: 11–13 (Hebrew).

Regehr, Ernie. 1980. "What Is Militarism?" In *Problems of Contemporary Militarism*, eds. Asbjorn Eide and Mark Thee. New York: St. Martin's Press.

Reiser, Stewart. 1989. *The Israeli Arms Industry*. New York: Holms and Meier.

Rekhess, Elie. 1995. "Israel's Arab Citizens and the Peace Process." In *Israel under Rabin*, ed. Robert O. Friedman. Boulder, Colo.: Westview Press.

Rhodes, Edward. 1995. "Constructing Peace and War: An Analysis of the Power of Ideas to Shape American Military Power," *Millennium* 24: 53–85.

Risse-Kappen, Thomas. 1994. "Ideas Do Not Float Freely: Transnational Politics, Domestic Structures, and the End of the Cold War," *International Organization* 48: 185–214.

Rock, Stephen R. 1989. *Why Peace Breaks Out: Great Power Rapprochement in Historical Perspective*. Chapel Hill: The University of North Carolina Press.

Rodinson, Maxime. 1982. *Israel and the Arabs*. New York: Penguin Books.

Rosenberg, David. 1995. "In Israel, Peace Won't Mean Prosperity," *New York Times (Section 3)*, March 5: 9.

Rosenberg, Justin. 1990. "A Non-Realist Theory of Sovereignty? Giddens' The Nation-State and Violence," *Millennium* 192: 249–259.

Rosenfeld, Henry, and Shulamit Carmi. 1976. "The Privatization of Public Means, the State-Made Middle Class, and the Realization of Family Values in Israel." In *Kinship and Modernization in Mediterranean Society*, ed. J. G. Peristiany. Rome: American University Field Staff, The Center for Mediterranean Studies.

Rosenhek, Zeev. 1996. *The Origins and Development of a Dualistic Welfare State: The Arab Population in the Israeli Welfare State*. Doctoral dissertation, Department of Sociology and Anthropology, The Hebrew University of Jerusalem (Hebrew).

Roumani, Maurice. 1979. *From Immigrant to Citizen: The Contribution of the Army to National Integration in Israel: The Case of Oriental Jews*. The Hague: Foundation for the Study of Plural Societies.

———. 1991. "The Military, Ethnicity, and Integration in Israel Revisited." In *Ethnicity, Integration, and the Military*, eds. Henry Dietz et al. Boulder, Colo.: Westview Press.

Ruggie, John Gerard. 1983. "Continuity and Transformation in the World Polity: Toward a Neorealist Synthesis," *World Politics* 35: 261–285.

Russett, Bruce. 1989. "Democracy, Public Opinion, and Nuclear Weapons." In *Behavior, Society, and Nuclear War*, eds. Philip E. Tetlock et al. New York: Oxford University Press.

————. 1990 (ed). *Grasping the Democratic Peace: Principles for a Post–Cold War World*. Princeton, N.J.: Princeton University Press.

————, and Zeev Maoz. 1990. "The Democratic Peace since World War II." In *Grasping the Democratic Peace: Principles for a Post–Cold War World*, ed. Bruce Russett. Princeton, N.J.: Princeton University Press.

Safran, Nadav. 1978. *Israel—The Embattled Ally*. Cambridge, Mass.: Harvard University Press.

Saleh, Samir Abdallah. 1990. "The Effects of Israeli Occupation on the Economy of the West Bank and Gaza Strip." In *Intifada: Palestine at the Crossroads*, eds. Jamal R. Nassar and Roger Heacock. New York: Praeger Publishers.

Sarkesian, Sam. 1984. "Two Conceptions of Military Professionalism." In *The Military, Militarism and the State: Essays in Honor of Morris Janowitz*, eds. Michael Louis Martin and Ellen Stern-McCrate. New York: Free Press.

Schiff, Rebecca L. 1992. "Israel as an 'Uncivil' State: A Reconsideration of Civil-Military Relations," *Security Studies* 1: 636–658.

————. 1995. "Civil-Military Relations Reconsidered: A Theory of Concordance," *Armed Forces and Society* 22: 7–24.

Schiff, Zeev. 1974. *The October Earthquake: The Yom-Kippur War*. Tel Aviv: Zmora Bitan Modan Publishers (Hebrew).

————, and Ehud Yaari. 1984. *A War of Deception*. Tel Aviv: Schocken Publishing House (Hebrew).

————, and Ehud Yaari. 1990. *The Intifada*. Tel Aviv: Schocken Publishing House (Hebrew).

Schild, Ozer. 1973. "On the Meaning of Military Service in Israel." In *Israel Social Structure and Change*, eds. Michael Curtis and Mordechai Chertoff. New Brunswick, N.J.: Transaction Books.

Schmitt, Carl. 1976. *The Concept of the Political*. New Brunswick, N.J.: Rutgers University Press.

Schwartzwald, Joseph, and Yehuda Amir. 1994. "Junior High School De-Segregation Experience and Interethnic Relations among Newly Recruited IDF Soldiers," *Megamot* 35: 359–374 (Hebrew).

Schweitzer, Avram. 1984. *Upheavals*. Tel Aviv: Zmora Bitan Modan Publishers (Hebrew).

Schweller, Randall L. 1993. "Tripolarity and the Second World War," *International Studies Quarterly* 37: 73–103.

Scruton, Roger. 1988. "Notes on the Sociology of War," *The British Journal of Sociology* 38: 259–309.

Segal, David R., et al. 1974. "Convergence, Isomorphism and Interdependence at the Civil-Military Interface," *Journal of Political and Military Sociology* 2: 157–172.

——— , and Naomi Verdugo. 1994. "Demographic Trends and Personnel Politics as Determinants of the Racial Composition of the Volunteer Army," *Armed Forces and Society* 20: 619–632.

Segev, Tom. 1986. *1949—The First Israelis*. New York: Free Press.

———. 1993. *The Seventh Million: The Israelis and the Holocaust*. New York: Hill and Wang.

Sella, Amnon, and Yael Yishai. 1986. *Israel the Peaceful Belligerent, 1967–79*. New York: St. Martin's Press.

Semyonov, Moshe, and Noah Lewin-Epstein. 1987. *Hewers of Wood and Drawers of Water: Noncitizen Arabs in the Israeli Labor Market*. Ithaca: Cornell University Press.

Shafir, Gershon. 1989. *Land, Labor and the Origins of the Israeli-Palestinian Conflict, 1882–1914*. Cambridge: Cambridge University Press.

Shalev, Aryeh. 1989. *Cooperation under the Shadow of Conflict: The Israeli-Syrian Armistice Regime 1949–1955*. Tel Aviv: Ma'arachot (Hebrew).

———. 1990. *The Intifada: Causes and Effects*. Tel Aviv: Papyrus Publishing House (Hebrew).

Shalev, Michael. 1984. "The Mid-Sixties Recession: A Political-Economic Analysis of Unemployment in Israel," *Machbarot Lemechkar Vlebikoret* 9: 3–54 (Hebrew).

———. 1989. "Jewish Organized Labor and the Palestinians: A Study of State/Society Relations in Israel." In *The Israeli State and Society: Boundaries and Frontiers*, ed. Baruch Kimmerling. Albany: SUNY Press.

———. 1992. *Labor and the Political Economy in Israel*. Oxford: Oxford University Press.

———. 1996. "Time for Theory," *Israel Studies* 2 (forthcoming).

——— , and Lev Grinberg. 1989. *Histadrut-Government Relations and the Transition from a Likud to a National Unity Government*. Tel Aviv University, Pinhas Sapir Center for Development.

Shalom, Zaki. 1996. *Policy in the Shadow of Controversy: The Routine Security Policy of Israel, 1949–1956*. Tel Aviv: Ma'arachot (Hebrew).

Shamir, Michal, and Asher Arian. 1982. "The Ethnic Vote in Israel's 1981 Elections," *Electoral Studies* 1: 315–331.

——, and Asher Arian. 1995. "Introduction." In *The Elections in Israel 1992*, eds. Asher Arian and Michal Shamir. Albany: SUNY Press.

Shapira, Anita. 1985. *The Army Controversy, 1948: Ben-Gurion's Struggle for Control.* Tel Aviv: Hakibbutz Hameuchad Publishing House (Hebrew).

——. 1986. "The Struggle for 'Jewish Labor'—Concept and Consequences." In *Conflict and Consensus in Jewish Political Life*, eds. Stuart A. Cohen and Eliezer Don-Yehiya. Ramat-Gan: Bar-Ilan University Press.

——. 1988. *Visions in Conflict.* Tel Aviv: Am Oved Publishers (Hebrew).

——. 1992. *Land and Power: The Zionist Resort to Force, 1881–1948.* New York: Oxford University Press.

Shapira, Rina, and Eva Etzioni-Halevy. 1973. *Who Is the Israeli Student?* Tel Aviv: Am Oved Publishers (Hebrew).

Shapiro, Ian, and Alexander Wendt. 1992. "The Difference That Realism Makes: Social Science and the Politics of Consent," *Politics and Society* 20: 197–223.

Shapiro, Yonathan. 1976. *The Formative Years of the Israeli Labour Party: The Organization of Power, 1919–1930.* London: Sage Publications.

——. 1977. *Democracy in Israel.* Ramat Gan: Massada (Hebrew).

——. 1980. "The End of a Dominant Party System." In *The Elections in Israel, 1977*, ed. Asher Arian. Jerusalem: Academic Press.

——. 1984a. *An Elite Without Successors—Generations of Political Leaders in Israel.* Tel Aviv: Sifriat Hapoalim (Hebrew).

——. 1984b. "Was the Yishuv a Constitutional Democracy? A Reply to Dan Horowitz," *Medina, Mimshal Viyahsim Benleumiyim* 23: 85–92 (Hebrew).

——. 1985. "Political Sociology in Israel: A Critical View." In *Studies of Israeli Society*, vol. 3: *Politics and Society in Israel*, ed. Ernest Krausz. New Brunswick, N.J.: Transaction Books.

——. 1991. *The Road to Power: Herut Party in Israel.* Albany: SUNY Press.

——. 1996. *Politicians as an Hegemonic Class: The Case of Israel.* Tel Aviv: Sifriat Hapoalim (Hebrew).

——, and Lev Grinberg. 1988. *The Full Employment Crisis 1957–1965: A Chapter in the Political Economy of Israel.* Tel Aviv: Tel Aviv University, Golda Meir Institute for Social and Labour Research (Hebrew).

Sharett, Moshe. 1978. *The Diaries of Moshe Sharett.* Tel Aviv: Sifriat Ma'ariv Library (Hebrew).

Sharett, Yaakov. 1988. *The State of Israel Is No More*. Tel Aviv: Tesher (Hebrew).

Shaw, Martin. 1984. "War, Imperialism and the State System: A Critique of Orthodox Marxism for the 1980s." In *War, State and Society*, ed. Martin Shaw. London: Macmillan Press.

————. 1987. "The Rise and Fall of the Military-Democratic State: Britain 1940–85." In *The Sociology of War and Peace*, eds. Colin Creighton and Martin Shaw. London: Macmillan Press.

————. 1988. *Dialectics of War: An Essay in the Social Theory of Total War and Peace*. London: Pluto Press.

————. 1991. *Post-Military Society: Militarism, Demilitarization and War at the End of the Twentieth Century*. Philadelphia: Temple University Press.

Sheffer, Gabriel. 1988. "Sharett, Ben-Gurion and the 1956 War of Choice," *Medina, Mimshal Viyahsim Benleumiyim*, 27: 1–27 (Hebrew).

Sheleg, Yair, and Allon Hadar. 1994. "The New Type of the National-Religious Young," *Kol Ha'ayr* August 12: 65–77 (Hebrew).

Shiffer, Shimon. 1984. *Snowball: The Story Behind the Lebanon War*. Tel Aviv: Edanim Publishers (Hebrew).

Shils, Edward. 1991. "The Virtue of Civil Society," *Government and Opposition* 26: 3–20.

Shimshoni, Jonathan. 1988. *Israel and Conventional Deterrence: Border Warfare from 1953 to 1970*. Ithaca: Cornell University Press.

Shlaim, Avi. 1983. "Conflicting Approaches to Israel's Relations with the Arabs: Ben-Gurion and Sharett, 1953–1956," *The Middle East Journal* 37: 180–201.

————. 1990. *The Politics of Partition: King Abdullah, the Zionists and Palestine 1921–1951*. New York: Columbia University Press.

————. 1994. *War and Peace in the Middle East: A Critique of American Policy*. New York: Whittle Books.

Silver, Allan. 1994. "Democratic Citizenship and High Military Strategy: The Inheritance, Decay, and Reshaping of Political Culture," *Democracy and Society* 2: 317–349.

Simon, Herbert, 1976. *Administrative Behavior: A Study of Decision-Making Processes in Administrative Organization*. New York: Free Press.

Sivan, Emmanuel. 1991. *The 1948 Generation: Myth, Profile and Memory*. Tel Aviv: Ministry of Defense (Hebrew).

Skocpol, Theda. 1977. "Wallerstein's World Capitalist System: A Theoretical and Historical Critique," *American Journal of Sociology* 82: 1075–1090.

——. 1979. *States and Social Revolutions: A Comparative Analysis of France, Russia and China.* Cambridge: Cambridge University Press.

——. 1985. "Bringing the State Back In: Strategies of Analysis in Current Research." In *Bringing the State Back In*, eds. Peter Evans et al. Cambridge: Cambridge University Press.

——. 1988. "Social Revolutions and Mass Military Mobilization," *World Politics* 40: 147–168.

——. 1992. *Protecting Soldiers and Mothers: The Political Origins of Social Policy in the United States.* Cambridge, Mass.: The Belknap Press of Harvard University Press.

Slater, Jerome. 1994. "The Significance of Israeli Historical Revisionism." In *Critical Essays on Israeli Social Issues and Scholarship—Books on Israel*, vol. 3, eds. Russell A. Stone and Walter P. Zenner. Albany: SUNY Press.

Smith, Antony D. 1981. "War and Ethnicity: The Role of Warfare in the Formation of Self Images and Cohesion of Ethnic Communities," *Ethnic and Racial Studies* 4: 375–397.

——. 1992. "Chosen People: Why Ethnic Groups Survive." *Ethnic and Racial Studies* 15: 436–456.

Smooha, Sammy. 1984a. "Three Approaches to the Sociology of Interethnic Relations in Israel," *Megamot* 28: 169–206 (Hebrew).

——. 1984b. "Ethnicity and the Military in Israel: Theses for Discussion and Research," *Medina, Mimshal Viyahsim Benleumiyim* 22: 5–32 (Hebrew).

——. 1985. "Existing and Alternative Policy Toward the Arabs in Israel." In *Studies of Israeli Society*, vol. 3: *Politics and Society in Israel*, ed. Ernest Krausz. New Brunswick, N.J.: Transaction Books.

——. 1993. "Class, Ethnic and National Cleavages and Democracy in Israel." In *Israeli Society: Critical Perspectives*, ed. Uri Ram. Tel Aviv: Breirot (Hebrew).

Sprinzak, Ehud. 1981. "Gush Emunim: The Tip of the Iceberg," *The Jerusalem Quarterly* 27: 28–47.

——. 1986. *Every Man Whatsoever Is Right in His Own Eyes: Illegalism in Israeli Politics.* Tel Aviv: Sifriat Hapoalim (Hebrew).

Sraya, Shmuel. 1954. "The Low-Scale War along the Borders." In *The Yearbook of the Association of Journalists.* Tel Aviv: Association of Journalists (Hebrew).

Starr, Harvey. 1994. "Revolution and War: Rethinking the Linkage Between Internal and External Conflict," *Political Research Quarterly* 47: 481–507.

Stepan, Alfred. 1978. *The State and Society: Peru in Comparative Perspective.* Princeton, N.J.: Princeton University Press.

————. 1988. *Rethinking Military Politics: Brazil and the Southern Cone.* Princeton, N.J.: Princeton University Press.

Stinchcombe, Arthur L. 1968. *Constructing Social Theories.* New York: Harcourt, Brace & World.

Stone, Russell A. 1982. *Social Change in Israel: Attitudes and Events, 1967–1979.* New York: Praeger Publishers.

Suchman, Mark C., and Dana P. Eyre. 1992. "Military Procurement as Rational Myth: Notes on the Social Construction of Weapons Proliferation," *Sociological Forum* 7: 135–161.

Sussman, Zvi. 1984. "Why Is the Burden of Security so Heavy upon Israel?" In *The Price of Power*, eds. Zvi Offer and Avi Kober. Tel Aviv: Ministry of Defense (Hebrew).

Swirski, Shlomo. 1981. *Orientals and Ashkenazim in Israel: The Ethnic Division of Labor.* Haifa: Machbarot Lemechkar Vlebikoret (Hebrew).

————. 1988. "The I.Q. Tests in Israel." In *The I.Q. Myth*, ed. Jeffrey Bloom. Haifa: Mifras (Hebrew).

————. 1989. *Israel: The Oriental Majority.* London: Zed Books.

————. 1990. *Education in Israel: Schooling for Inequality.* Tel Aviv: Breirot (Hebrew).

————. 1993. "Tomorrow." In *Israeli Society: Critical Perspectives*, ed. Uri Ram. Tel Aviv: Breirot (Hebrew).

————. 1995. *Seeds of Inequality.* Tel Aviv: Breirot (Hebrew).

Szymanski, Al. 1977. "Capital Accumulation on a World Scale and the Necessity of Imperialism," *The Insurgent Sociologist* 7: 35–53.

Tal, David. 1990. *Israel's Response to Infiltrations into Its Territory from Jordan and Egypt, 1949–1956.* Unpublished M.A. thesis, Department of History, Tel Aviv University (Hebrew).

Talmud, Ilan. 1985. *Between Politics and Economy: Public Consent versus Ideological Distinction in Israel.* Unpublished M.A. thesis, Department of Sociology, Tel Aviv University (Hebrew).

Tarrow, Sidney. 1994. *Power in Movement: Social Movements, Collective Action and Politics.* New York: Cambridge University Press.

Taylor, Charles. 1984. "Foucault on Freedom and Truth," *Political Theory* 12: 152–183.

Teachman, Jay D., et al. 1993. "The Selectivity of Military Enlistment," *Journal of Political and Military Sociology* 21: 287–309.

Teitelbaum, Raul. 1984. "The Price of Occupation," *Machbarot Lemachshava Socialistit* 7: 9–10 (Hebrew).

Tessler, Mark. 1994. *A History of the Israeli-Palestinian Conflict.* Bloomington: Indiana University Press.

Teveth, Shabtai. 1971. *Moshe Dayan.* Tel Aviv: Schocken Publishing House (Hebrew).

———. 1992. *Shearing Time/Calaban.* Tel Aviv: Shabtai Teveth (Hebrew).

Therborn, Goran. 1976. "What Does the Ruling Class Do When It Rules?" *The Insurgent Sociologist* 6: 3–16.

Thompson, Edward Palmer. 1984. "Notes on Exterminism: The Last Stage of Civilization." In *Exterminism and Cold War*, ed. Edward Palmer Thompson. London: Verso.

Thompson, Richard H. 1989. *Theories of Ethnicity: A Critical Appraisal.* Westport, Conn.: Greenwood Press.

Thomson, Janice E. 1990. "State Practices, International Norms and the Decline of Mercenarism," *International Studies Quarterly* 34: 23–47.

———. 1994. *Mercenaries, Pirates, and Sovereigns: State-Building and Extraterritorial Violence in Early Modern Europe.* Princeton, N.J.: Princeton University Press.

Tilly, Charles. 1978. *From Mobilization to Revolution.* New York: McGraw-Hill.

———. 1985a. "War and the Power of Warmakers in Western Europe and Elsewhere, 1600–1980." In *Global Militarization*, eds. Peter Wallensteen et al. Boulder, Colo.: Westview Press.

———. 1985b. "War Making and State Making as Organized Crime." In *Bringing the State Back In*, eds. Peter Evans et al. Cambridge: Cambridge University Press.

———. 1992. *Coercion, Capital, and European States, AD 990–1992.* Cambridge, Mass.: Basil Blackwell.

———. 1994. "Citizenship, Identity, and Social History." The New School for Social Research, Center for Studies of Social Change (Working Paper No. 205).

———. 1995a. "Invisible Elbow." The New School for Social Research, Center for Studies of Social Change (Working Paper No. 221).

———. 1995b. "State-Incited Violence, 1900–1999," *Political Power and Theory* 9: 161–179.

———. 1995c. "Democracy Is a Lake." In *The Social Construction of Democracy, 1870–1990*, eds. George Reid Andrews and Herrick Chapman. New York: New York University Press.

———. 1995d. "Globalization Threatens Labor's Rights," *International Labor and Working-Class History* 47: 1–23.

Titmus, Richard M. 1976. "War and Social Policy." In *Essays on the Welfare State*, ed. Richard M. Titmus. London: George Allen and Unwin.

Tocqueville, Alexis de. 1967. "Democracy and the Army." In *Garrisons and Government: Politics and Military in New States*, ed. Wilson C. McWilliams. San Francisco: Chandler Publishing Company.

Toffler, Alvin, and Heidi Toffler. 1993. *War and Anti-War*. New York: Little, Brown.

Touval, Saadia. 1980. "Mediators in the Israeli-Arab Conflict: Requisites for Success." In *Israel—A Developing Society*, ed. Asher Arian. Jerusalem: Academic Press.

Trimberger, Ellen Kay. 1977. "State Power and Modes of Production: Implications of the Japanese Transition to Capitalism," *The Insurgent Sociologist* 7: 85–98.

Trop, Zvi. 1989. "What Is the Real Meaning of the Defense Budget?" *Politica* 26: 52–53 (Hebrew).

Tzahor, Zeev. 1994. *Vision and Reckoning: Ben-Gurion's Ideology and Politics*. Tel Aviv: Miskal-Sifriat Hapoalim (Hebrew).

Unger, Amiel. 1993. "The Power of Unwillingness," *Politica* 51: 34–37 (Hebrew).

Urieli, Nachman, and Amnon Barzilay. 1983. *The Rise and Fall of the Democratic Movement for Change*. Tel Aviv: Reshafim (Hebrew).

Vagts, Alfred. 1959. *A History of Militarism*. New York: Free Press.

Van-Doorn, Jacques. 1975. "The Decline of the Mass Army in the West," *Armed Forces and Society* 1: 147–157.

———. 1976. "The Military and the Crisis of Legitimacy." In *The Military and the Problem of Legitimacy*, eds. Gwyn Harries-Jenkins and Jacques Van-Doorn. London: Sage Publications.

Wagner, Harrison R. 1974. "Dissolving the State: Three Recent Perspectives on International Relations," *International Organization* 28: 435–466.

Wald, Emanuel. 1987. *The Curse of the Broken Vessels*. Tel Aviv: Schocken Publishing House (Hebrew).

———. 1994. *The Owl of Minerva*. Tel Aviv: Miskal (Hebrew).

Wallach, Yehuda. 1987. "Trends in the Development of the Israeli Security Doctrine," *Skira Hodshit* 3–4: 24–30 (Hebrew).

Wallerstein, Immanuel Maurice. 1974. *The Modern World System*. New York: Academic Press.

Waltz, Kenneth. 1979. *A Theory of International Politics*. New York: Addison-Wesley.

———. 1988. "The Origins of War in Neorealist Theory," *Journal of Interdisciplinary History* 18: 615–628.

Weber, Max. 1972. *From Max Weber: Essays in Sociology*, eds. H. H. Gerth and C. W. Mills. New York: Oxford University Press.

Weede, Erich. 1992. "Some Simple Calculations on Democracy and War Involvement," *Journal of Peace Research* 29: 377–383.

————. 1993. "The Impact of Military Participation on Economic Growth and Income Inequality: Some New Evidence," *Journal of Political and Military Sociology* 21: 241–258.

Weizmann, Ezer. 1975. *For You the Sky, For You the Land*. Tel Aviv: Sifriat Ma'ariv Library (Hebrew).

————. 1981. *The Battle for Peace*. Tel Aviv: Edanim Publishers (Hebrew).

————. 1987. "Leaders' Absence of Belief and Missing Chances," *Politica* 14–15: 6–8 (Hebrew).

Wellman, Israel. 1985. "Hesder Yeshivas: Confusion and Obedience," *Yediot Aharonot Supplement*, May 31: 34–35 (Hebrew).

Wendt, Alexander E. 1987. "The Agent-Structure Problem in International Relations Theory," *International Organization* 41: 335–370.

————. 1992. "Anarchy Is What States Make of It: The Social Construction of Power Politics," *International Organization* 46: 391–425.

————. 1994. "Collective Identity Formation and the International State," *American Political Science Review* 88: 384–396.

————. 1995. "Constructing International Politics," *International Security* 20: 71–81.

Williams, Robin M. 1994. "The Sociology of Ethnic Conflicts: Comparative International Perspectives," *Annual Review of Sociology* 20: 49–79.

Wohlforth, William C. 1994/95. "Realism and the End of the Cold War," *International Security* 19: 91–129.

Wolfe, Alan. 1973. *The Seamy Side of Democracy: Repression in America*. New York: David McKay.

————. 1974. "New Directions in the Marxist Theory of Politics," *Politics and Society* 4: 131–160.

————. 1977. *The Limits of Legitimacy: Political Contradictions of Contemporary Capitalism*. New York: Free Press.

————. 1984. "Perverse Politics and the Cold War." In *Exterminism and Cold War*, ed. Edward P. Thompson. London: Verso.

Wolfsfeld, Gadi. 1988. *The Politics of Provocation: Participation and Protest in Israel*. New York: SUNY Press.

Yaacobi, Gad. 1989. *On the Razor's Edge*. Tel Aviv: Edanim Publishers (Hebrew).

Yanai, Natan. 1969. *Split at the Top*. Tel Aviv: Lewin-Epstein Publishers (Hebrew).

———. 1982. *Political Crises in Israel*. Jerusalem: Keter Publishing House (Hebrew).

Yaniv, Avner. 1989. "What Happened to Israel's Deterrence?" *Politica* 26: 6–9 (Hebrew).

———. 1994. *Politics and Strategy in Israel*. Tel Aviv: Sifriat Hapoalim (Hebrew).

———, and Zeev Maoz. 1984. "Processes of Decisionmaking and Escalation in Democracy: The Case of Israel's Policy toward Syria, 1948–1984." Paper delivered at the annual convention of the Israeli Association of Political Science (Hebrew).

Yariv, Aaron. 1985. "War by Choice—War with no Choice." In *War by Choice*, ed. Josef Alpher. Tel Aviv: Hakibbutz Hameuchad Publishing House (Hebrew).

Yatziv, Gadi. 1986. *The Heart of the Matter—Essays on Socialism and Democracy in Israel*. Tel Aviv: Adam Publishers (Hebrew).

Yemini, Ben-Dror. 1986. *Political Punch*. Haifa: Mifras (Hebrew).

Yinon, Yoel, and Nili Freedman. 1977. "Why Do Kibbutz-Born Soldiers Perform Better Than Do City-Born in the Army?" *Megamot* 23: 110–118 (Hebrew).

Yishai, Yael. 1985. "The Labor Party and the Lebanon War," *Armed Forces and Society* 11: 379–397.

———. 1987. *Interest Groups in Israel: The Test of Democracy*. Tel Aviv: Am Oved Publishers (Hebrew).

Yogev, Amnon. 1989. "An Alternative Battlefield," *Politica* 26: 18–21 (Hebrew).

Young, Nigel. 1984. "War Resistance, State and Society." In *War, State and Society*, ed. Martin Shaw. London: Macmillan Press.

Yuval-Davis, Nira. 1985. "Front and Rear: The Sexual Division of Labor in the Israeli Army," *Feminist Studies* 11: 649–675.

Zak, Moshe. 1994. "The Missing Opportunities to Achieve Jordanian-Israeli Peace," *Ma'ariv*, July 26: 6 (Hebrew).

Zamir, Danny. 1987. "The Kibbutz-Born Soldiers and the Military Service," *Ma'arachot* 312–313: 18–20 (Hebrew).

Zarhi, Shaul. 1991. "Dogmatic Approaches to Economic Policy," *Yaad* 8: 44–51 (Hebrew).

Zeitlin, Maurice. 1980. "On Classes, Class Conflict, and the State: An Introductory Note." In *Classes, Class Conflict, and the State: Empirical Studies in Class Analysis,* ed. Maurice Zeitlin. Cambridge, Mass.: Winthrop Publishers.

Zukerman-Bareli, Haya, and Tova Bensky. 1989. "'Parents Against Silence': Conditions and Processes Leading to the Emergence of a Protest Movement," *Megamot* 32: 27–42 (Hebrew).

Zweig, Ferdynand. 1969. *Israel: The Sword and the Harp: The Mystique of Violence and the Mystique of Redemption, Controversial Themes in Israel.* London: Heinemann.

NEWSPAPERS

Al Ha'mishmar: July 1951; July 1955 (Hebrew).

Davar: July 1951; July 1955 (Hebrew).

Globes: March 31, 1995 (Hebrew).

Ha'aretz: May 19, 1995; June 16, 1995; March 29, 1996 (Hebrew).

Ha'aretz Supplement: April 12, 1996 (Hebrew).

Ha'boker: July 1951; July 1955 (Hebrew).

La'merchav: July 1951; July 1955 (Hebrew).

Ma'ariv: May 11, 1995 (Hebrew).

Status: The Magazine of Managerial Thought, June 1995 (Hebrew).

Yediot Aharonot: July 1951; July 1955; September 1993–September 1996 (Hebrew).

Yediot Aharonot Supplement: May 31, 1985; April 19, 1996 (Hebrew).

Index

A

Abdullah (King of Jordan), 60
Accountability Operation, 235n. 10, 235n. 11
Adam, Yekutiel, 150
Agranat Commission, 155
Ahdut Ha'Avoda (Unity of Labor Party), 84, 103–104, 110, 112, 133–34. *See also* Alignment
Alignment, 103–104, 109, 132–34, 151–53, 155–56, 159–60, 162–63, 171–72, 181, 232n. 6, 233n. 12, 234n. 5. *See also* Labor Party; Mapai Party
Allon, Yigal, 110, 131
anarchy, 2–4, 6, 13, 18, 217
Anderson, Robert, 78
Arab Democratic Party, 201
Arafat, Yasir, 175, 191
Arens, Moshe, 182, 236n. 18
Armistice Agreement (1949), 59–60, 65–66, 68, 70, 77
Armistice Commission, 65–66, 68, 109
Ashkenazi Jews. *See* under specific titles
austerity and rationing regime, 29, 32, 37, 51–52, 56, 92, 213

B

Baghdad Pact, 67
Barak, Ehud, 235n. 10
Byroade, Henry, 68
Begin, Menachem, 109, 152–53, 156, 162–63, 169, 171, 180
Beilin, Yossi, 175, 205
Ben-Gurion, David, 36, 39, 40–42, 44, 48, 50–51, 55, 60, 65–67, 69, 70–75, 77–78, 80–82, 85, 87–89, 91, 93, 102–106, 109, 111–12, 119, 133
Black Panthers, 145, 149–51, 154
border frictions between Israel and Arab states: general, 59–60, 63–68, 234n. 4; Israel-Egypt, 57, 73–75, 77–79, 108–10, 138–39, 144–47; Israel-Jordan, 57, 66–67, 107–108; Israel-Lebanon, 166–68, 172, 235n. 10 (*see also* Accountability Operation; Grapes of Wrath; Hezbollah); Israel-Palestinian Authority, 206; Israel-Syria, 68–69, 106–108, 77, 145–47, 170, 228n. 1. *See also* reprisal raids and under specific titles
Britain, Middle East policies of, 61, 69, 74–75, 78, 234n. 4
British Mandate, 17, 26, 37